AF251058

# ENGLAND ON FIRE

## A VISUAL JOURNEY THROUGH ALBION'S PSYCHIC LANDSCAPE

## STEPHEN ELLCOCK

## MAT OSMAN

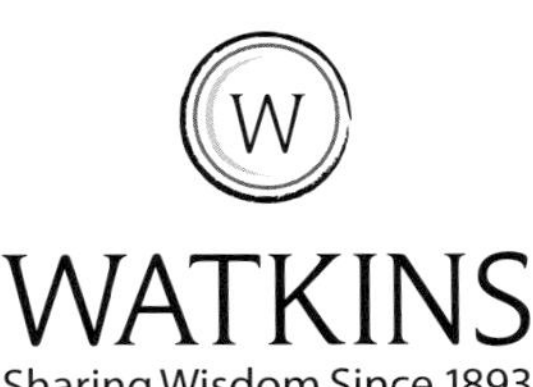

### WATKINS

Sharing Wisdom Since 1893

**England on Fire**
Stephen Ellcock & Mat Osman

First published in the UK and USA in 2022 by
Watkins, an imprint of Watkins Media Limited
Unit 11, Shepperton House, 83–93 Shepperton Road
London  N1 3DF

enquiries@watkinspublishing.com

Design and typography copyright © Watkins Media Limited 2022
Image selection copyright © Stephen Ellcock 2022
Text copyright © Mat Osman 2022
For copyright of the artwork see the Picture Credits which is to be
regarded as an extension of this copyright

The right of Stephen Ellcock and Mat Osman to be identified as the
Authors of this text has been asserted in accordance with the Copyright,
Designs and Patents Act of 1988.

All rights reserved. No part of this book may be reproduced in any form or
by any electronic or mechanical means, including information storage and
retrieval systems, without permission in writing from the publisher, except
by a reviewer who may quote brief passages in a review.

| | |
|---|---|
| Publisher & Managing Editor | Fiona Robertson |
| Commissioning Editor | Adam Gordon |
| Assistant Editor | Brittany Willis |
| Designer | Josse Pickard |
| Proofreading & indexing | Kelly Thompson |
| Extended captions | Maisie McGregor |
| Short captions & picture credits | Emma Thakara |
| Chapter opener typography | Josse Pickard |
| Production | Uzma Taj |

A CIP record for this book is available from the British Library

ISBN: 978-1- 78678-428-5

10 9 8 7 6 5 4 3 2 1

Typeset in Adobe Jenson
Printed in Bosnia and Herzegovina
Colour repro by Rival Colour UK


www.watkinspublishing.com

# CONTENTS

*This book is dedicated to Jackie, my fellow
exile and eternally revolting peasant x*

Stephen Ellcock, January 2022

# ABOUT THE AUTHORS

STEPHEN ELLCOCK is a London-based curator, writer, researcher and online collector of images who is in the process of creating an ever-expanding, virtual museum of art that is open to all via social media. He is the author of *All Good Things*, *The Book of Change* and, with Cécile Poimboeuf-Koizumi, *Jeux de Mains*. His method of image curation is based on thousands of hours of archival research as well as an intuitive approach that combines pattern-making and collage with what might be described as channelling and spell-casting, having something in common with Tarot, astrological charts and other forms of divination.

MAT OSMAN is a writer and musician. His debut novel, *The Ruins*, came out in 2019 and the follow-up, *The Ghost Theatre*, is due in 2023. He's a founder member of the British band *Suede* and composes music for film and TV.

# INTRODUCTION

WORDS. WORDS HAVE ALWAYS BEEN ENGLAND'S SOFT POWER.

The tendrils of the English language spread themselves further around the globe than the gunships of Empire ever managed. From Shakespeare to Stormzy, from the Brontës to the Beatles and from Kipling to the Kinks, English words have fallen like rain across the globe and then washed the world's riches back into England's gutters. These viral words hid a multitude of sins. If the English called a pirate a privateer then he was free to plunder and burn and kill. Call a slaver a tradesman and it was only the balance sheet that need be scrutinized. But William Blake and the other artists knew it: words are just the sheen on the surface and underneath a stranger, truer language lurks – the strong draught of imagery.

This is a book, in part, about English art. Two words that together strike fear into discerning hearts, what with its hunting dogs and tall ships and haywains and horses. Its old white men in old white ruffs with their women always two paces behind. But Stephen Ellcock's knowledge starts where most people's ends. In the wild corners and the forgotten lanes. Among the dispossessed and the excluded. He has scoured England's dark corners for the nation's true nature and what he has found is something more furious and magical than any Shakespeare play. Here is an Albion unhinged, where magic and rebellion

and destruction are the horses to which the country is hitched. In place of that tired rogues' gallery of Lords and Ladies, we find images made by unknown artists or nameless groups. Standing stones and forgotten photographic plates. Chalk horses and discarded film stills.

This, then, is a very English rebellion of the nameless many against the privileged few. It's no surprise that of all the peoples of the world it was the English who embraced Saturnalia so wildly. That Roman festival of social upheaval – bosses becoming servants, serfs taking over grand houses – plays on ideas that beat at England's unspoken heart. Upheaval, reversal, ridicule and chaos. Dog-headed huntsmen and trees that walk. Cars blazing in Mayfair streets while dinosaurs roam Crystal Palace. Think of the images here as a kind of visual Saturnalia, where the incoherent fever-dream of England's 99% rules over this green, unpleasant land.

Everywhere among these images order is overthrown. Gardens are reclaimed by weeds, cities are set afire and ships are wrecked. The mind's order is overthrown too. An unholy trinity of drugs, madness and humour gives us the peculiarly British surrealism that peppers this book. Butterflies draw airy carriages as the cow jumps over the moon.

Many, if not most, of these extraordinary images were new to me and with every thrill of unique discovery came a pang of regret that we only have these scraps. Stephen's years of research in obscure archives and down web rabbit holes have dug up these gems, but how many more went unrecorded? For centuries the work of women, of working men, of marginalized communities, of anyone outside power's rigid paradigm, was erased, more likely to be used for firewood or scrap paper than displayed. How many geniuses were born, blossomed and died without leaving a scratch of their art behind for us? Which Coventry Kahlo, which Plymouth Picasso should be hanging in the National Gallery? Ghost works lost in smoke and salt spray. It is, then, all the more important to cherish those pieces from outside the mainstream that Stephen has unearthed here. They're a secret history of this country, like those handwritten notes you find in library books that say "not so!" or "yes, but …"

Stephen juxtaposes and weaves imagery around itself, teasing out narratives and finding wild connections in a kind of visual language. This collocation of old and new, male and female, insider and outsider spins tales and tells jokes; it banters, theorizes and explains. It's a language that speaks to England's subconscious and which we understand in some kind of deep, pre-verbal core. So what's a poor writer to do, in trying to accompany these carefully constructed image-stories, without words bringing them down to earth again?

Well, in my case, I mainly just hung on and enjoyed the ride. I've paired each of Stephen's chapters with a text inspired in part by his imagery and in part by long conversations about the meanings hidden therein. The texts are tangential; they wander off down odd side roads, provoked by a scene or a sentence of Stephen's that sparked my imagination. I hope they illuminate some hidden side of each chapter but the true heart of this book beats in the interplay of images. The texts are meant as seasoning rather than explanation.

Like a teenager sulking in their room, England is in one of its periodic spasms of insularity – but no matter, we've been here before. Scattered across these pages is a new breed of artists who are sowing the seeds of a changed England. They are the "green shoots of recovery" that politicians are always spying. Often of colour or from the margins, almost all from outside the art establishment, this is a generation who paint a bolder, wilder nation. With the twin scalpels of anger and humour, they're cutting away the bloated flesh of old ideas. Where they're leading us, and where their psychic ancestors explored before us, is a new land – an enchanted, enchanting, maddening, quickening, furious, funny and fabulous England.

An England on fire …

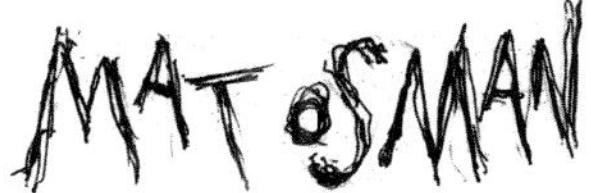

# 1

## OUT OF DARKNESS

PREVIOUS PAGE

**1** *Wolf Moon* (one of a triptych)  2020
Cathy de Monchaux (b.1960)  Copper wire, paper, elastoplast and paint

**ENGLAND IS A SHIPWRECK: A BROKEN ABSENCE RISING FROM A BLACK SEA WITH LIGHTNING FOR ITS BOWS AND STORMWINDS FOR ITS STERN.**

The tattered rigging is crowned with tempests that dump oceans of rain onto mile upon mile of silent trees. Cymbal-crash of waves and brassy gales call to us out across the seas.

So, we pull ourselves, salt-raw and wave-beaten, out onto a midnight shore. The stony beach is ringed with cliffs like castle walls, and the rain and stars are poor shelter for us castaways. No friendly desert island this, but a land built for giants and then abandoned and overgrown and sodden and treacherous.

The wreckage creaks in the surf as we make for the safety of the interior. But the broken teeth of mountain crags and the long scars of funeral barrows tell the tale; we have washed up on a battleground, pitted by long-forgotten wars. Herds of vast white horses gallop forever across the rolling hills – through Uffington and Westbury and Cherhill – with their riders thrown and the reins flapping wild. Blank-faced caves spew bats and dragon's breath. Anarchic nature runs wild, Albion is unhinged.

We sleepwalk amid England's dreaming, trekking through forests so thick that it might be day or night or both at once. These are the places that clothe nightmares, where everything is too huge and too dark and too old. Here, the mythical and the everyday live side by side, in this place where history's light doesn't reach: lions lay down with lambs; green men peer from paths that snake away into shadow; the forest floor is littered with dragons' teeth and unicorn bones. And always the invitation to get lost. Follow the flash of deer tail down bosky lanes and let the trees' fingers close around you. Dive into black river water and surrender to the undertow. Birds for guides, sycamore seeds for way markers.

We escape, breathless, into the hills, where the sky seems close enough to touch and ospreys hunt down angels. We are all marooned here – motherless children playing in the ruins. Stone edifices echo to the sound of *ring a ring o' roses* and kids play hide-and-seek around the hillfort beeches. Darkness falls but no one is here to call us home.

Whoever was here before left a land incomprehensible. There seems no way to read the stones and the storms, the cairns and the carvings. All that's left is to look on in awe.

England is a shipwreck, endlessly crashing into waves of rock, and we are its flotsam…

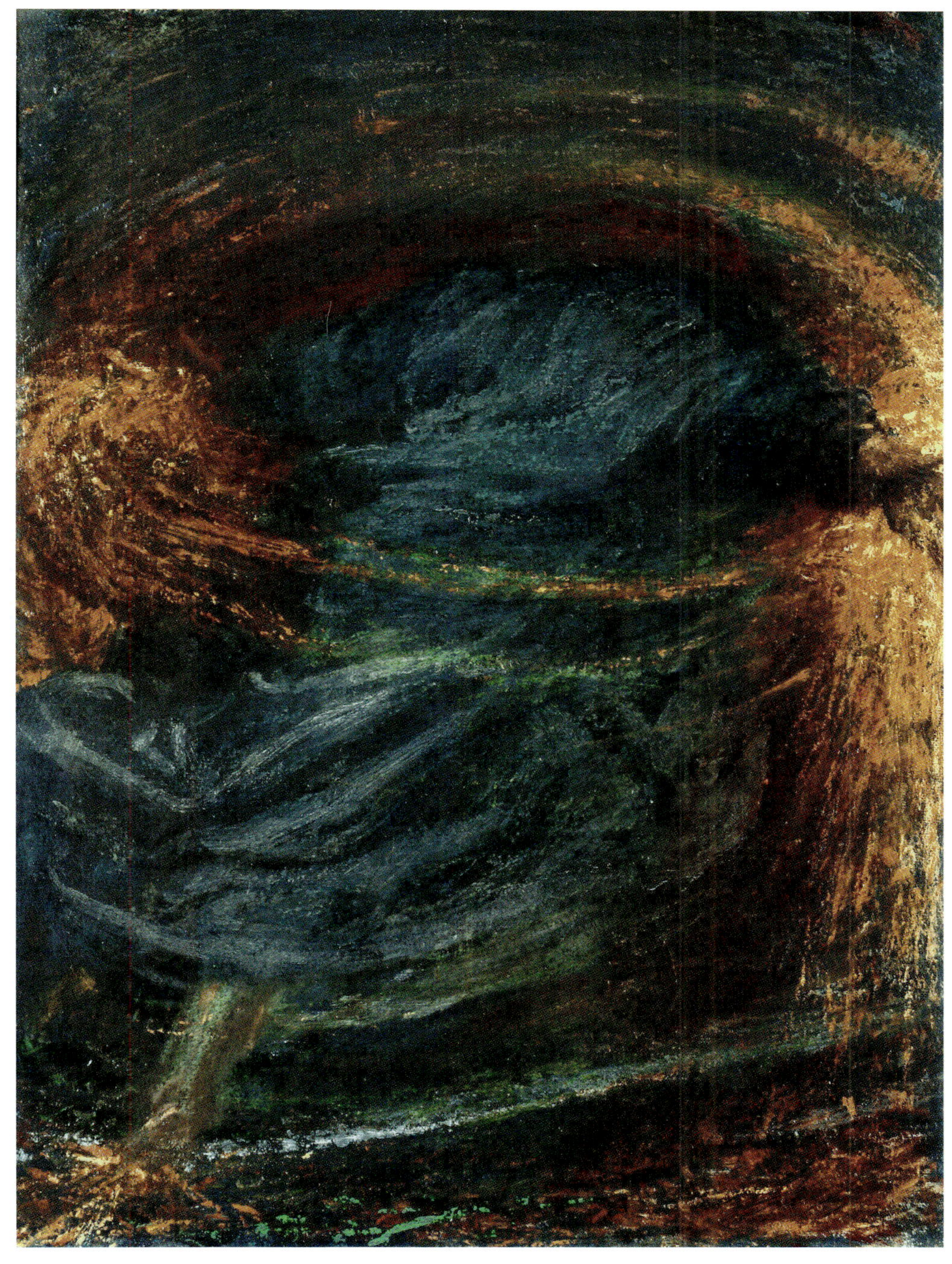



**2**  *The Sower of the Systems* *c.*1902
George Frederick Watts (1817–1904)  Oil on canvas

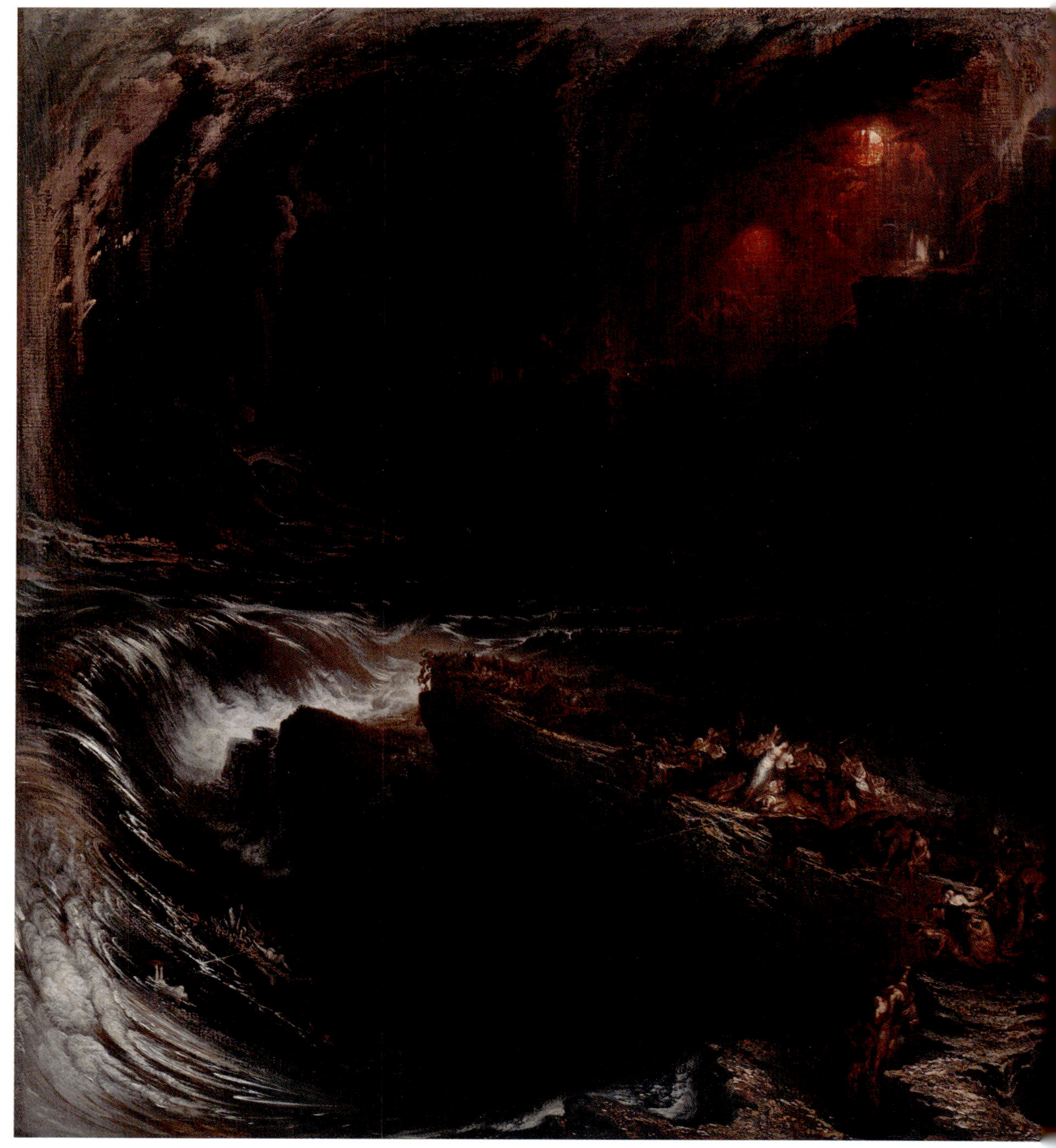

ENGLAND ON FIRE

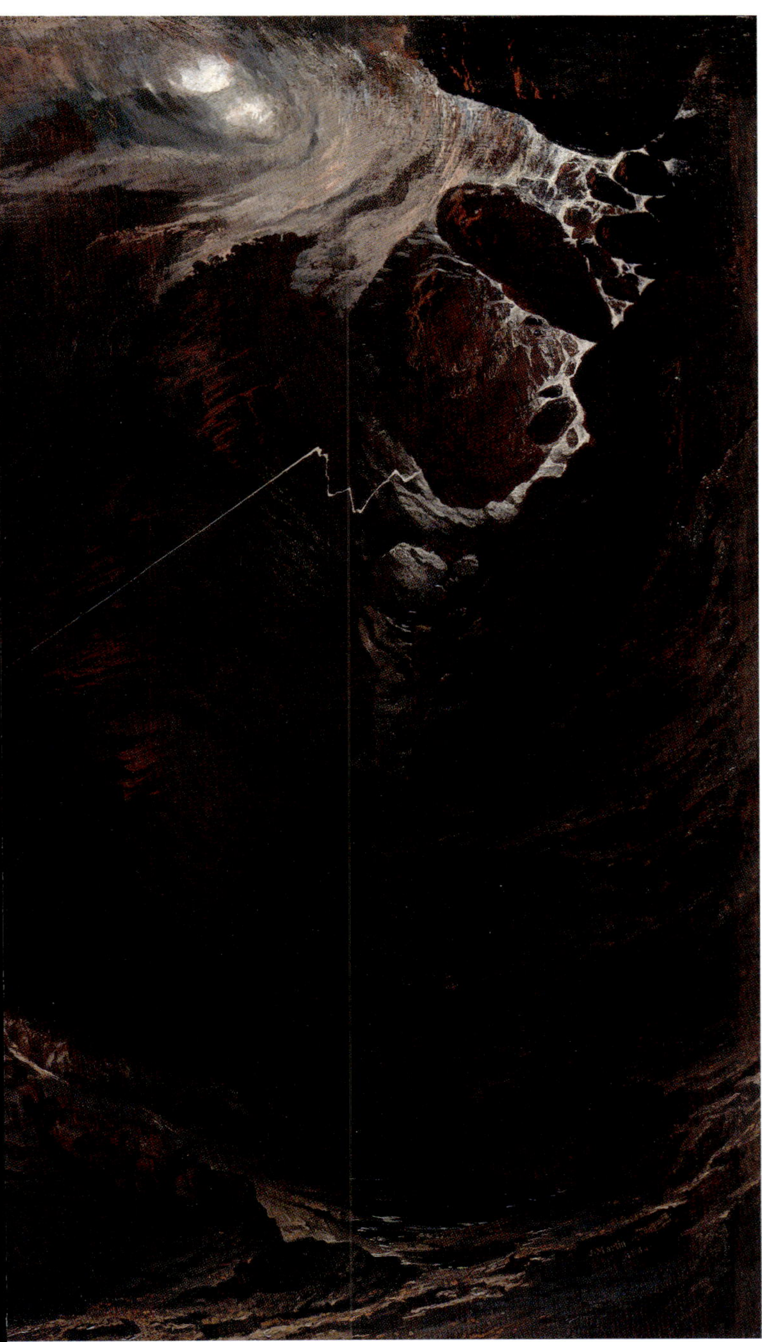



John Martin, an ardent believer in natural religion, here presents the dual power of God and the natural landscape. Man appears in miniature, reaching for mercy and drowning in the force of the water, which refers both to the biblical flood and to Martin's own belief in an historic flood caused by a comet colliding with the sun and moon.

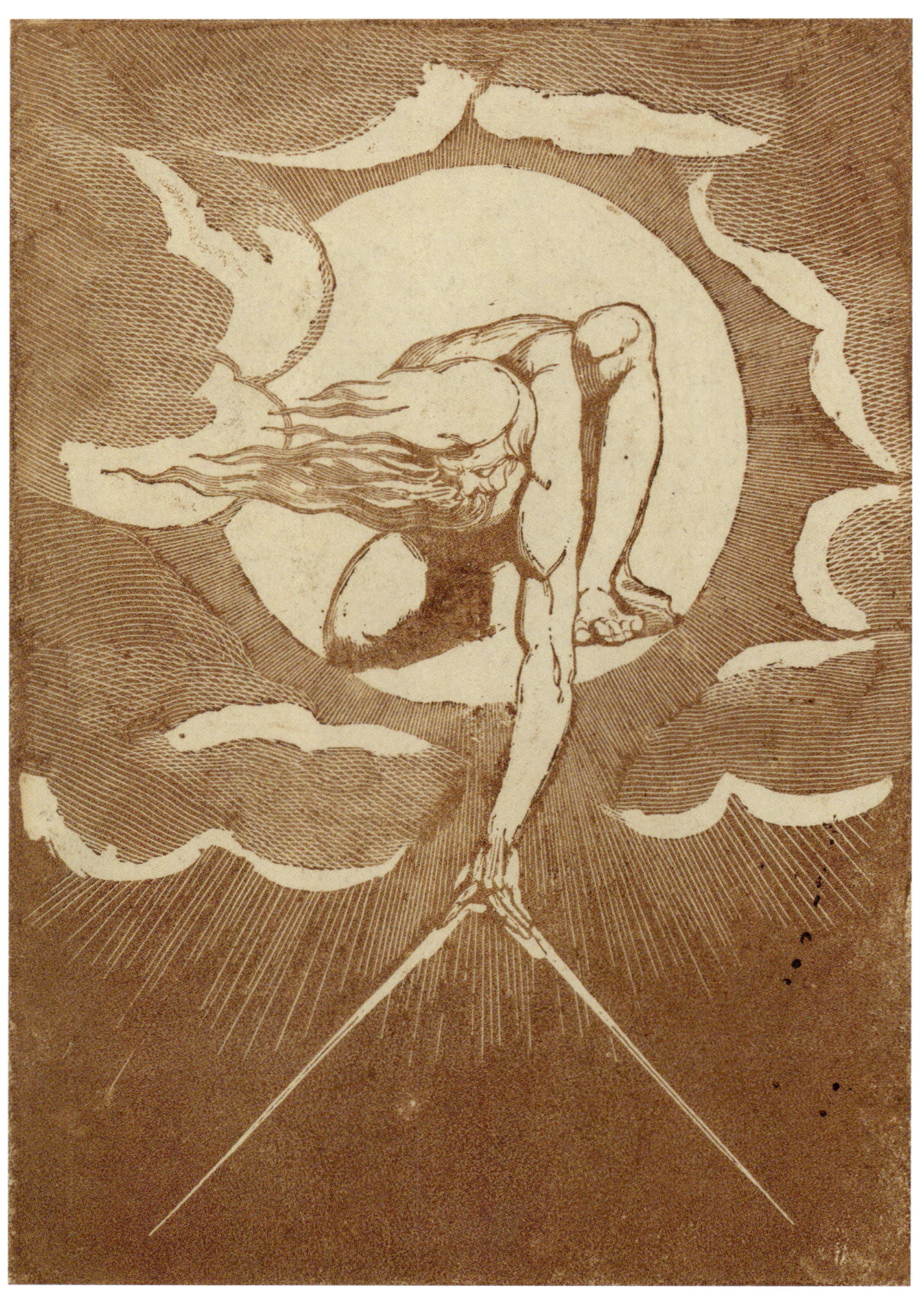

**4**  *Europe. A Prophecy, Frontispiece Proof Impression  c.1820*
William Blake (1757–1827)  Relief etching with pen and black ink

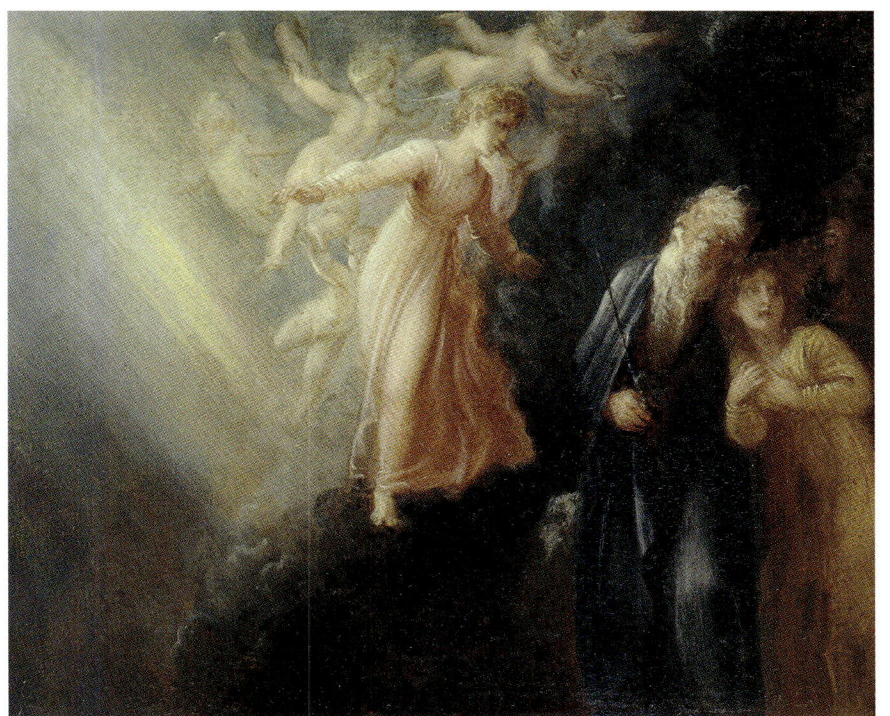

5  *Prospero, Miranda and Ariel, from the Tempest, Act I, scene II*  c.1799
Thomas Stothard
(1755–1834)
Oil on panel

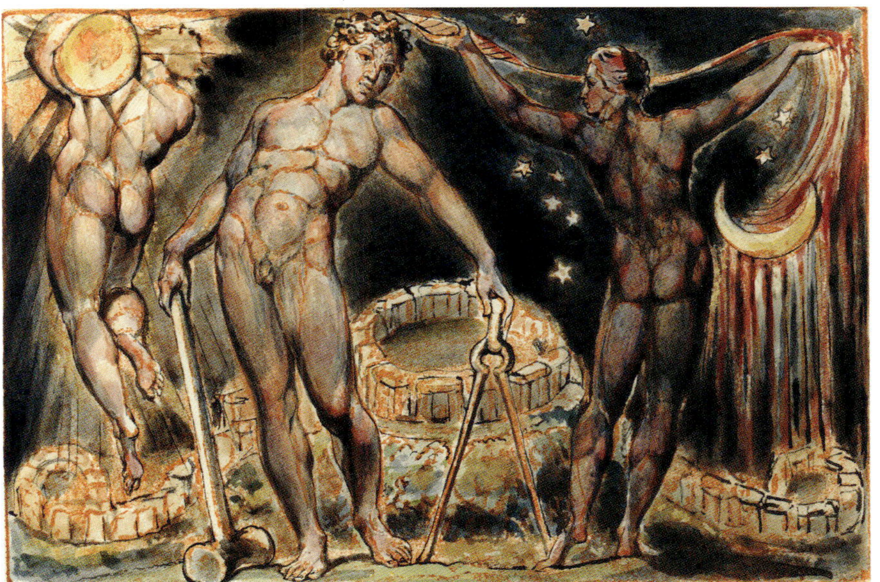

6  *Jerusalem, Plate 100*
1804–20
William Blake
(1757–1827)
Relief etching with monoprinted colour

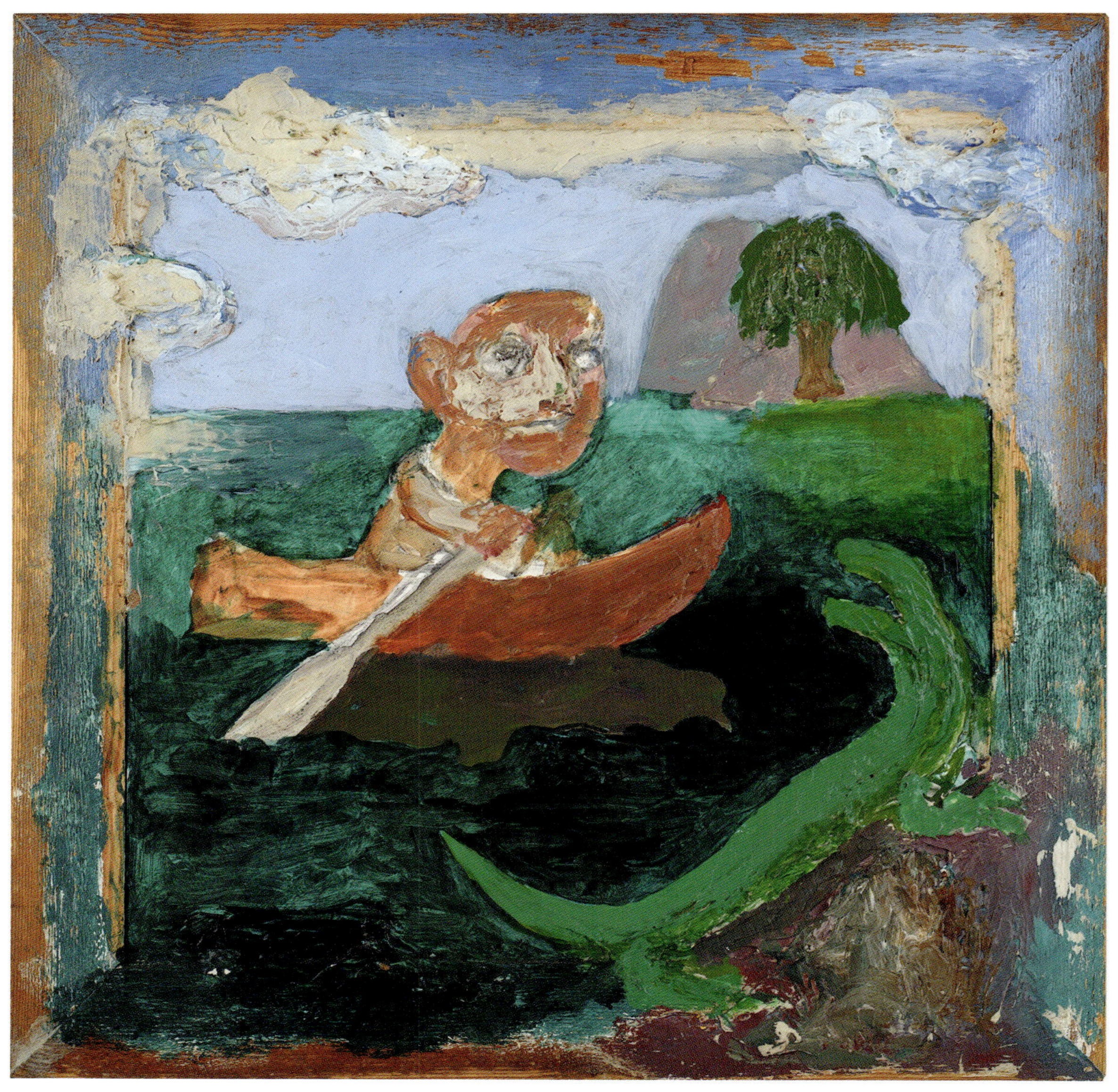

7   *Boat and Lizard*  *c*.1972
Ken Kiff (1935–2001)
Mixed media on board



8   *The Green Dragon*  1910
Arthur Rackham (1867–1939)
Pen and ink with wash

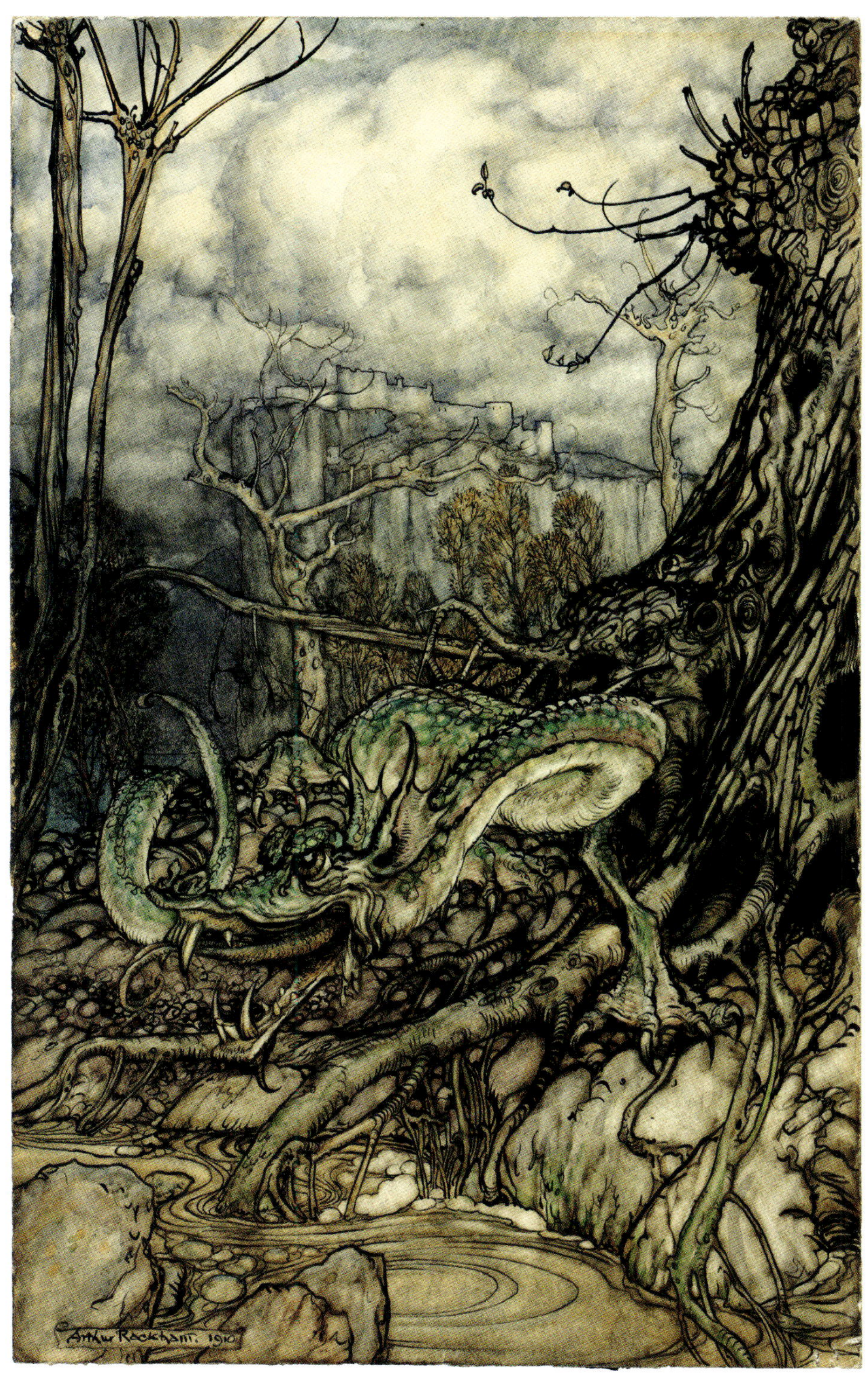

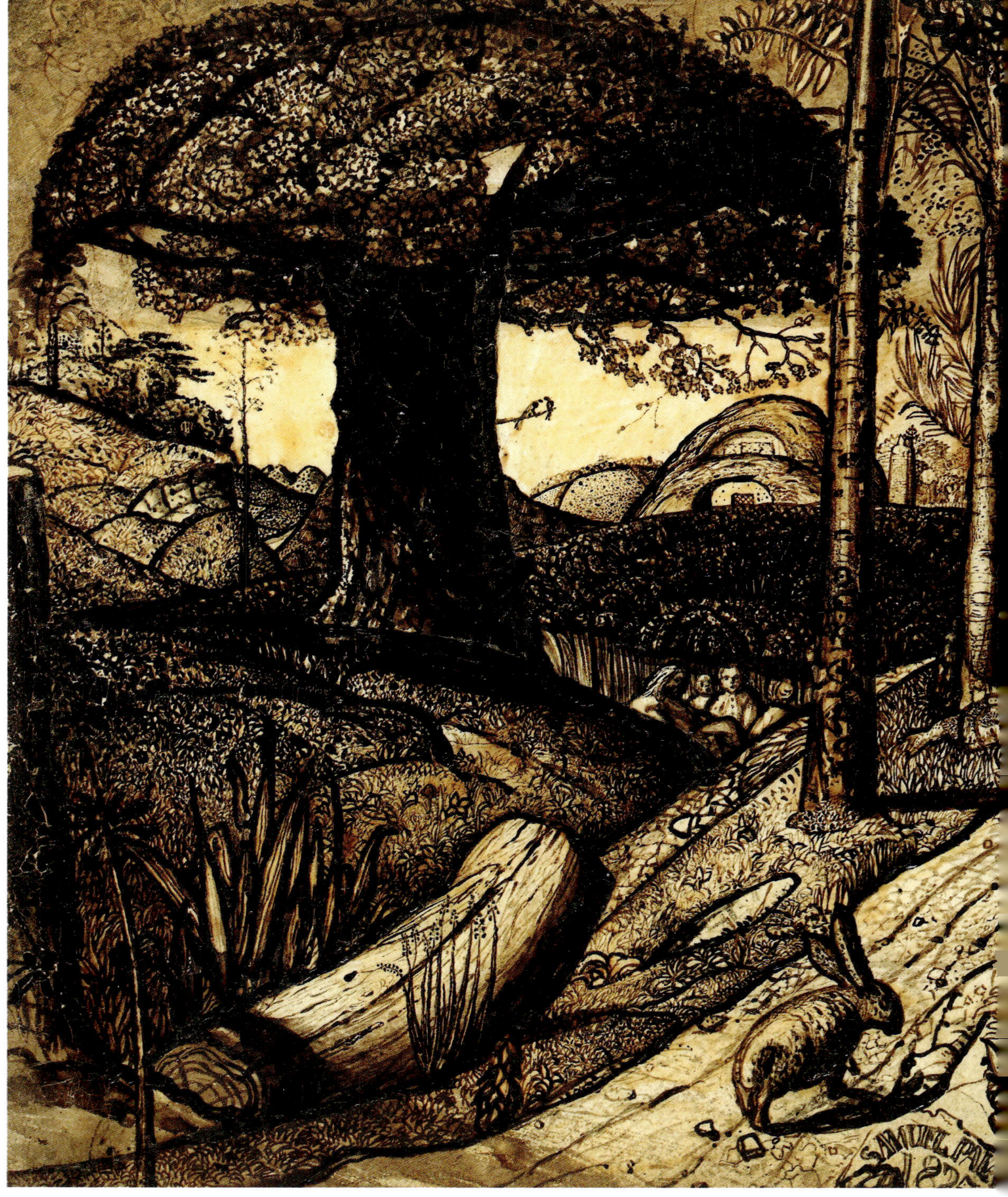

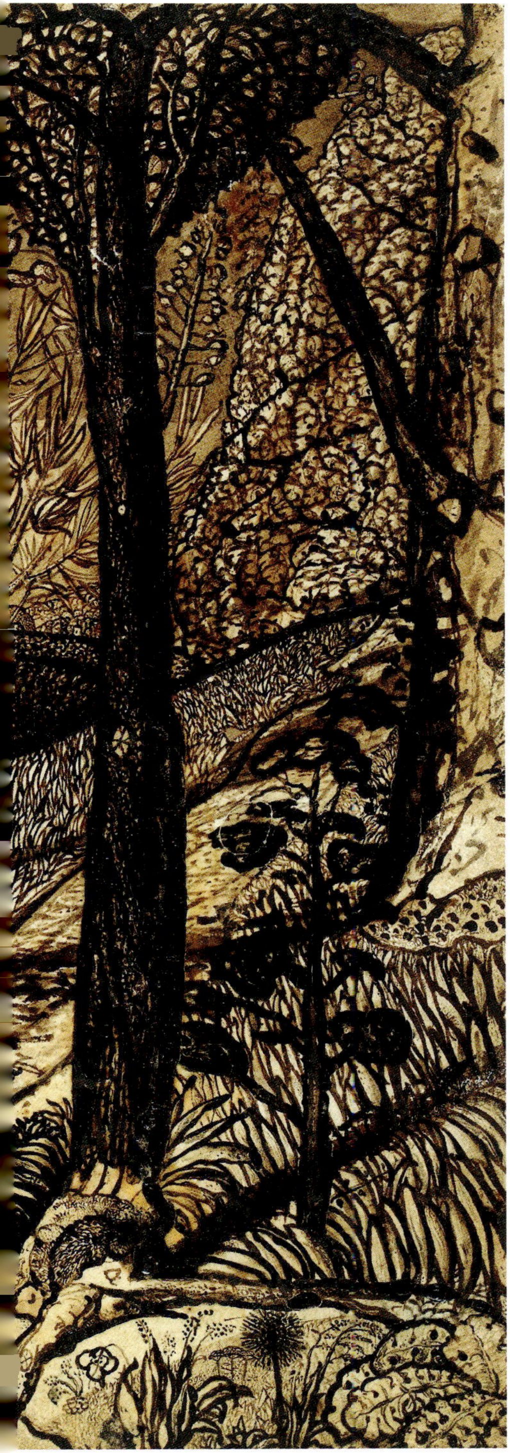

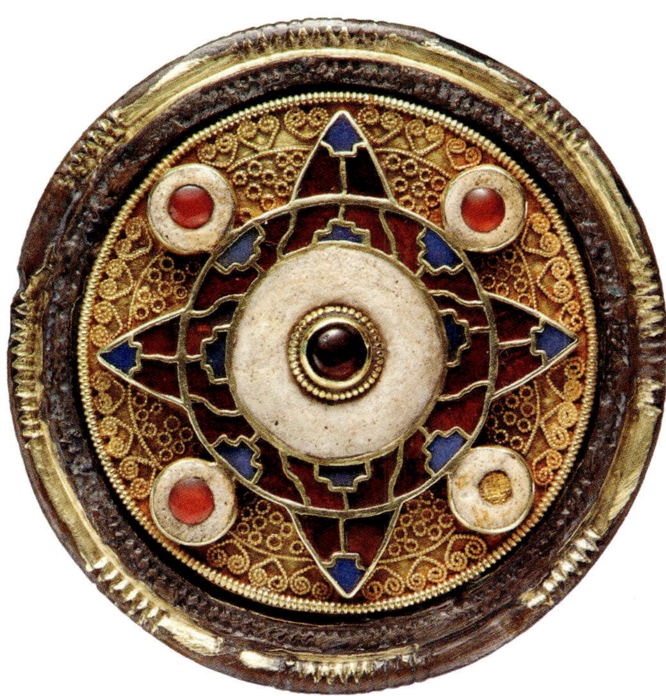

**9** *Early Morning*  1825
Samuel Palmer (1805–81)
Gum and sepia ink

**10** *Anglo Saxon Disc Brooch*  Early 7th century
Artist unknown
Gold with garnets, glass and niello

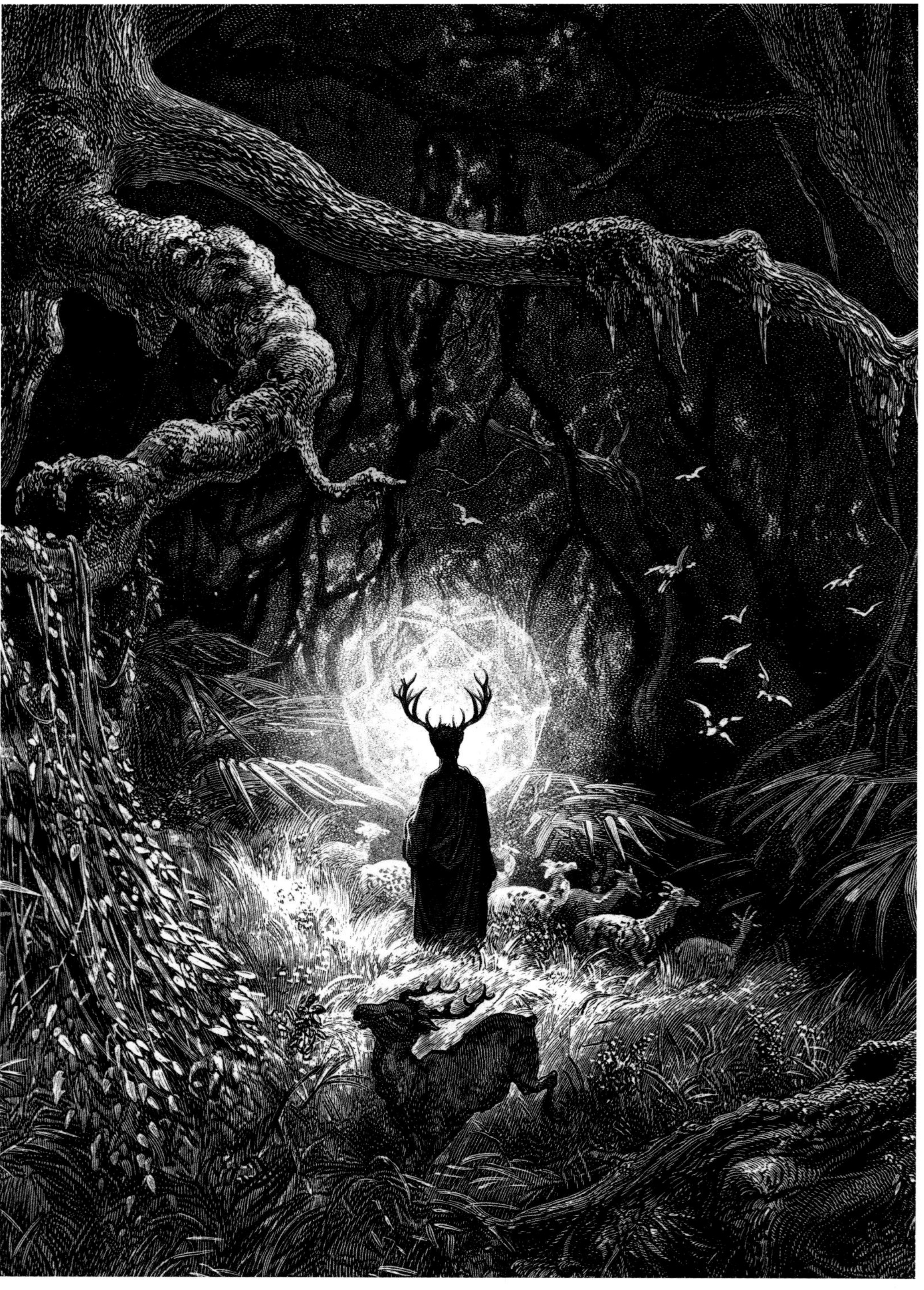

**11** *Fount*  2021
Dan Hillier (b.1973)
Giclée print

**12** *Donati's Comet*  1859
William Turner of Oxford (1789–1862)
Watercolour and gouache over graphite

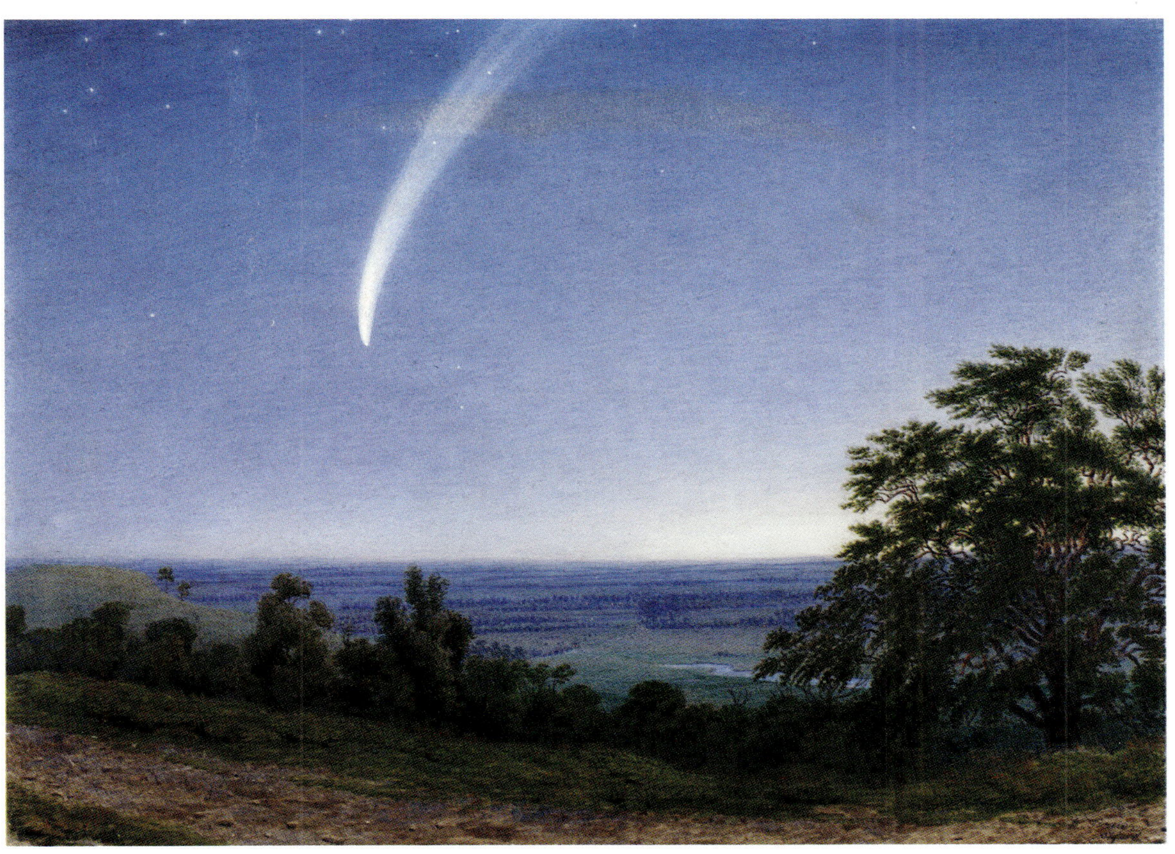

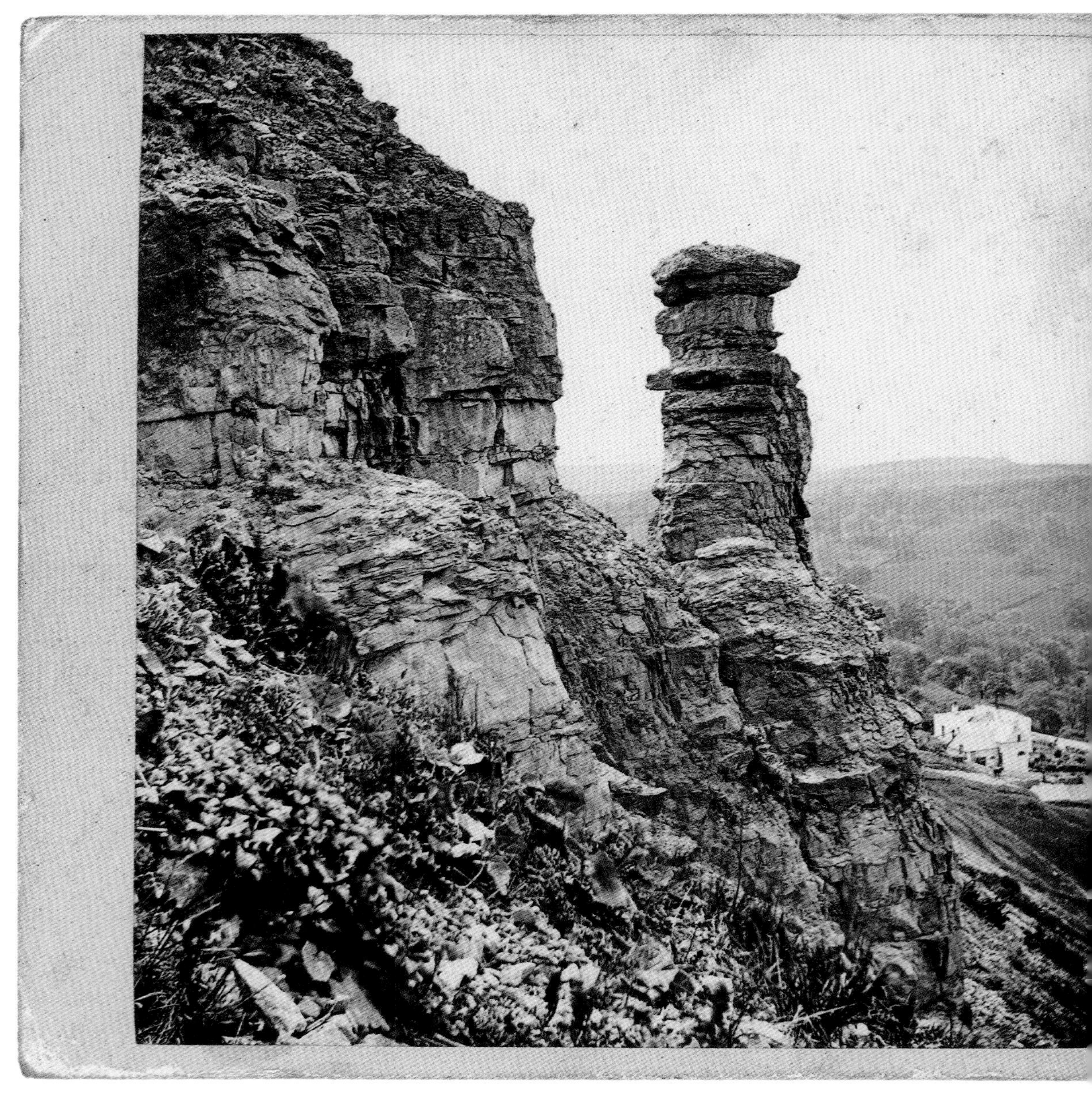

**13** *Devil's Chimney, from a Group of Eleven Early Stereograph Views of British Landscapes* 1850s–1920s Artist unknown Photographs

It is believed that the Devil's Chimney, a limestone rock formation in Leckhampton, Gloucestershire, sits atop the Devil's dwelling place. Legend has it that he would throw stones at Sunday churchgoers from the top of the crooked rock stack, only to have them hurled back at him, forcing him to the depths below. The stack functions as a chimney through which smoke from the fires of hell spurts into the world above.

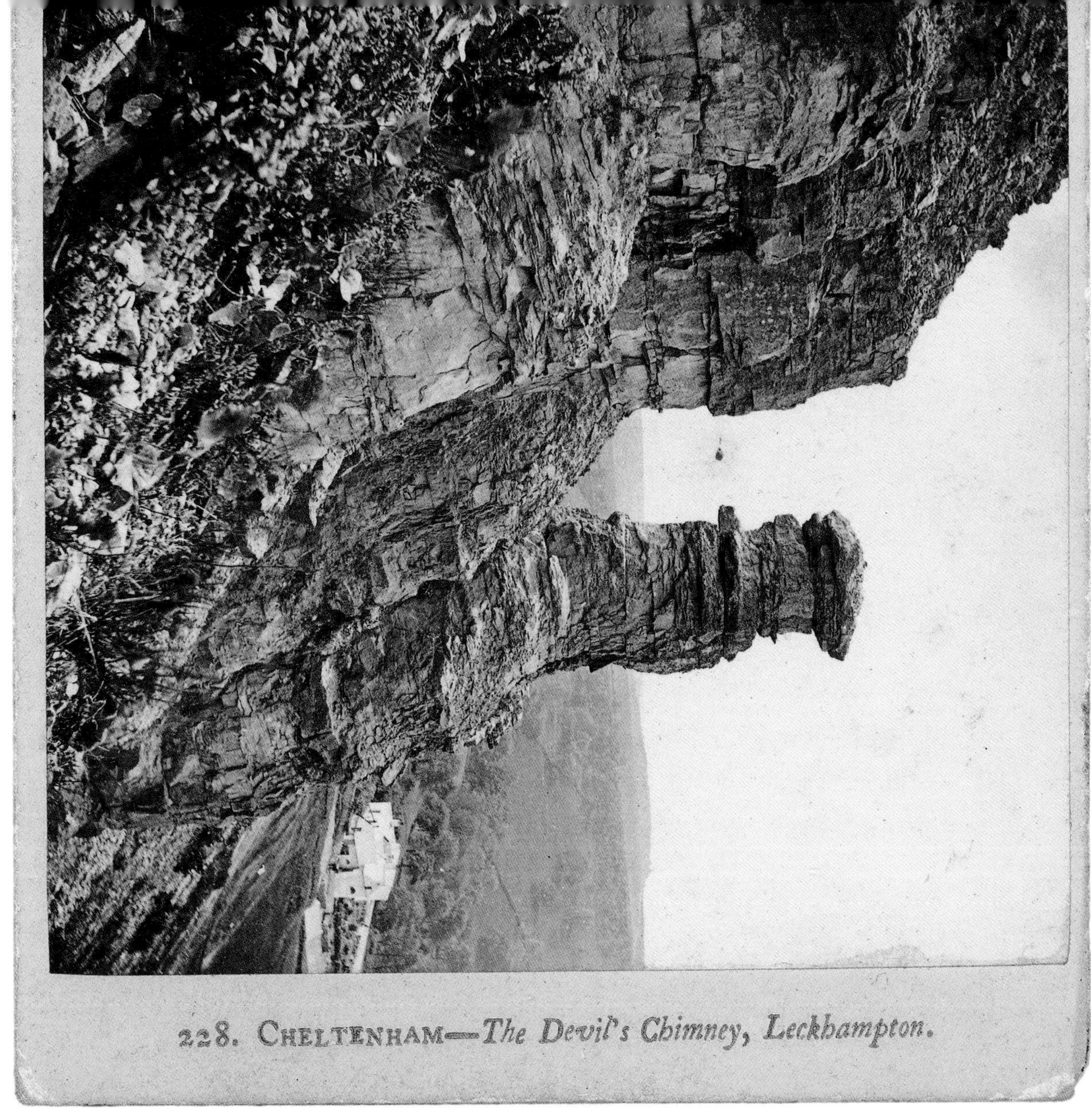

228. CHELTENHAM—The Devil's Chimney, Leckhampton.

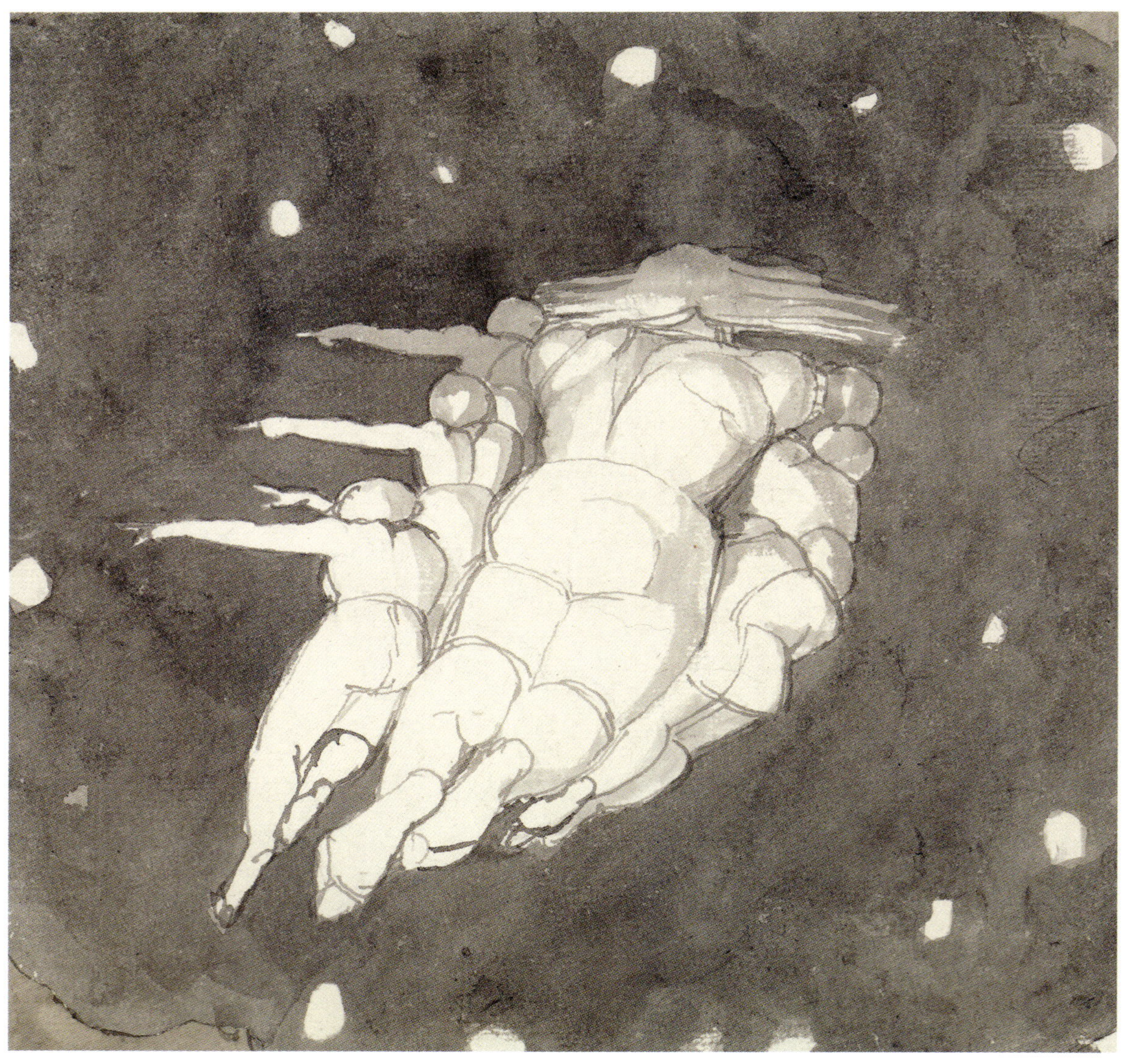

**14** *The Creation of the Heavens*  *c.*1790
John Flaxman (1755–1826)
Grey ink and grey wash on paper

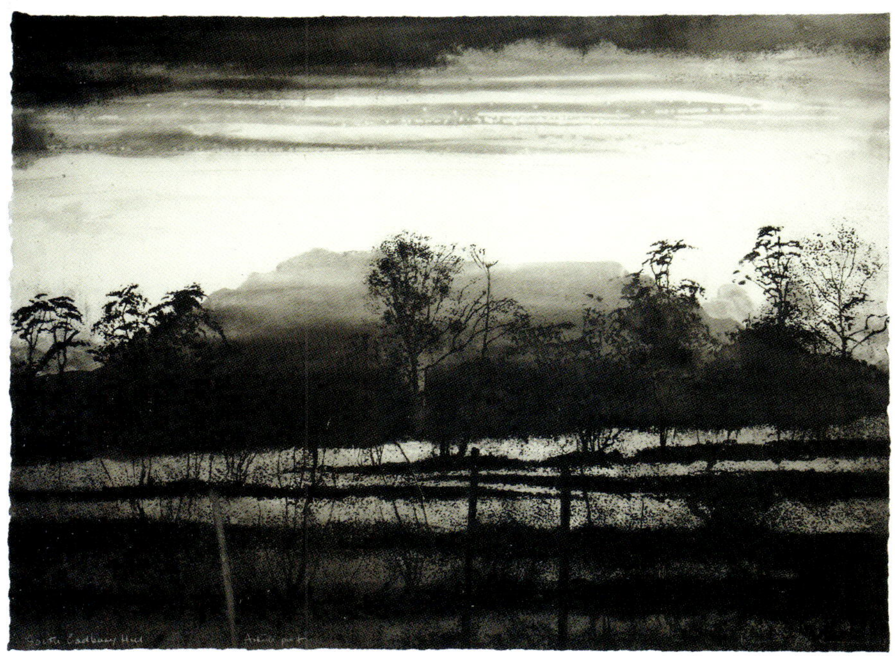

15 *South Cadbury Hill* 1993
Norman Ackroyd
(b.1938)
Etching

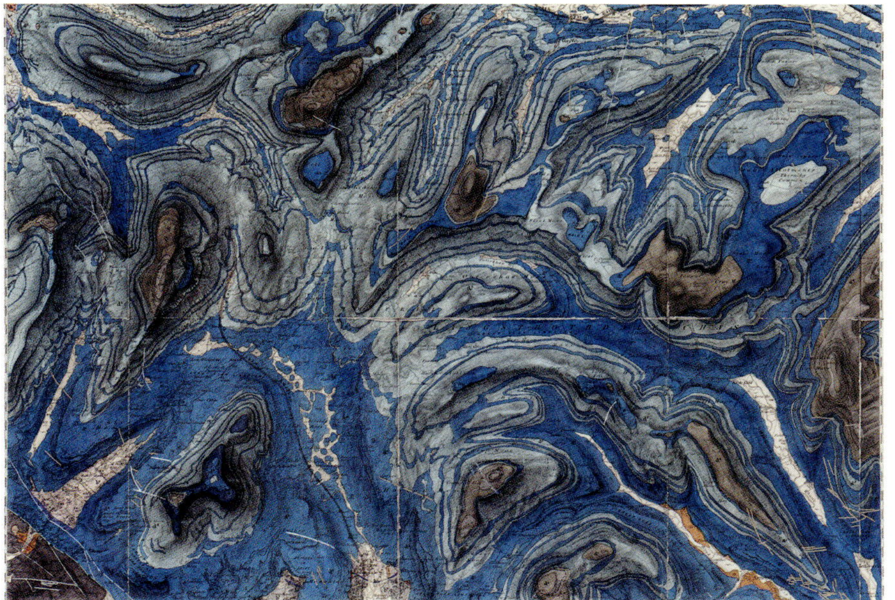

16 *Map from the Geological Survey of Great Britain and Ireland: 97. Richmond, Yorkshire, SW Quad.* 1889
Great Britain, Ordnance Survey Office Map mounted on linen

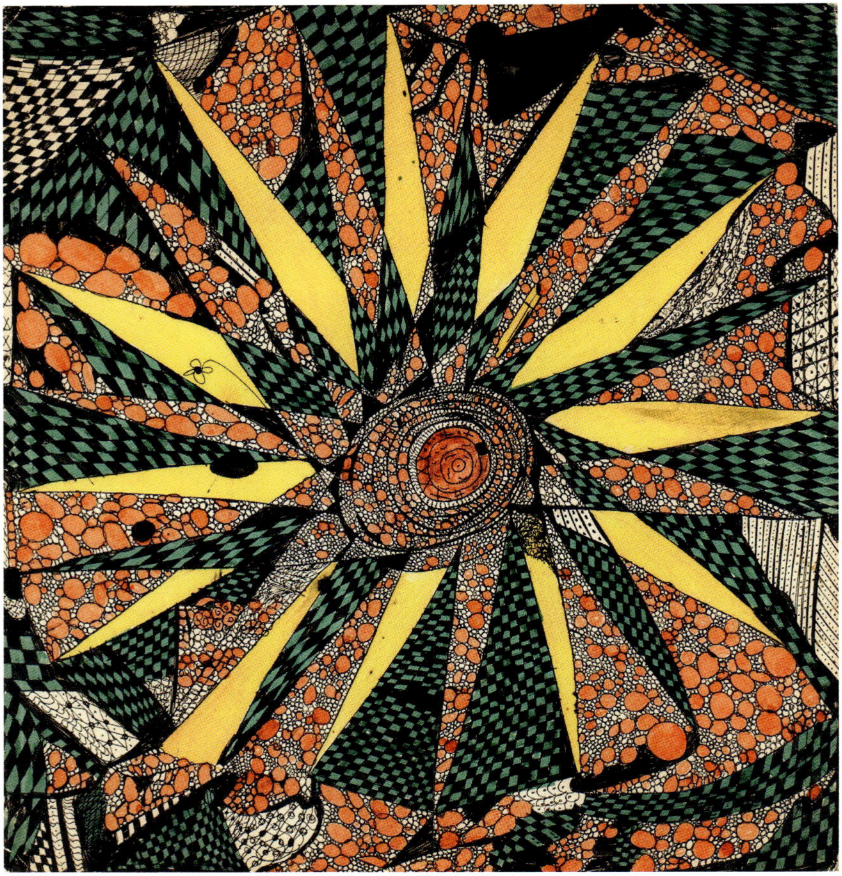

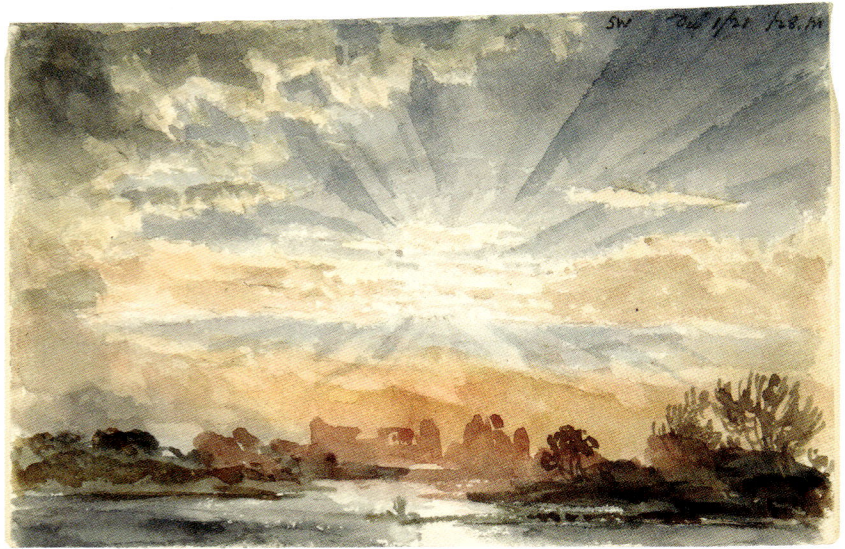

**17** *Untitled* *c.*1945
Madge Gill
(1882–1961)
Ink on paper

In 1920, the year after
the loss of her stillborn
daughter, Madge Gill
became possessed by the
spirit guide Myrninerest.
Much of Gill's work
was produced in
trance conditions
under the influence of
Myrninerest, and she
often used the name as
a signature. In later life,
Gill worked as a medium
in her neighbourhood of
Upton Park, London.

**18** *Landscape with
Rising Sun*  1828
Joseph Michael Gandy
(1771–1843)
Watercolour
over graphite

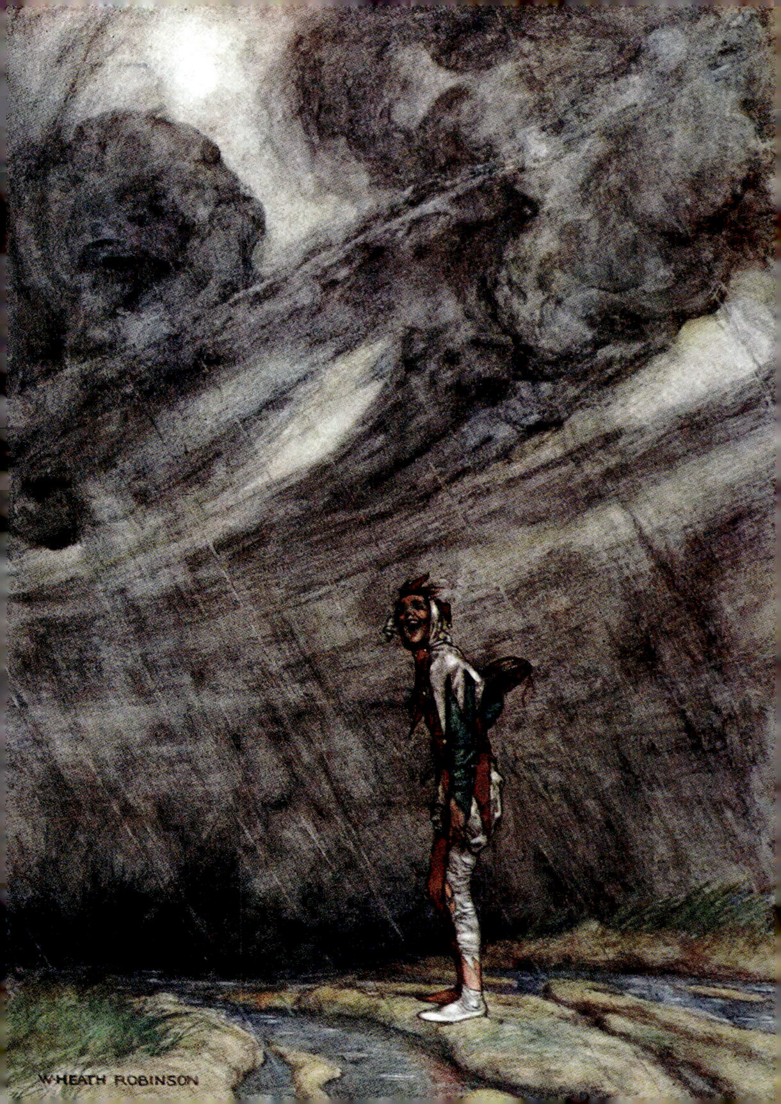

W·HEATH·ROBINSON

# 2

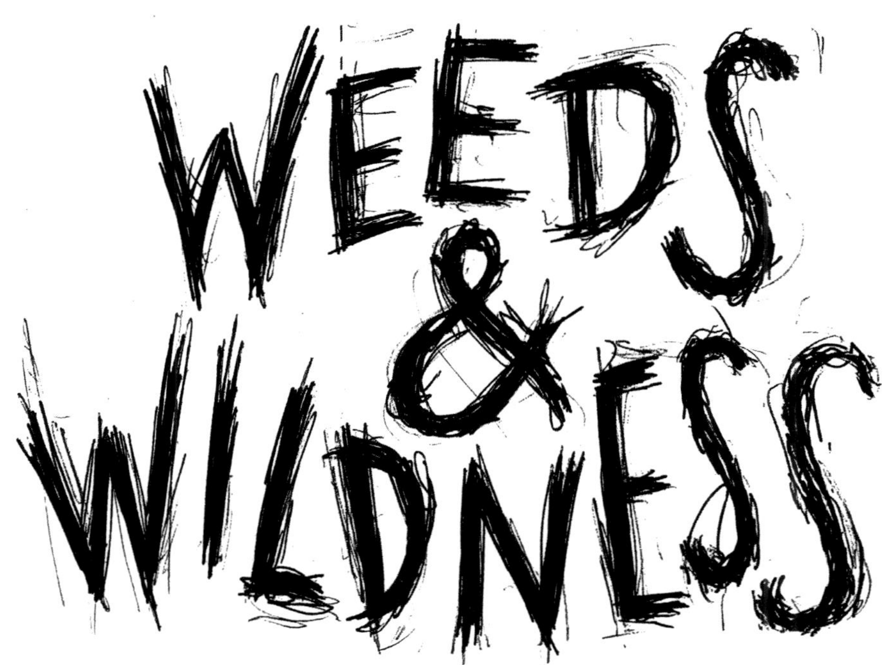

# WEEDS & WILDNESS

PREVIOUS PAGE

**19** *Clown (sings) "For the Rain it Raineth Every Day", from Shakespeare's* Twelfth Night
1908  William Heath Robinson (1872–1944)  Lithograph with colour

ENGLAND IS A BODY WITH ALL THE
SOFTNESSES AND HIDDEN PLACES
THAT BODIES POSSESS.

We scramble over ribs of tree trunk and roll breathless down breasts of hill. We wander through soft miles of fields, which are cave-mouthed and tree-haired. We bathe in those rock-pool eyes and river tears; the rainbow brows are comet-lit.

But a body is a living thing, and living things grow and bloom and age and wither. They can be injured. The mines cut England to the bone (bone is chalk, and marrow is soil), and the forest was torn up to build future shipwrecks. The body sags and blemishes. Quicksilver changes *flash* like lightning storm: hail, sungleam, squall. All these moods as capricious as a boy-king's but always, at the end, returning to the rain.

Over and over we see the same shapes tattooed across England's skin: nature's economy of pattern. Bare tree branches are maps of arteries, are forks of lightning, are estuaries seen from a hawk's eye, are cracks in river ice, are lungs, are WiFi networks. Whirlpools are whorls of hair, storms brew in teacups and sycamore seeds spin like helicopters. England's palette – blue, green, brown – is daubed everywhere: in eyes and skies, in fur and feathers.

Every body has its ages. In young spring, everything grows too fast, pale shoots push up through death, and cabbage whites struggle out of pupae shrouds. Everything reaching for the sun, freckling and burnishing and burning. Summer promises maturity; as with the lives of England's people, its prime is brief and broken. In the middle age of autumn, England's skin begins to taste of dying things. Whisky, peat and veins of mould. Oil-slick leaves rotting in the crook of dead branches. The exuberant nakedness of spring's youth is now clothed in the sombre plaid of ploughed fields.

And always everything rushing downhill into winter: England's home screen. Greyed over and wrinkled, but gentler too now that the old wounds have dulled and smoothed. Our aching joints mean rain, and it always rains. Rain is the soft filter that smears and confuses and melds and hides. Rain that transfigures sea into sky into cloud into land into wild, wild dreams.

England is a body with only its scars and broken bones holding it together.

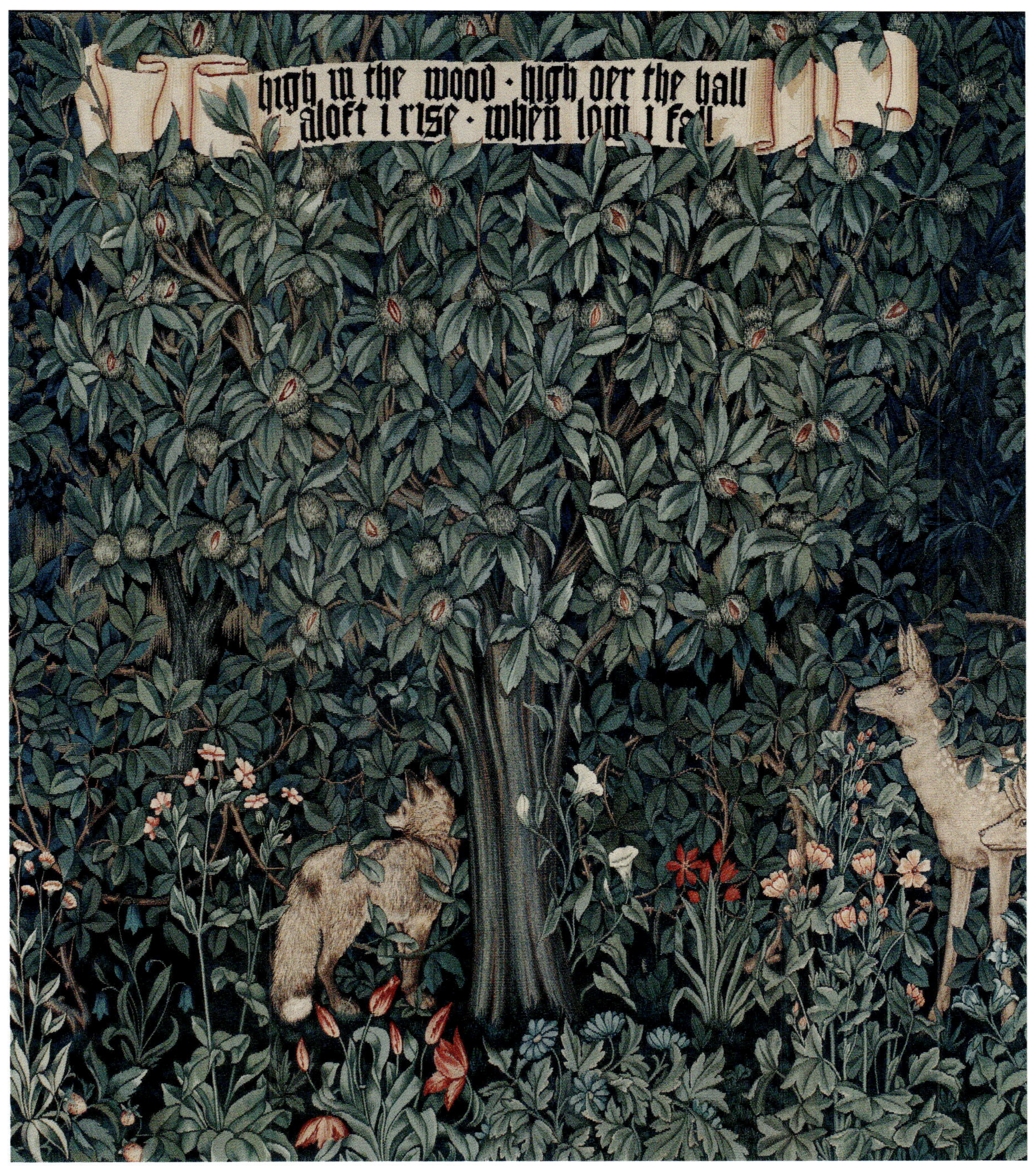


**20**  *Tapestry: Greenery*  1892  John Henry Dearle (1859–1932)
Designed for William Morris & Co.  Wool and mohair; tapestry weave

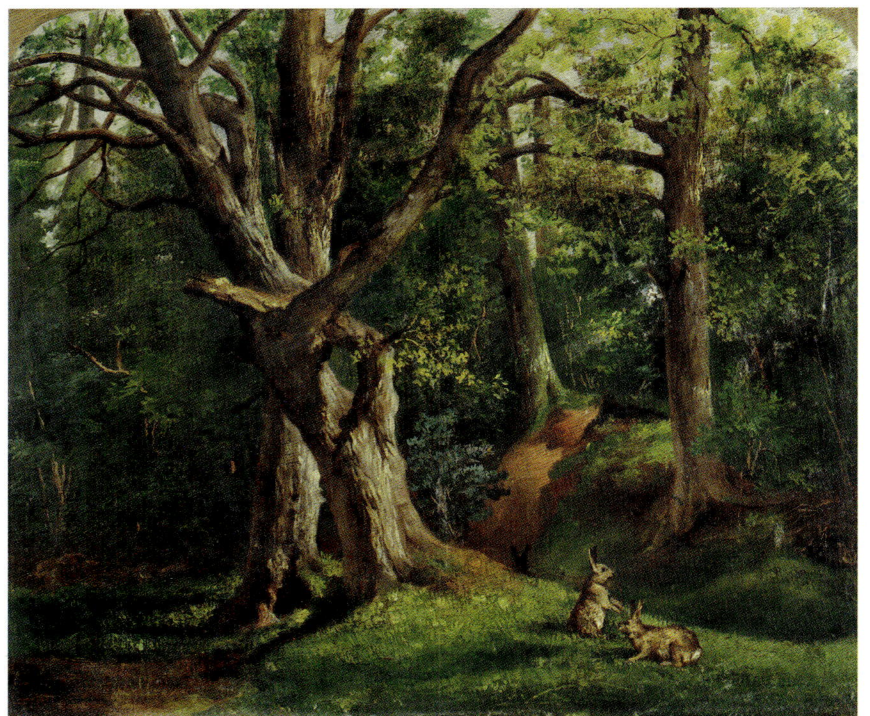

**21** *Woodland Scene
with Rabbits* c.1862
Hubert von Herkomer
(1849–1914)
Oil on canvas

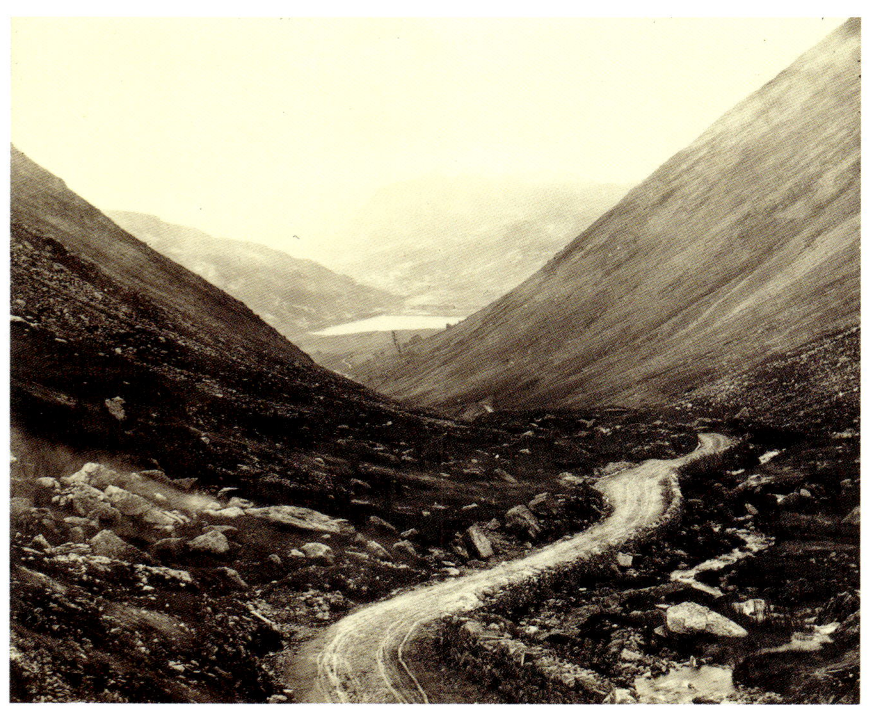

**22** *Kirkstone Pass,
Westmoreland* 1857
Roger Fenton
(1819–69)
Salted paper print

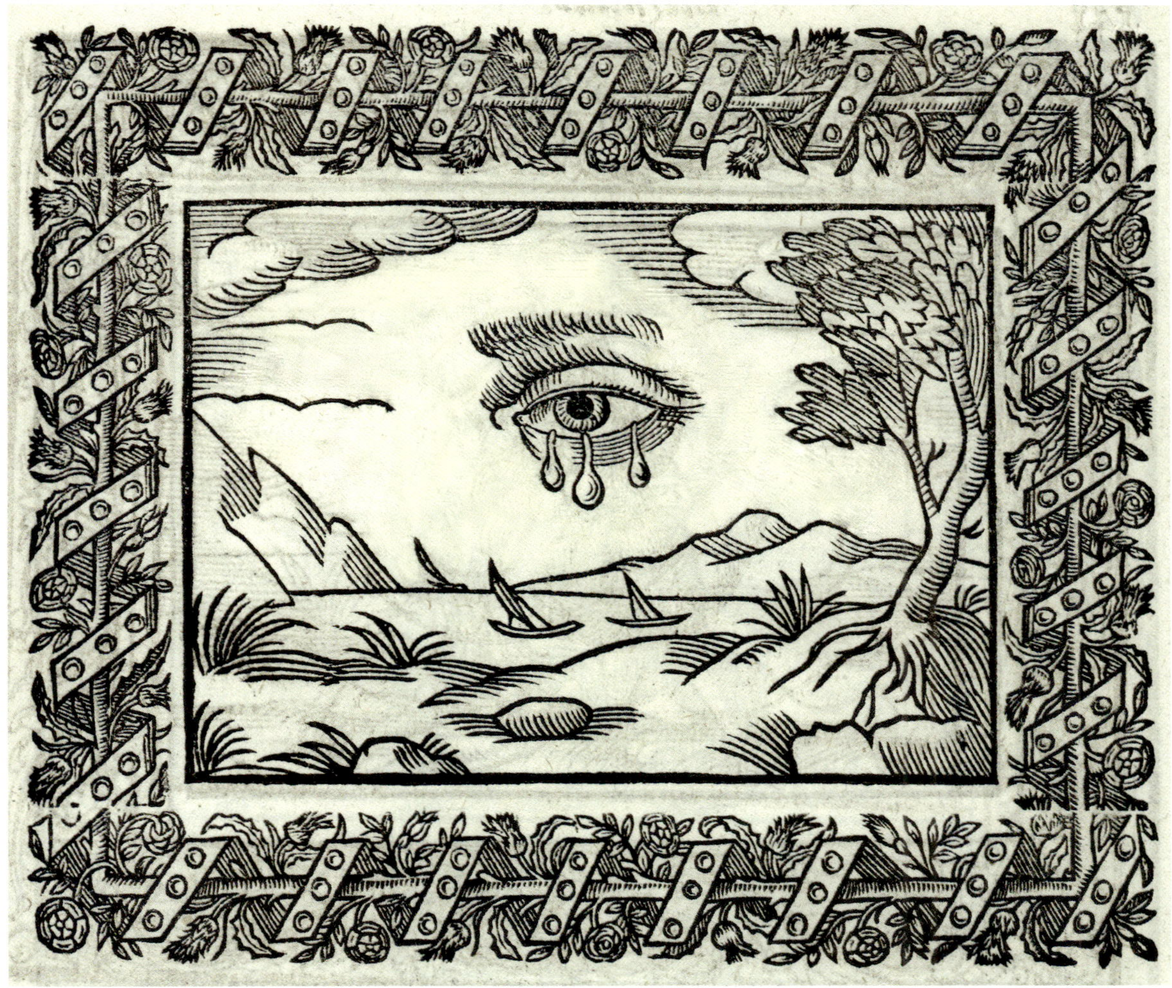

23 *Minerva Britannia* 1612
Henry Peacham (*c.*1576 – *c.*1643)
Book illustration

Emblem books, an early modern extension of the medieval bestiary, became very popular in western Europe in the seventeenth century. They were typically composed of three elements: an image, a motto, and a text drawing parallels between the two. Peacham's *Minerva Britannia* was dedicated to Henry, Prince of Wales, and utilizes multiple symbols to present a single idea on each page. This image is paired with the motto *"Hei mihi quod vidi"*, which can be roughly translated as "Woe is me, the things I have seen". The image represents the tears of a thwarted lover.

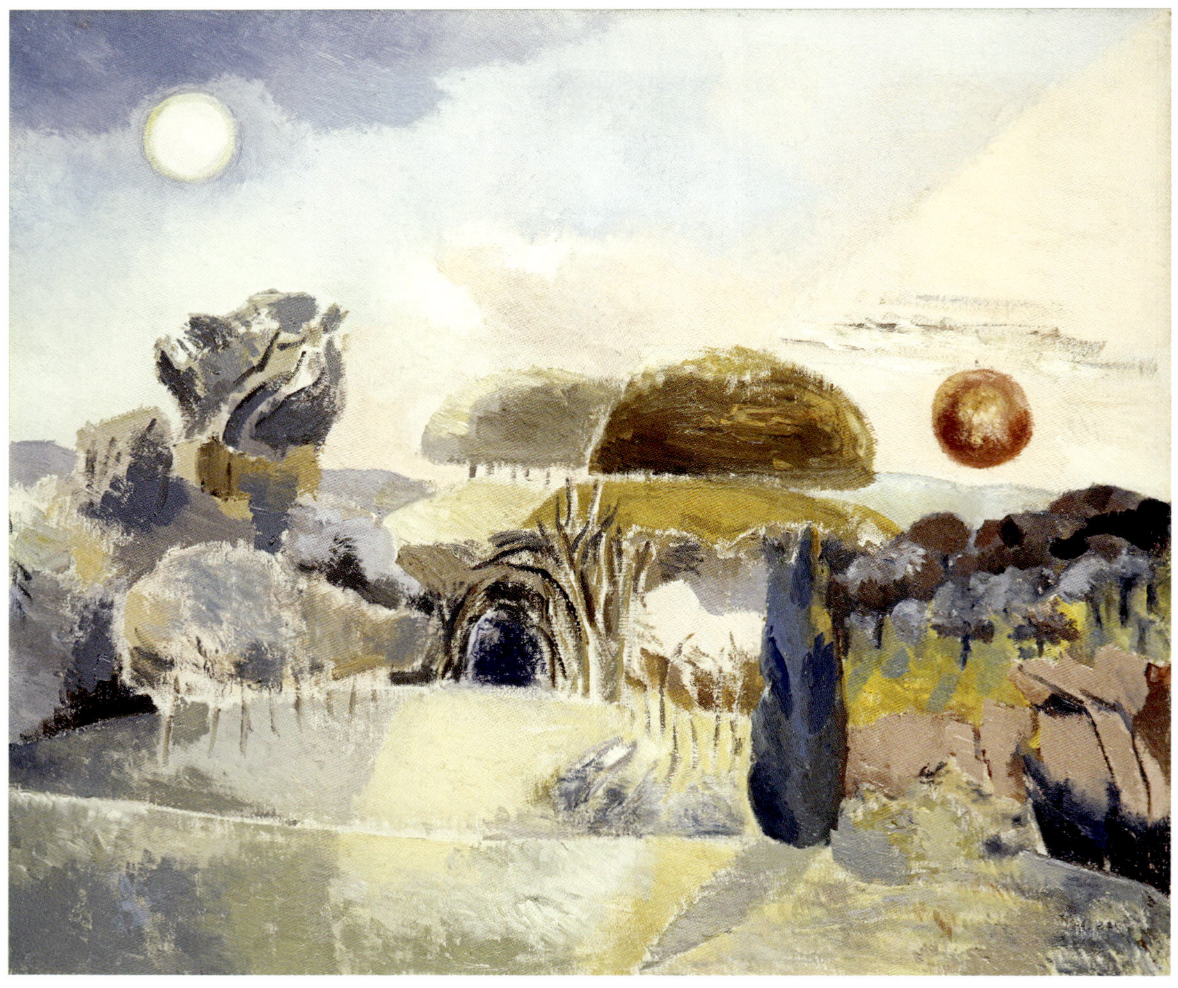

24  *Landscape of the Vernal Equinox (III)*  1944
Paul Nash (1889–1946)
Oil on canvas

Nash enshrines in vibrant oils the shape of England's ancient landscape, with Oxfordshire's Wittenham Clumps featuring on the horizon of his painting. His colour choice evocatively depicts processes of temporal change, as spring takes over from winter, and the moon replaces the sun in the duochromatic sky.



25  *Journey to Avebury*  1973
Derek Jarman (1942–94)
S8mm film

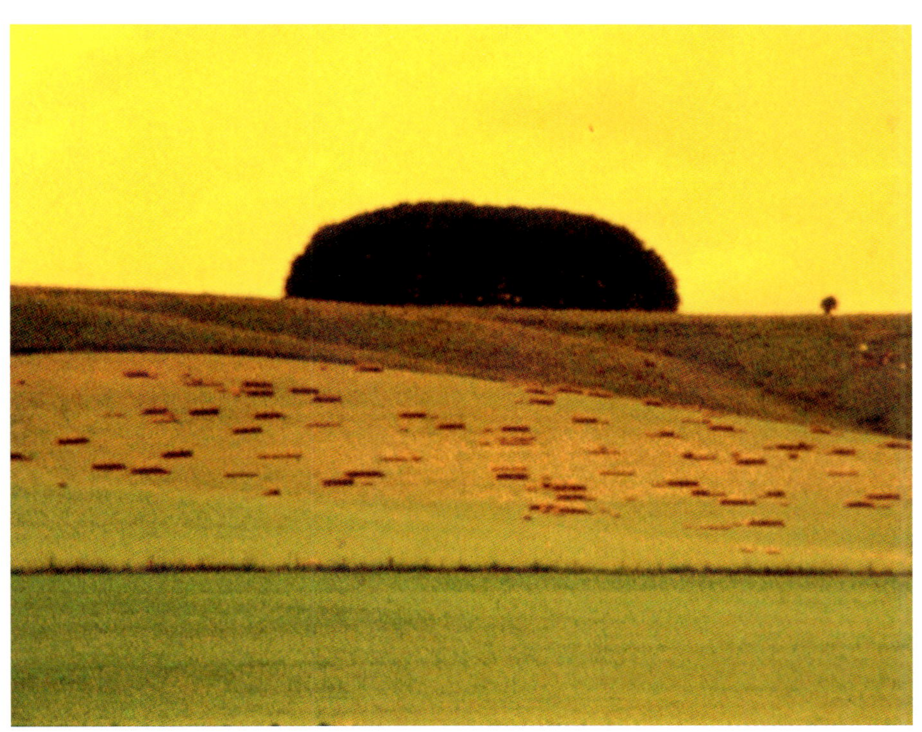

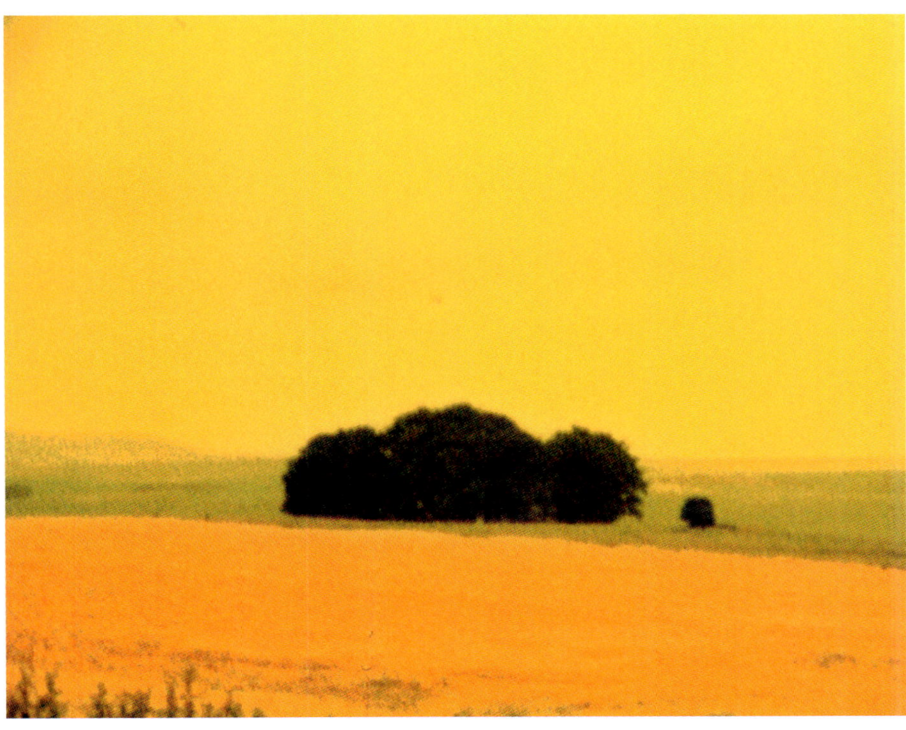

WEEDS & WILDNESS

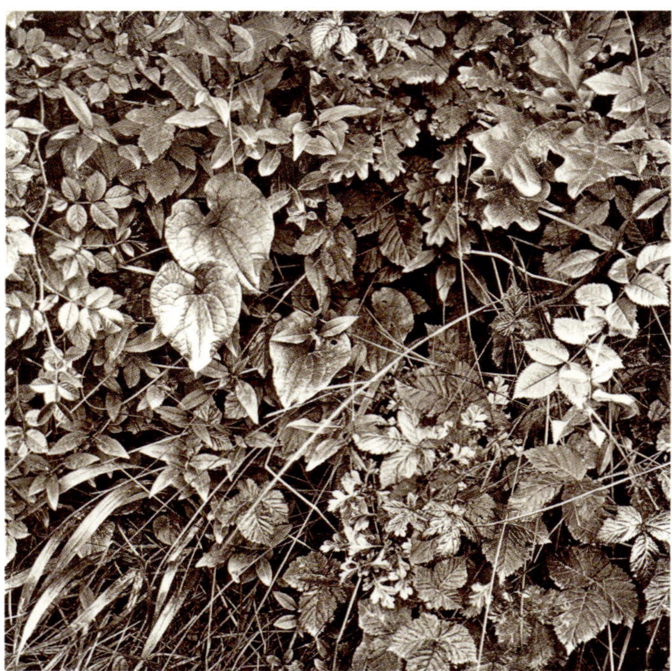

**26**  *Hedgerow Study*  *c.*1888
Frederick H. Evans (1853–1943)
Platinum print photograph

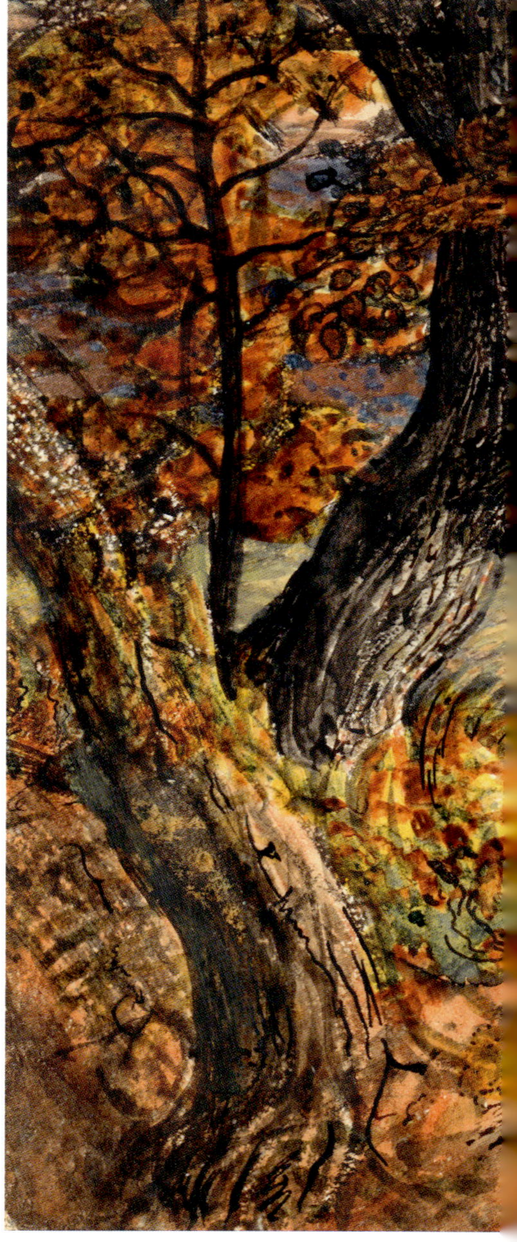

**27**  *The Weald of Kent*  *c.*1833–4
Samuel Palmer (1805–81)
Watercolour and gouache on paper

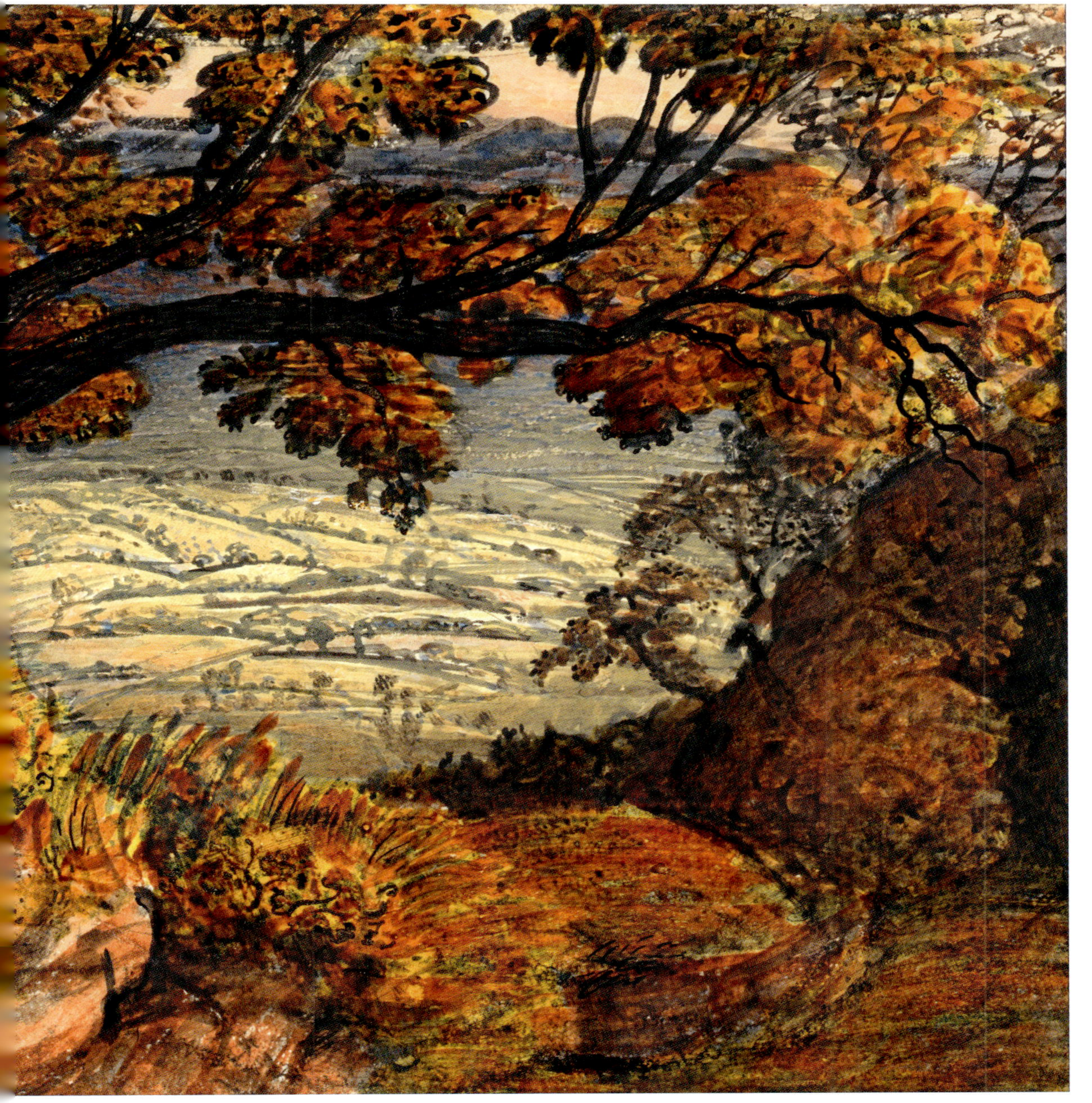

WEEDS & WILDNESS

28  *Scenes from the Passion: A Few Days
Before Christmas*  2002–03
George Shaw (b.1966)
Humbrol enamel on board

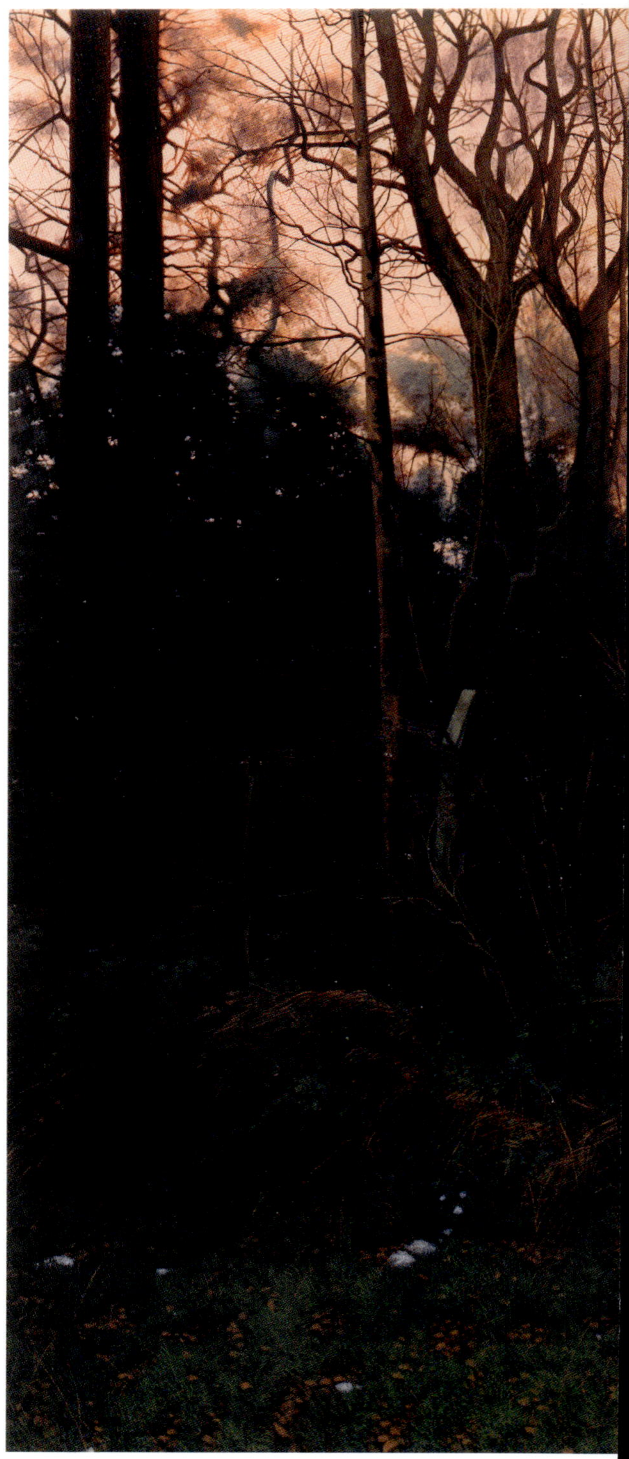

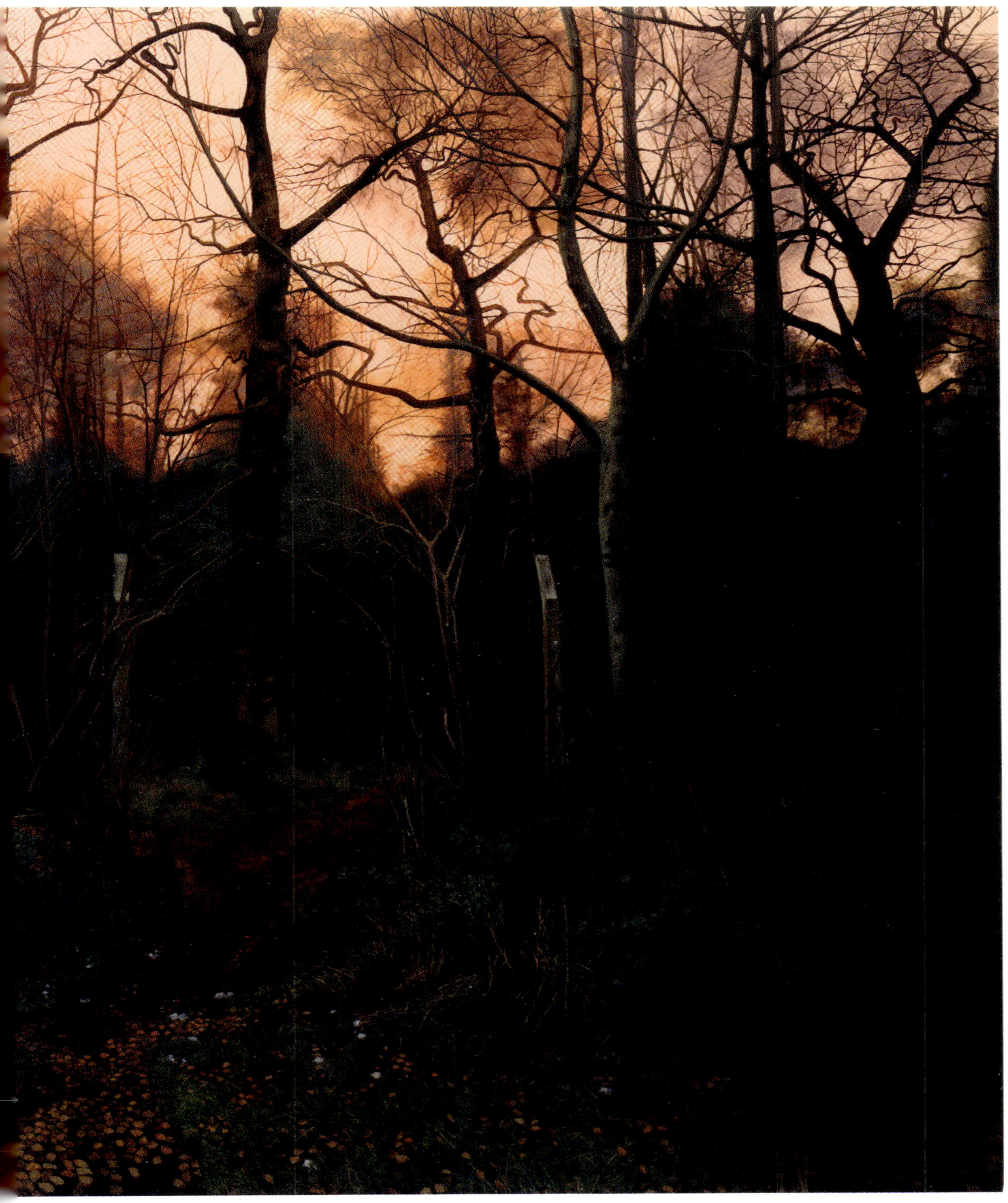

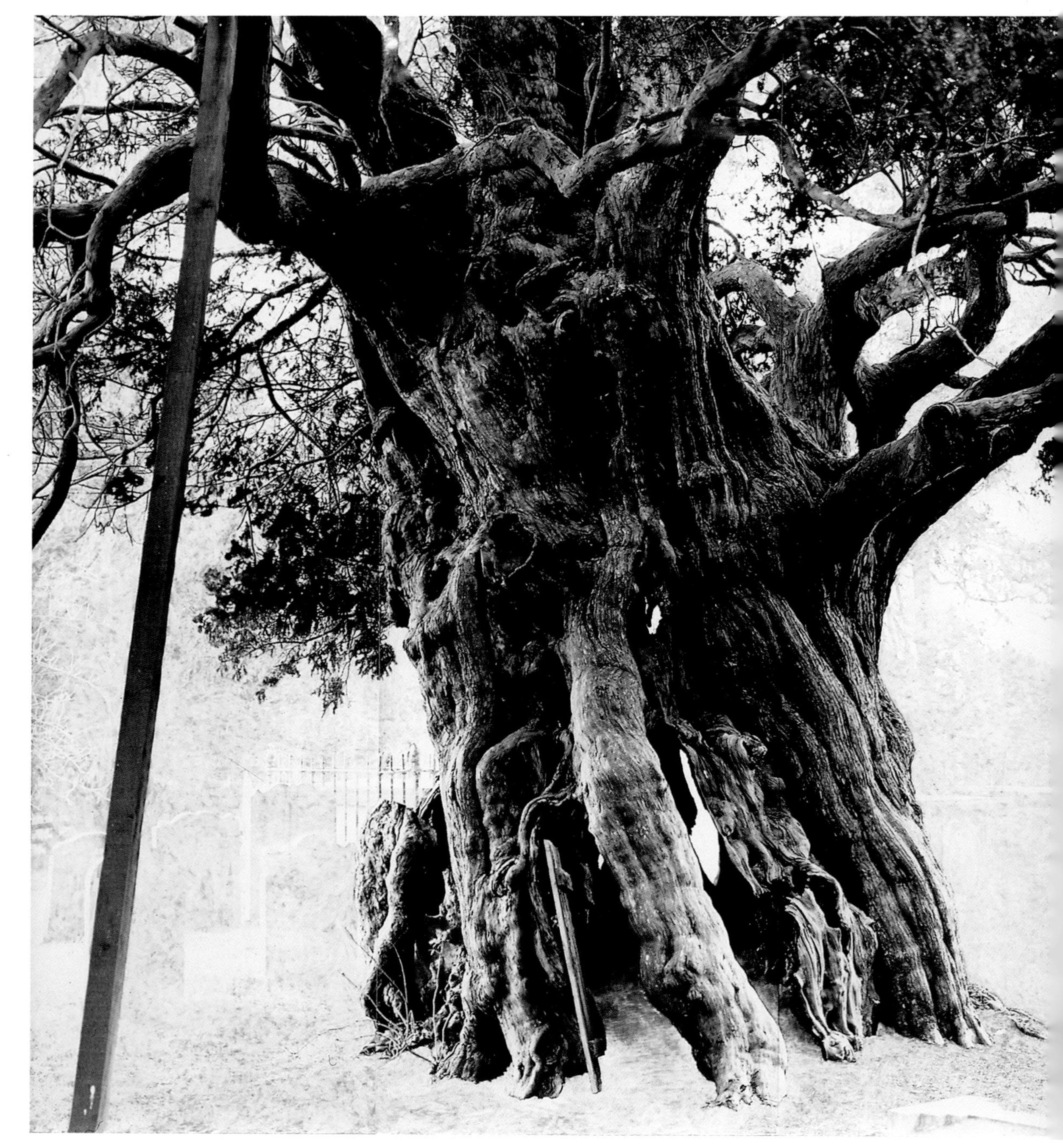

29  *Crowhurst*  2006
Tacita Dean (b.1965)
Gouache on fibre-based photograph mounted on paper

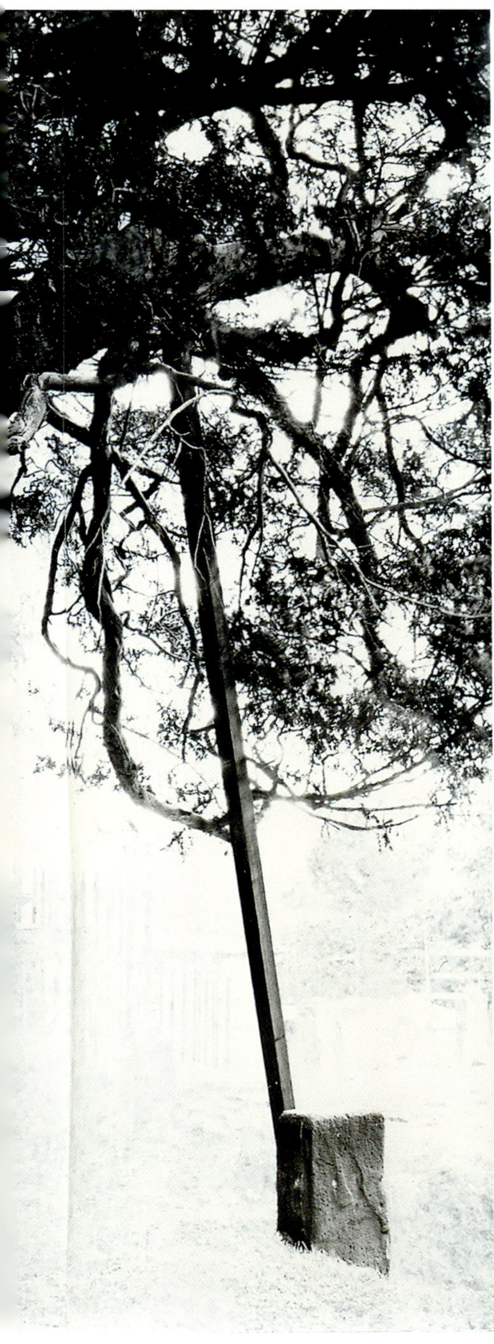

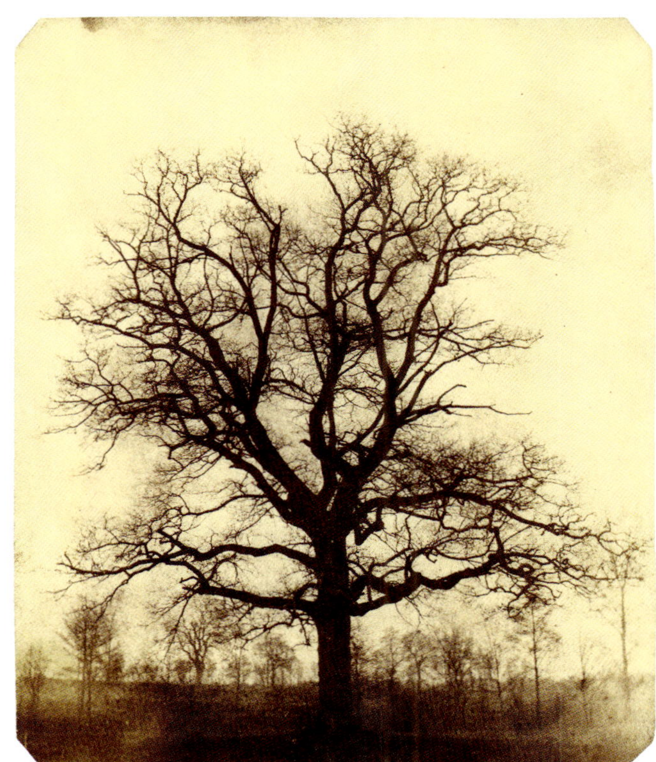

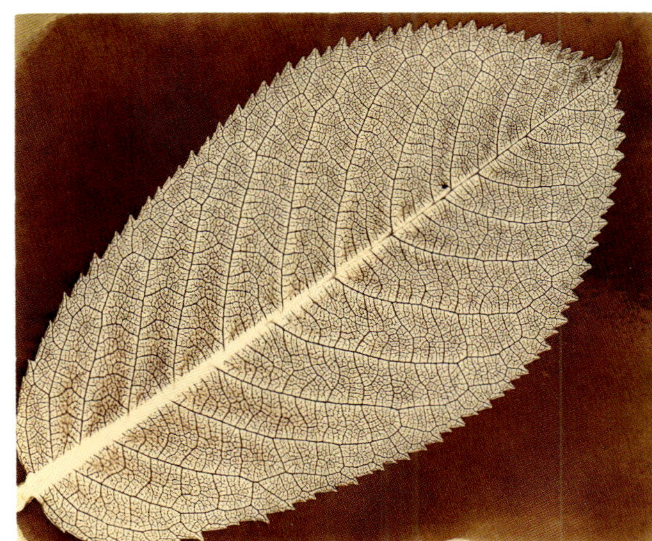

**30a** *An Oak Tree in Winter* 1842–3   **30b** *Leaf* 1839
William Henry Fox Talbot (1800–77)
Salted paper print and calotype negative

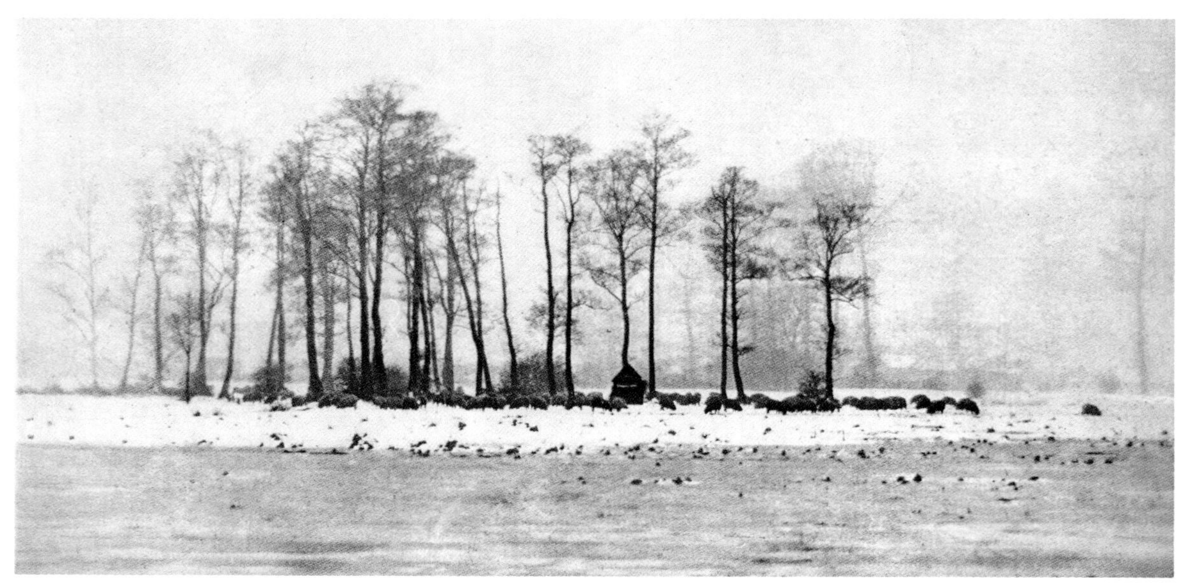

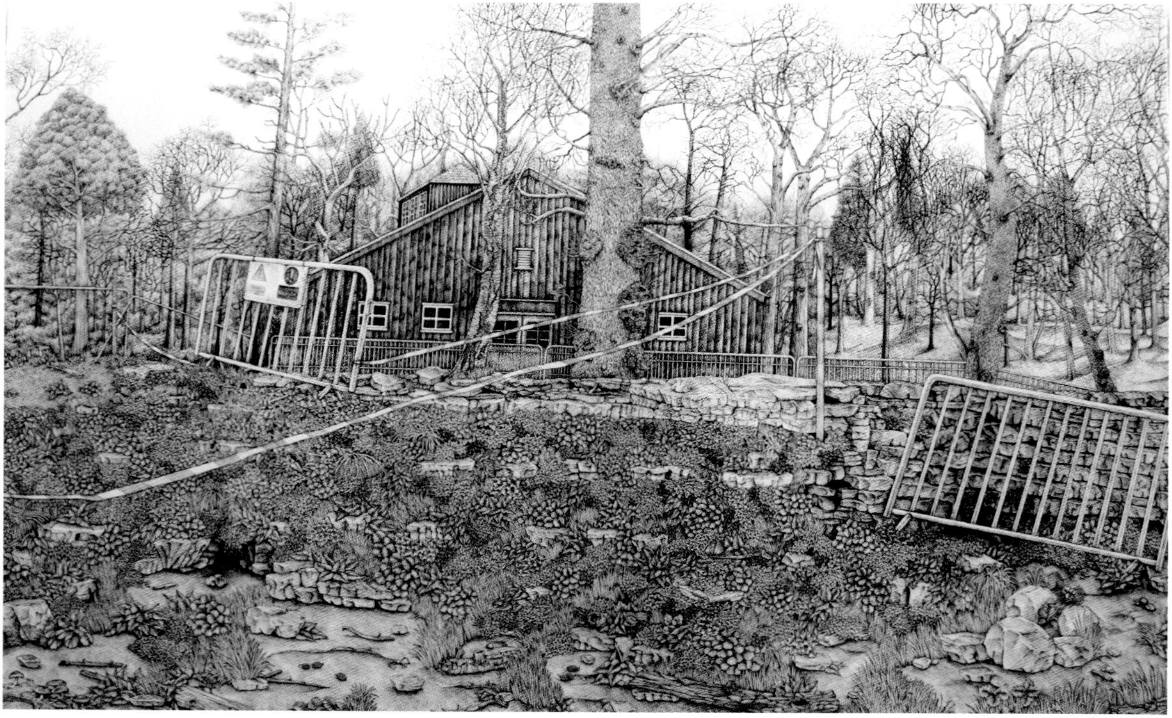

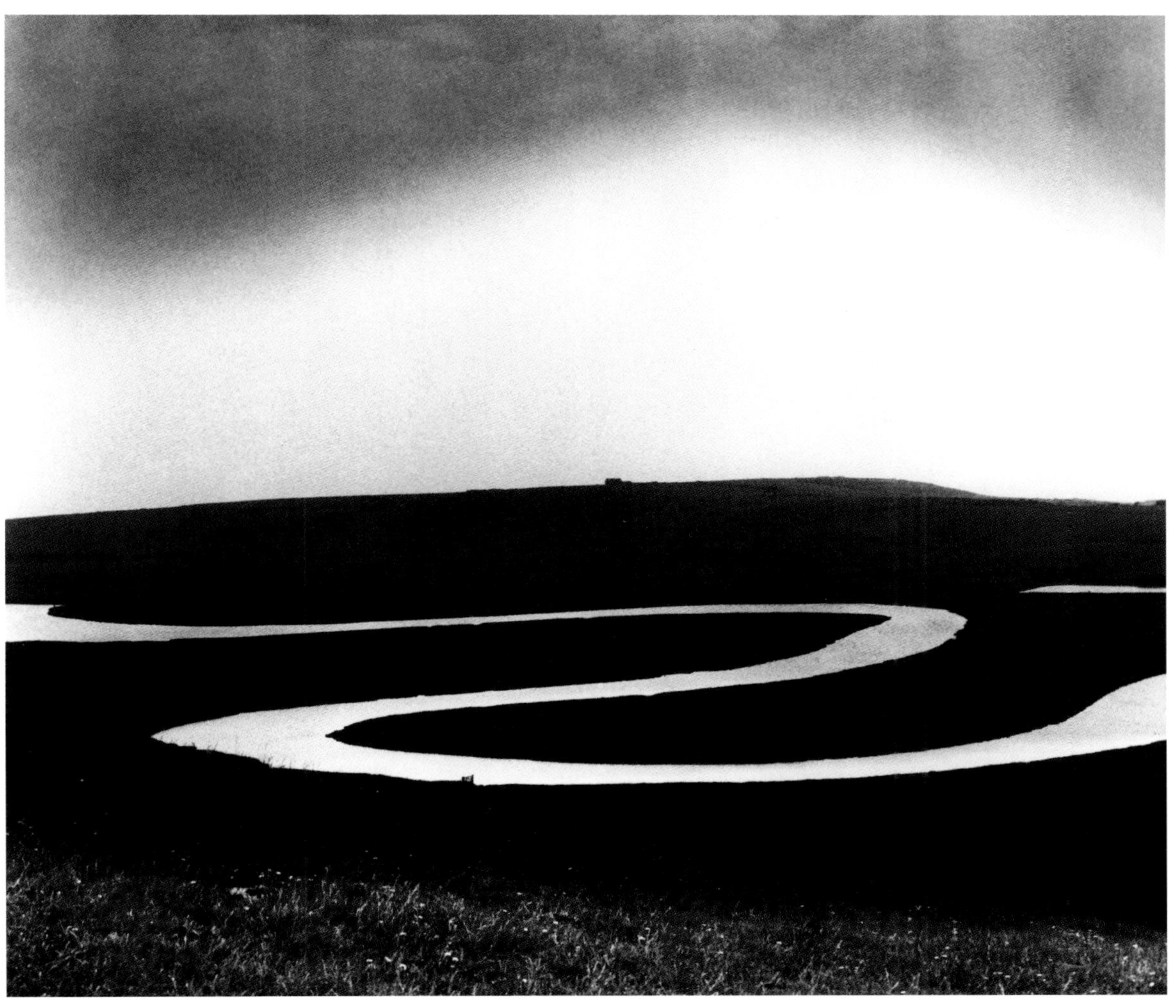

32  *Cuckmere River*  1963
Bill Brandt (1904–83)
Silver gelatin print

Brandt, known for his photographs of the female nude, here presents the Cuckmere River as integral to England's curving body. Its various bends cut through the dark landscape, meandering toward its mouth, which lies at the entrance to the English Channel. Despite the river's name purportedly deriving from the Old English word for "fast-flowing", Brandt's image fixes the river in a moment of seemingly enduring tranquillity.

33  *Though the Way is Lost*  2015
Olivia Kemp (b.1990)
Ink on paper

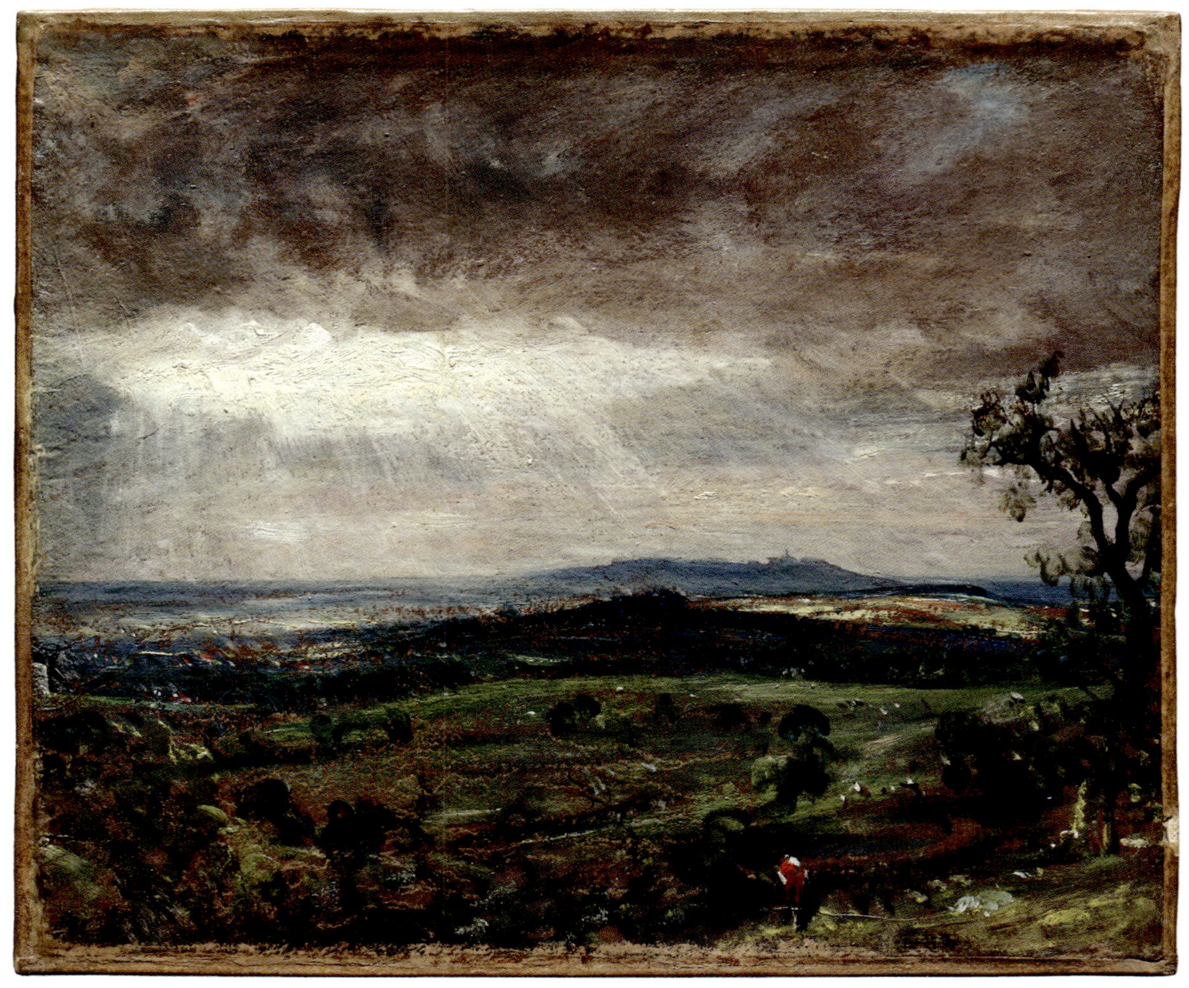

**34** *Hampstead Heath looking towards Harrow*  1821
John Constable (1776–1837)
Oil on paper laid on board, red ground

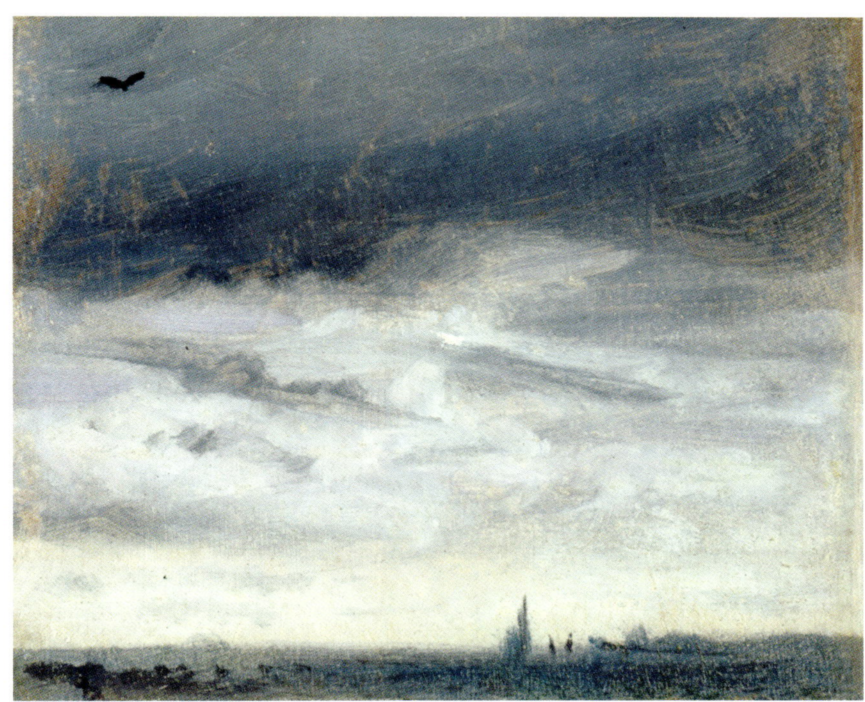

35 *A Grey Day*  *c.*1845
Lionel Constable
(1828–87)
Oil on canvas

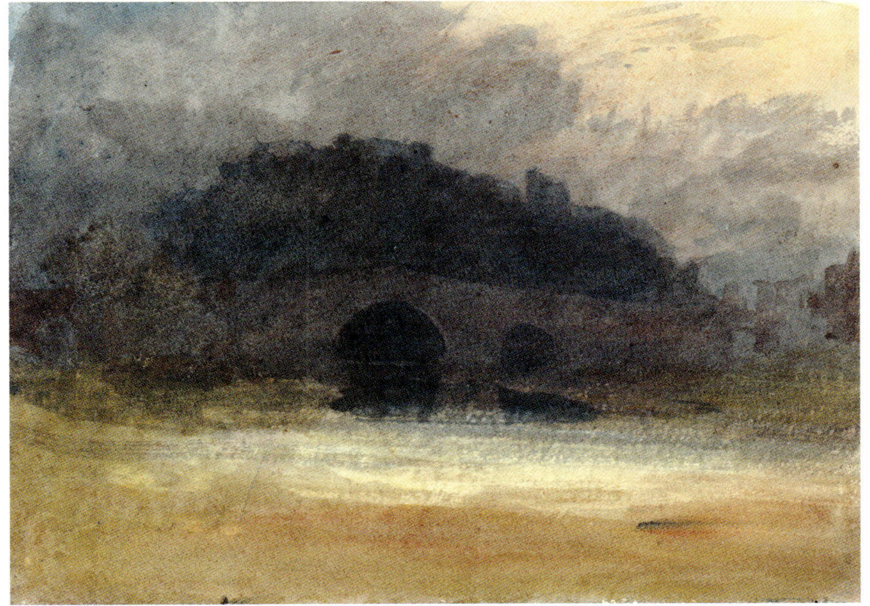

36 *Evening Landscape*
*c.*1798–9
Joseph Mallord
William Turner
(1775–1851)
Watercolour on paper

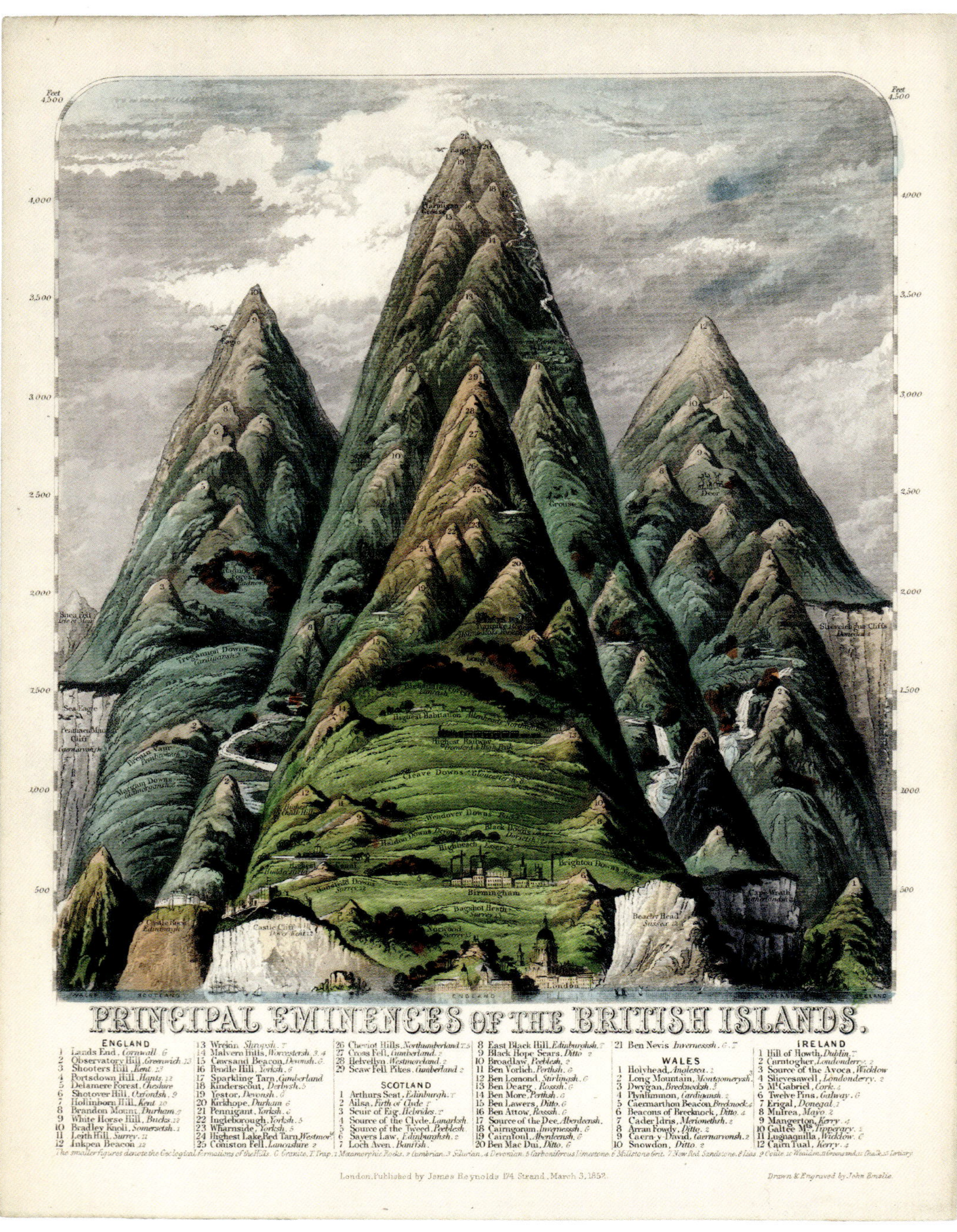


**37** *Principal Eminences of the British Islands* 1852
John Emslie (1813–75)  Colour engraving

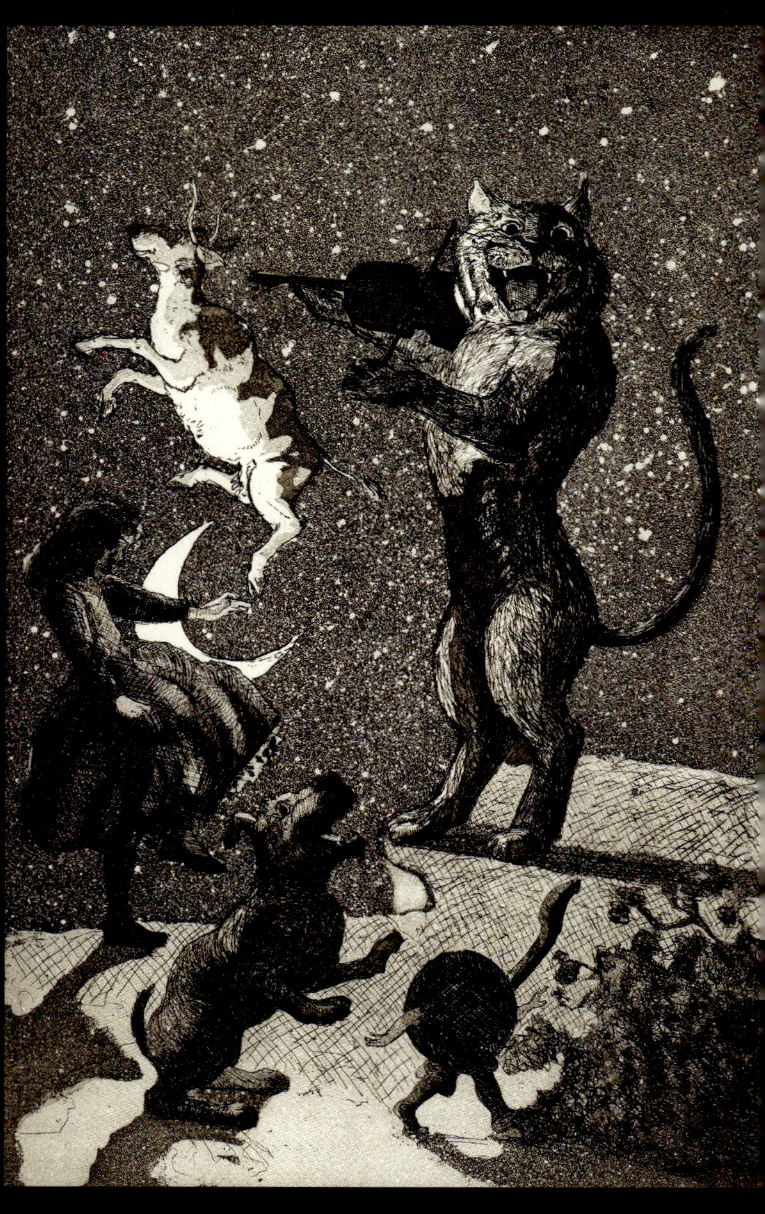

# 3

# REBELLIOUS NATURE

PREVIOUS PAGE

38 *Hey Diddle Diddle* 1989 From the *Nursery Rhymes* series
Paula Rego (b.1935) Etching and aquatint on paper

**ENGLAND IS A SHALLOW GRAVE WITH WILD FLOWERS FOR A HEADSTONE.**

We head to Tyburn, drawn by the sound of children singing and the scent of flowers. We arrive as dusk falls and find a boy in the graveyard, swinging from the branches of an elm that has burst the broken teeth of headstones. He watches us as he swings – back and forth, back and forth – and says, "See how lush it is at your feet, where the wildflowers open and twist and climb? Every living thing was dead once, and England carries death in every green shoot." The boy leaps from the branch with a flourish and lands on all fours. He places his ear to the ground and raises a hand to us. "Here, where the land has been fed by a thousand executions, the underground sings with a morbid ripeness." He smiles up at us. "It was here the triffids ran wild." In a moment he's scampering away toward Hyde Park, nimble as a deer. He calls over his shoulder, "Come, night is no time to be out."

He's right about that. Hyde Park is sullen and sodden. We hear his voice from the lightless route ahead. "Maybe the park is named for Dr Jekyll's own dark undergrowth," he calls as he skips along concrete paths crumbling into marshland. From every side comes the glint of dark water. The Tyburn Boy leaps from tussock to tussock, easy as a goat, but we have to watch our steps in the dark. "Don't look down," he calls from the gloom, "It's all dead armies and crawling things beneath the surface."

We daren't look down because those creatures we thought had been tamed or broken, well, under the stars they seep back like bog water into the quietnesses. We are the interlopers here, and England is a marooned ark full of older, odder beings.

As dusk deepens into night, will o' the wisps flicker awake. A pale green light – the colour of money and sickness. All at once the isle is full of noises. It's a wilderness orchestra: gull cry and wolf howl over the percussion of broken bones. Leaves crackle like fire and trees fall. The city is a marshland lit by fire and we're assailed from all sides. Nettle burn and adder sting. Vines that coil around unwary ankles, and dark, dank lakes with eyeless things that wait patiently in the depths. Foxes and magpies steal trinkets from our bags, and if we sleep for an hour then moss grows over our ears and thistledown clogs our eyes. "Come on," calls the boy, "keep moving. This is no place to stop."

England is a shallow grave marked by dead flowers in a jar.

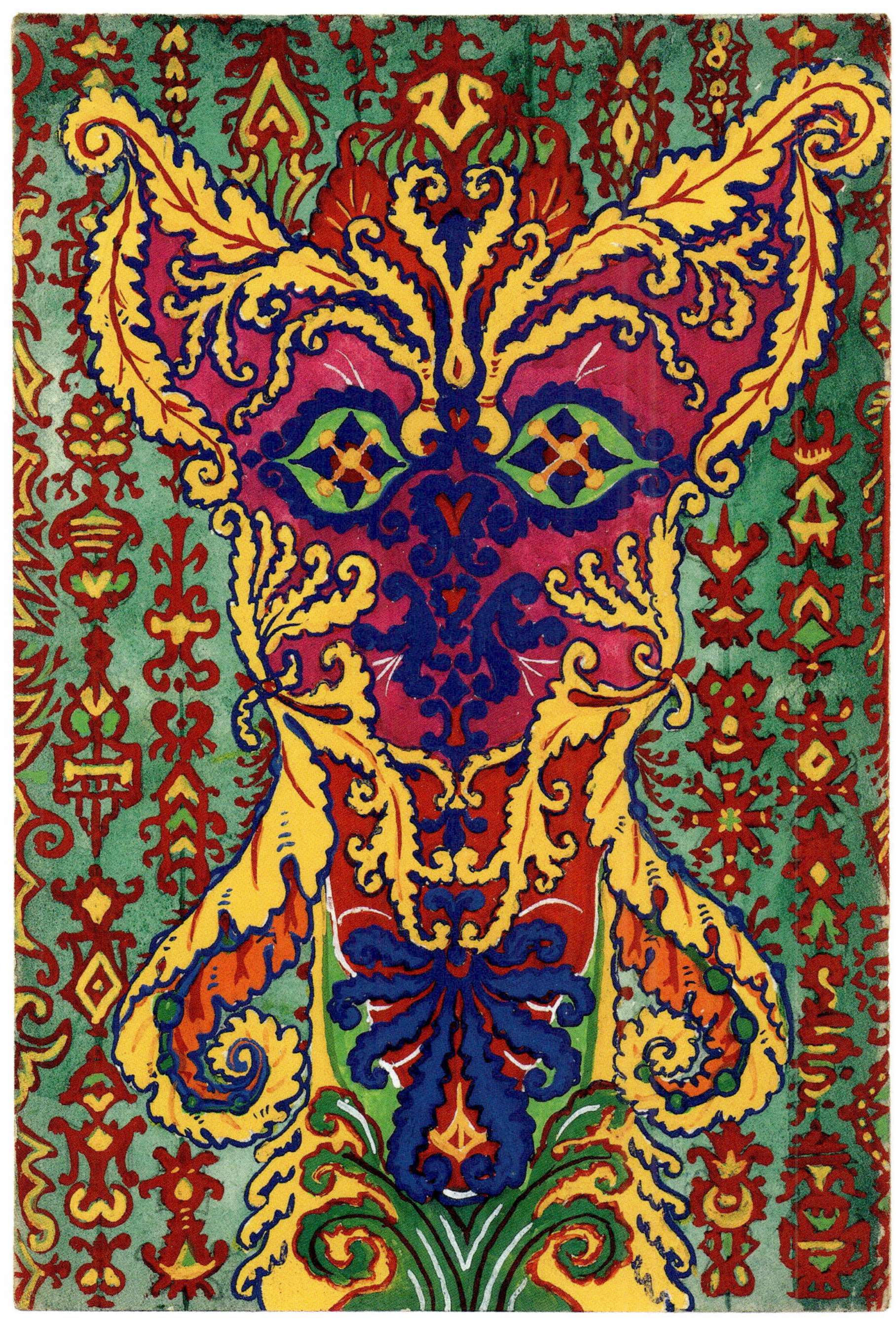

**39**  *A cat standing on its hind legs, formed by patterns supposed to be in the "early Greek" style  c.1925–39*
Louis Wain (1860–1939)  Gouache

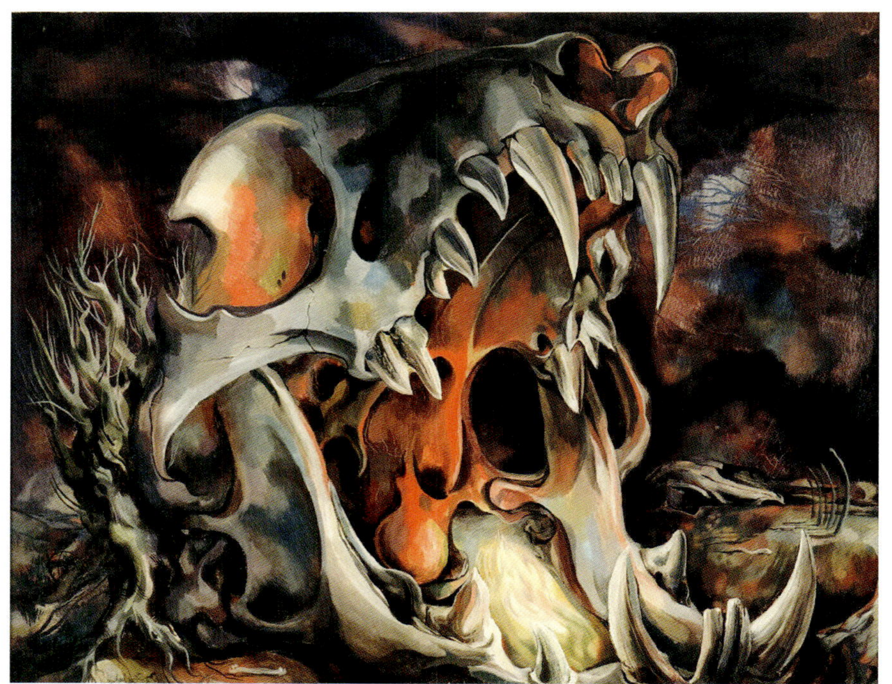

**40** *Skull Vision* 1943
Michael Ayrton
(1921–75)
Oil on panel

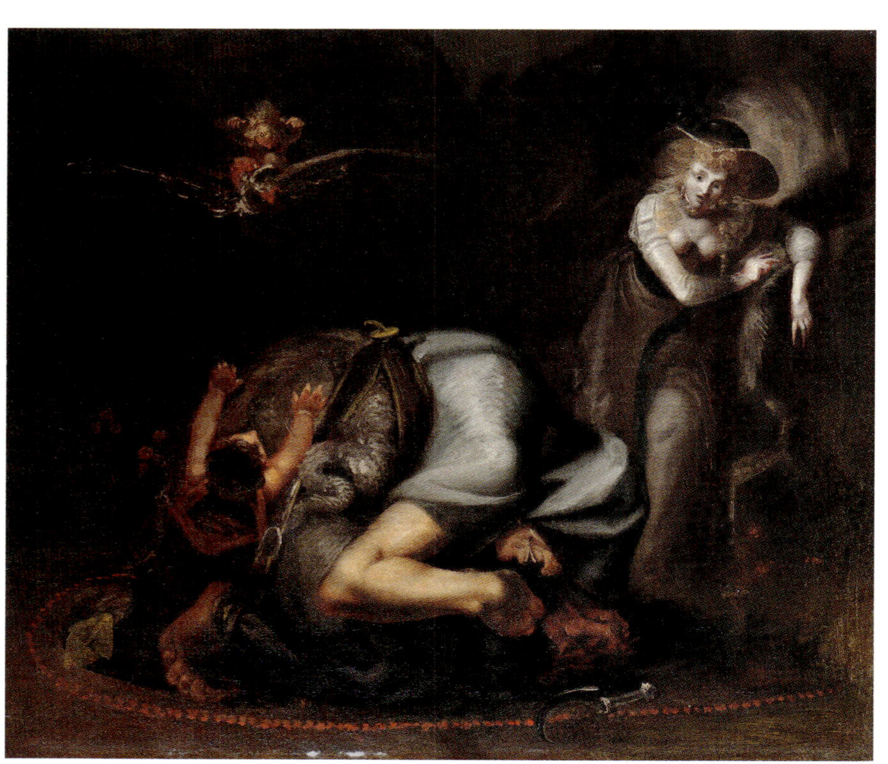

**41** *The Mandrake,
a Charm* 1785
Henry Fuseli
(1741–1825)
Oil on canvas

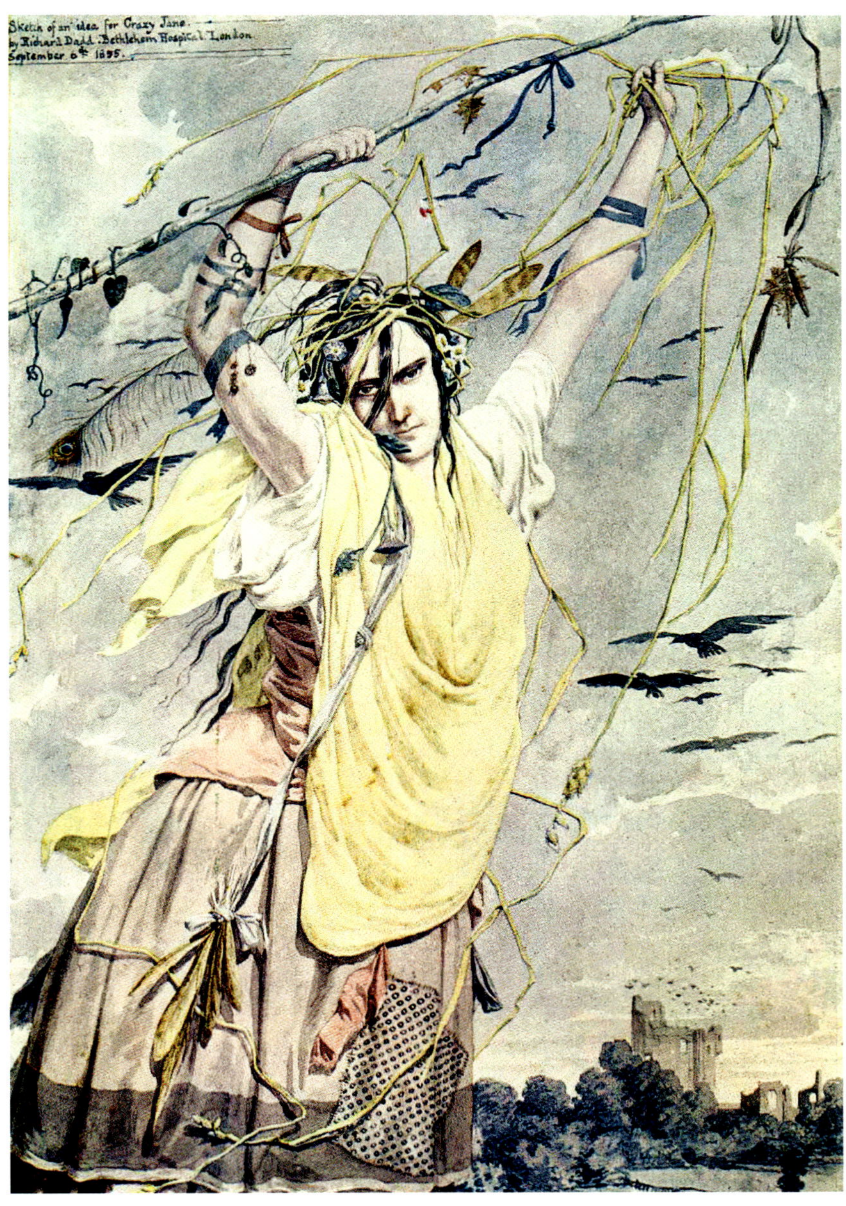



**42** *Sketch of an Idea for Crazy Jane* 1855
Richard Dadd (1817–86)
Watercolour on paper

Dadd's Crazy Jane, based on the ballad "Poor Crazy Jane", about a girl who was driven to insanity by being abandoned by her lover, is a wistful imagining of madness. Dadd himself had spent over a decade in Bethlem Royal Hospital by the time he painted this image, having murdered his father in 1843 during a psychotic episode.

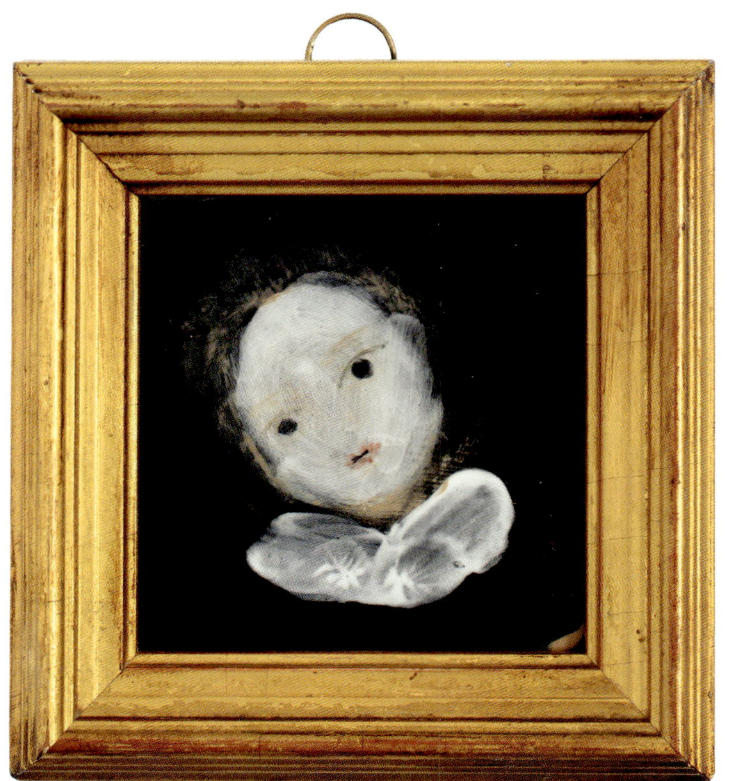



In the early nineteenth century, at the age of seventeen, Romantic writer Thomas de Quincey met Ann of Oxford Street, a sex-worker known now only through De Quincey's 1821 memoir *Confessions of an Opium Eater*. The addition of two bat wings to Goldsmith's glazed-clay portrait of De Quincey recall biographer and critic Leslie Stephen's view of him flying like "a bat on the wings of prose … to the true poetic region".

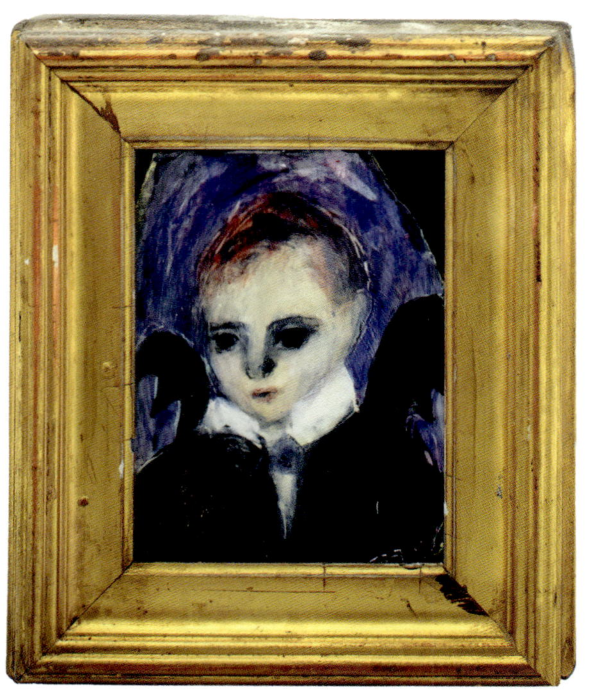

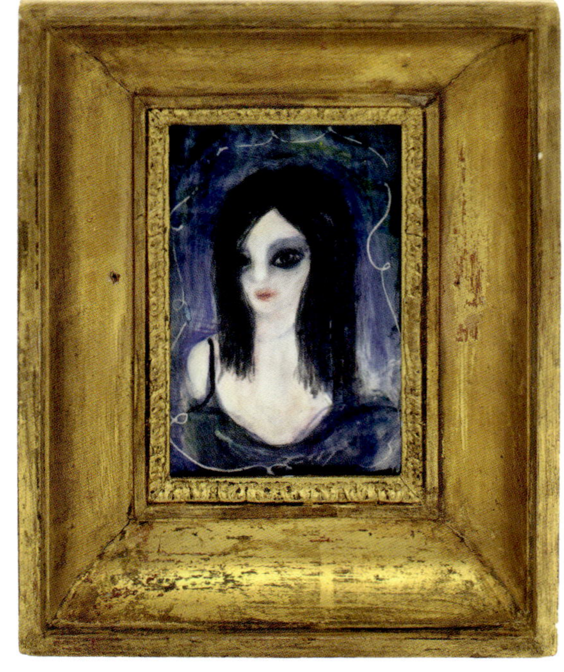

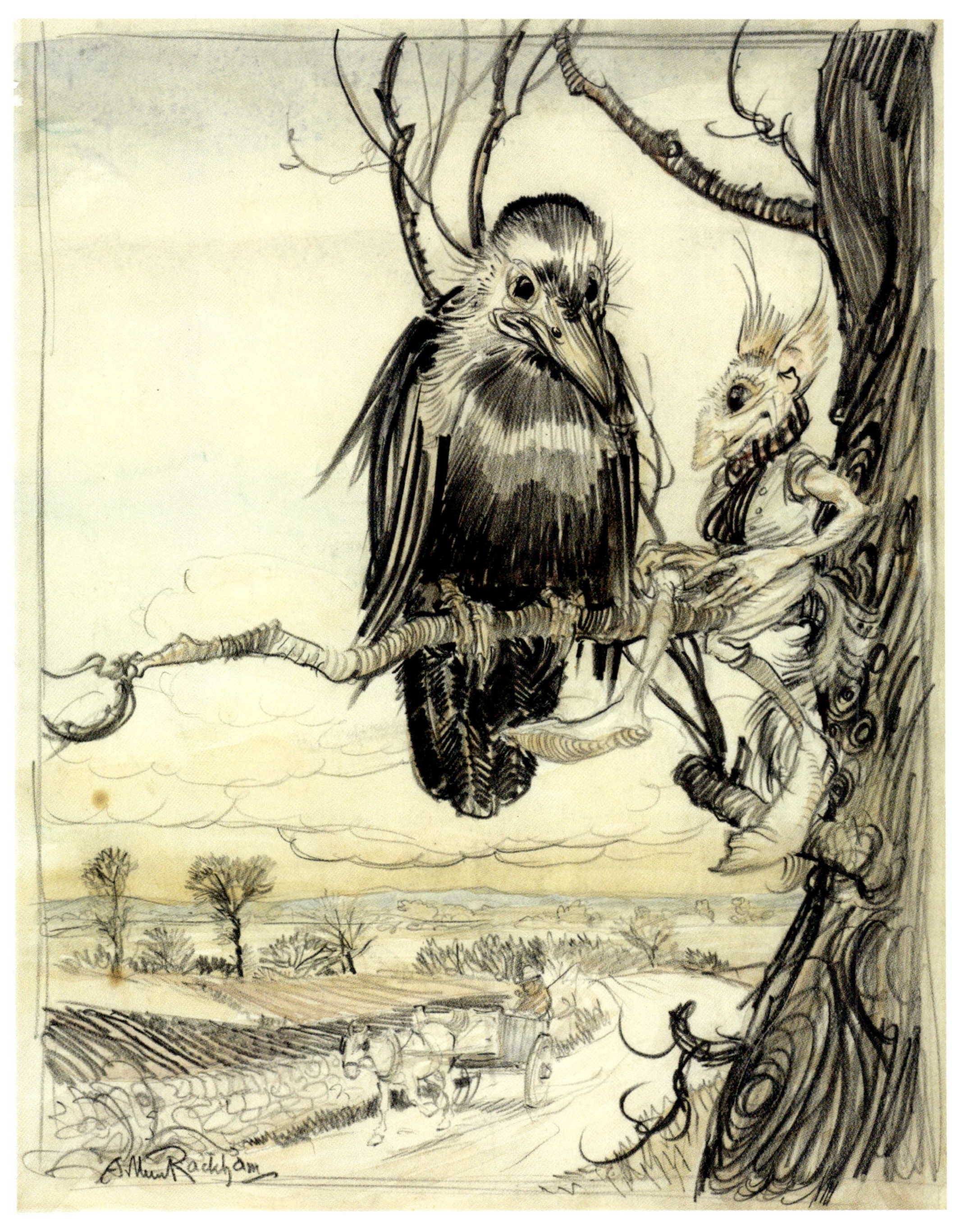

**44** *A Squirrel and a Crow*  1913
Arthur Rackham (1867–1939)  Ink and graphite

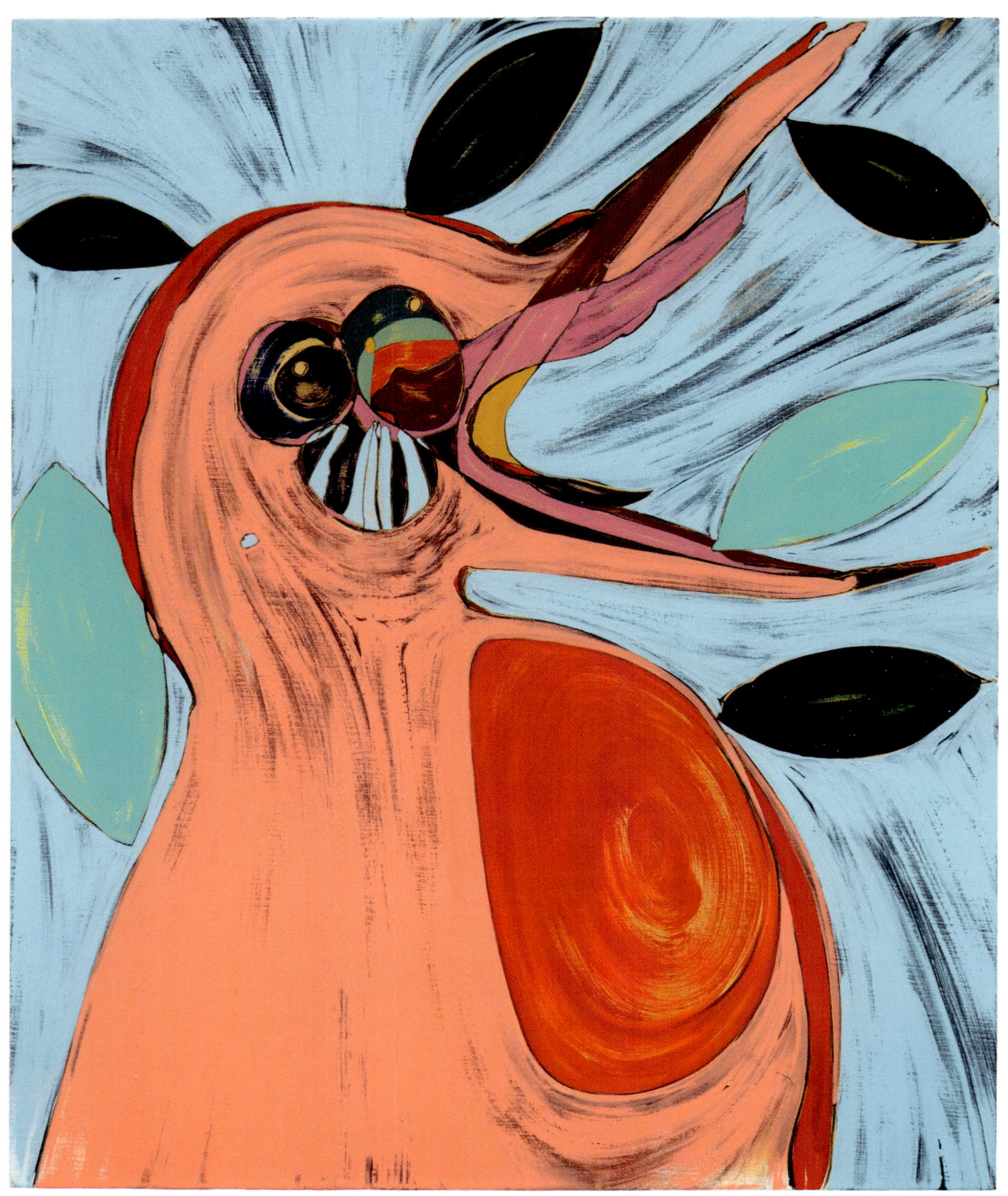

**45** *Bird Call* 2021
Nicola Tyson (b.1960)
Acrylic on linen

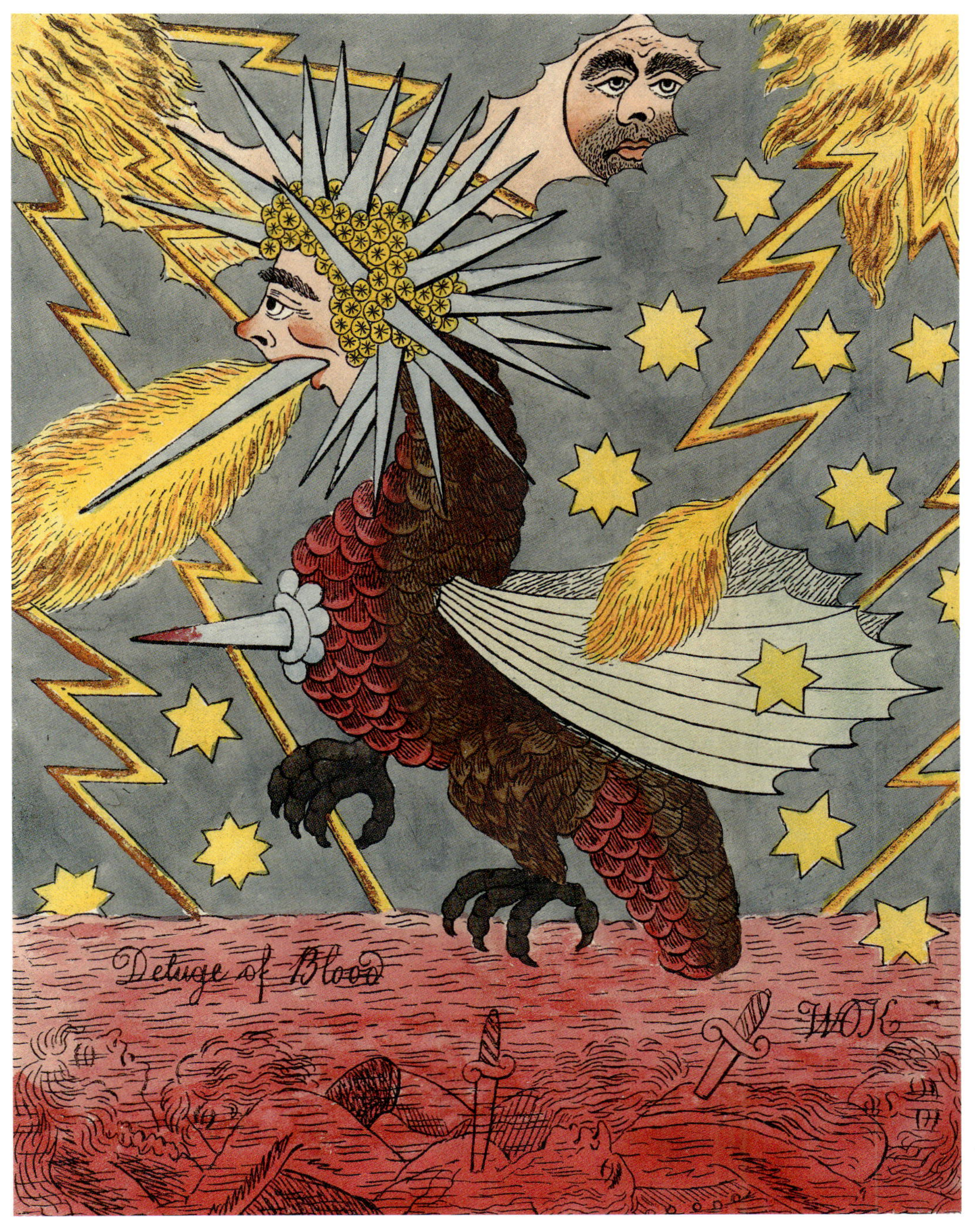


**46**  *A Vision, Vide, the Monster of Slaughter, the Distress of Nations; Deluge of Blodd*  1796 William O'Keefe (active 1794–1807)  Caricature of Prime Minister William Pitt the Younger  Etching with watercolour on paper

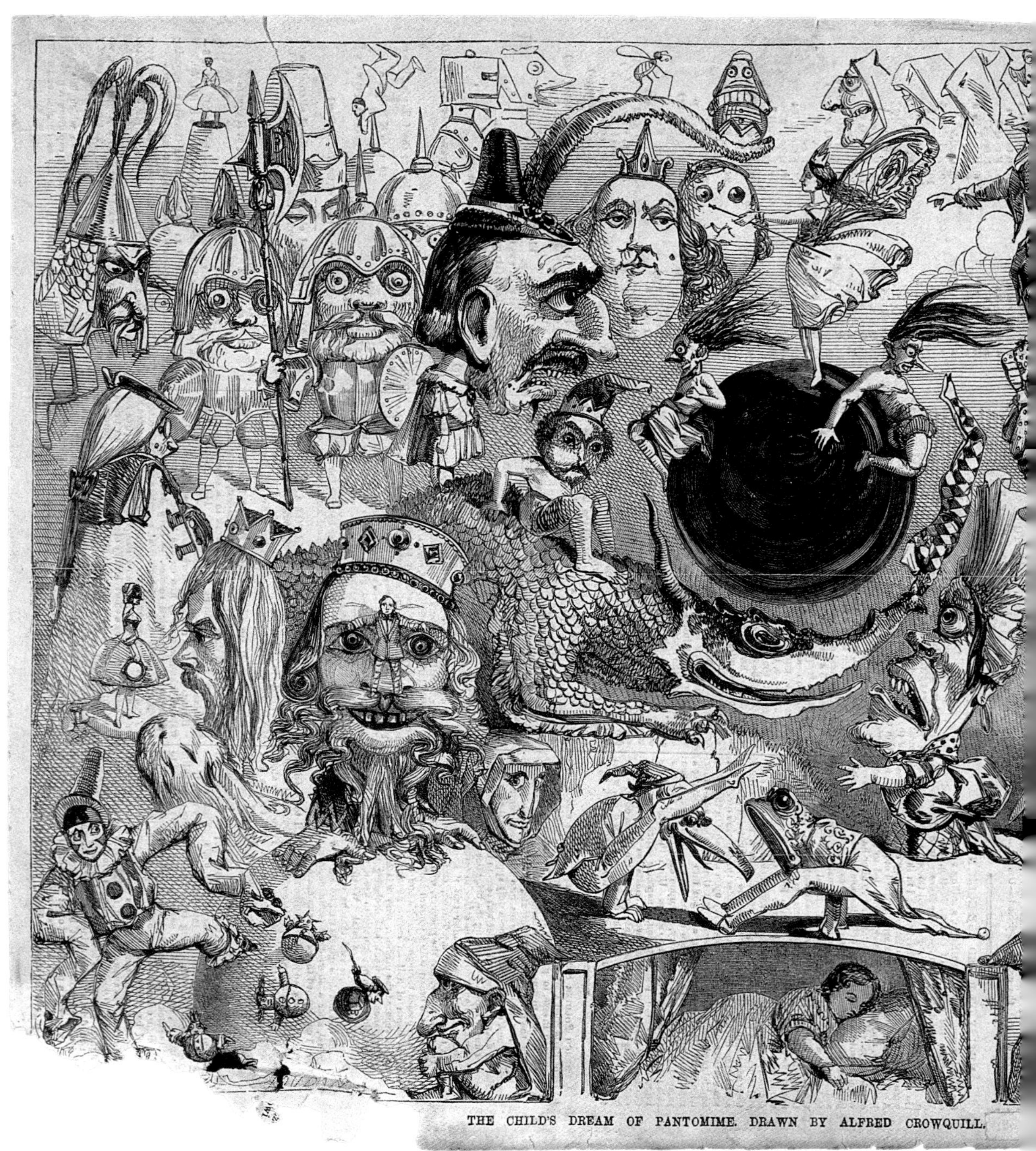

THE CHILD'S DREAM OF PANTOMIME. DRAWN BY ALFRED CROWQUILL.

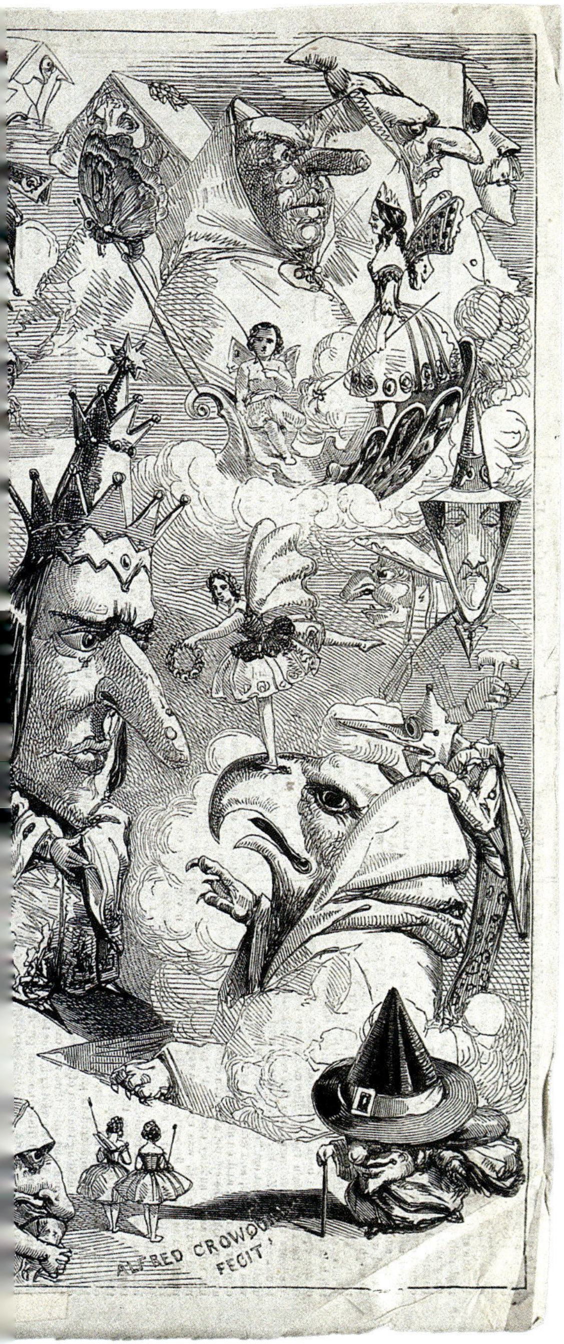

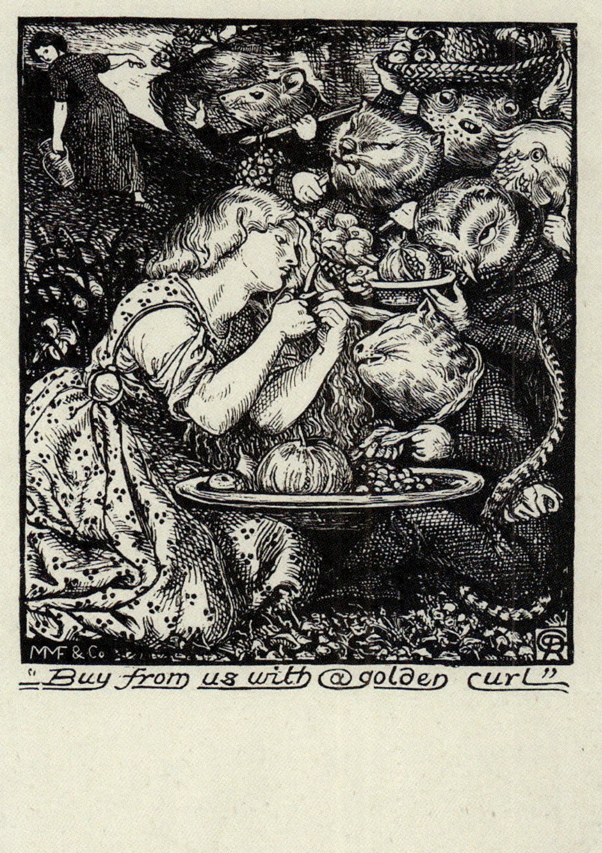


**47**  *The Child's Dream of Pantomime*  1859
Alfred Crowquill (pseudonym of
Alfred Henry Forrester 1804–72)
Wood engraving

**48**  *Buy from Us with a Golden Curl (frontispiece to*
**Goblin Market and other Poems** *by Christina
Rossetti) c.*1861–2
After Dante Gabriel Rossetti (1828–82)
Wood engraving

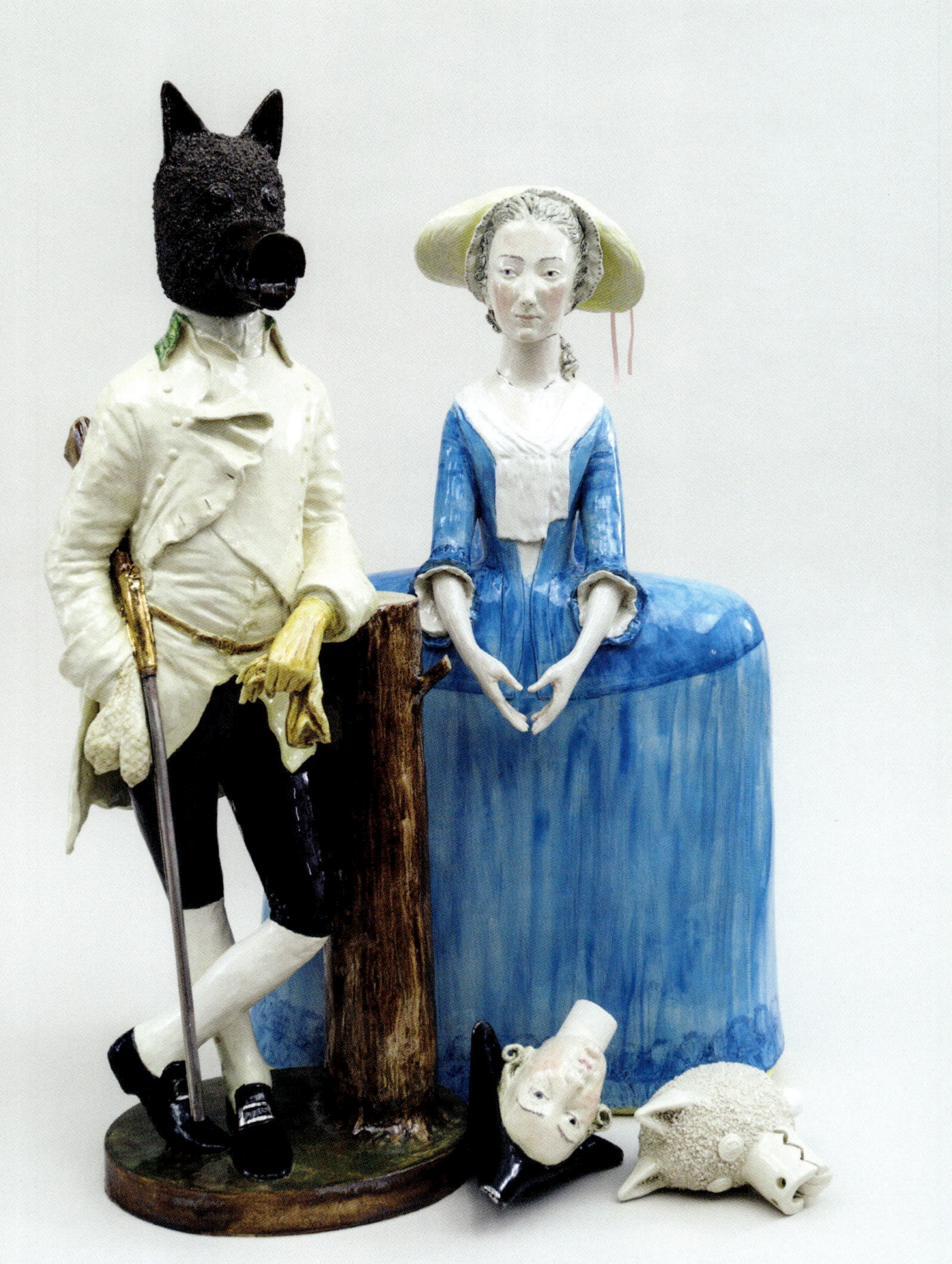

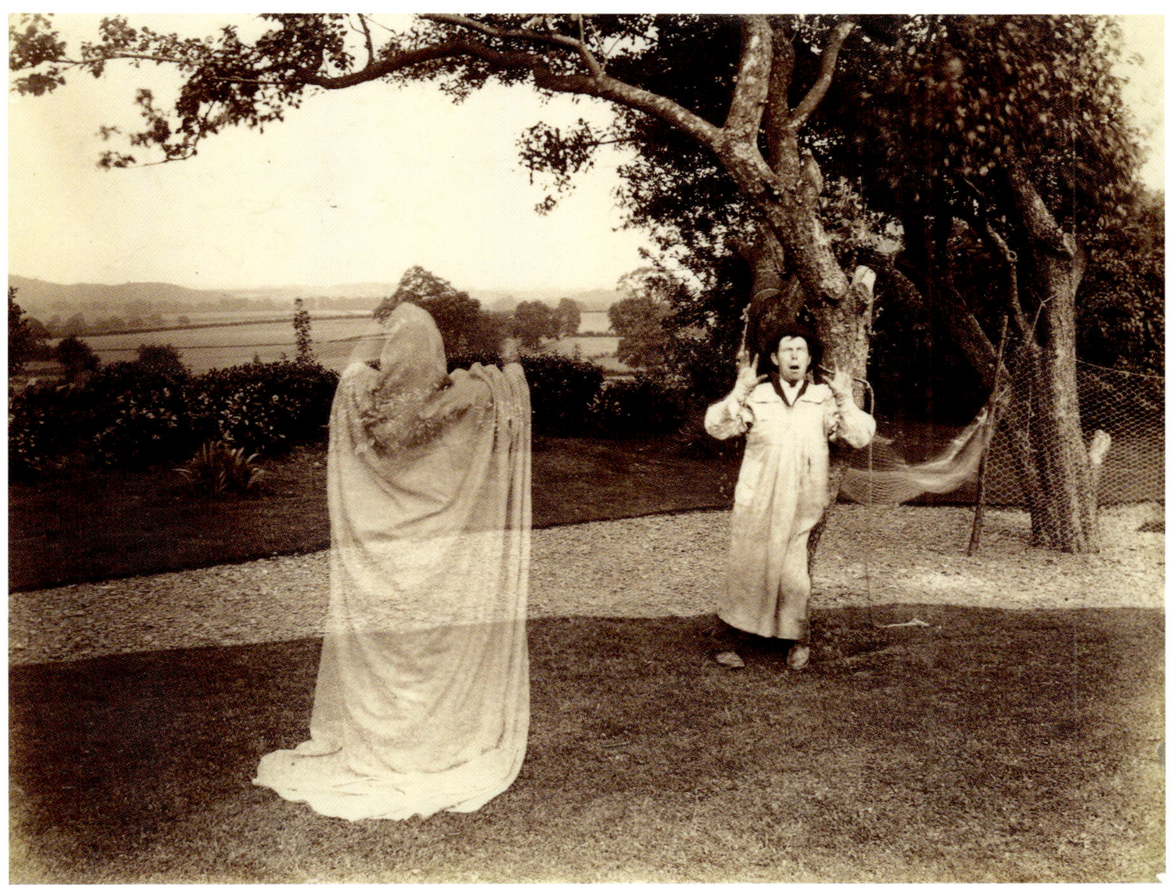

**49**  *Amateurs Playing Ghost Scene*  1887
W.S. Hobson (active 1850s–80s)
Albumen silver print

A Victorian and Edwardian fad, spirit photography utilized multiple exposure techniques to give the illusion of a ghostly or spectral presence manifesting within the image. Hobson's photograph is likely to be a parody, satirizing the genre in a more burlesque manner than the typically posed portraits.

**50**  *Mr and Mrs Andrews*  2021
Claire Partington (b.1973)
Glazed earthenware and mixed media

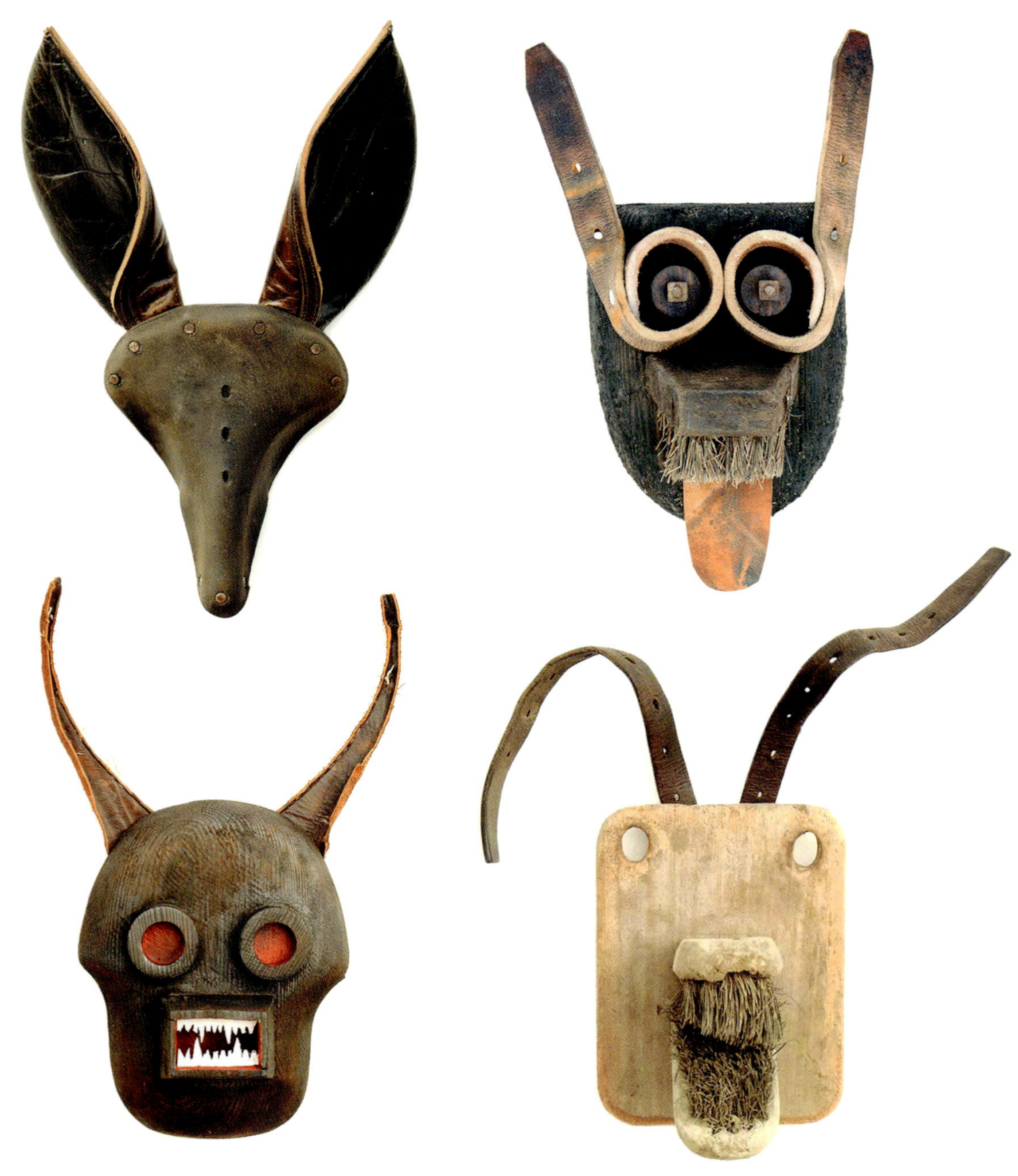

**51** Clockwise from top left: *Saddle Shuck, Cousin of Yard Broom Shuck, Yard Broom Shuck, Tribal Shuck*
September–October 2019  From the *Black Shuck* series
John Douglas Piper (b.1964)  Mixed media (found objects from East Anglian farms)

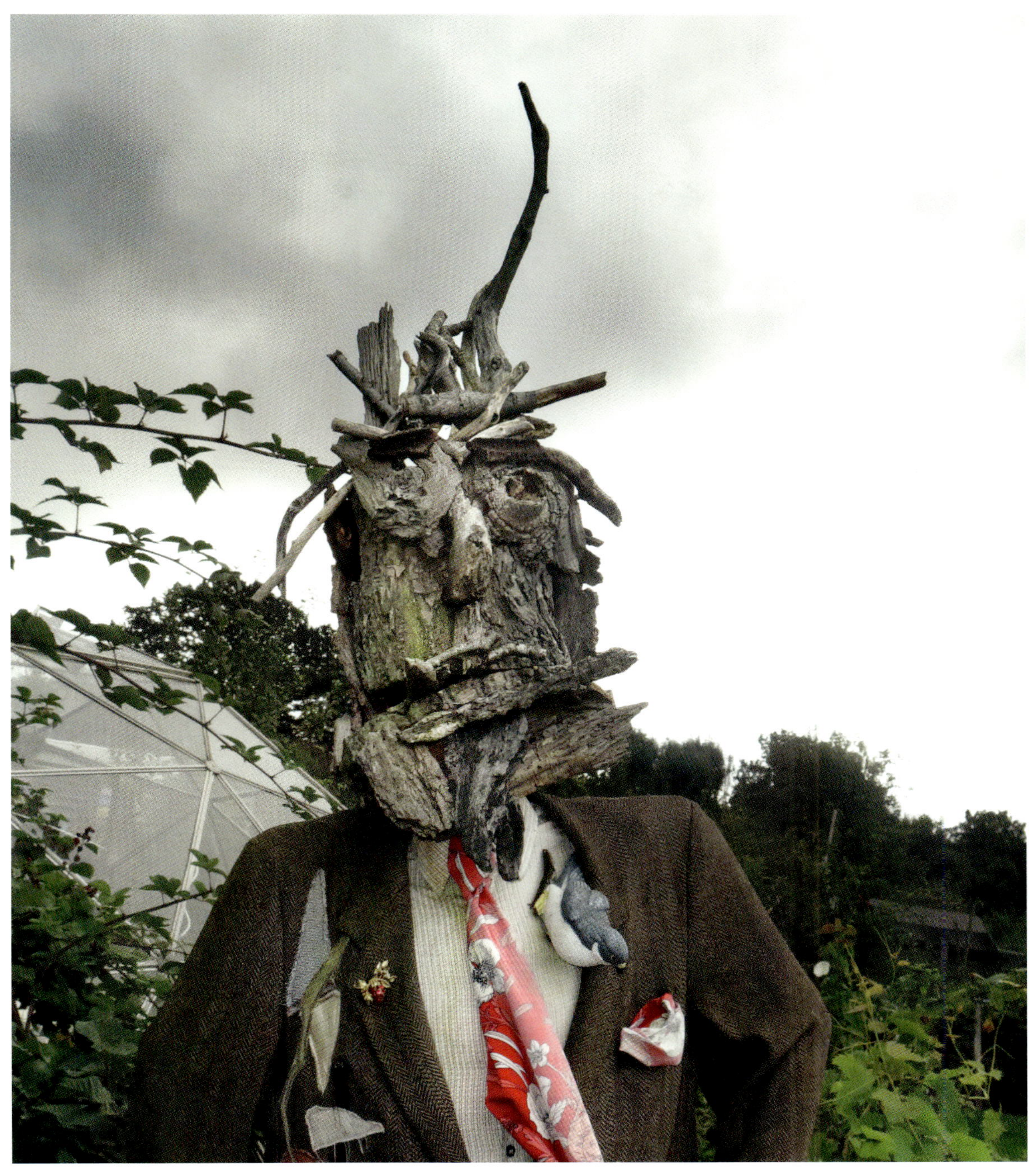

**52**  *New Barnet*  2021  From *The Scarecrow* series
Max Reeves (b.1966)
Colour photograph

REBELLIOUS NATURE

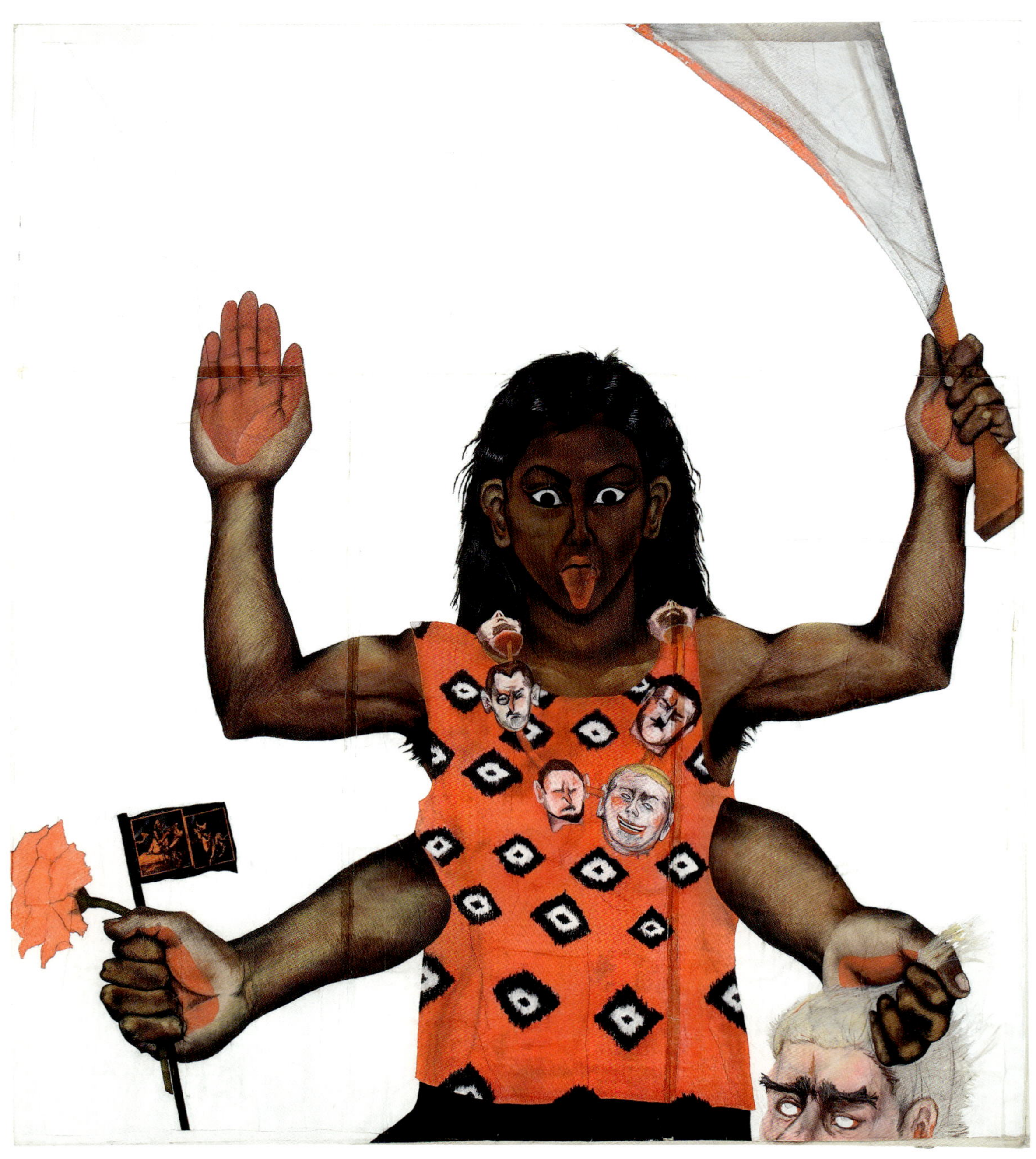

53 *Housewives with Steak-knives*  1984–5
Sutapa Biswas (b.1962)
Oil, acrylic, pastel, pencil, collage and house paint on paper mounted onto canvas

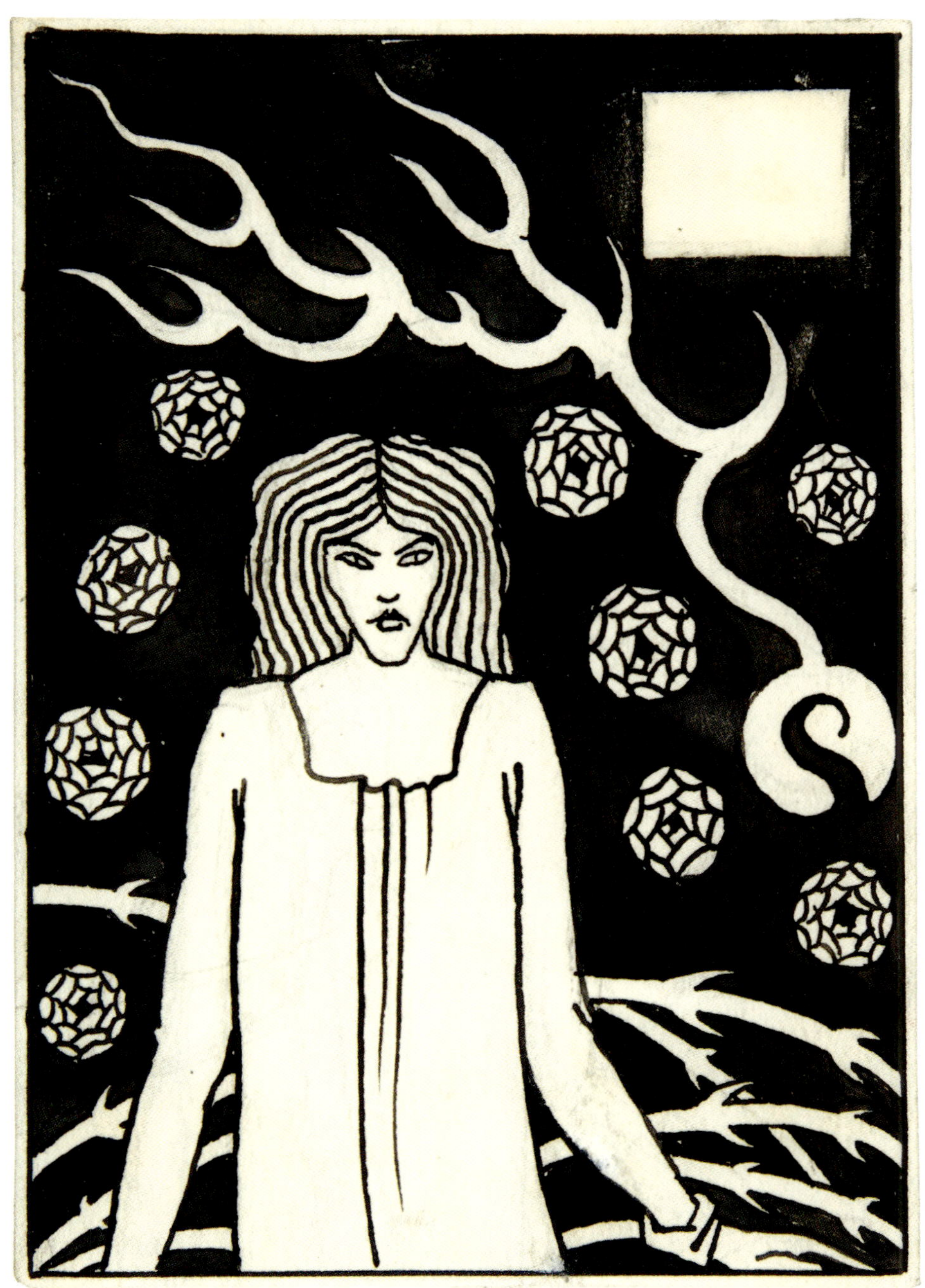

**54**  *Young Woman Surrounded by Briars, Lightning and Roses*  1893–4
Aubrey Vincent Beardsley (1872–98)
Pen and carbon black ink, brush and wash, over graphite

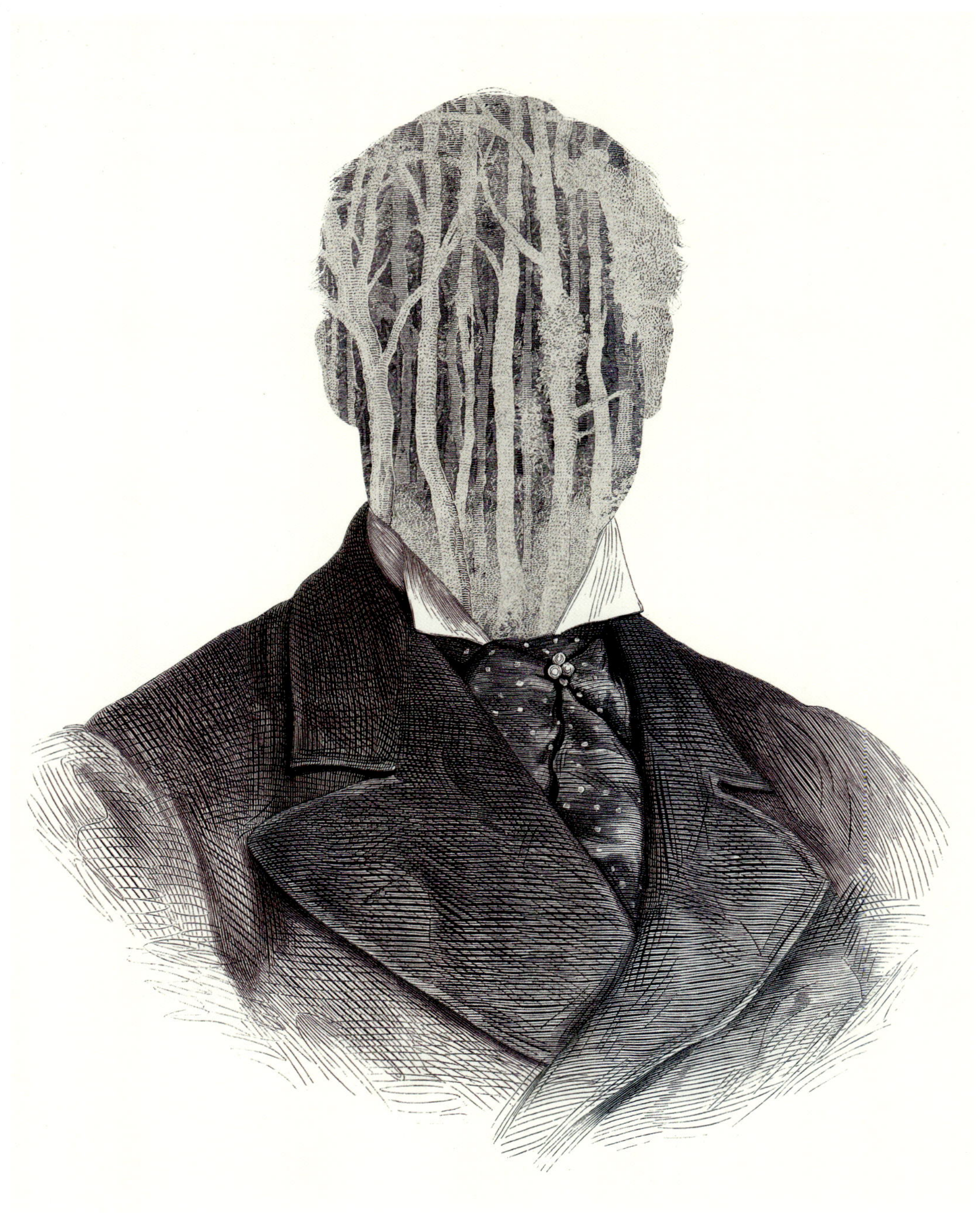

**55** *Ghost* 2016
Dan Hillier (b.1973)  Screen print

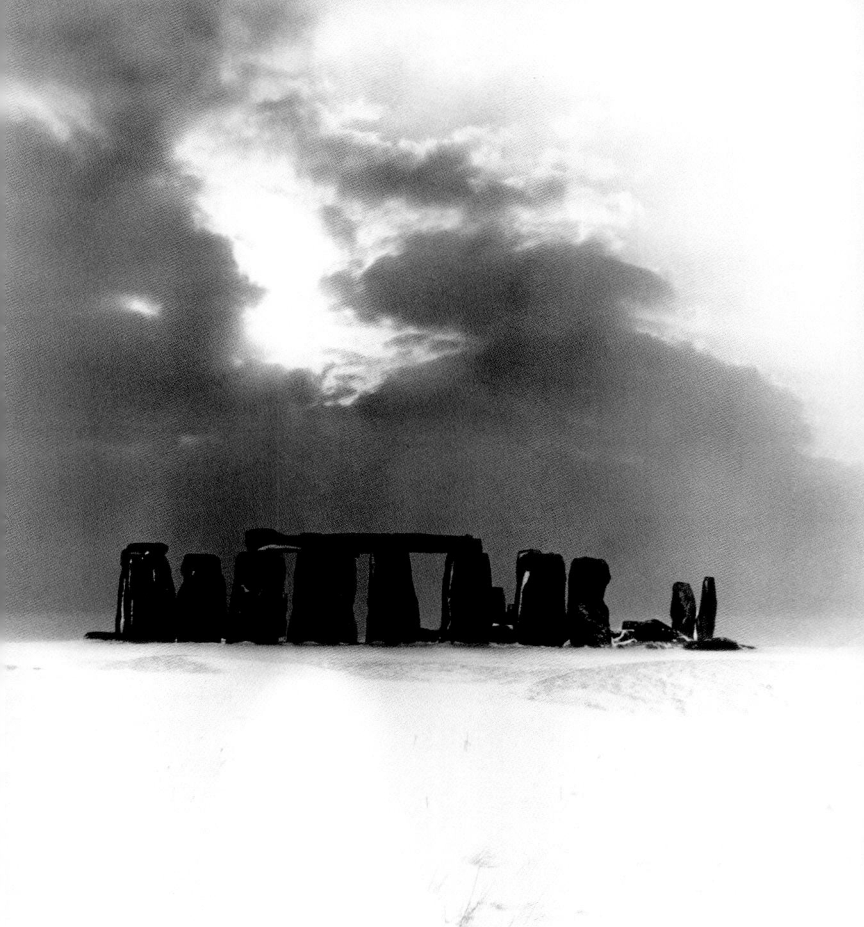

# 4

# STONES

EN*LA*D *S A C*D*. A CODE WHOSE
KEY IS LOST, WITH STONE RINGS
FOR DOTS AND CARVED LINTELS
FOR DASHES.

On a bright and shining morning the Tyburn boy leads us toward the stone circle. It's the mystery that draws us to Stonehenge, of course – a chance to walk through a secret text that our ancestors could have read as easily as we would a road sign. Some Neolithic binary language has smuggled an entire library into these sarsen stones. The circle pulls us in from the desert of the plains, but we find that we're not the first to come here seeking answers. Others throng the stones, shouting wild theories across each other, the competing interpretations rising to a white-water roar. The boy cups his hands and bellows, "This place is an amplifier. It traps ancient rites within its circle and then feeds them back upon themselves until they build to a howl more devastating than any tempest."

A gang of dress-up druids yell a counter-argument: "The stones are a battery, dude". They claim that the ring is a spiritual power source that harnesses the magnetic ley lines that converge here and they charge their smartphones through its centuries-old magic. A girl with a spray can paints over Satanic carvings and bemoans the standard of druidic graffiti but it was ever thus.

Lovers see a meeting place, futurists dream of a landing site. Historians guide us into sacred spots and tell us that if we stand *there* and *there* then we'll become the hands of the world's earliest clock. Ravers stop their dancing for a second to claim that if the bass were to drop at the precise moment of solstice then we'd all see the face of God. Louder and louder ring the theories; everyone declares that only *they* have the key to unlock the stones, but still they stand, silently sleeping.

All these claims and counterclaims share a common ground. They assume that the desire to drag stones the size of estate cars miles across the rubble of England must have been driven by *meaning*. They suppose that if we search hard enough the truth will be revealed. But meaning isn't everything, isn't even, maybe, the most important thing. There are other, more ravenous drives. Awe. Terror. Beauty. Stones that swoon and sing and dance and weep.

What it was that people once saw here is lost to us, so we must worship at the altar of the unknown. When the eeriness is all that's left to us, then it's the eeriness that becomes our god.

En*la*d *s a c*d* that never had a key at all.

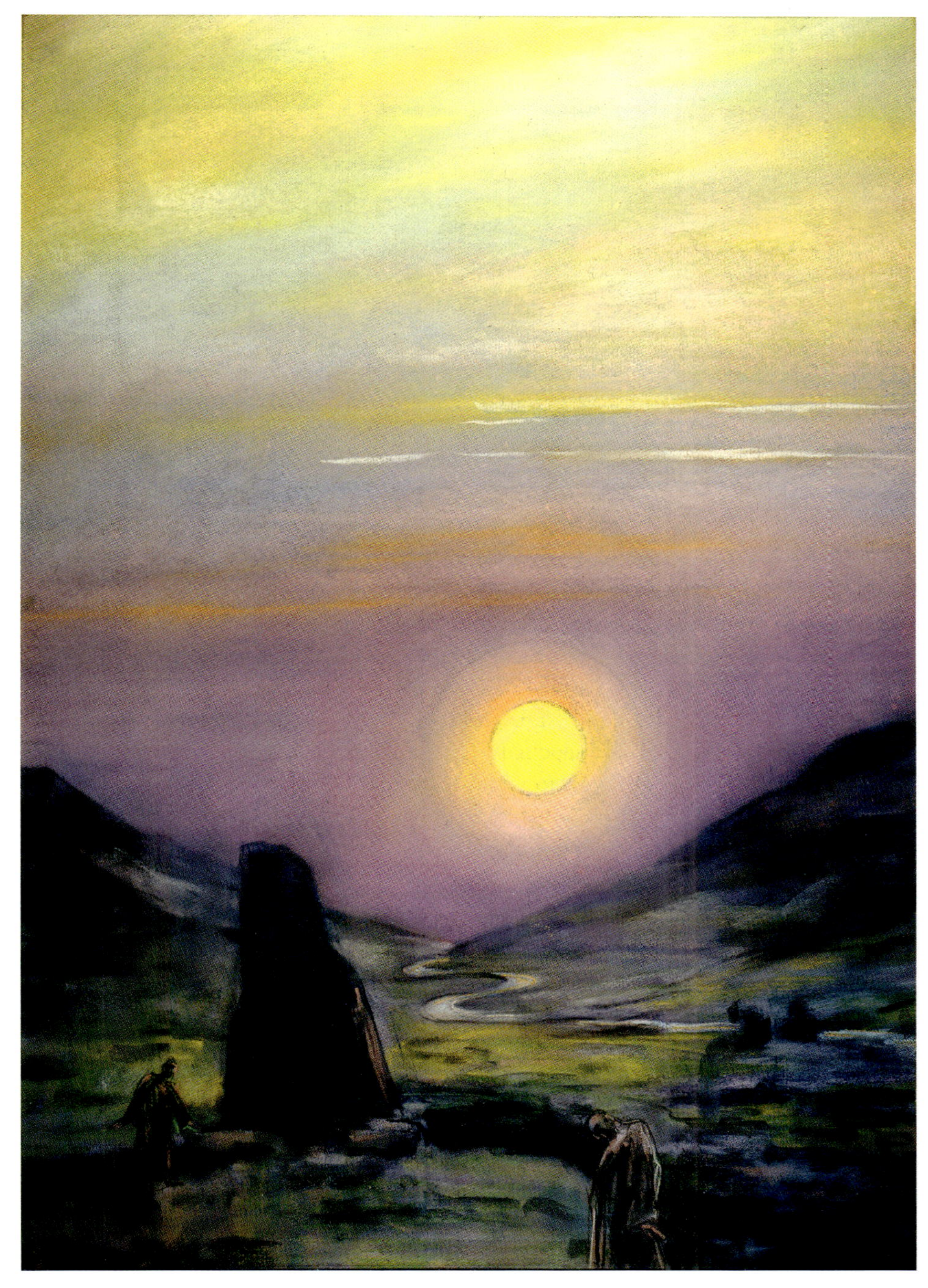

**57**  *Druidesque*  1955
Austin Osman Spare (1886–1956)  Pastel on paper

 *The Devil's Den*  2021
Ben Edge (b.1985)
Oil on canvas

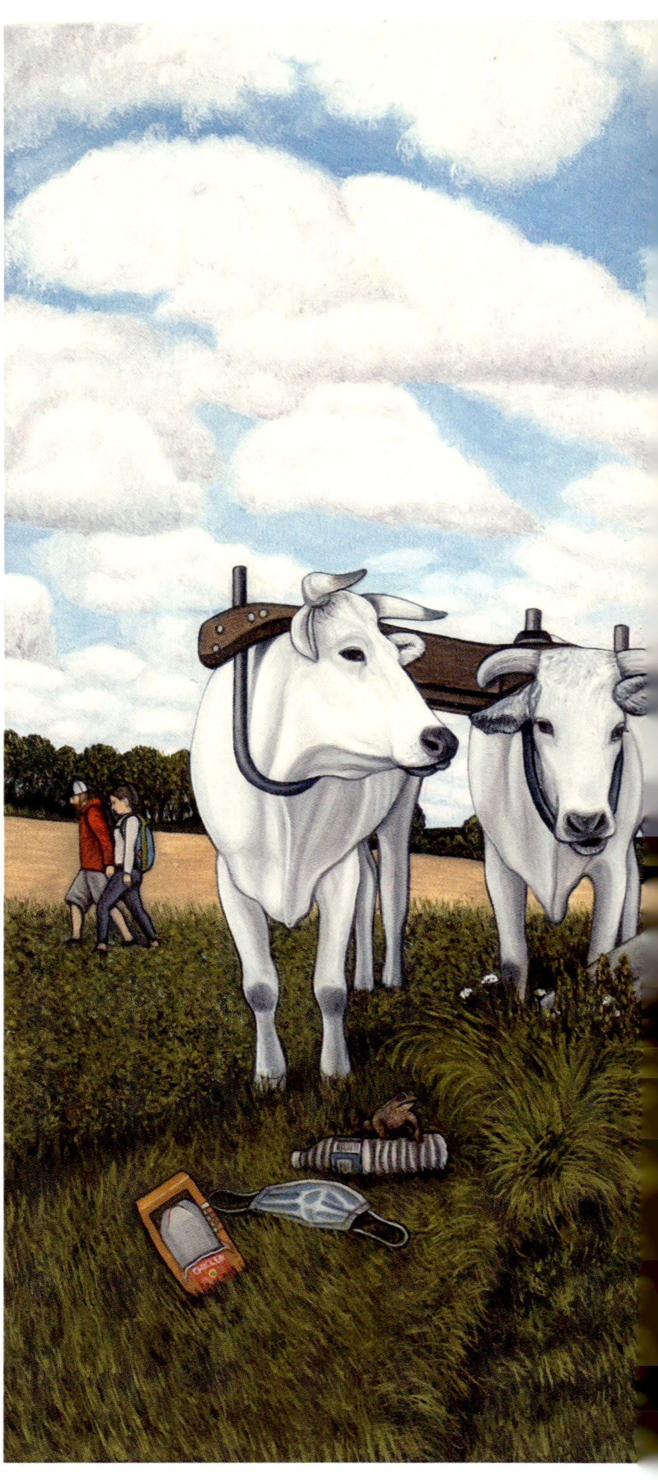

The subject of Edge's painting is a
Neolithic burial chamber in Wiltshire,
close to Avebury and not far from
Stonehenge. According to legend, each
night at midnight the Devil comes with a
team of eight oxen and each time tries and
fails to remove the capstone. The Devil
has long been associated with ancient
stone monuments through the Church's
condemnation of pagan practices.

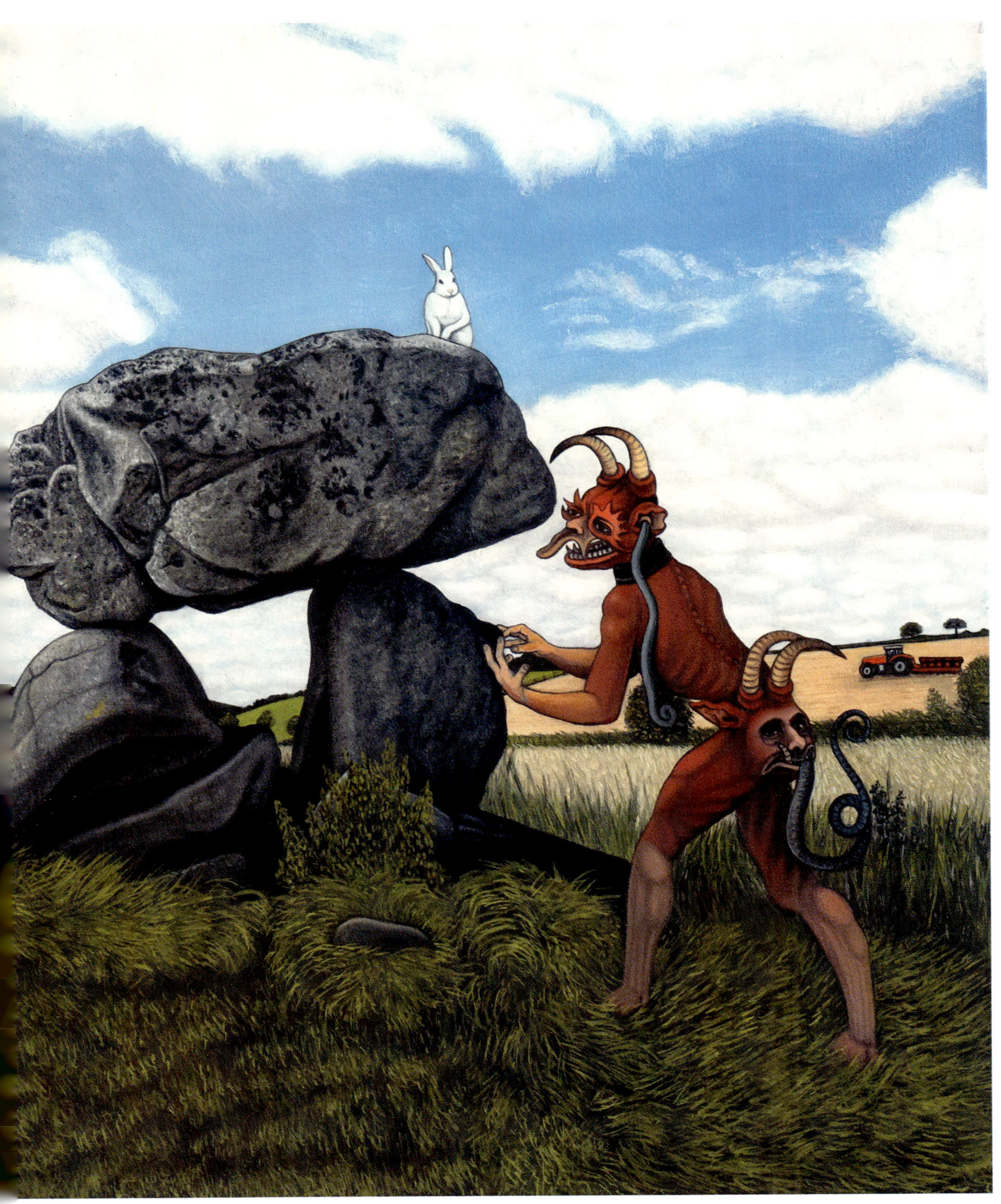

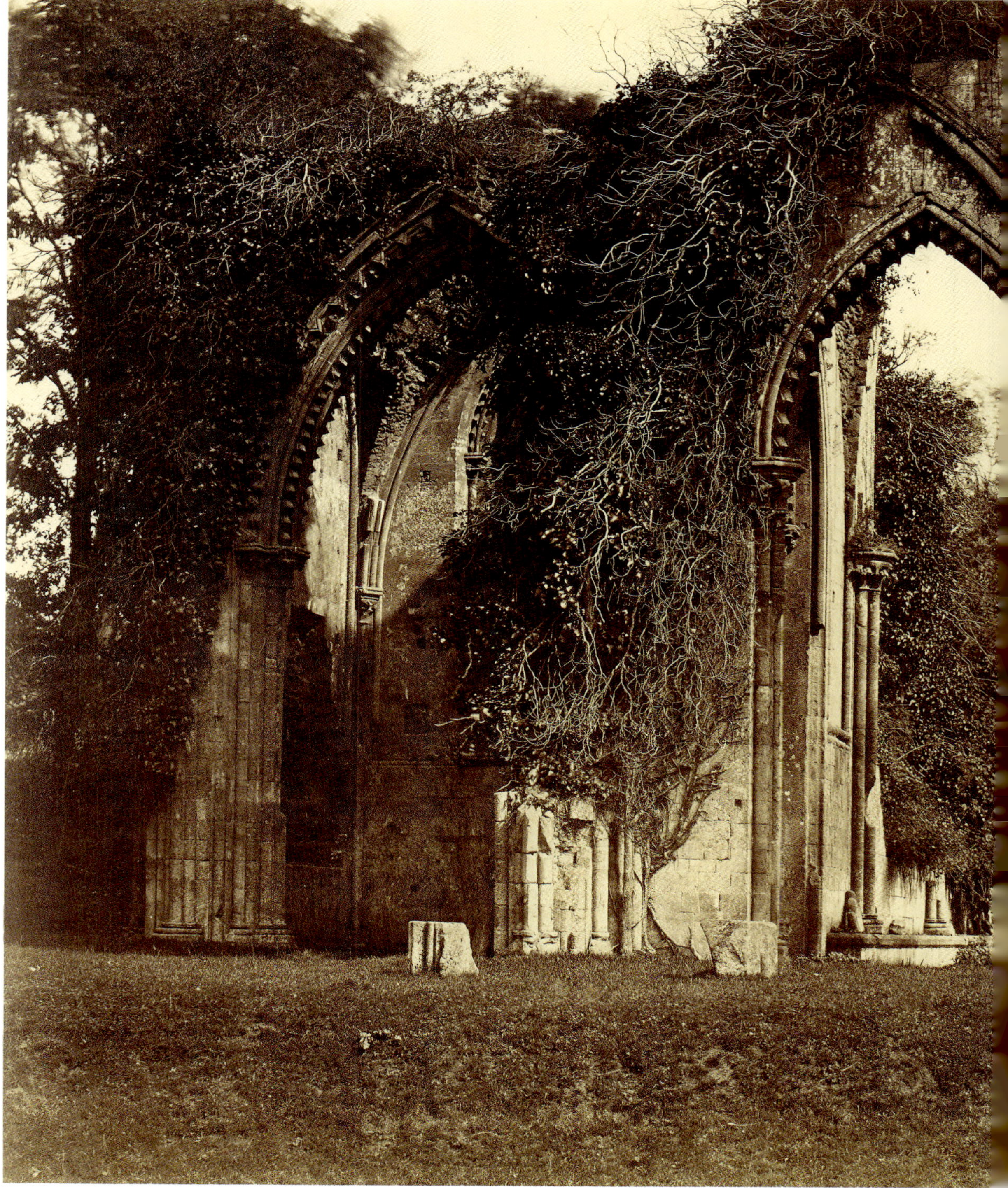

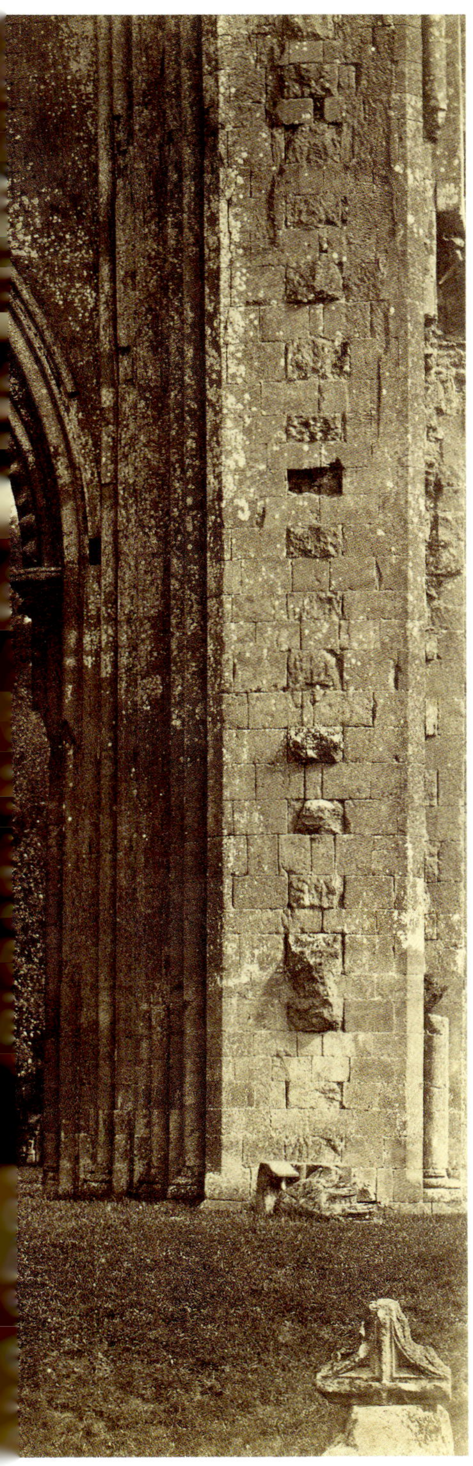

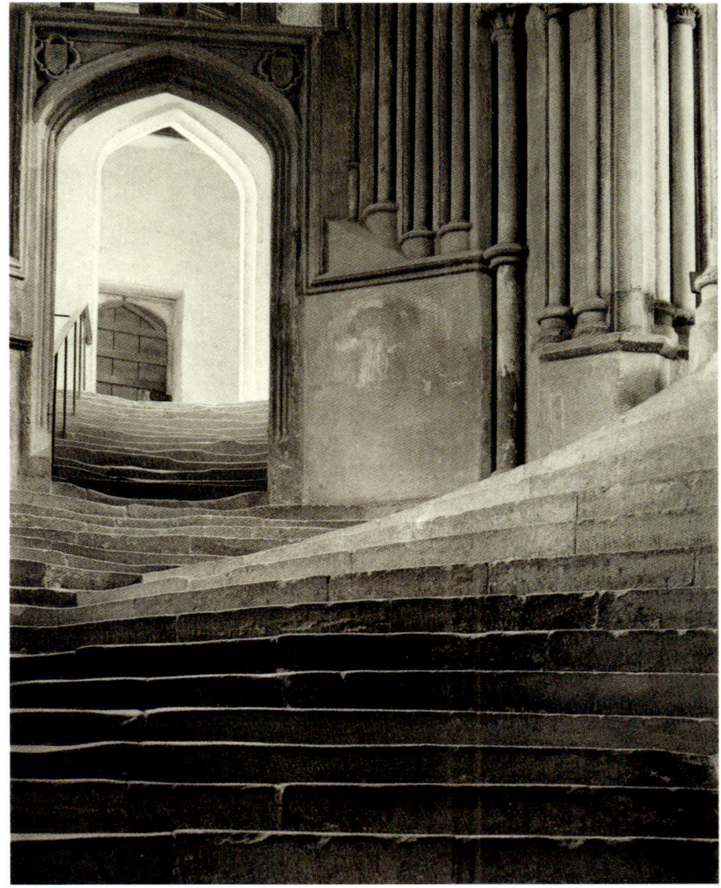

**59**  *A Sea of Steps, Wells Cathedral*  1903
Frederick H. Evans (1853–1943)
Platinum print photograph

**60**  *Glastonbury Abbey,
Arches of the North Aisle*  1858
Roger Fenton (1819–69)
Albumen silver print

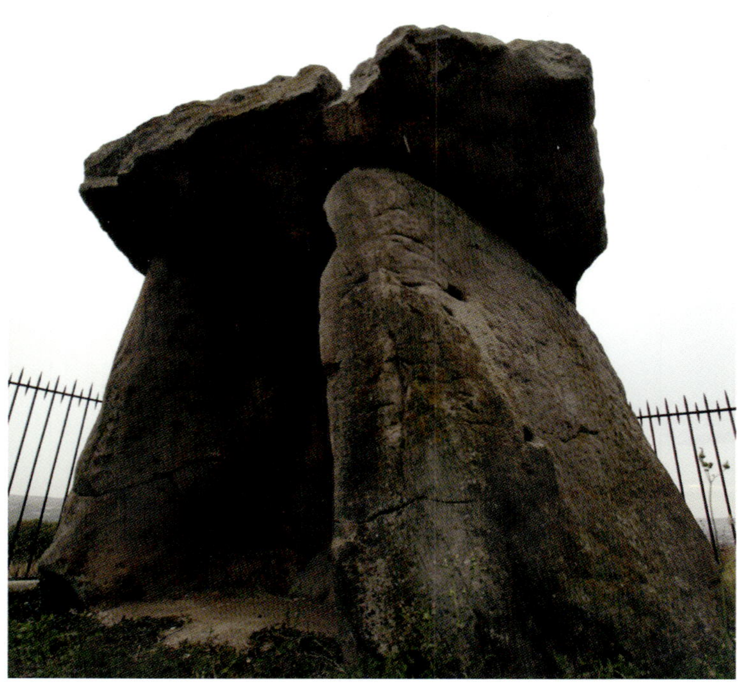

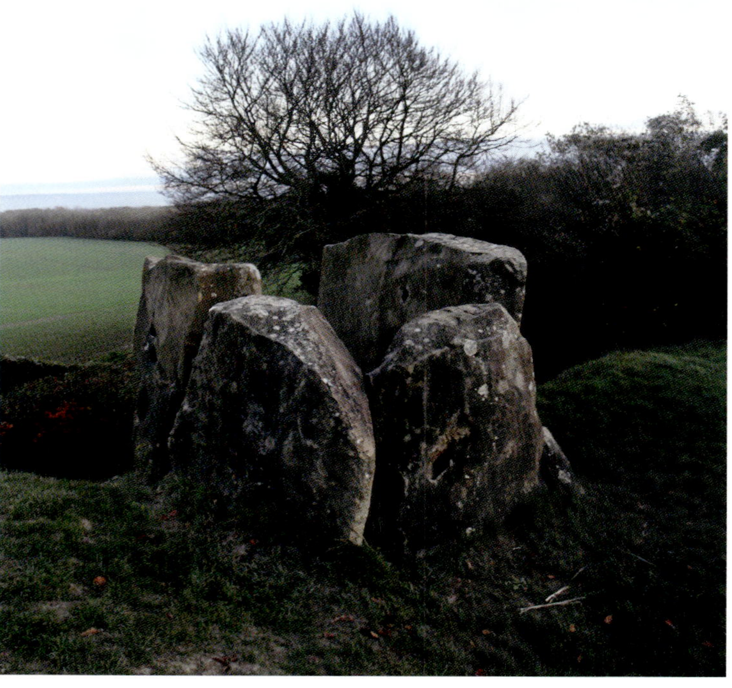

**61**  *Coldrum Long Barrow, Kent*  2021
*Kit's Coty House, Kent*  2021
From *The Book of Charles* series
Max Reeves (b.1966)
Colour photographs

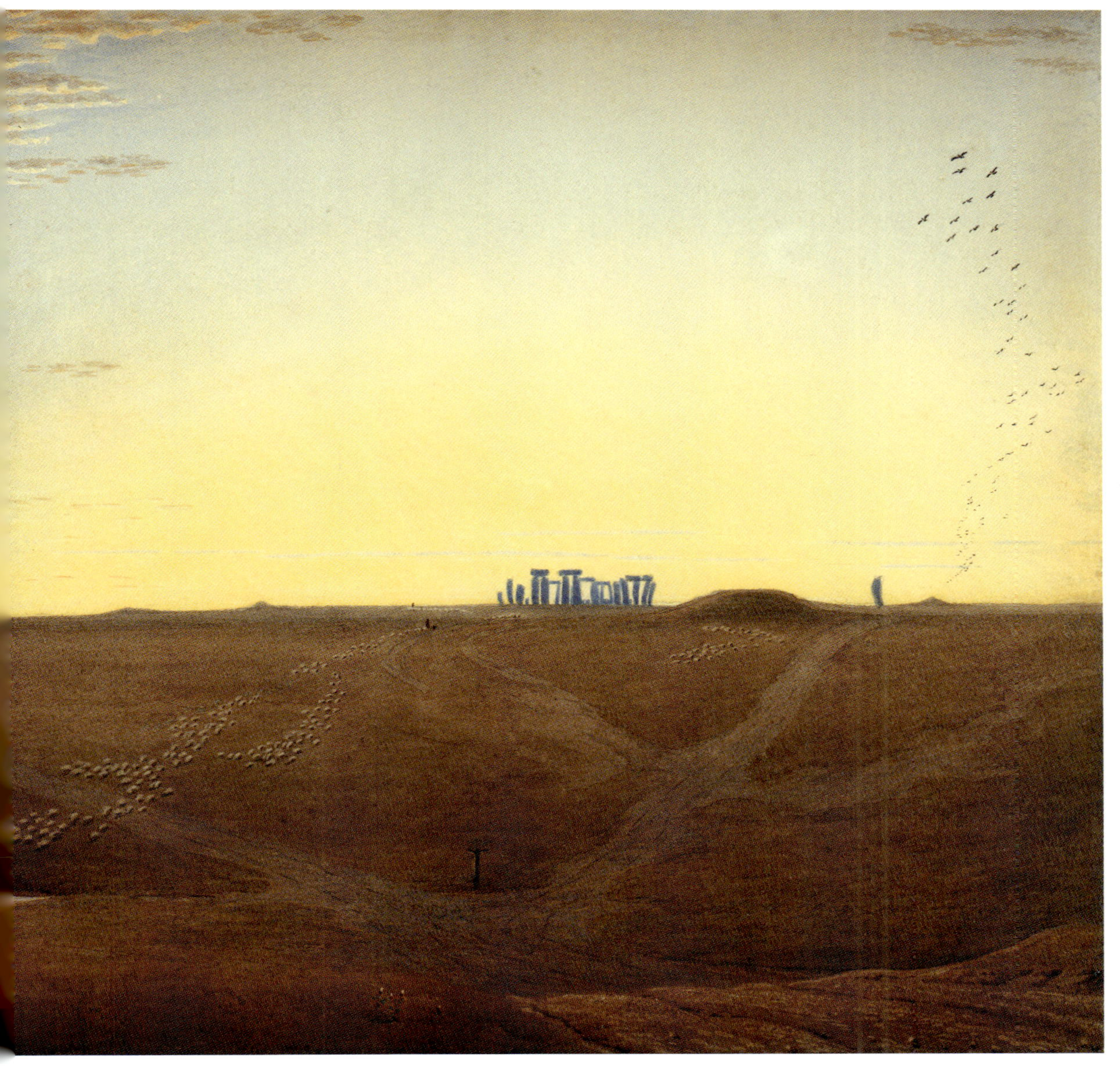

62  *Stonehenge-Twilight*  *c.*1840
William Turner of Oxford (1789–1862)
Watercolour

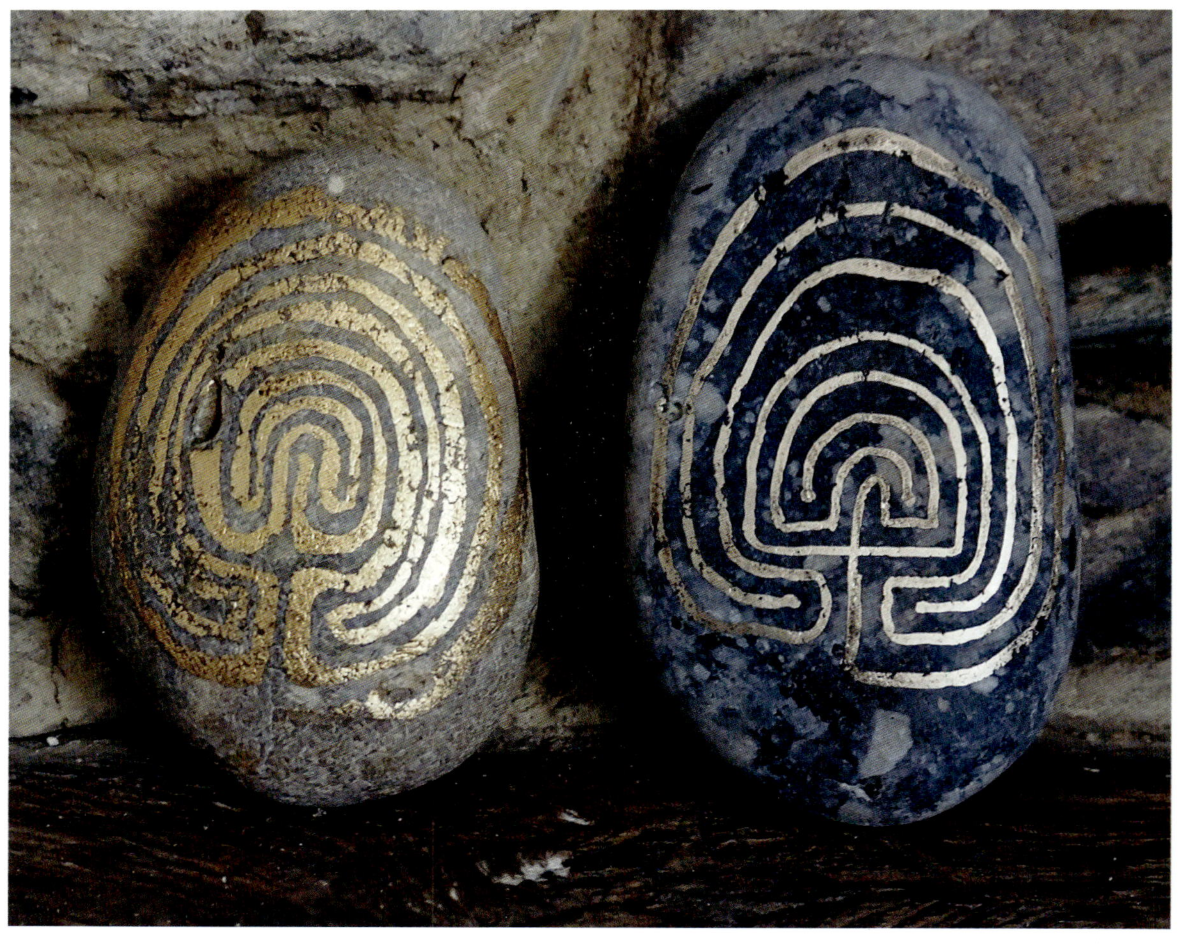

**63** *Labyrinth Stones:*
*the path and the walls*  2021
Jackie Morris (b.1961)
Beach stones and gold leaf

The stones used by Morris in these works were found on beaches, where they were returned by the artist once decorated with gold. She traces mazes across the smooth surfaces, highlighting the stones' almost cosmic quality in their dappled colouring. Placed for strangers to find, Morris' labyrinth stones become relics, mapped with mystical signage from which to determine significance.

**64**  *Landscape with Antiquities (Lamorna)*  1955
Ithell Colquhoun (1906–88)
Oil on canvas

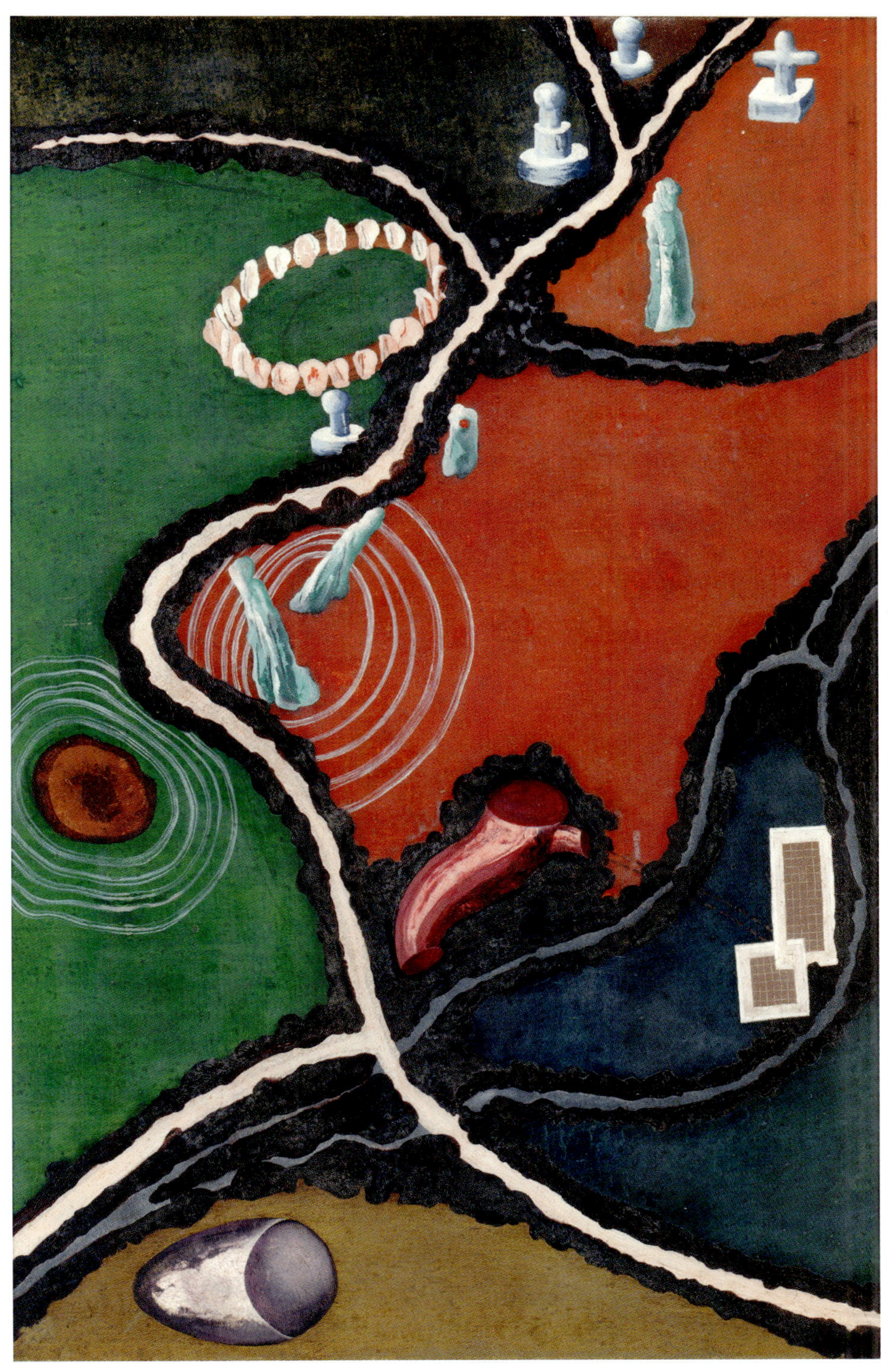

STONES

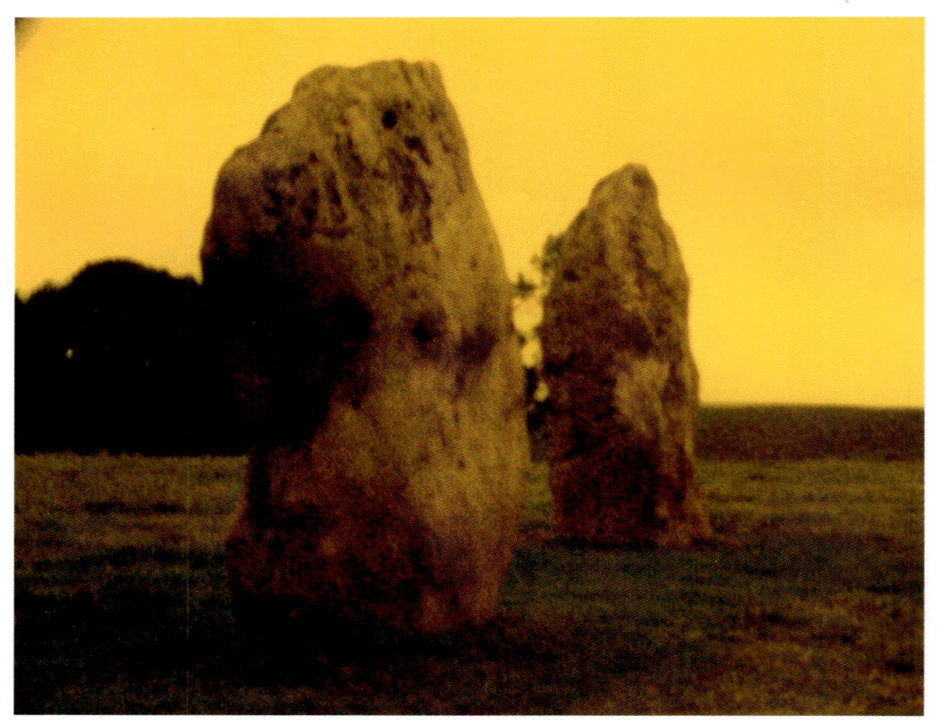

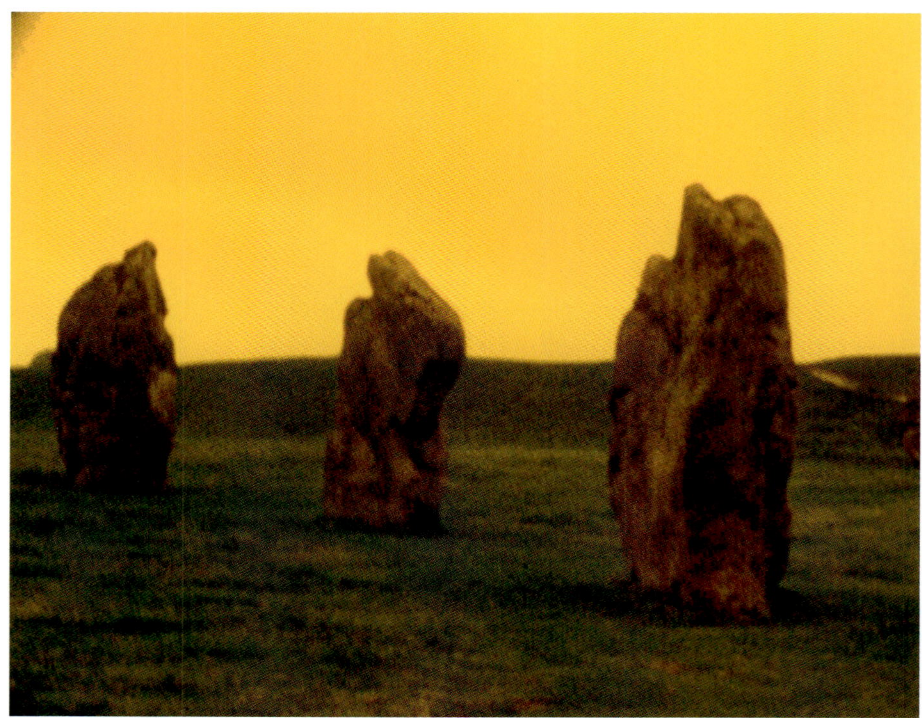

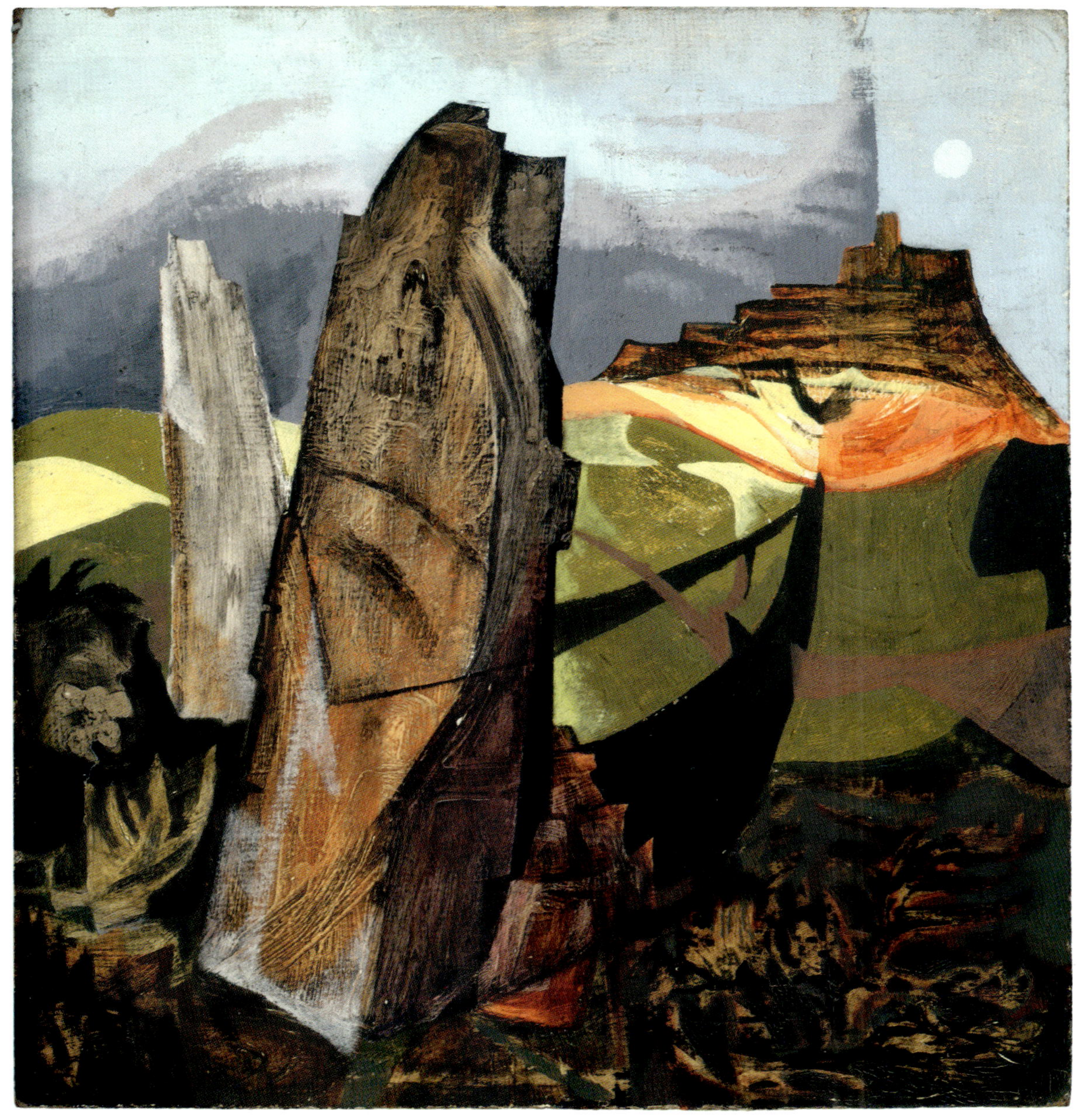

**65**  *Two Menhirs*  c.1950
Bryan Wynter (1915–75)  Oil on board

**66**  *Journey to Avebury*  1973
Derek Jarman (1942–94)  S8mm film

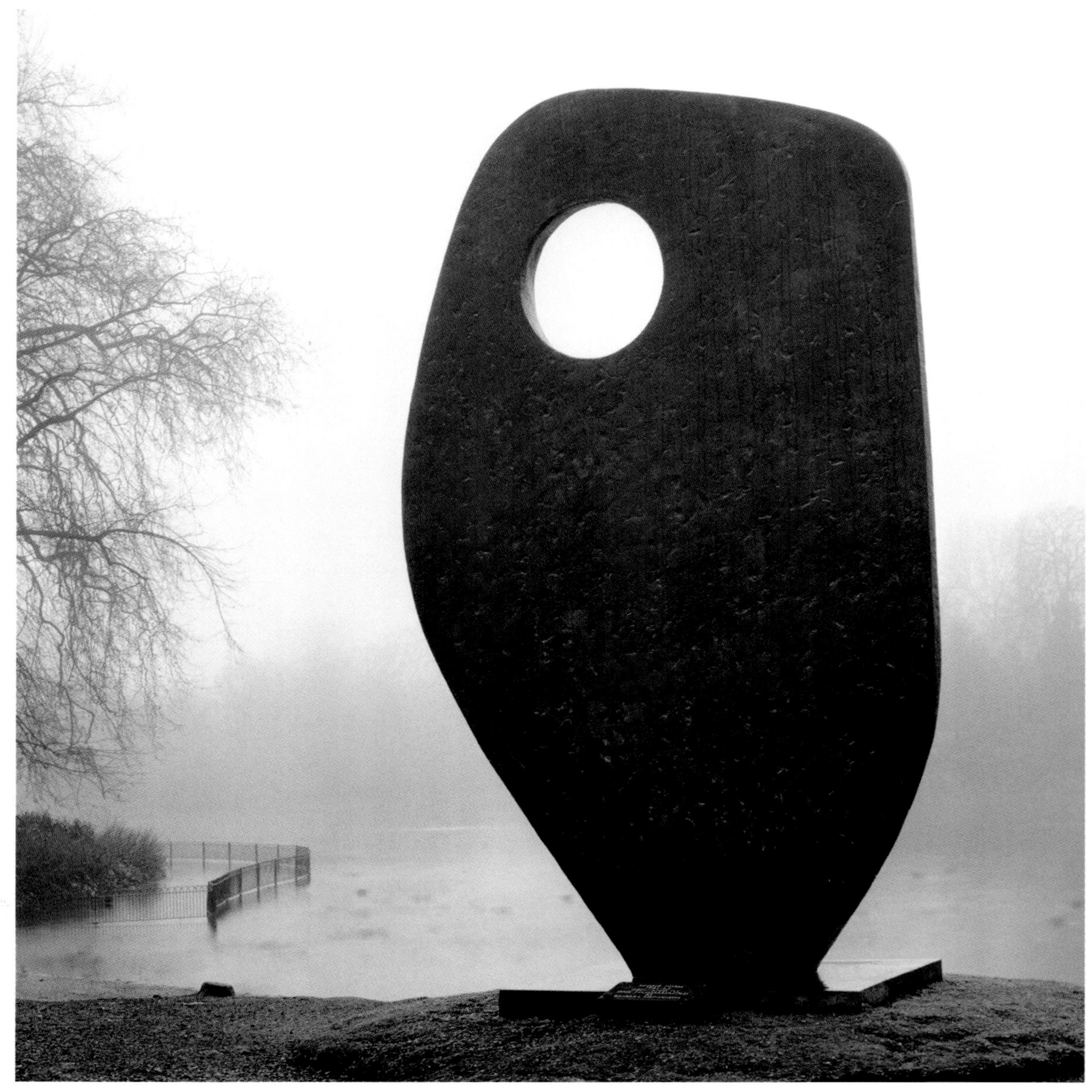

**67**  *Single Form by Barbara Hepworth, Battersea Park*  2008
Michael Gray (b.1961)
Black and white photograph

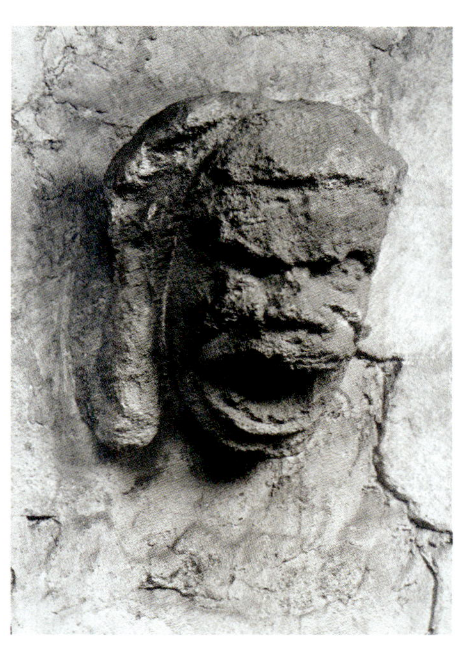

**68**  *Ely Cathedral: A Grotesque*  1903
Frederick H. Evans (1853–1943)
Half-tone print

**69**  *When the Earth had Many Moons*  1990
Jamie Reid (b.1947)
Colour Xerox collage

A form of modern iconoclasm, Reid's art urges its
collective viewers to mobilize. Famous for his work with
the Sex Pistols in the 1970s, Reid makes clear in this piece
the human search for identity and meaning, as astronomy
collides with England's deep history.

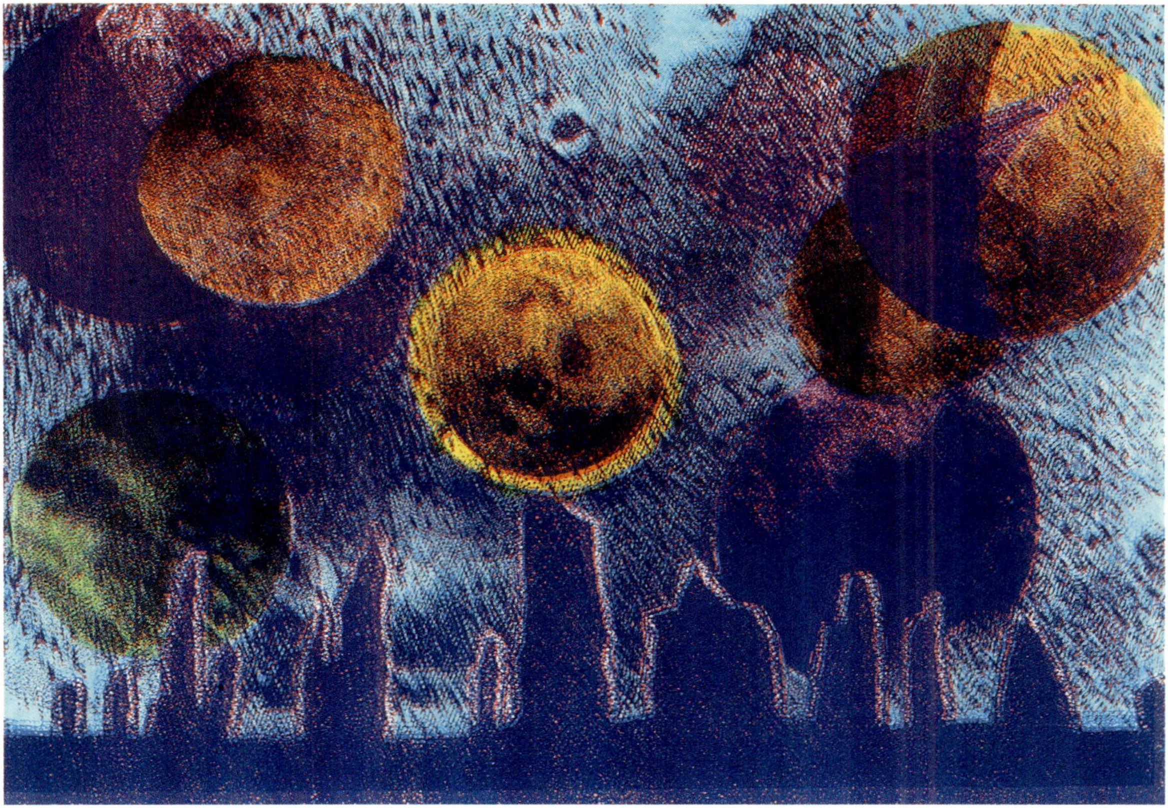

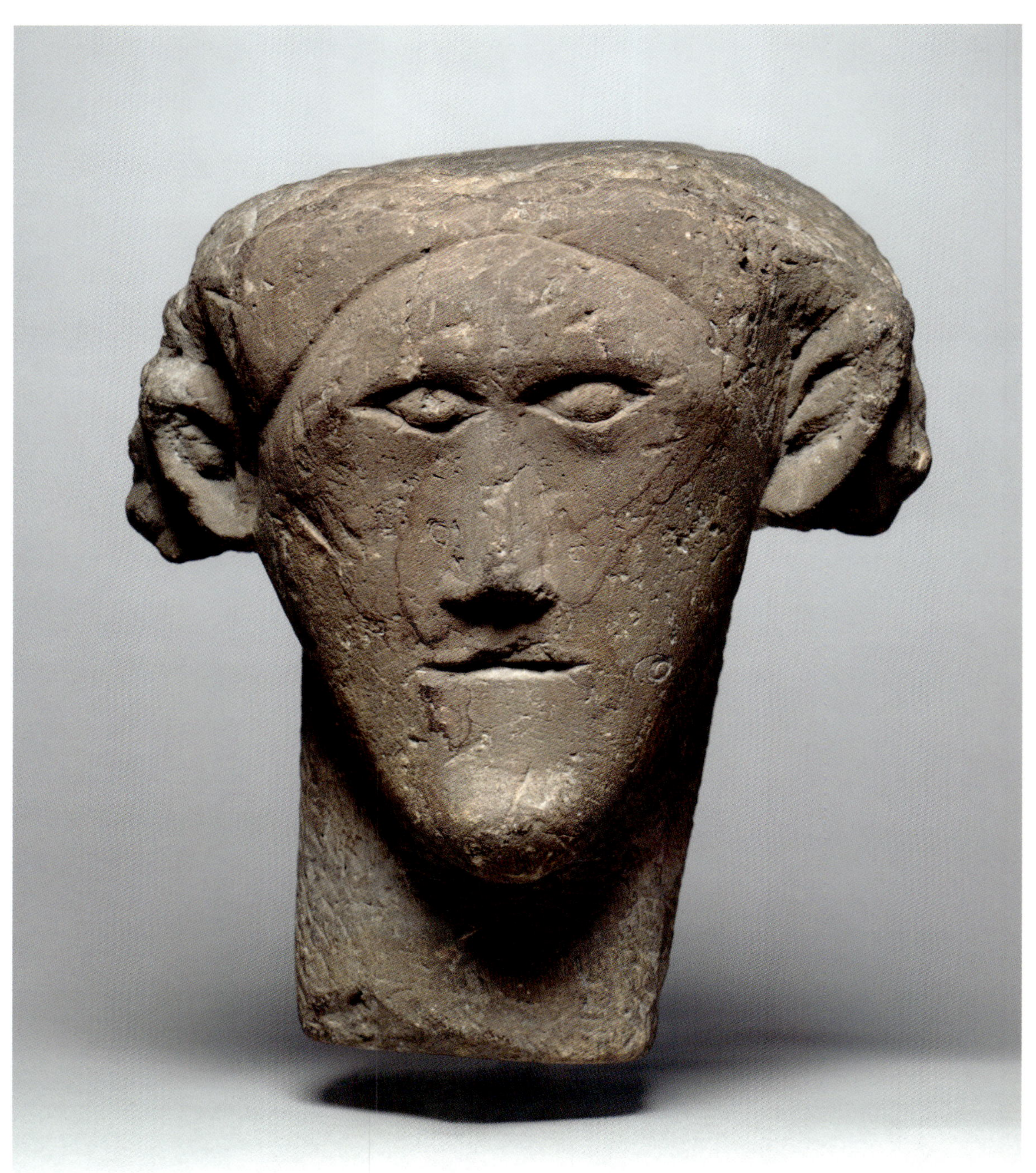

**70**  *Celtic Head*  *c.*100–300AD
Artist unknown  Sandstone with traces of original red paint

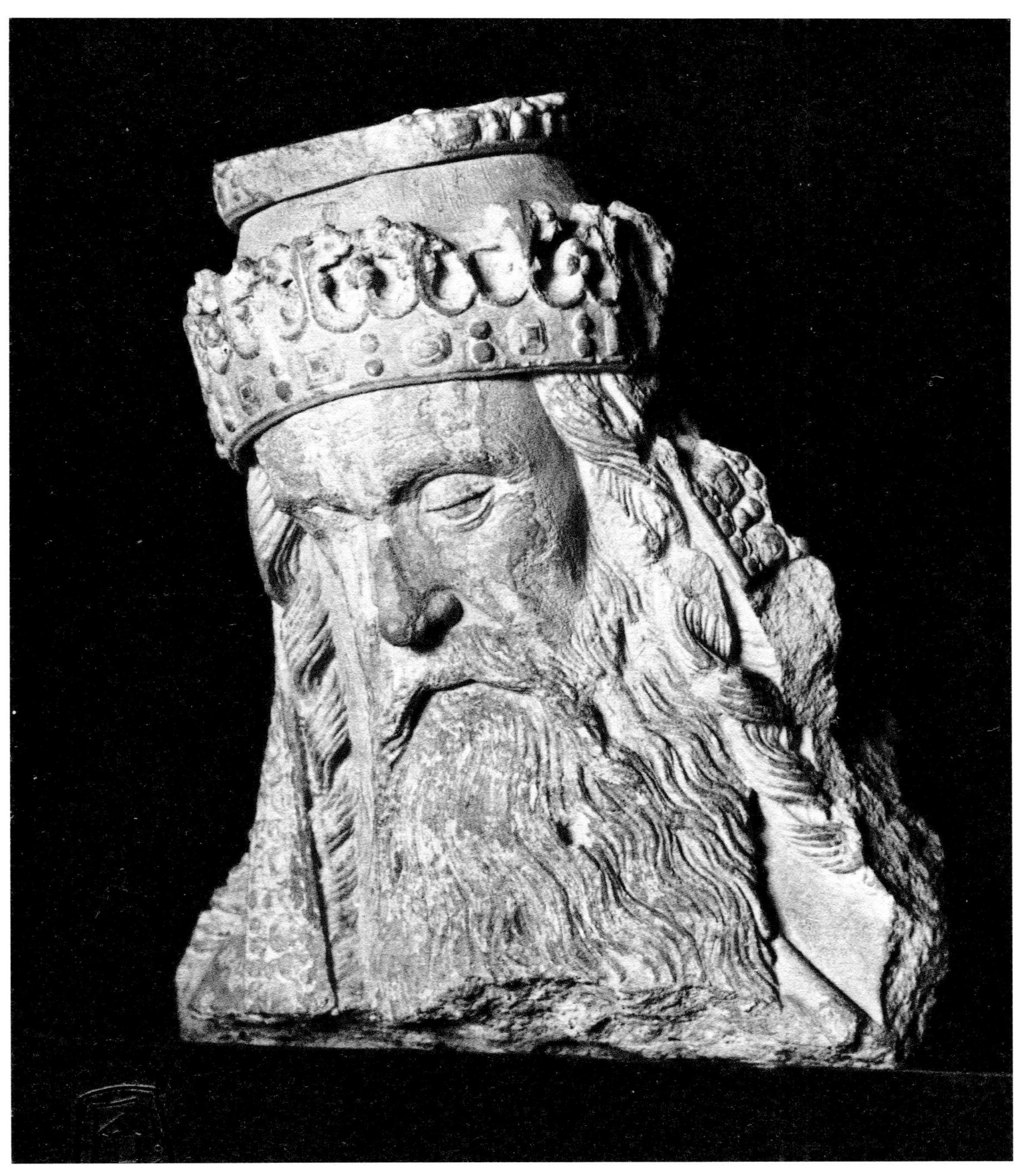

**71**  *Carved Head, Winchester*  late 11th–early 12th century, photographed c.1900
Frederick H. Evans (1853–1943)  Platinum print photograph

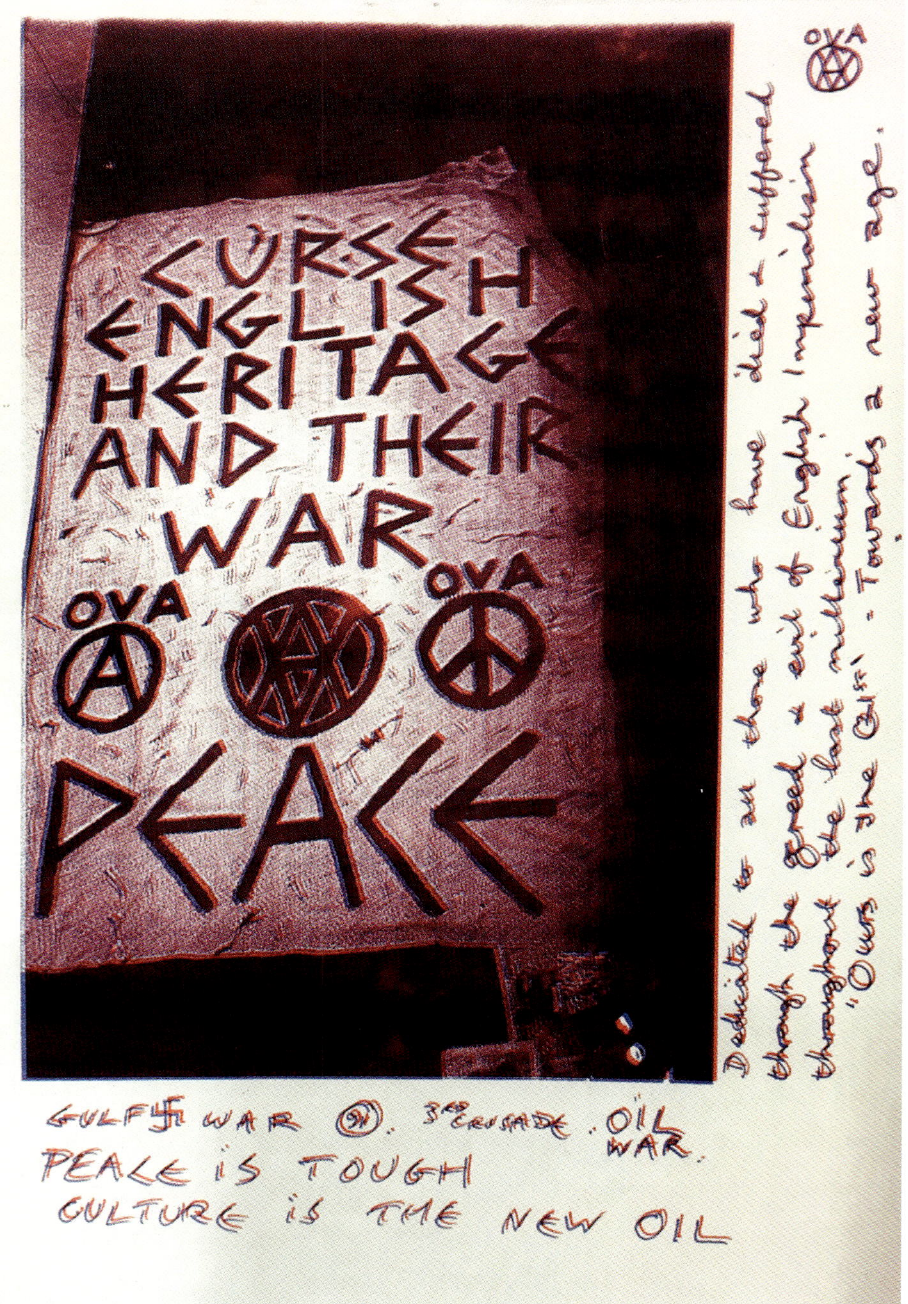


**72** *Curse English Heritage* 1990
Jamie Reid (b.1947)  Colour Xerox

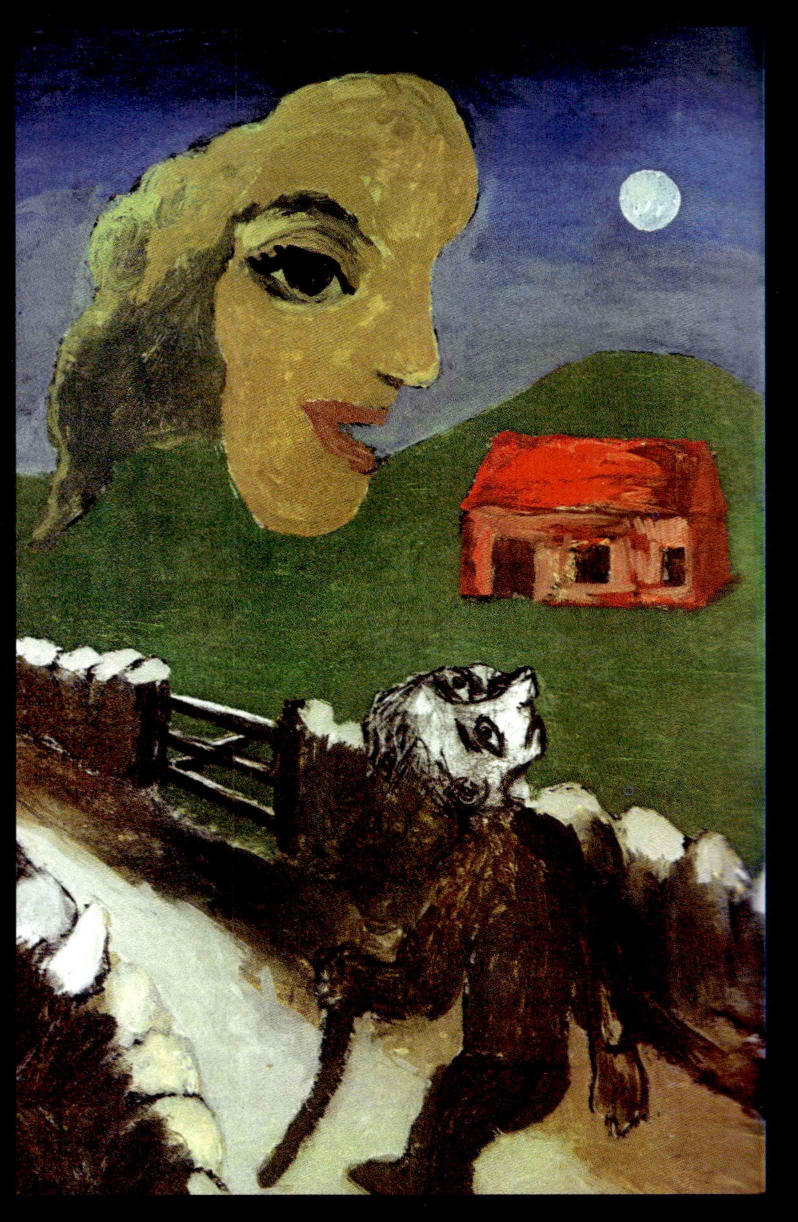

# 5

# THE WAY

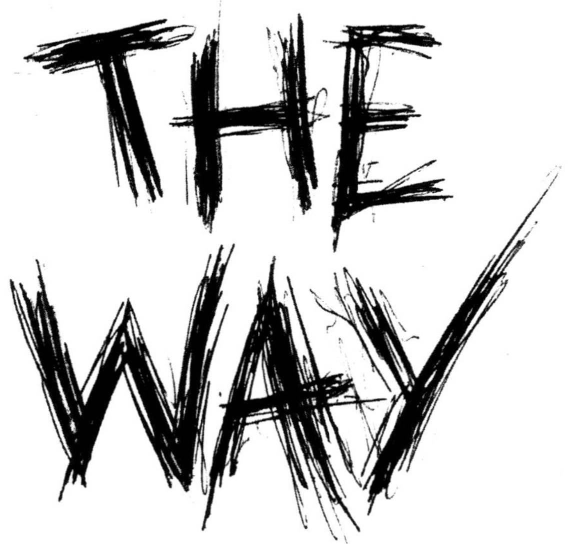

ENGLAND IS A MAZE WITH NO
ENTRANCE AND NO EXIT.

We stroll along a deserted Oxford Street where the grass grows through cracks in the pavement and fallow deer stand as still as the mannequins in the department store windows.

"Do you know how a street like this is born?" asks the Tyburn boy, as swallows dart through the columns outside Selfridges.

"First of all, centuries back, mice scurried from hole to hole. They barely bent the grass underfoot but it was enough to make just the merest rumour of a path. Of course, predators spotted that flattened grass and smelled the scent of prey." The Tyburn boy sniffs the air and bares his teeth.

"Wildcats were here, and stoats and foxes and wolves too. Lions once, long ago. So, then heavier feet trampled the bent grass into a tunnel. The flattened path marked the directions of desire – hunter and prey had scribbled sentences across the woods. A language of terror and violence. Then came the men, too lazy to hack a path through the forest. Instead they were led by the hunting tracks, at first alone and then with their livestock and carts. The ground was worn bare by centuries of travel. Horses' hooves pounded and compressed and formalized the old animal tracks. This path goes here and this path goes there. They began to cross and chatter, to share information and tell tall tales. Over time they joined up with others and the paths interweaved until, like arteries, they fed every inch of England's body. Now you could walk from sea to sea without ever touching vegetation. Speed the film up. More people, more horses, more cattle. Carts, carriages, cars. Lorries, tankers, processions. These random patterns – mouse-track tracings – become official and gain names. Now there is stone beneath your feet: brick and cobble and tarmac. Planks leap over streams and tunnels dive through hills. Now the turnpikes go up. Road tax and access rights, toll roads with automatic number-plate recognition."

The boy stops to look in the window of TK Maxx. He whispers, seemingly to himself. "Every step that we take here is echoed back, through tyres and men and horse and cattle, back to the dance of predator and prey. This, here, is a rabbit-run. Sales reps in Skodas trace the ancient deer tracks of Arden, now an A-road. Planes taxi along runways that were once the shortest route between two molehills. A million dead feet guide our path."

England is a maze that we walk without ever once escaping.

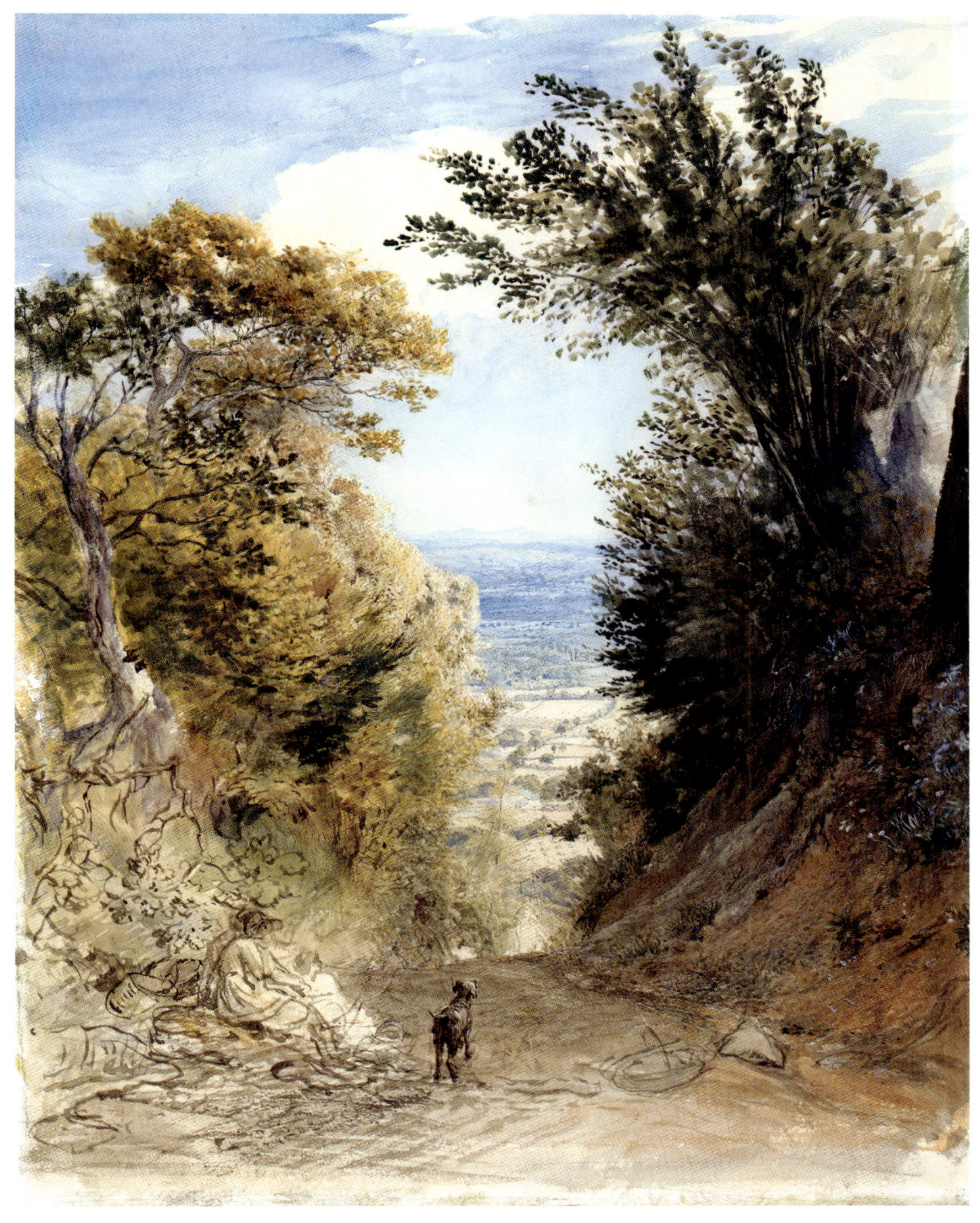

**74**  *View from Rook's Hill, Kent*  1843
Samuel Palmer (1805–81)  Watercolour with gouache, pen, brown ink and graphite  

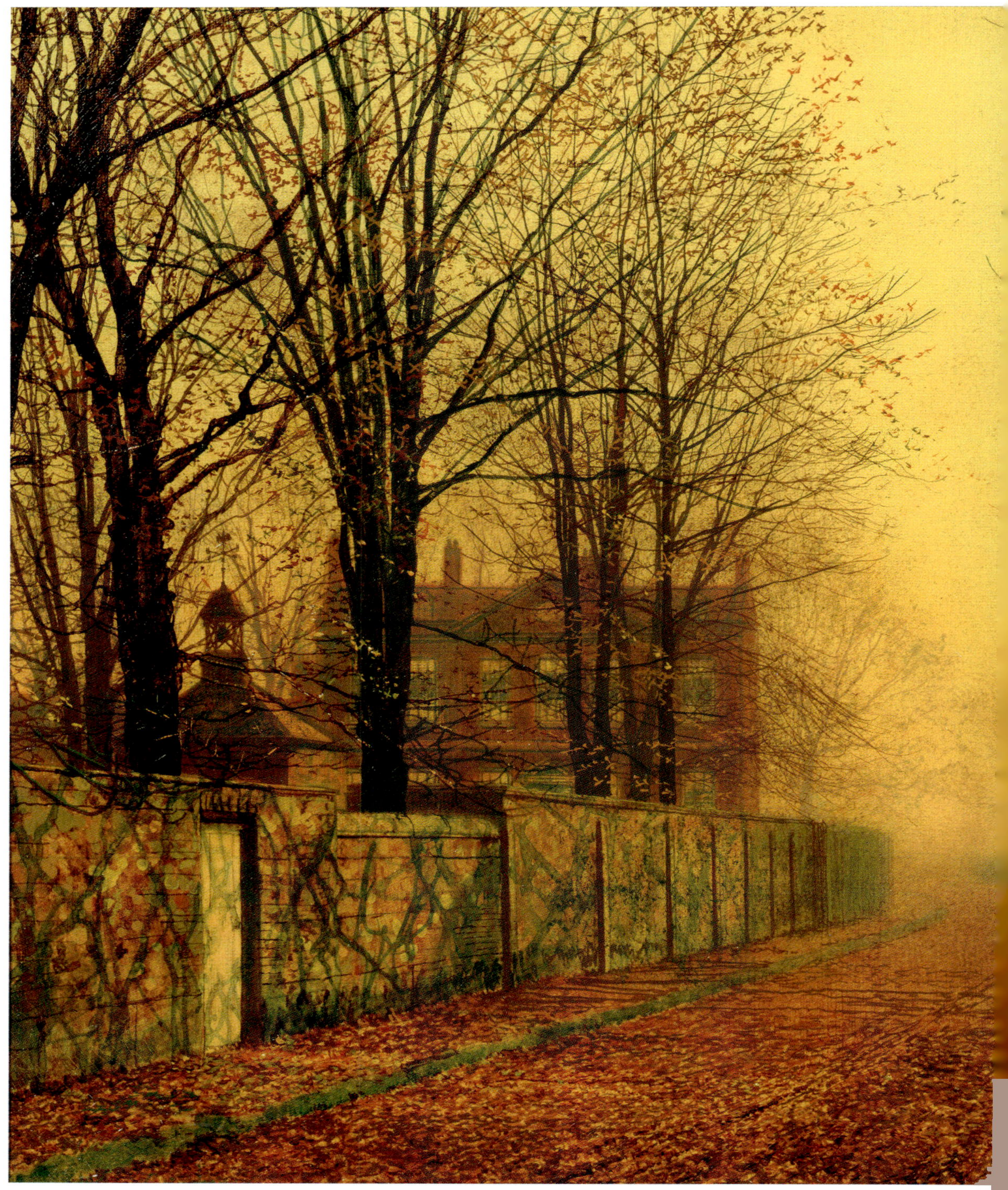

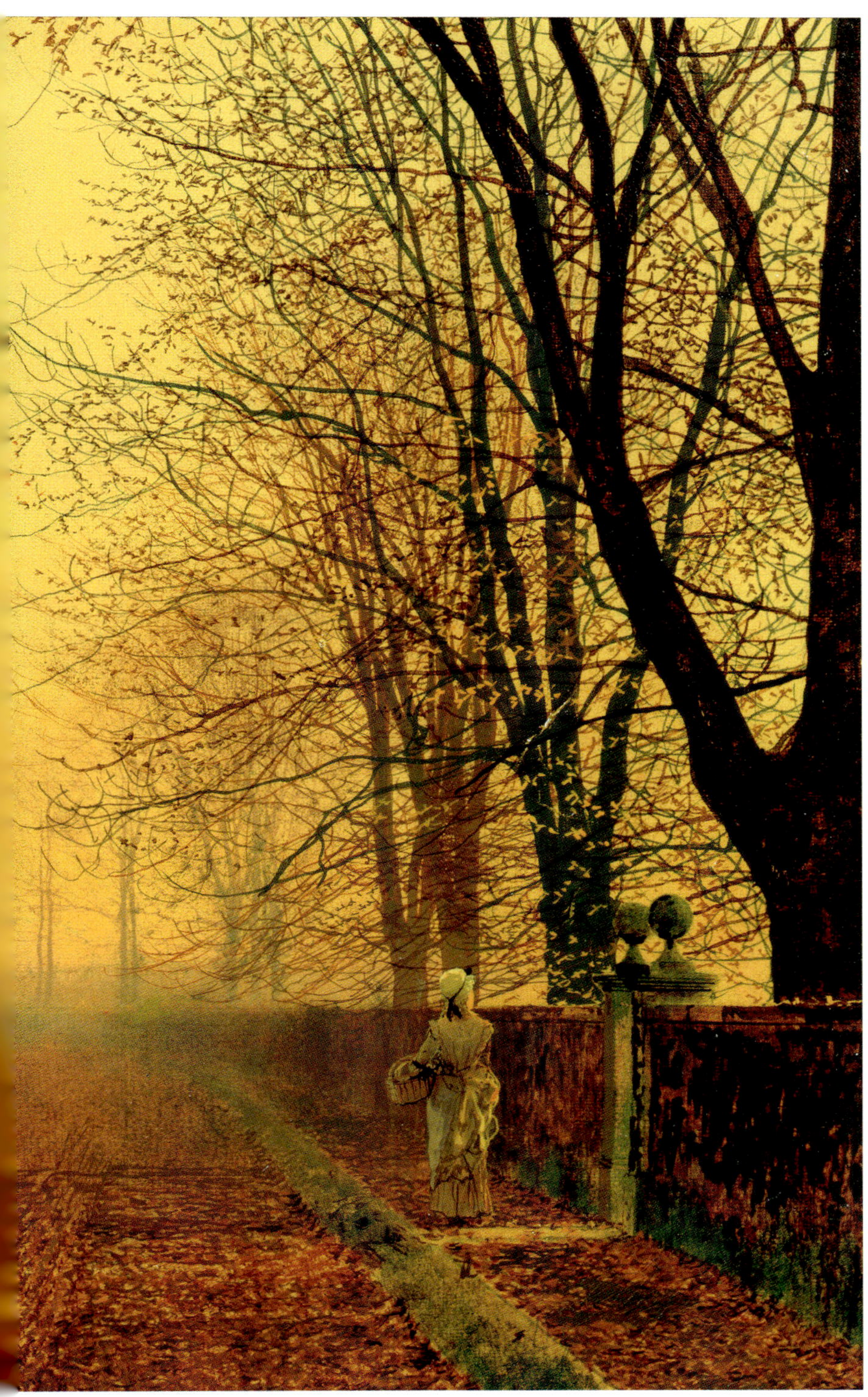

75 *Evening Glow*  c.1884
John Atkinson
Grimshaw
(1836–93)
Oil on canvas

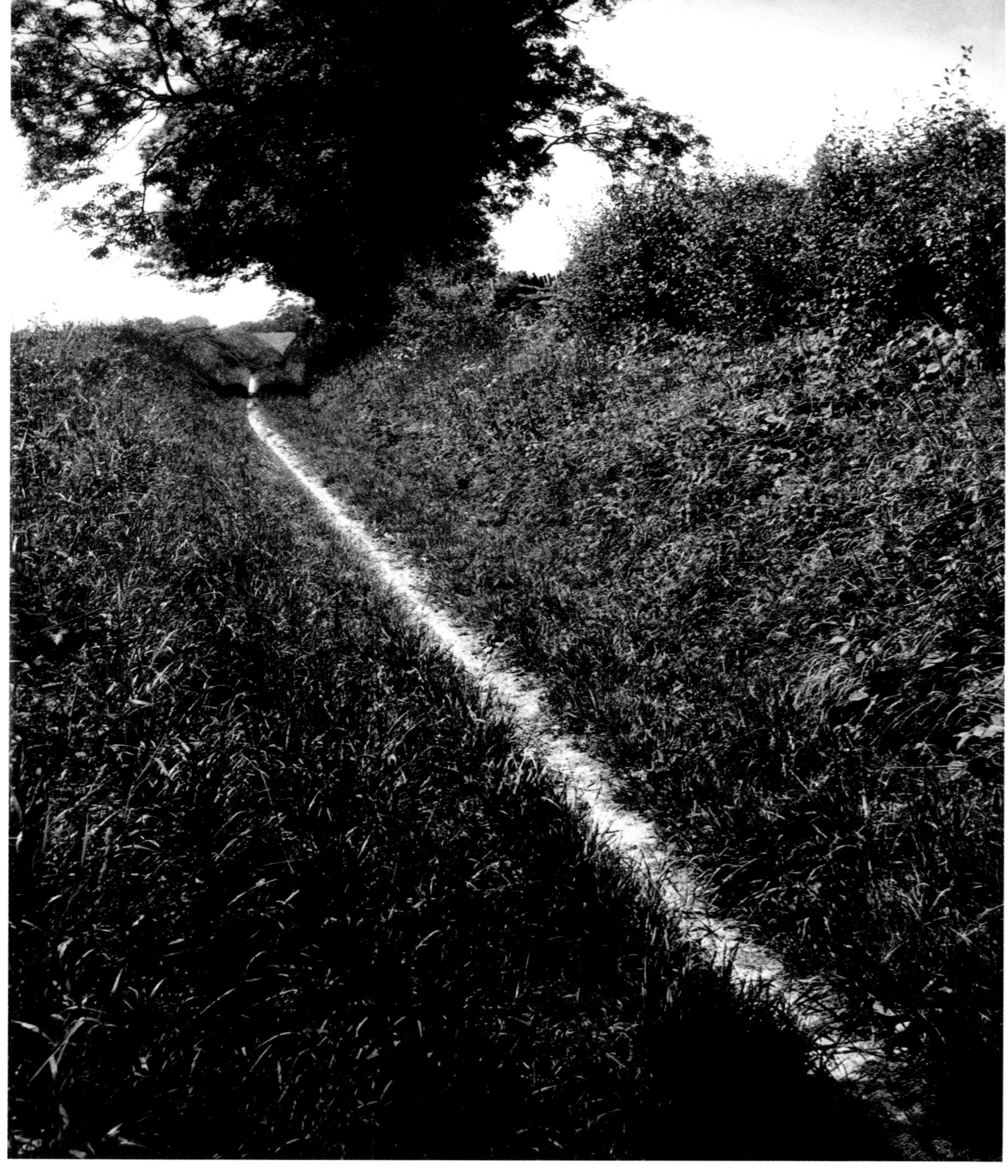

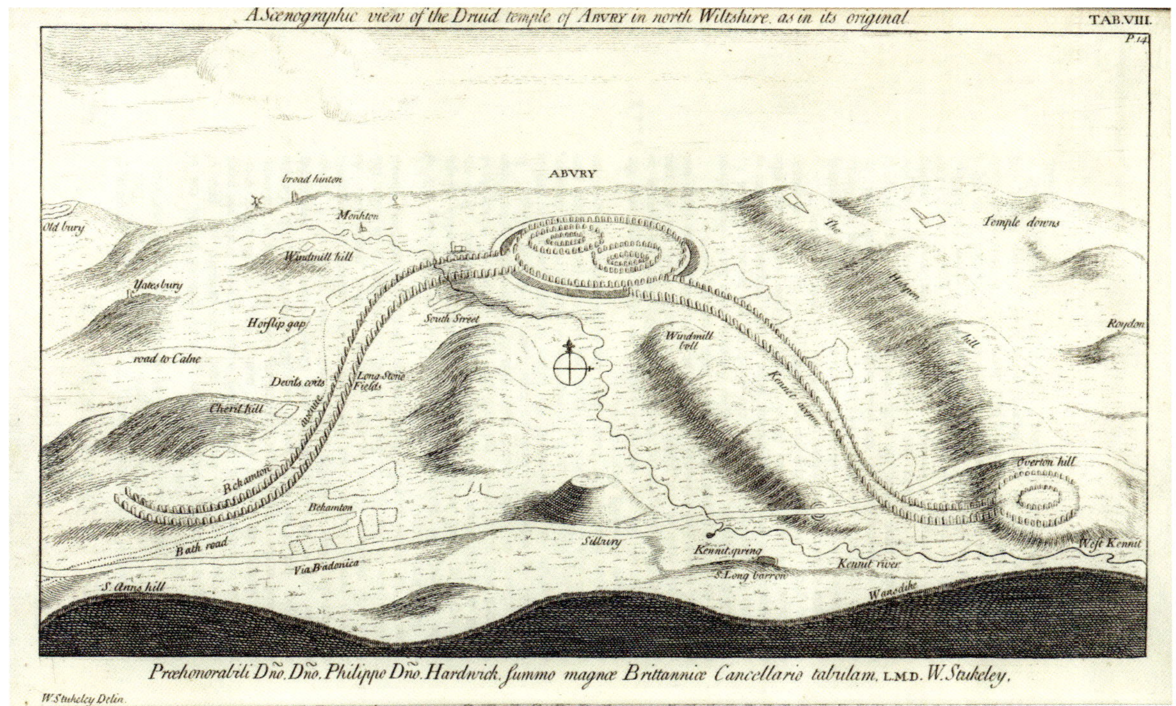


**76** *A Scenographic view of the Druid temple of Abury in north Wiltshire as in its original* 1743
William Stukeley (1687–1765)
Engraving

Stukeley believed that the plan of Avebury formed the shape of a huge two-headed serpent, but to prove his point in this image he had to distort the landscape to make it appear more symmetrical. At the time he was studying the stones of Avebury, many were being removed for use as building material, so his drawings (despite such distortions) offer a valuable record of the prehistoric sites that had existed in his day but are now lost.

**77** *The Pilgrim's Way* 1950
Bill Brandt (1904–83)
Vintage gelatin print

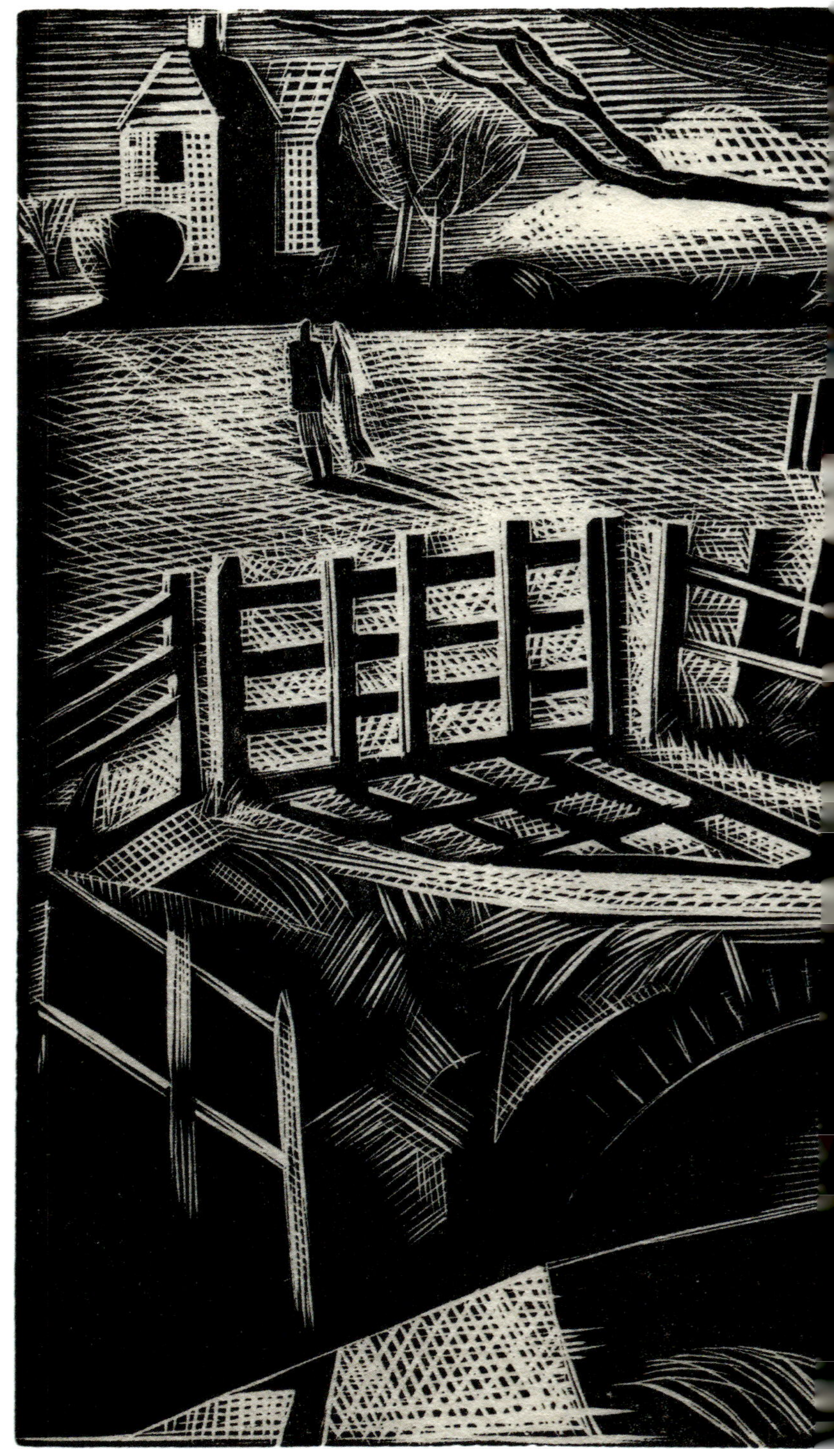

78 *Dyke by the Road*  1922
Paul Nash (1889–1946)
Wood engraving

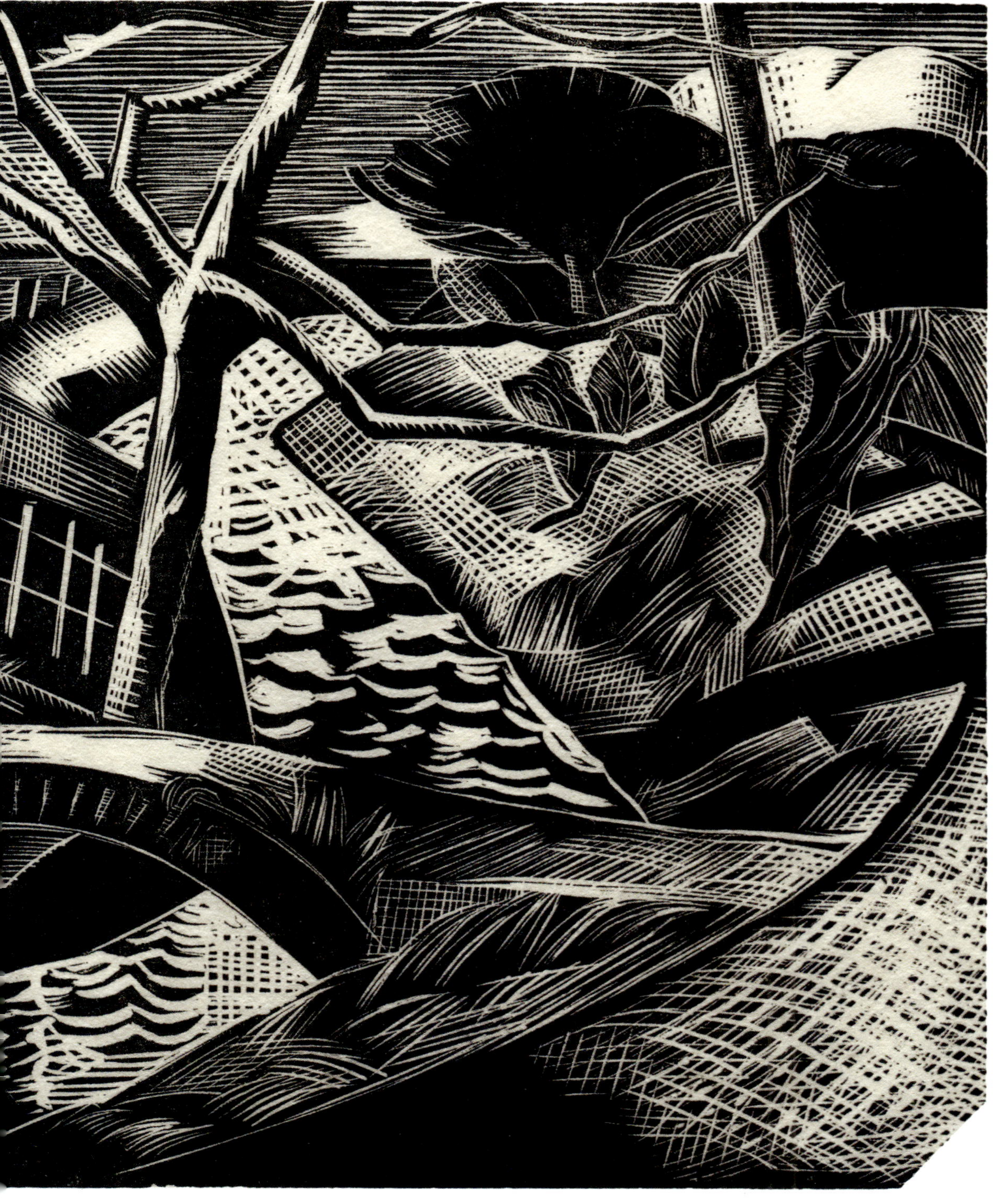

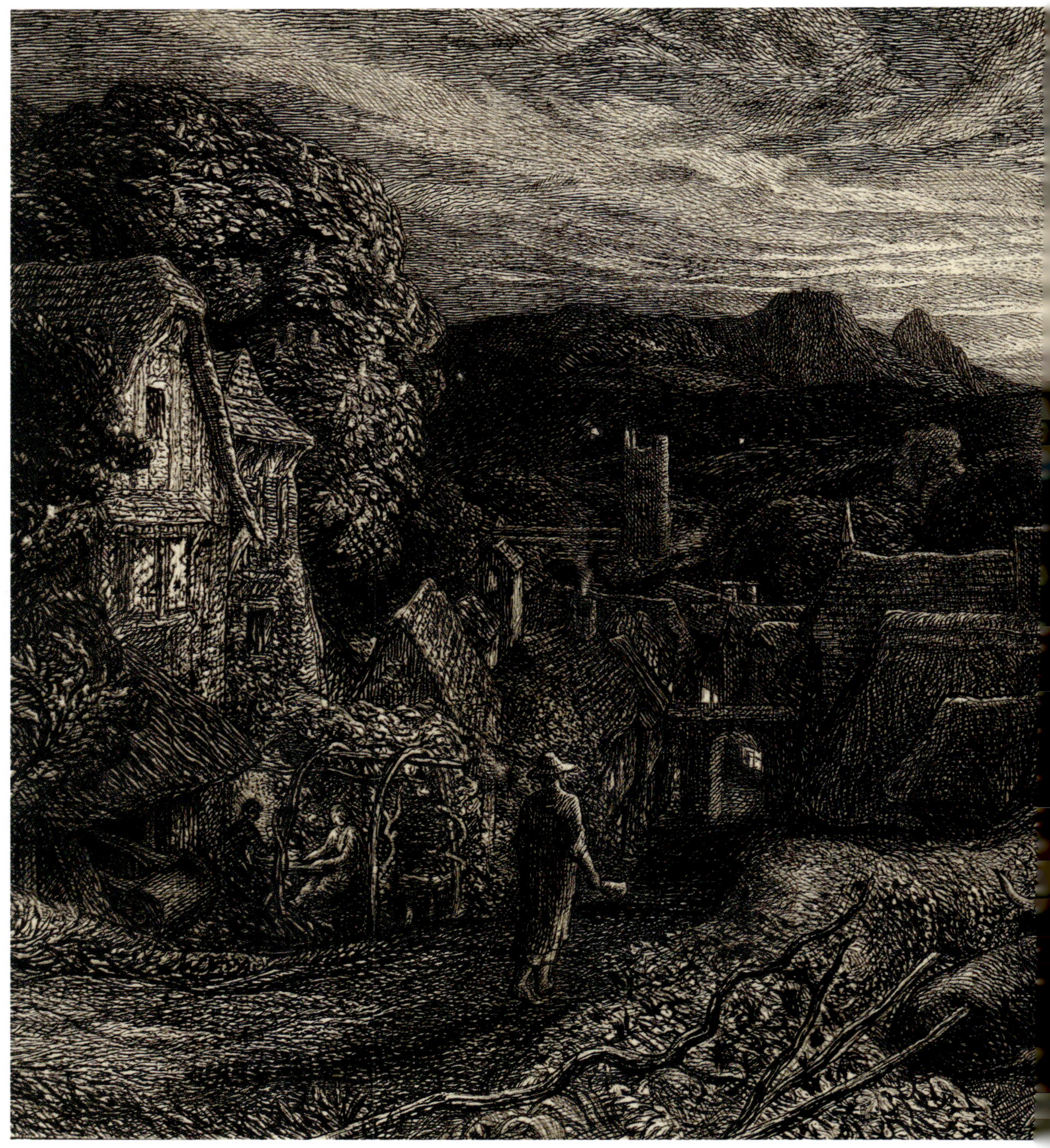

ENGLAND ON FIRE

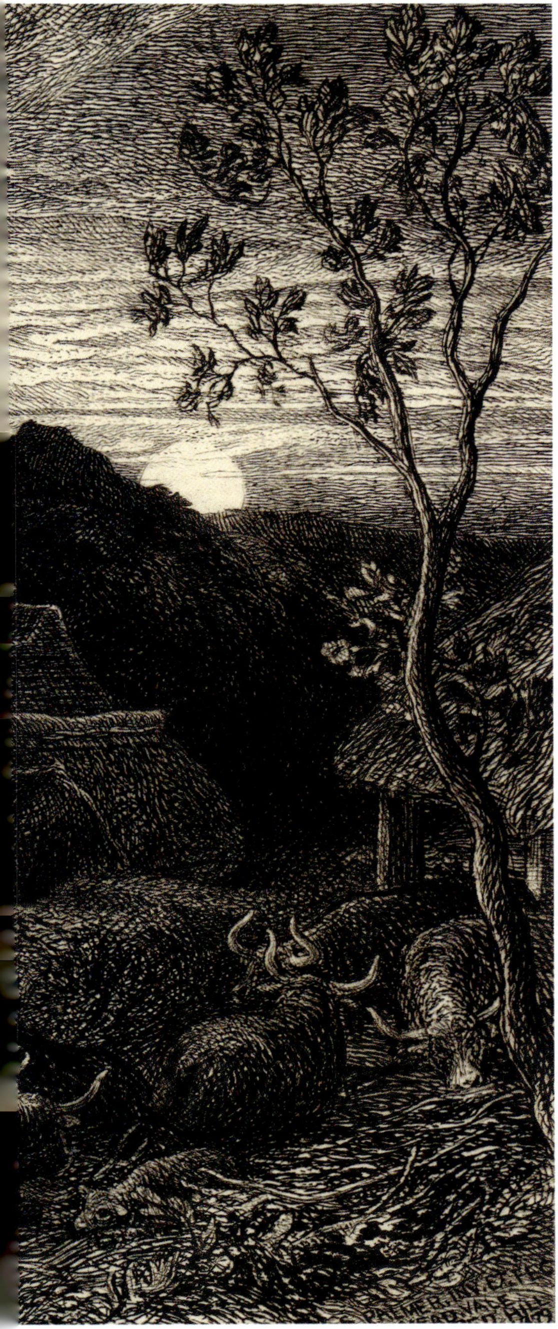

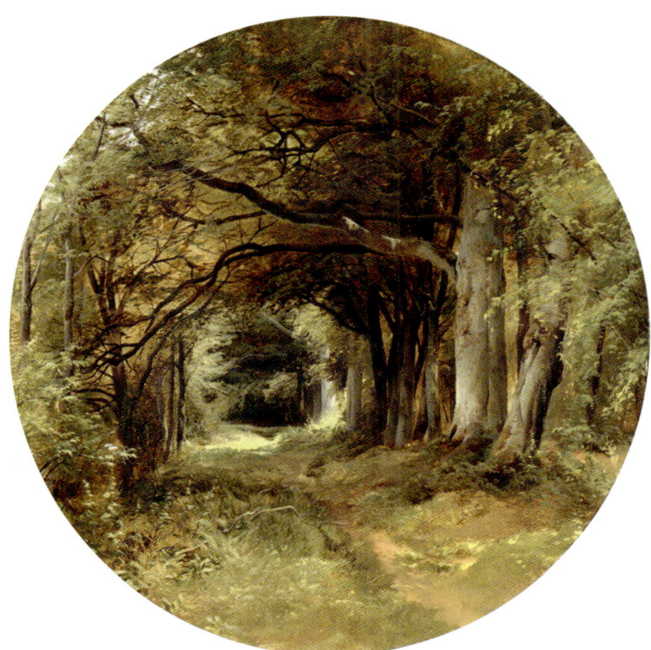

79 *Approach to Hastings*  Undated
George Barret Jr (1767–1842)
Watercolour, pen and brown ink on paper

80 *The Bellman*  1879
Samuel Palmer (1805–81)
Etching and dry point, with plate tone on paper

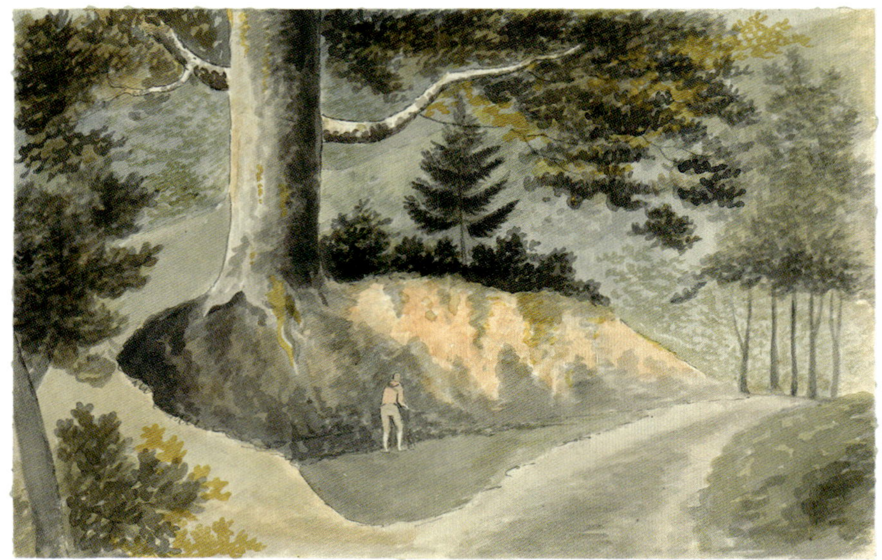

81 *Road in the Forest* Undated Edward Francis Burney (1760–1848) Watercolour, pen and black ink on paper

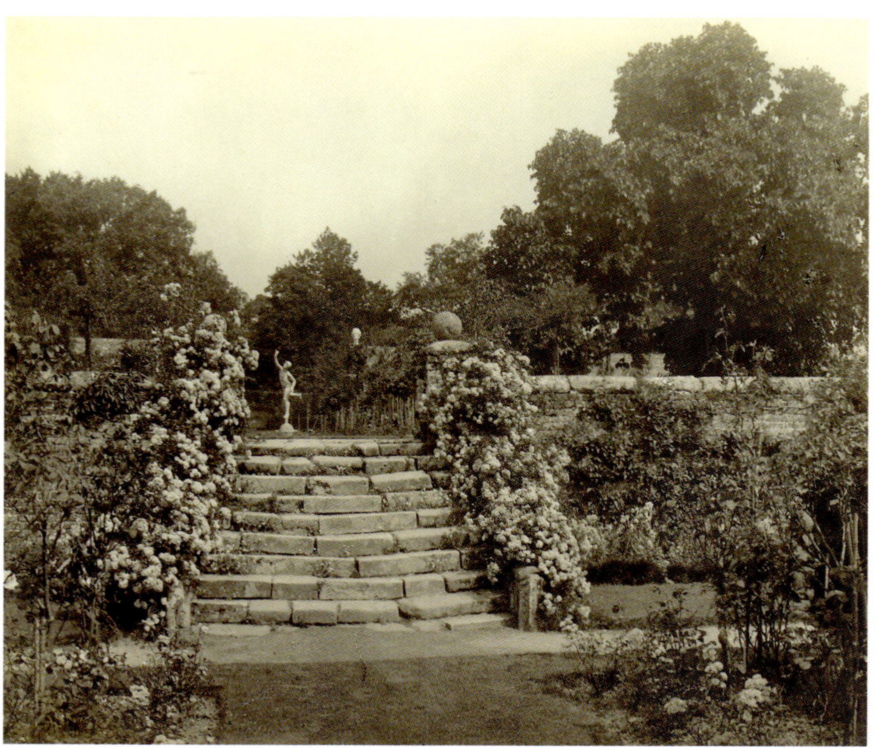

82 *Herstmonceux Castle, Sussex, Steps to the Upper Garden* 1918 Frederick H. Evans (1853–1943) Gelatin silver print

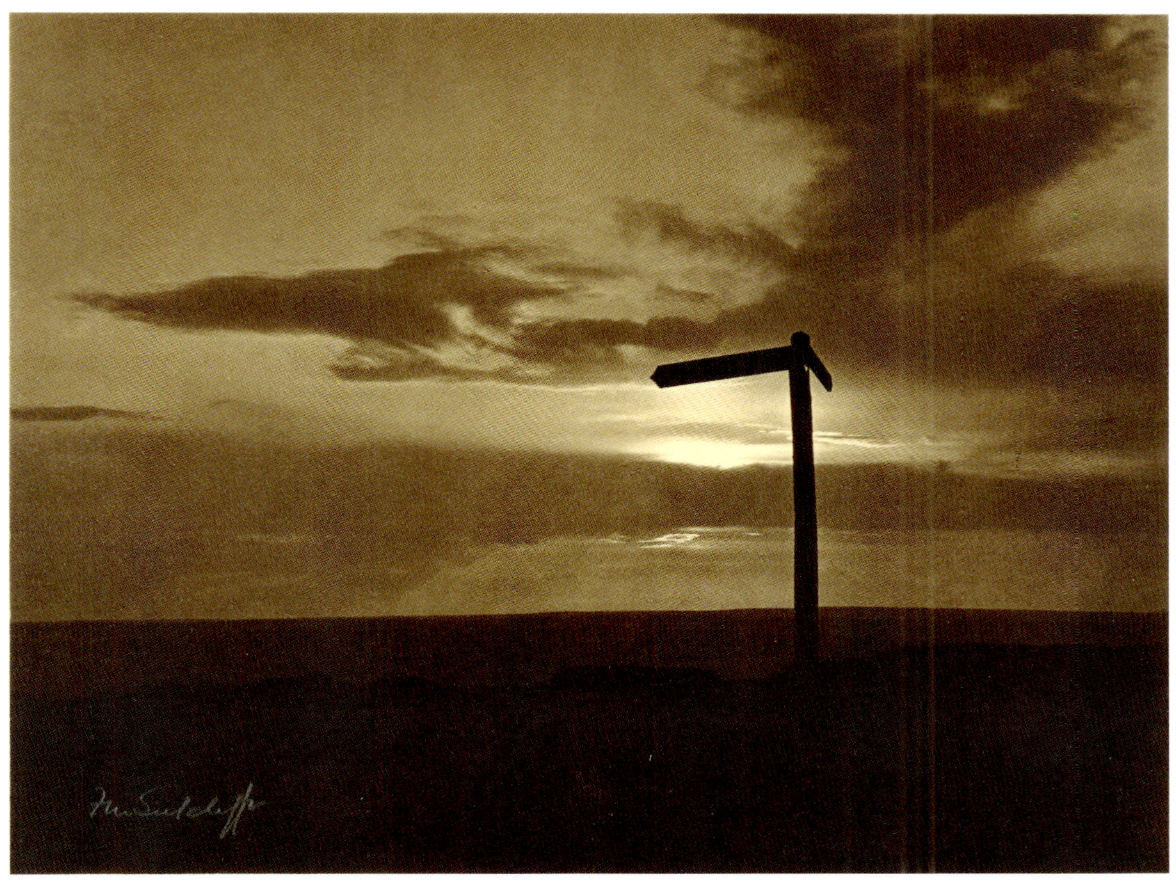

**83** *Quo Vadis?* *c.*1895
Frank Meadow Sutcliffe
(1853–1941)
Gelatin silver print

Sutcliffe's image evokes a deep sense of being on the move, as the sun sets behind two arrows pointing in opposing directions. According to the apocryphal Acts of Peter, "*Quo vadis?*" ("Where are you going?") was the question posed by St Peter when the resurrected Christ appeared to him on the Appian Way.

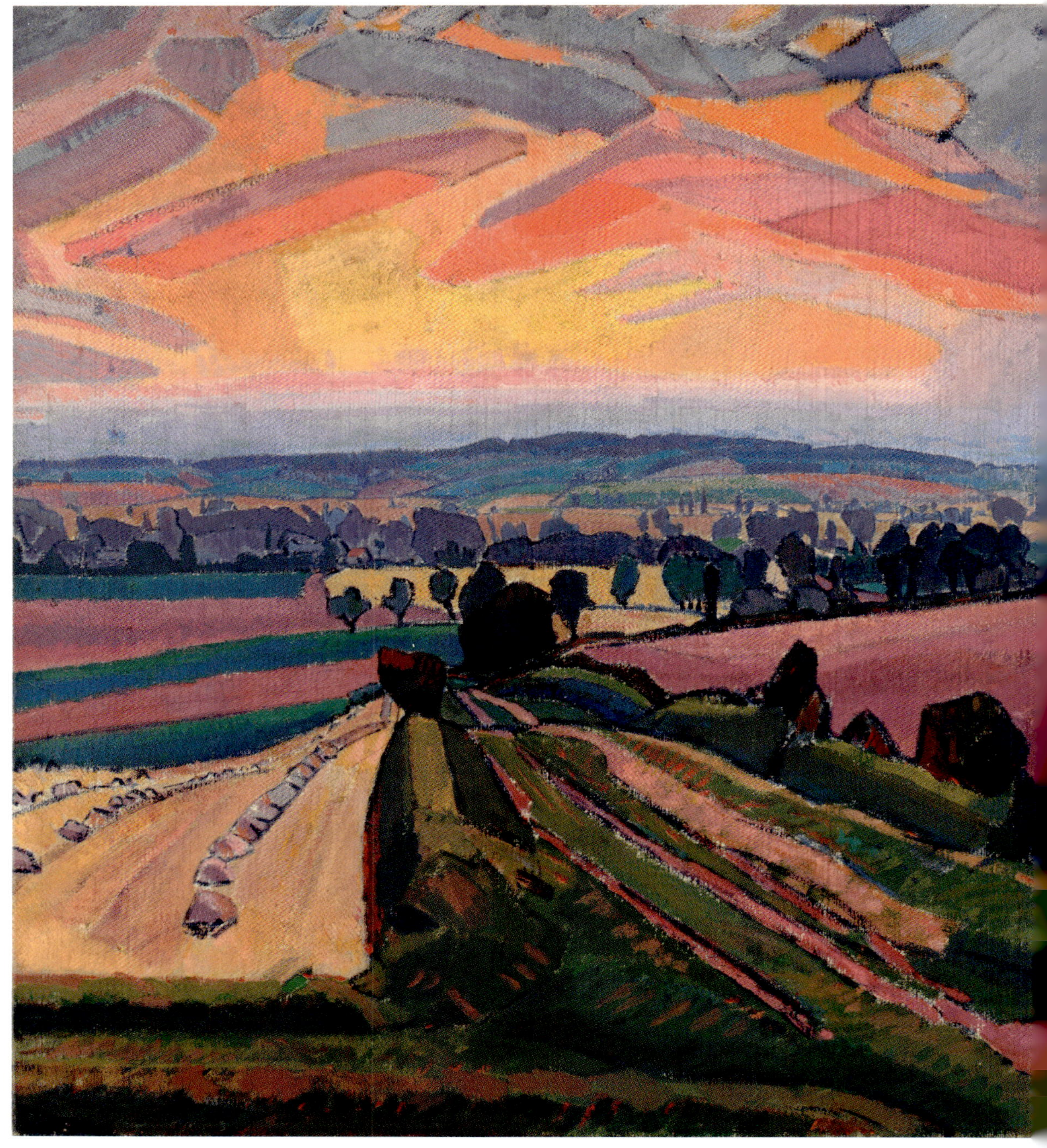

ENGLAND ON FIRE

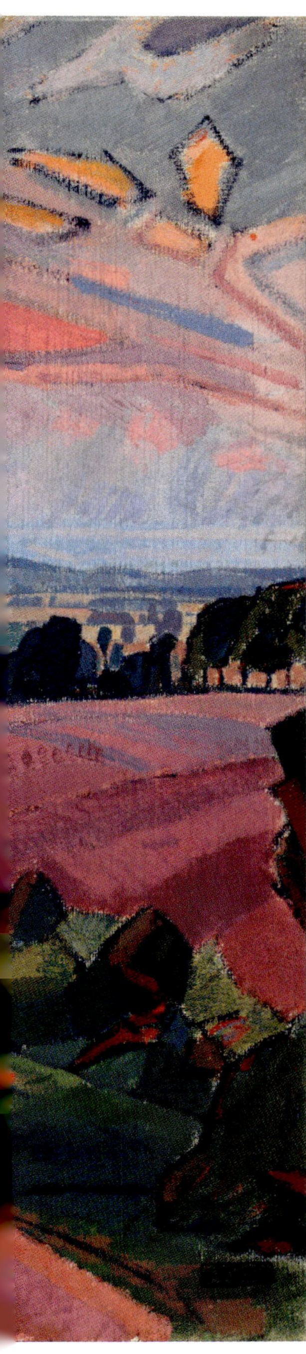

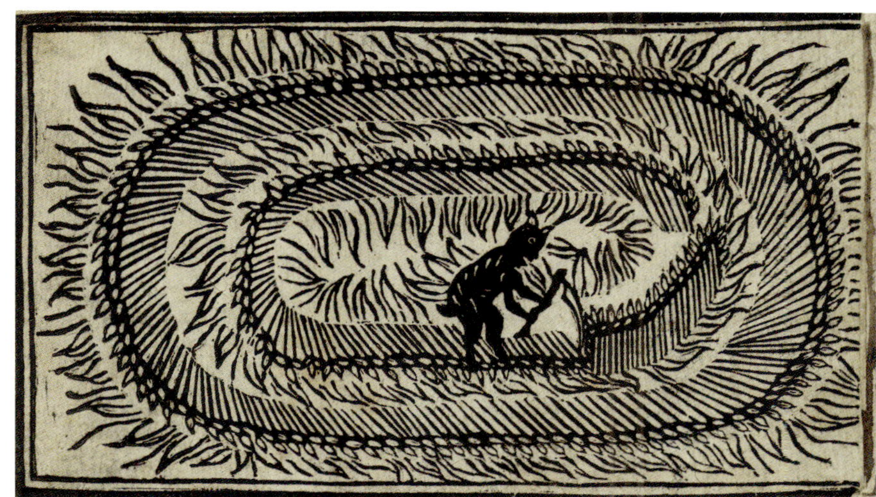

**84**  *The mowing-Devil, or, Strange news out of Hartford-Shire …*  1678
Artist unknown
Woodcut

Perhaps the first known image of a crop circle, like those that appeared across England in the 1970s and 80s, this woodcut illustration depicts a mysterious event that occurred in Hertfordshire in 1678. According to a pamphlet of the time, a local farmer was looking for someone to mow his field of oats. When the first man he attempted to hire demanded too high a price, the farmer exclaimed, "The devil shall mow it rather than thee!" During the night the fields were seen to be lit by a strange glow, as if they were on fire, and the next day the farmer emerged to find his crops neatly mowed and stacked.

**85**  *The Icknield Way*  1912
Spencer Gore (1878–1914)
Oil on canvas

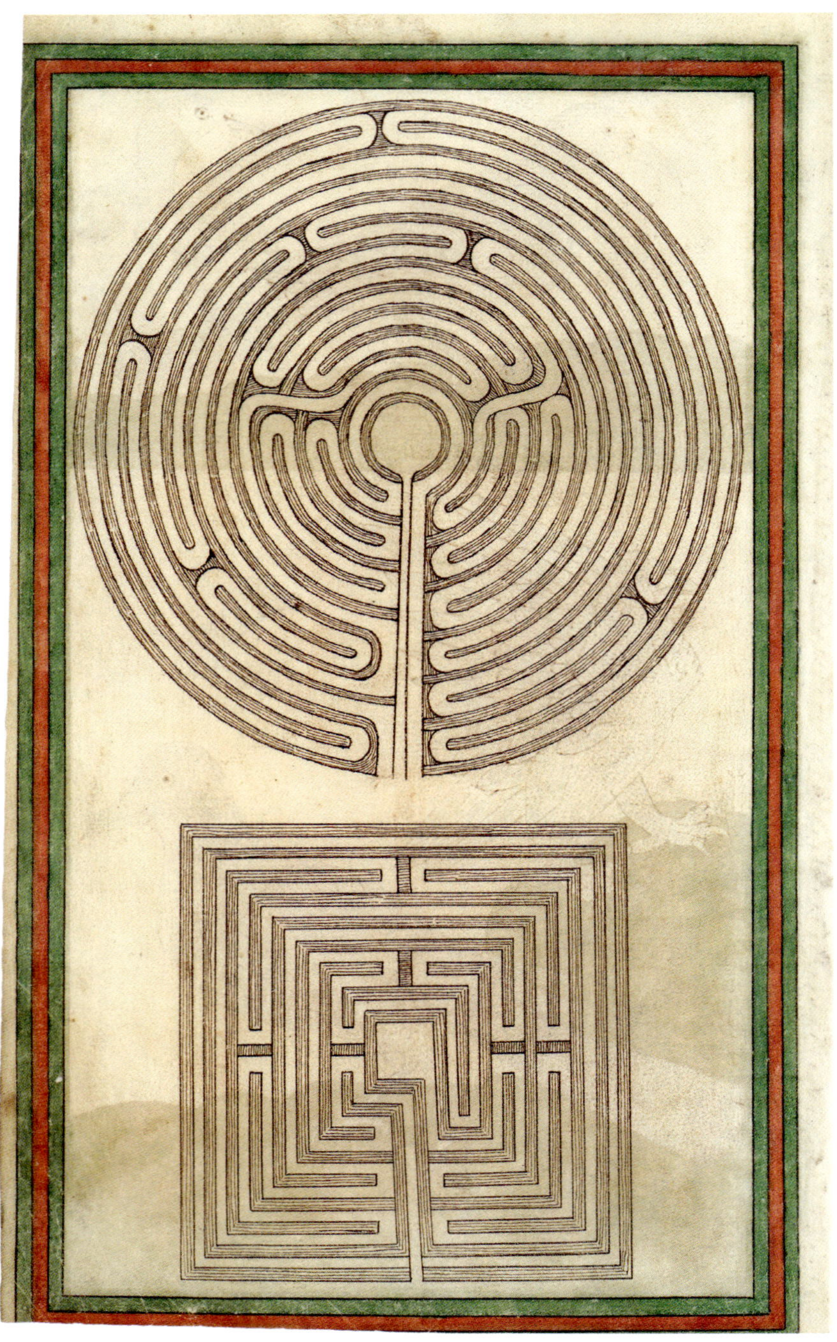

**86** *Maze from* The Trevelyon Miscellany  1608
Thomas Trevelyon (b. *c.*1548)
Engraving

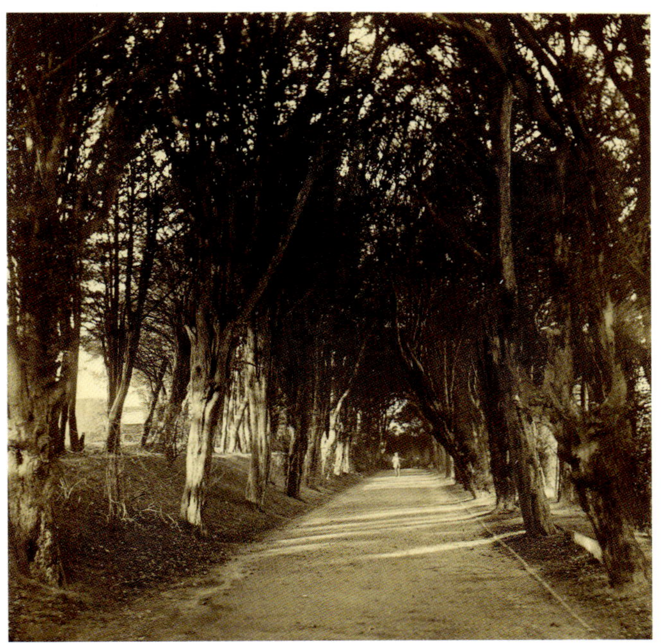

87  *The Dark Walk; Stonyhurst*  1856–8
Roger Fenton (1819–69)
Albumen silver print

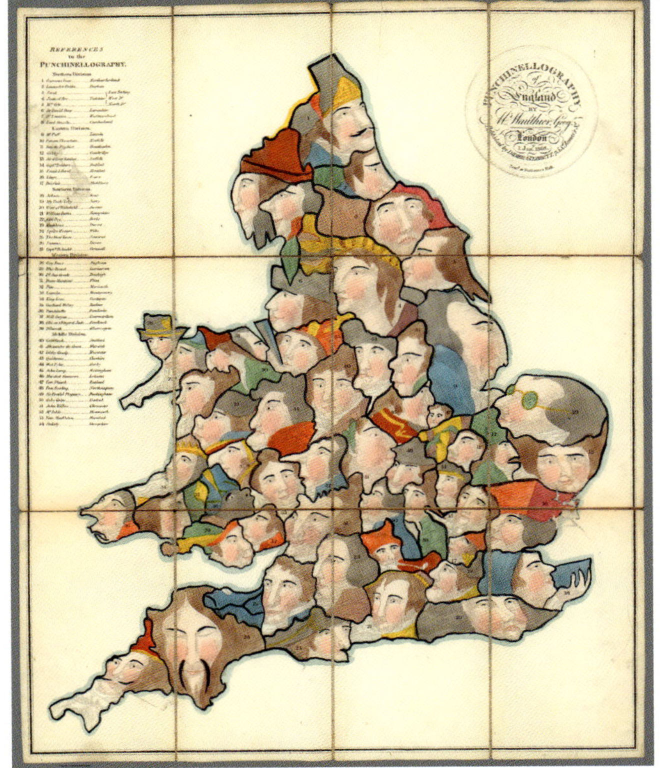


88  *Punchinello-graphy of England*  1808
John M. Wauthier (active 19th century)
Engraving

Here, a map of the counties of England
and Wales is presented in the form of
portraits of various figures from history,
literature and folklore. It featured in a
board game, produced by Peter Didier
and William Tebbett, and first advertised
in January 1808, in which players would
pick a counter from a bag – each counter
being named for one of the characters
– and then proceed to list the principal
towns of the associated county. There is
no clear correlation between character and
location – Cardinal Wolsey is Radnor, for
example, while Joan of Arc is Yorkshire.

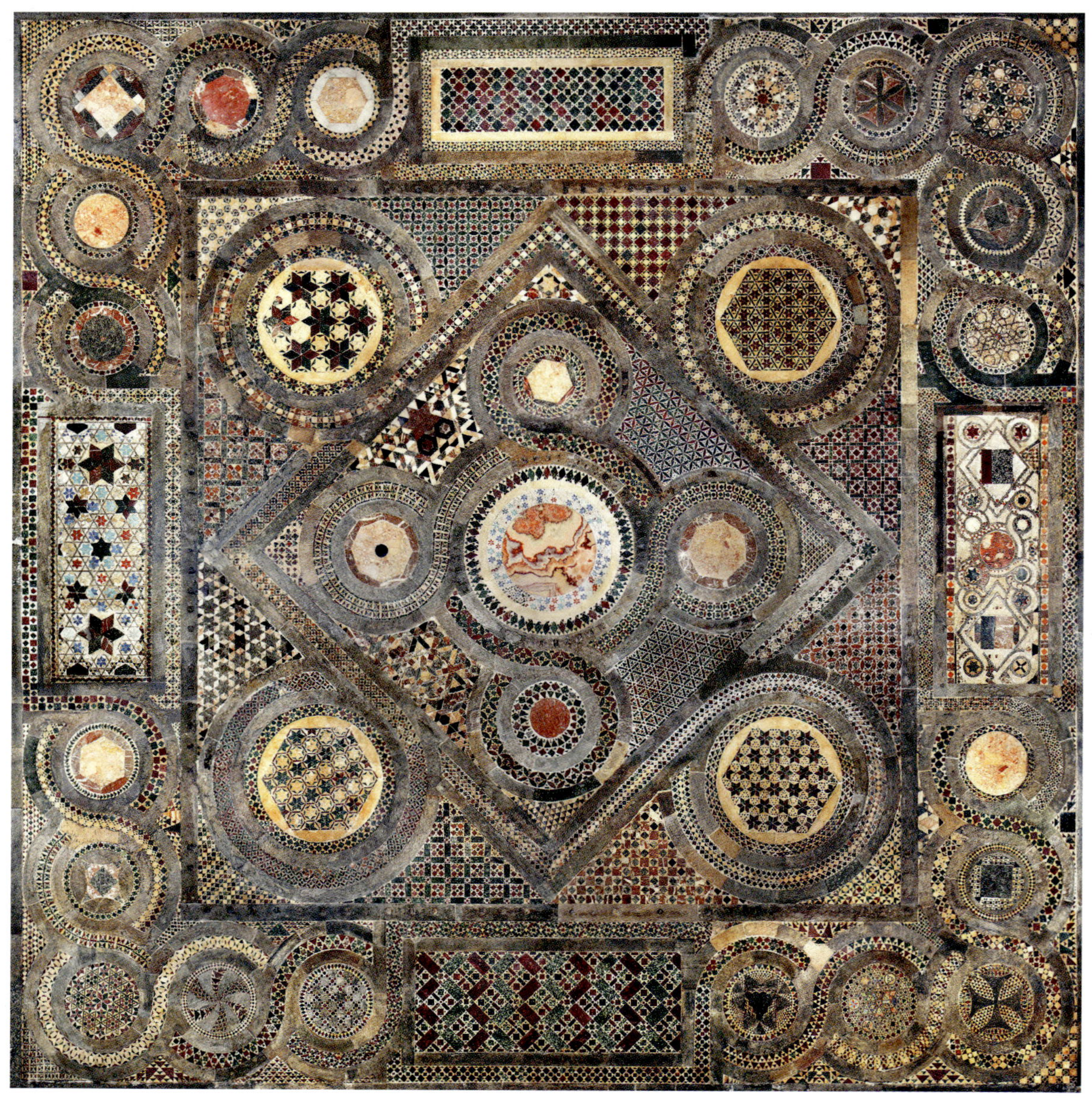

**89**  *The Cosmati Pavement at Westminster Abbey*  1268
Odoricus of Rome (13th century)
Opus sectile work

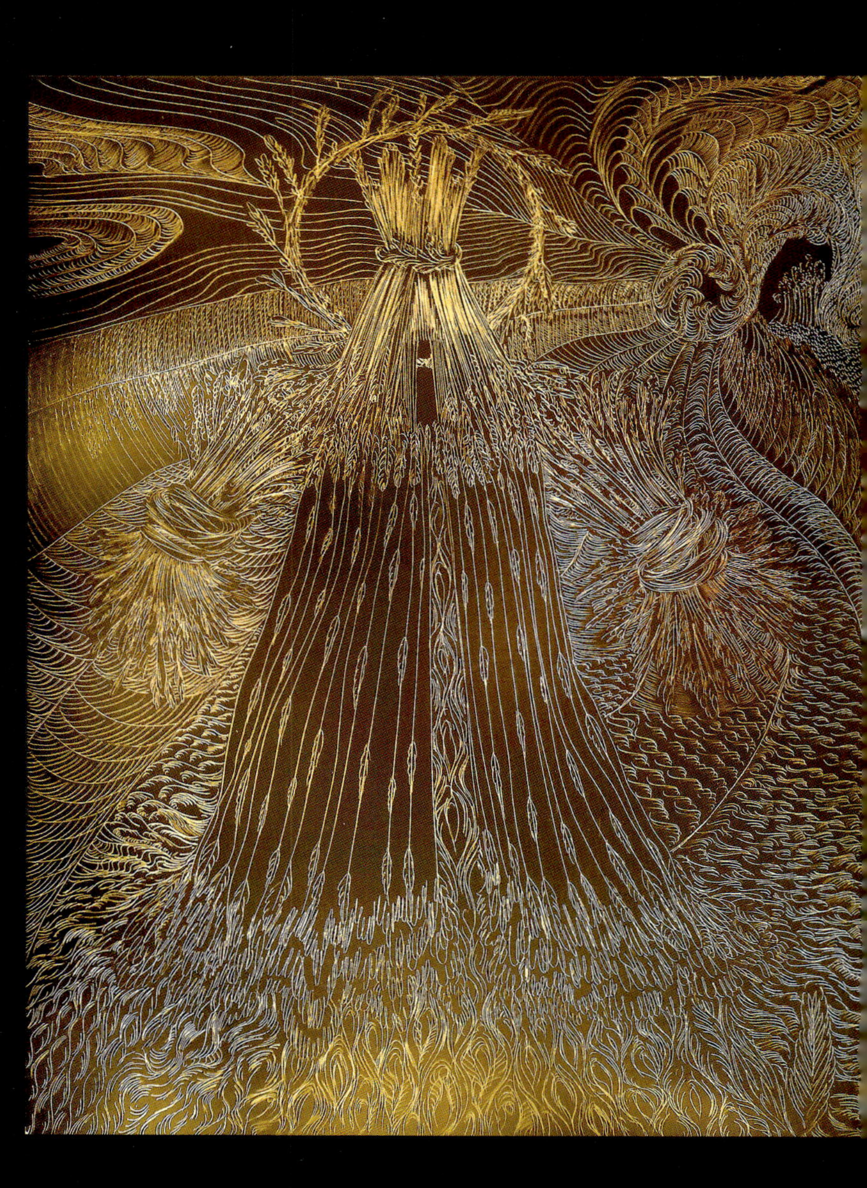

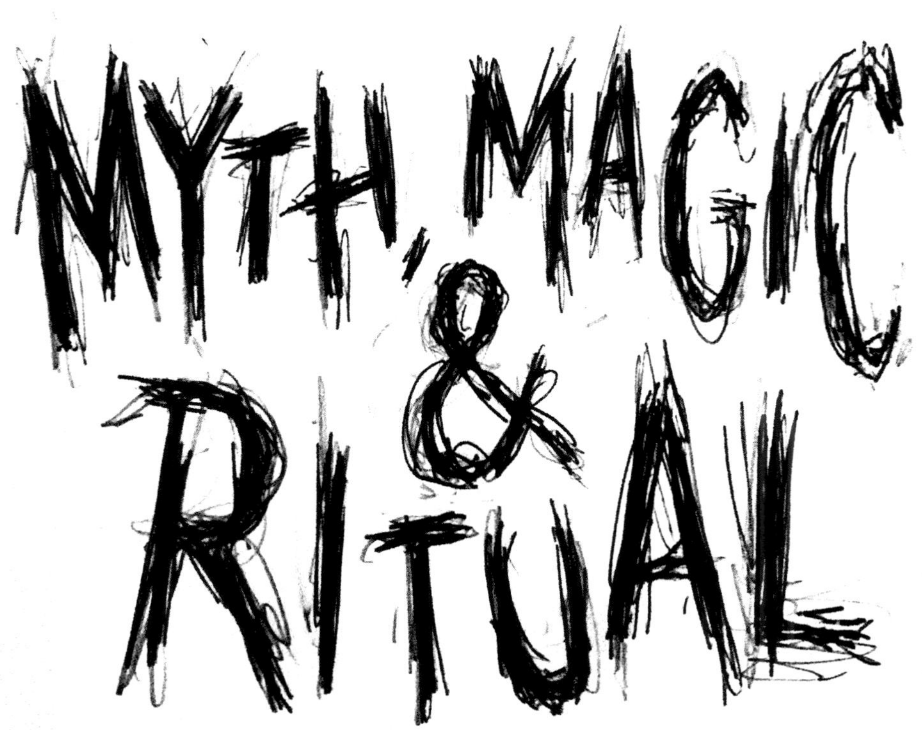
6
MYTH, MAGIC & RITUAL

ENGLAND IS AN IMMIGRANT SONG. A BASTARD, BLENDED LAND MADE UP OF FOREIGN MYTHS AND FANTASTICAL CREATURES.

At night, around the camp fire, the Tyburn boy tells stories to ward off the dark. Old tales of heroes and beasts and lovers and death. Where did they come from, these English myths? They came from across the waters in tiny storm-tossed boats like so many refugees. Look, there, the Morris Dancers are all the way from Turkey (Moorish Dancers, really, mangled by a million mishearings). They dodged the coastguards and bailed the water from their craft with runcible spoons. Their tatters and rags are sodden, these refugees from Islamic tales. But once here they'll twist and unravel through the land, scattering their dark-magic spells in pub car parks where the men drink Carling as the kids eat their crisps.

The cliffs ring to the sound of Punch thwacking at the sides of the Dover-bound container lorry with his truncheon. *That's the way to do it! That's the way to do it!* They all piled in at Calais – Punch and Judy and the rest of them, full of wild glee and senseless violence. There are no bluebirds flying over the white cliffs; like so many symbols of Albion, the song was written by an outsider, an American who'd never seen Dover, writing about a bird that never visits these shores. So, of course, the English took the tune to their hearts.

Still the myths come. These crossbreed stories are the ones we love the best. St George and the Dragon, those old co-dependents, ride in on the back of a donkey. St George is a Turk, shivering in clammy England, and the dragon is from even further afield, who knows where? From the blank spaces on the map where it reads "Here Be Monsters", perhaps. Whatever. He's a refugee from somewhere. No matter that he has no papers, the Welsh will put him on their flag anyway.

Bastard myths, bastard stories, bastard heroes. These strangest of bedfellows breed fresh mongrel traditions. Beltane begets May Day, Saturnalia births Christmas, Samhain beds down with the Gunpowder Plot (the perfect English festival really – equal parts fire and failure, with a foreign name to blame it on).

All traditions were new once, no family is truly young. England will grind every story beneath the harrow, back into the soil, and let strange wild blooms burst forth.

England is an immigrant song that changes us with every singing.

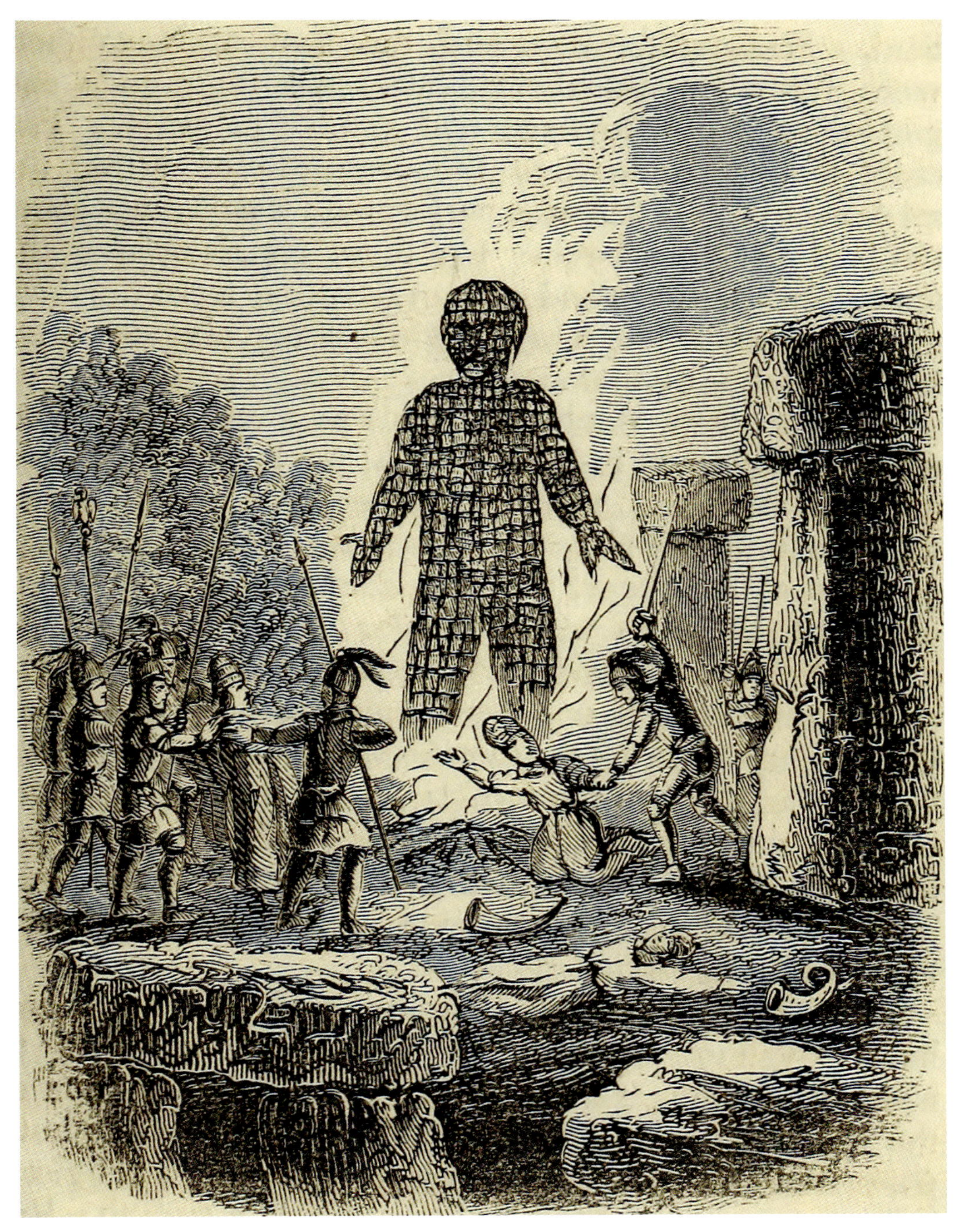

**91** *Romans Destroying the Druids*  1860
John Warner Barber (1798–1885)  Engraving

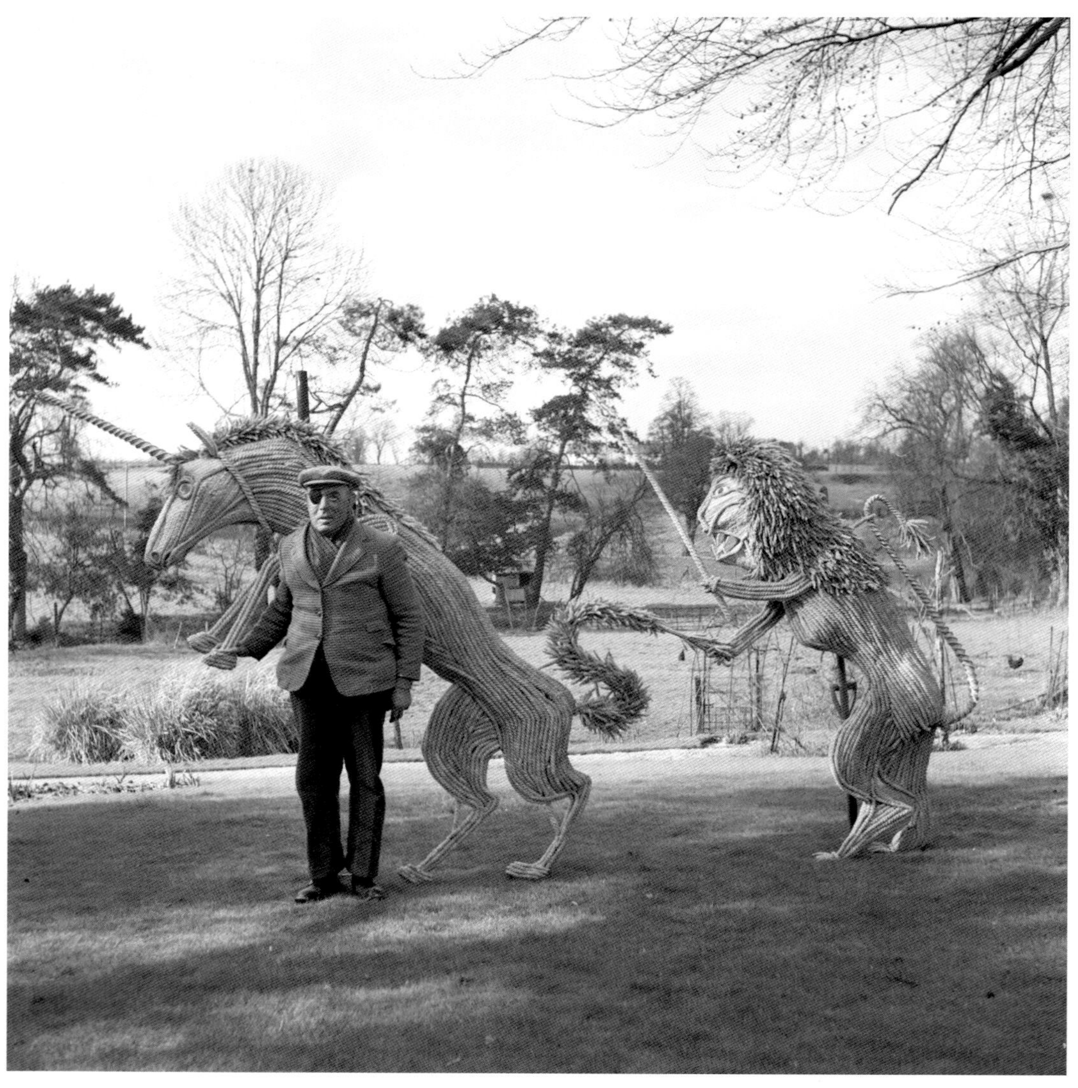

**92**  *Fred Mizen aged 60 from Bardfield, Braintree, Essex, with straw effigies of the Lion and the Unicorn  c.1951*
John Tarlton (1914–80)
Black and white photograph from 60mm x 60mm negative

Mizen was foremost a maker of corn dollies, widely associated with the harvest rituals of pre-industrial Europe. This photograph by Tarlton of Mizen with his Lion and Unicorn effigies, produced for the Festival of Britain, presents a unique portrayal of Britishness and the Union, interestingly with the Lion (representing England) shown in a stance of attack against the Unicorn (Scotland).

**93**  *The Witch Sycorax from Shakespeare's* **The Tempest**  late 19th–early 20th century
Arthur Rackham (1867–1939)  Ink with colour wash drawing

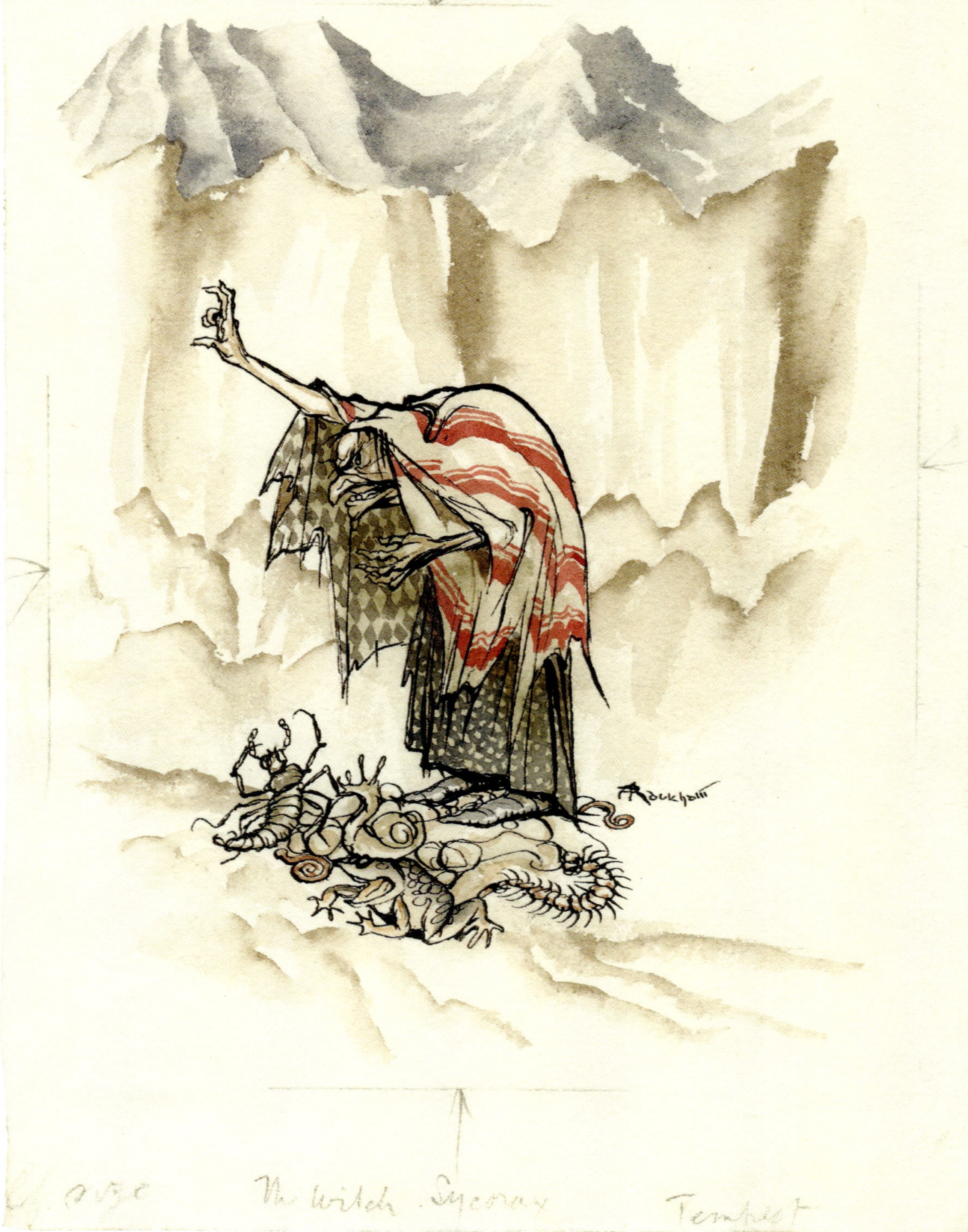

½ size
The Witch Sycorax
Tempest

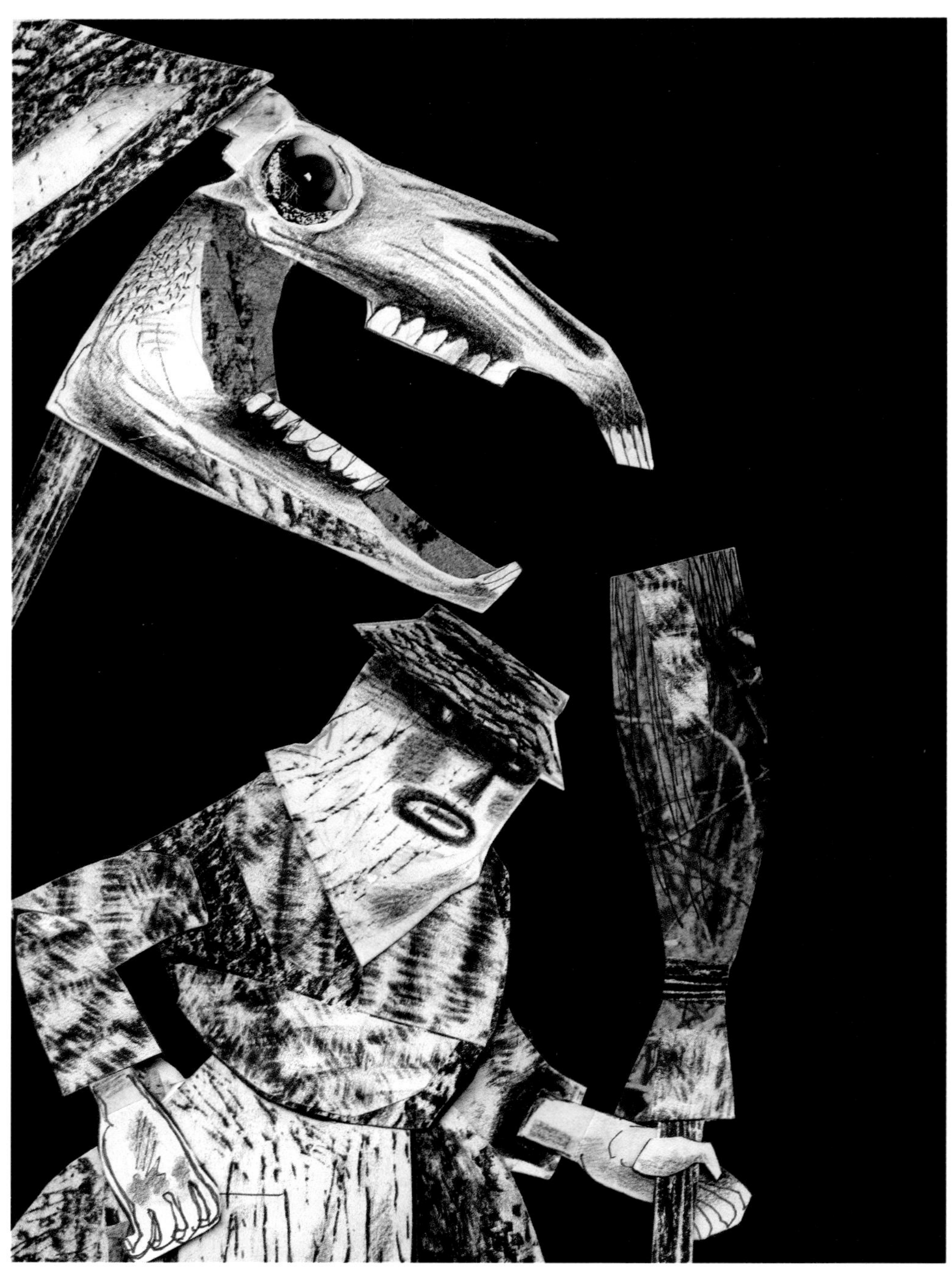

**94** *Mari Lwyd revellers conjured in stop-motion maquettes
made for the first performance of "The Mare's Tale"* 2013
Clive Hicks Jenkins (b.1951)  Ink, wax crayon and pencil on card

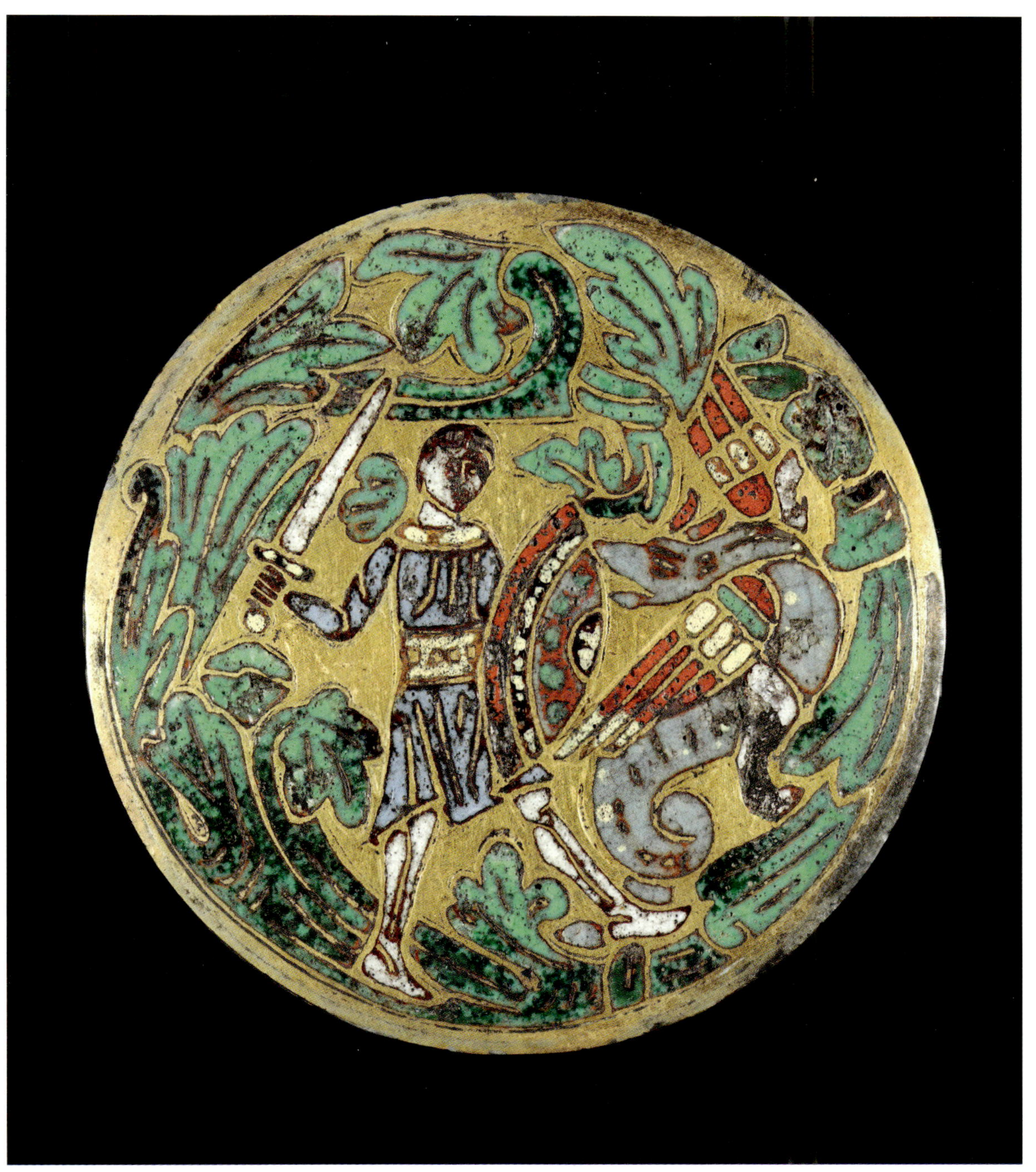

95   *Warrior (Possibly St George) Fighting a Dragon*  *c.*1170–80
Artist unknown
Gilded copper, champlevé enamel

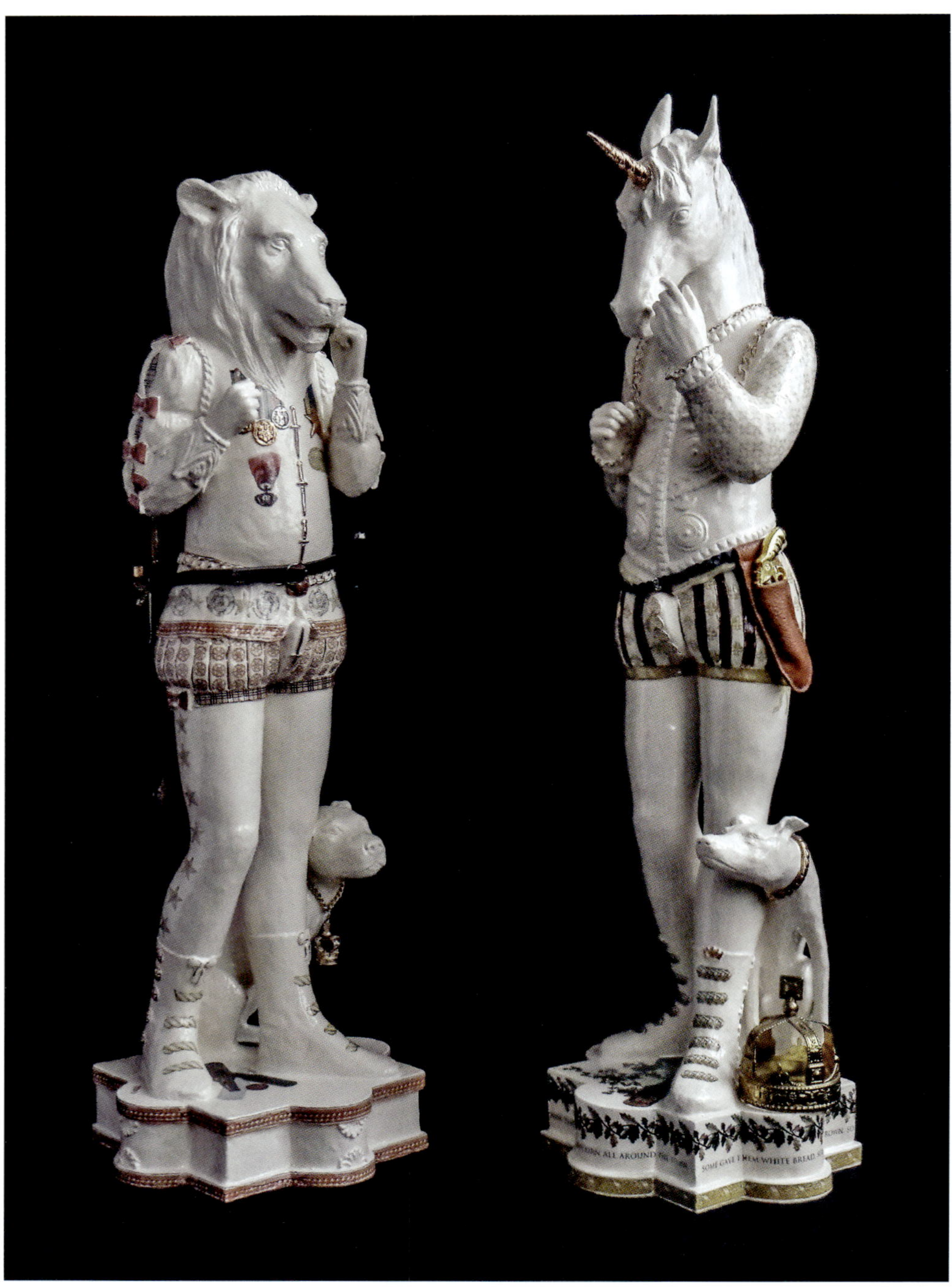

**96** *The Lion and the Unicorn* 2013
Claire Partington (b.1973)  Glazed earthenware and mixed media

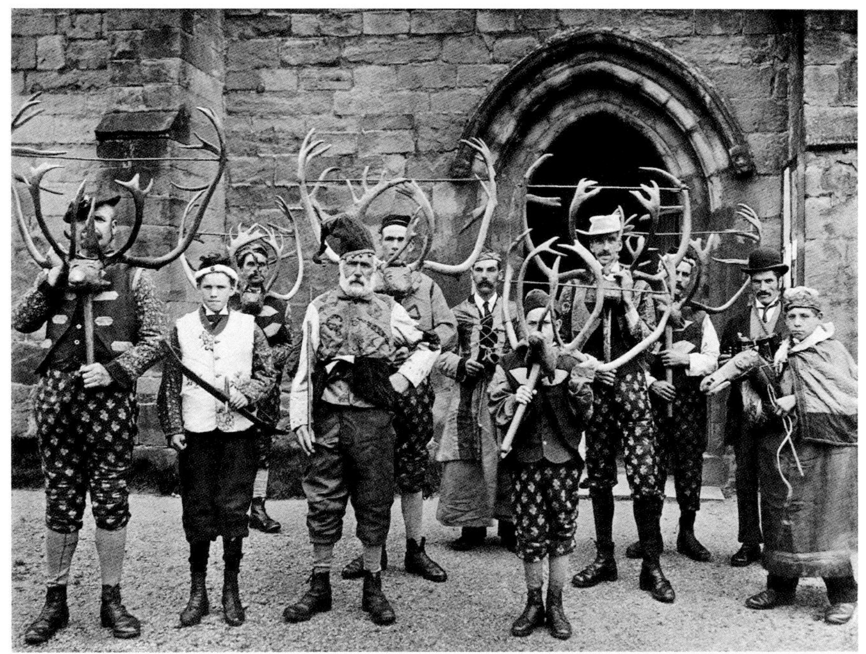

97   *Abbot's Bromley
Horn Dance*  c.1900
John Benjamin Stone
(1838–1914)
Platinum print
photograph

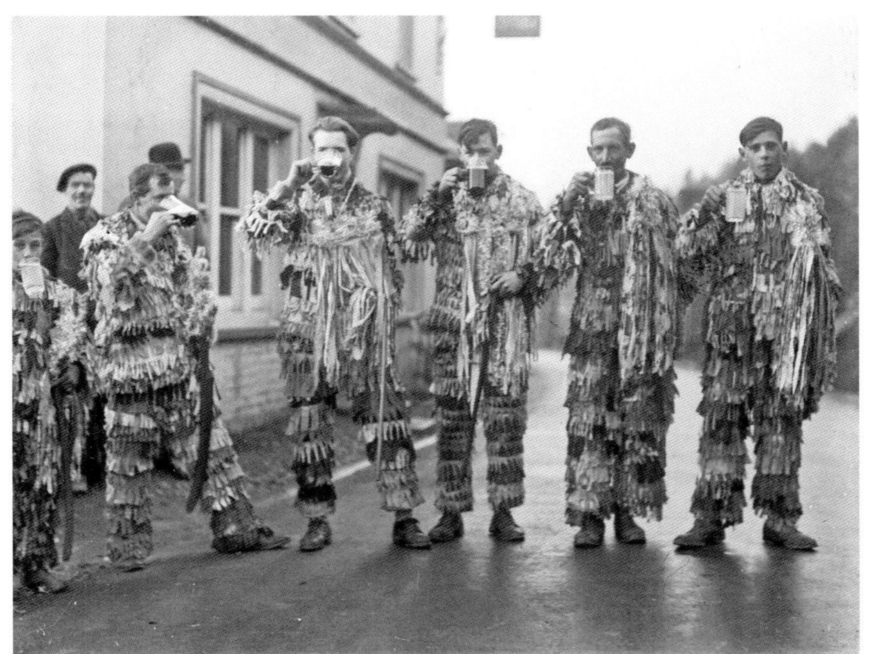

98   *Long Parish Mummers*
1920s–30s
George Long
(active 1910–50)
Glass plate negative

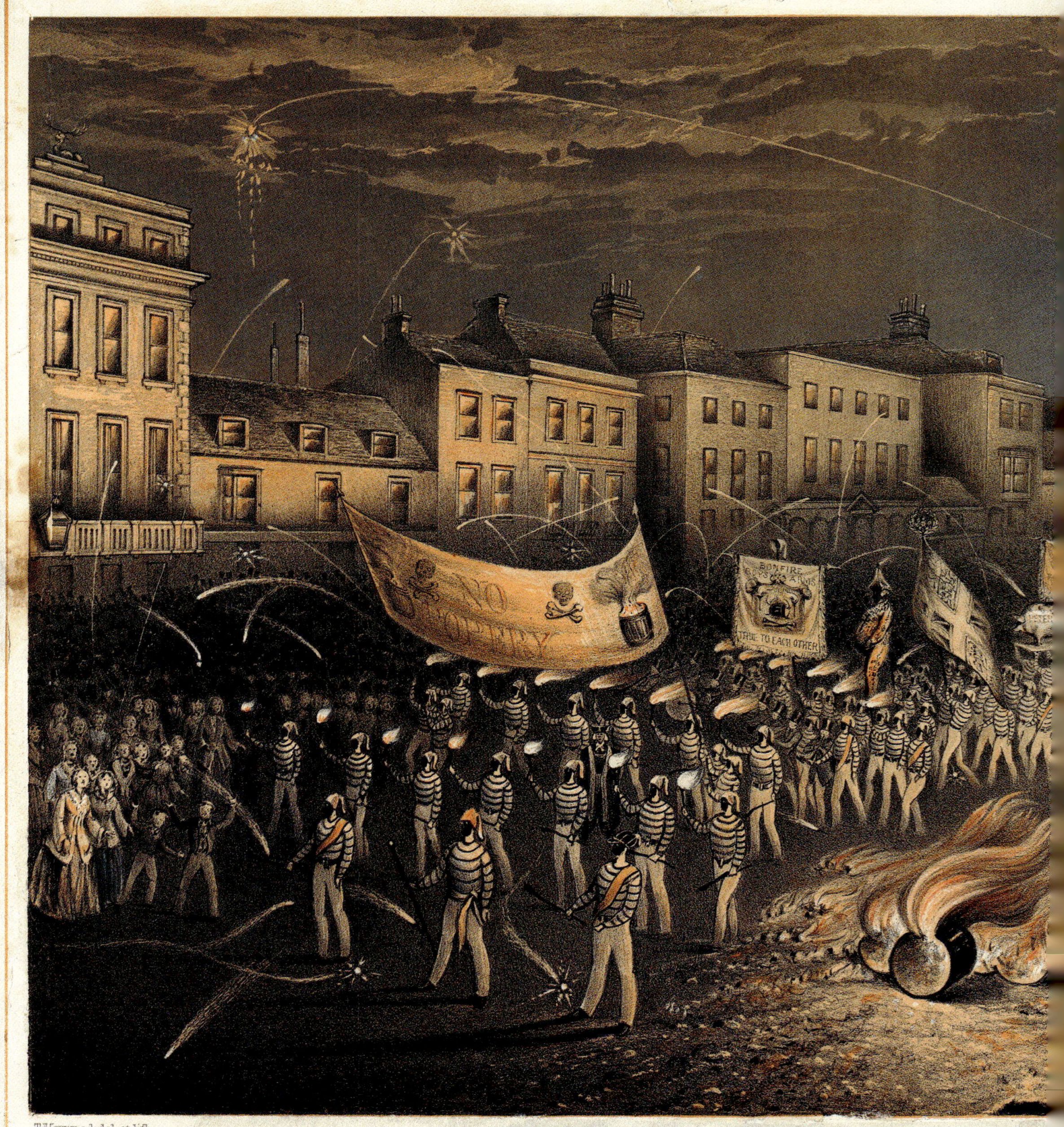


THE PROCESSION OF THE LEWES BONFIRE

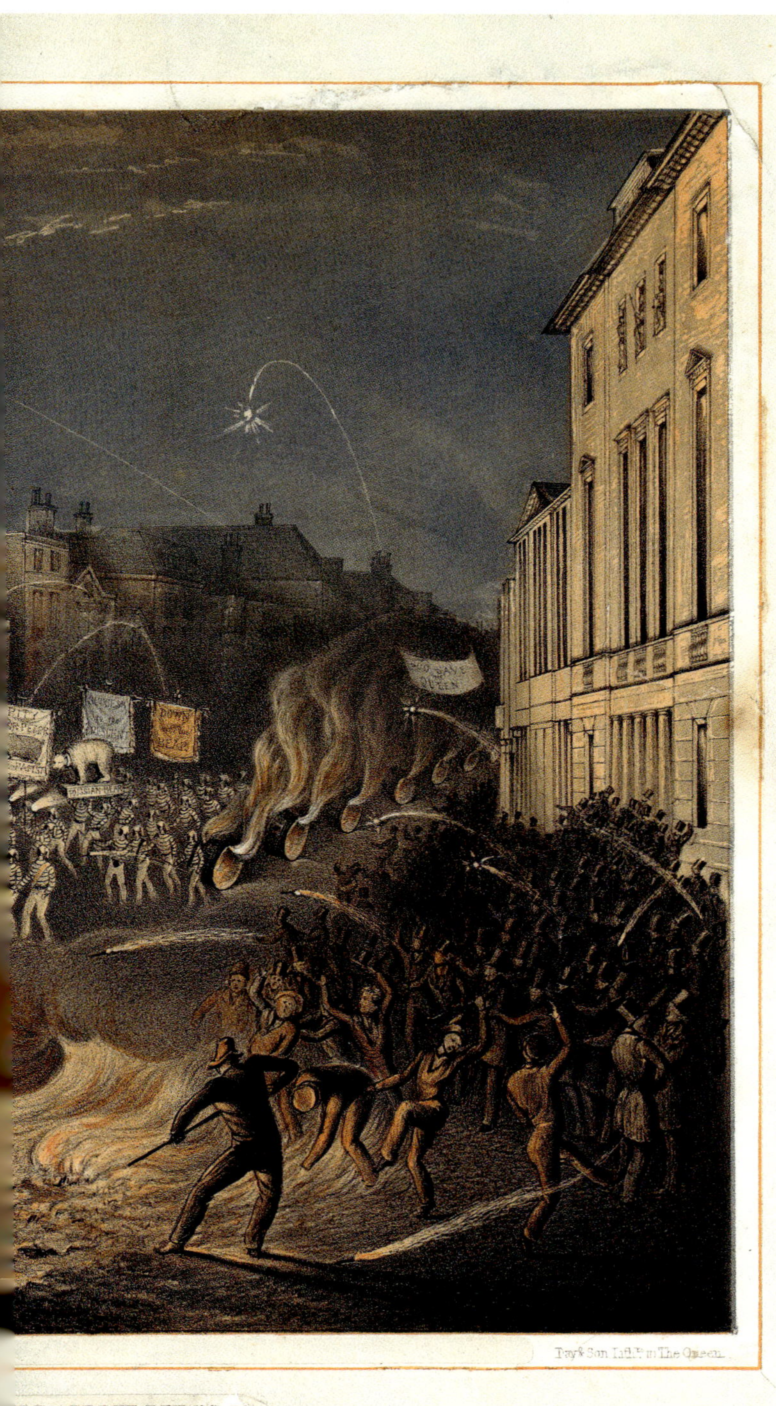


**99**  *The Procession of the Lewes Bonfire Boys*  1853
Thomas Henwood (1797–1861)
Lithograph

This work was produced in the same year as the first two Bonfire Societies were founded in Lewes, following years of riots and chaos spurred on in large part by the notorious "bonfire boys". To this day animosity survives between the bonfire boys or belles and the local authorities, the former fiercely continuing their proclamations of "No Popery", as in Henwood's image.

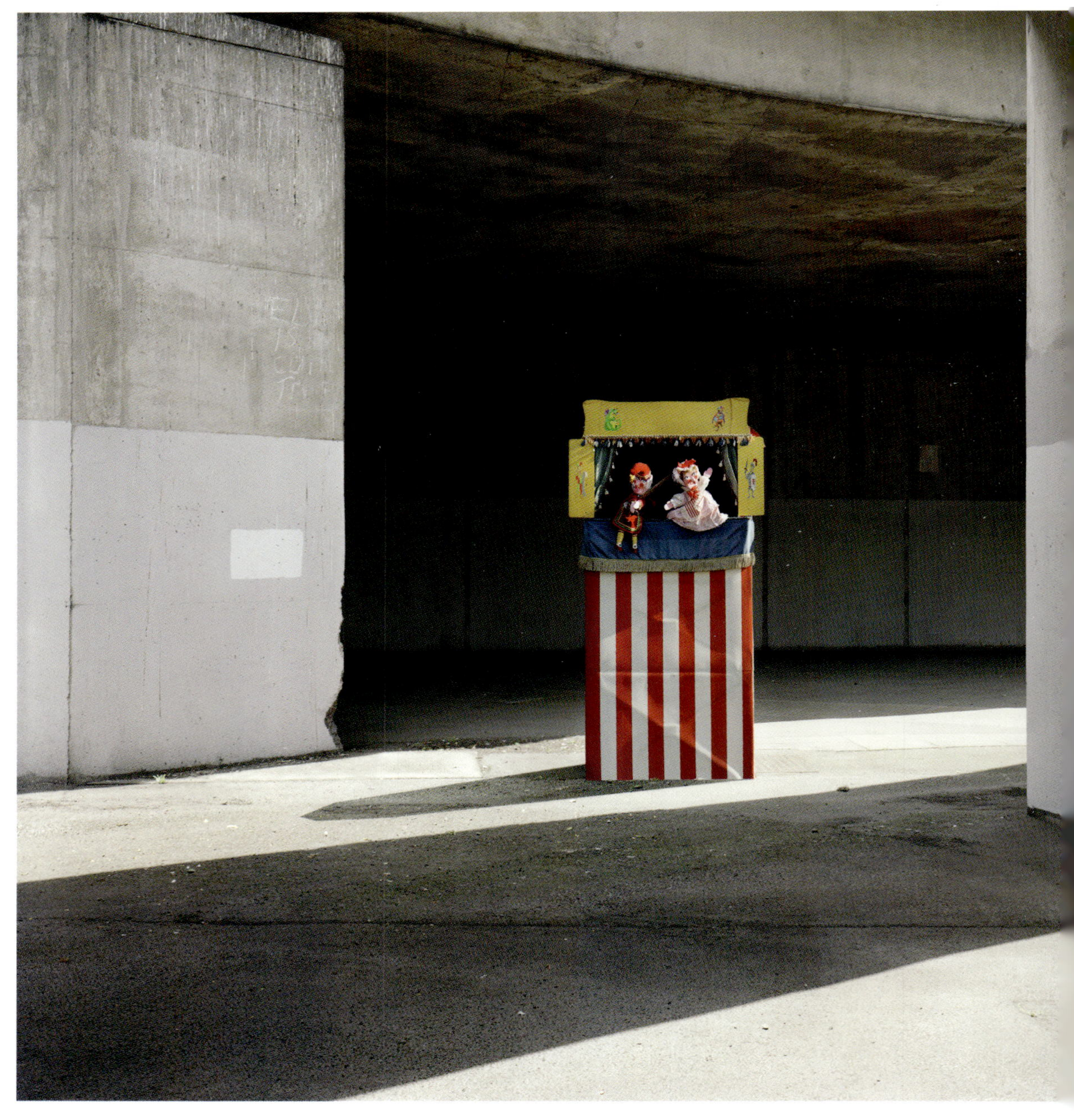

**100**  *Disparate Remedies*  2006
Nick Waplington (b.1965)
C-type photograph

Waplington places a Punch and Judy set in the Thamesmead estate of southeast London where Stanley Kubrick shot *A Clockwork Orange*. The clownish, horror-like nature of much long-established children's entertainment is emphasized by Waplington, who exports the slapstick puppets from their traditional seaside setting to an indistinct, audience-less, urban landscape.

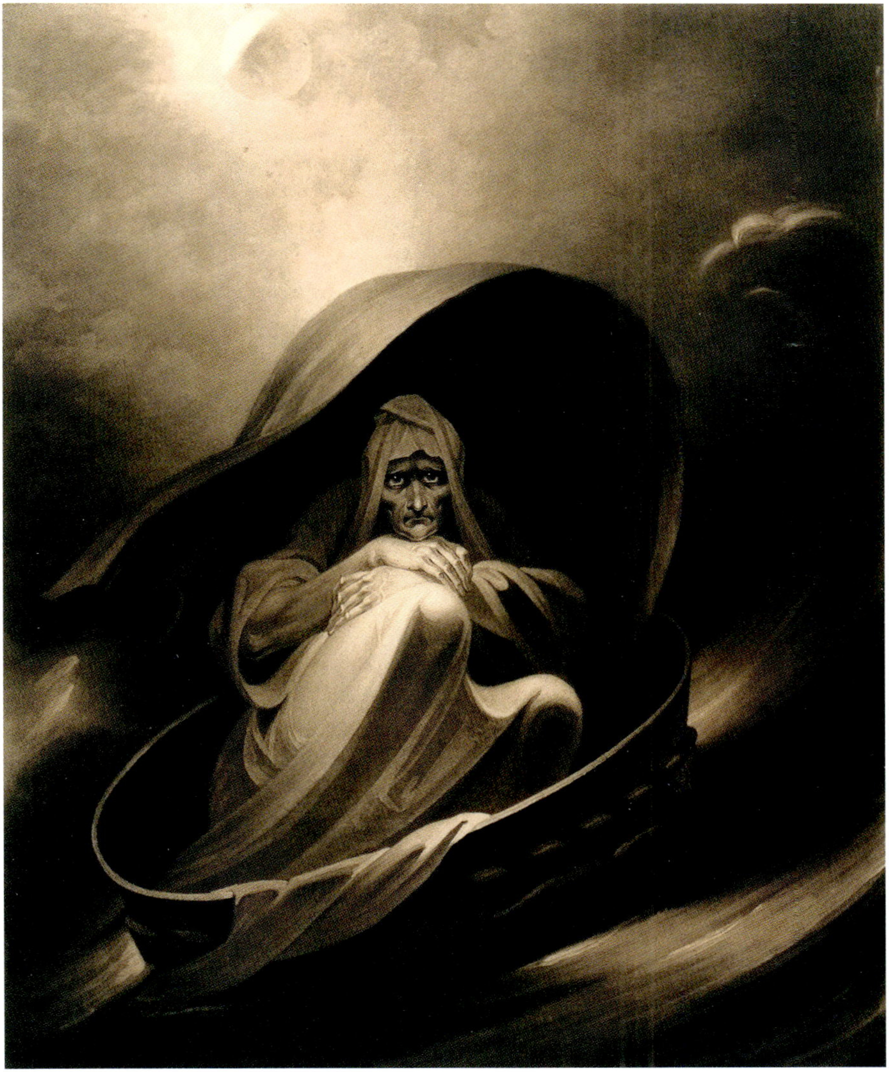

**101**  *A Witch Surfing on a Sieve*  1807
C. Turner after John James Halls (active 1791–1834)
Mezzotint

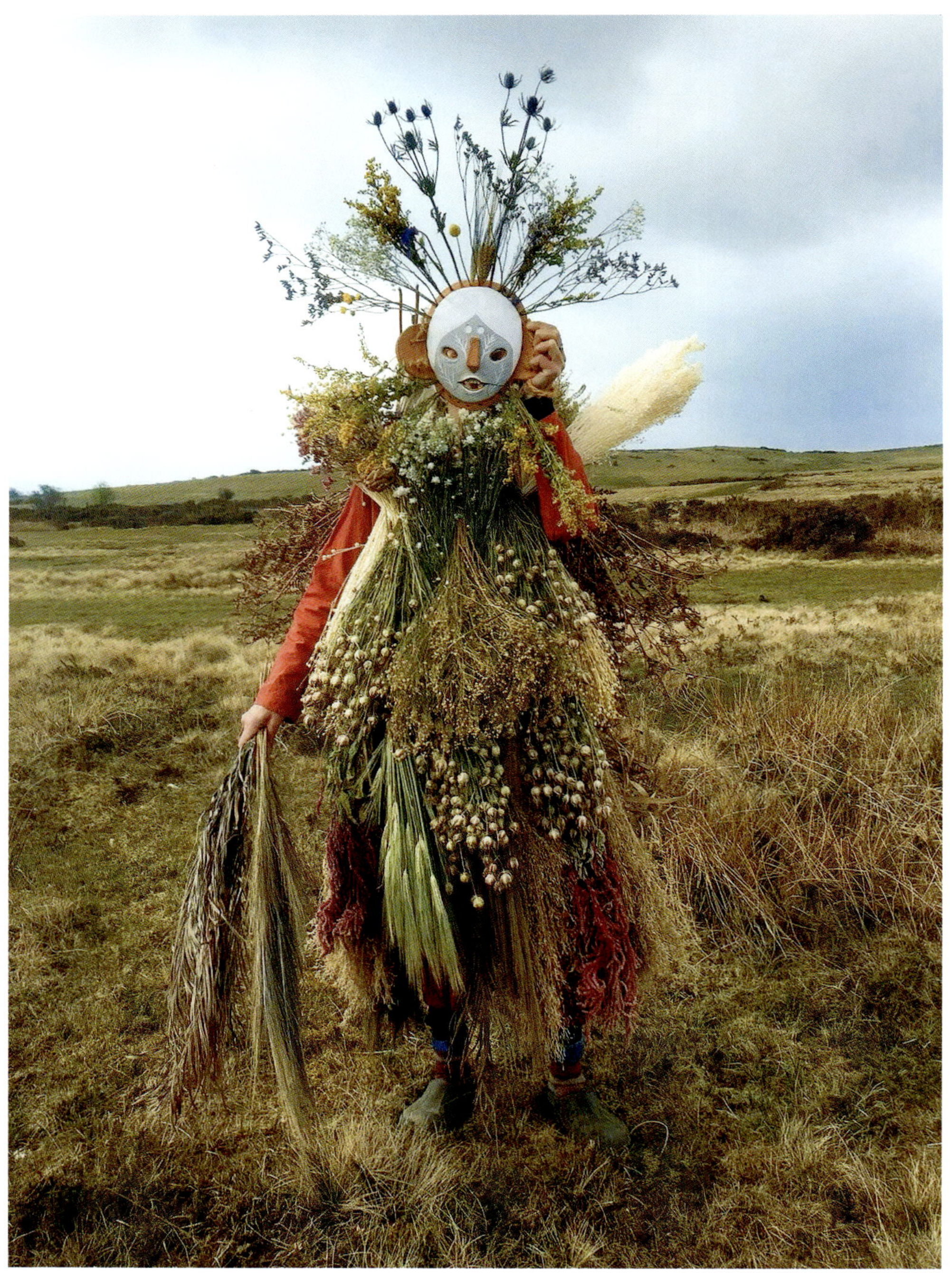

**102**  *The Seed Guardian*  2021
Holland Otik (b.1989)
Colour photograph of soil-ritual costume made of ceramic, textile and dried UK flora

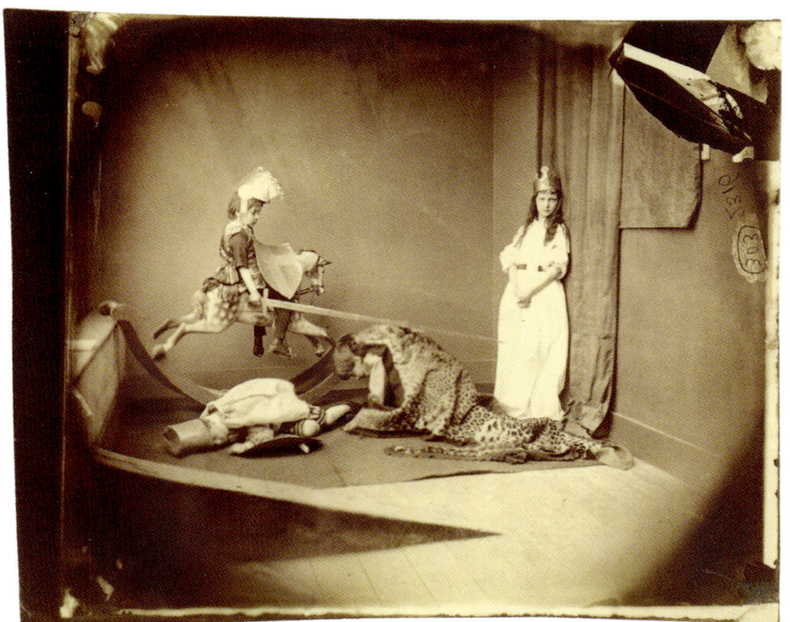



**103** *St George and the Dragon*  1875
Lewis Carroll
(pseudonym of Charles
Lutwidge Dodgson
1832–98)
Albumen silver print

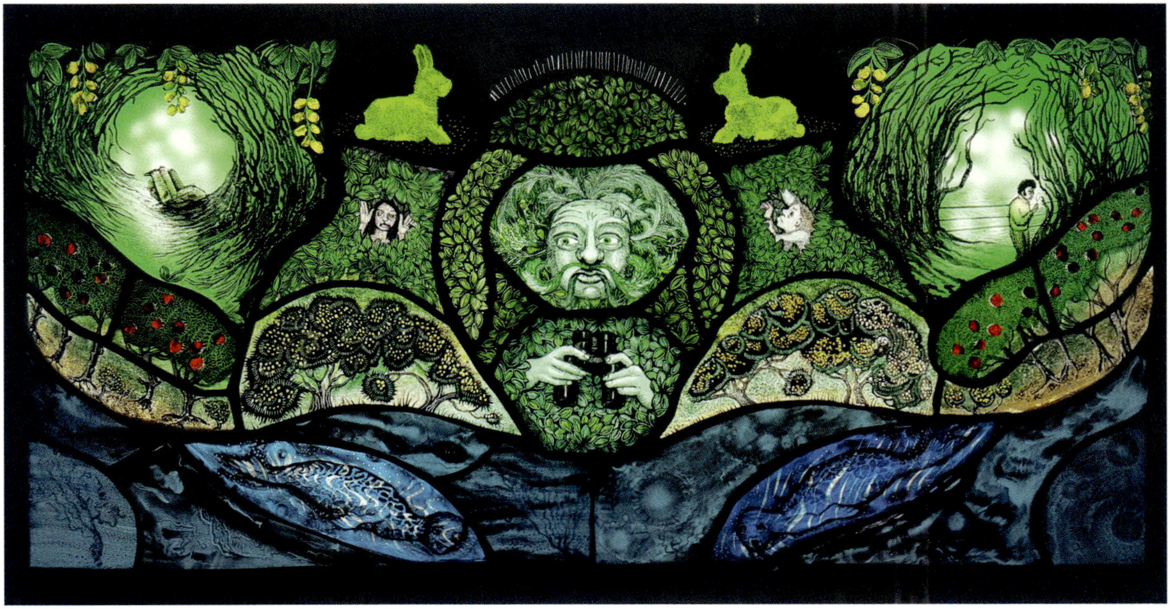

**104** *Green Man Searches for Wilderness*  2020
Pinkie Maclure (b.1961)
Stained glass light box

The Green Man, traditionally a symbol of rebirth and growth, clutches binoculars in a search for an implied lost wilderness. The allegorical irony here is perhaps a symptom of Maclure's self-confessed wish to challenge, inspire and amuse those who view her work, using storytelling as a means to mitigate internal frustration.

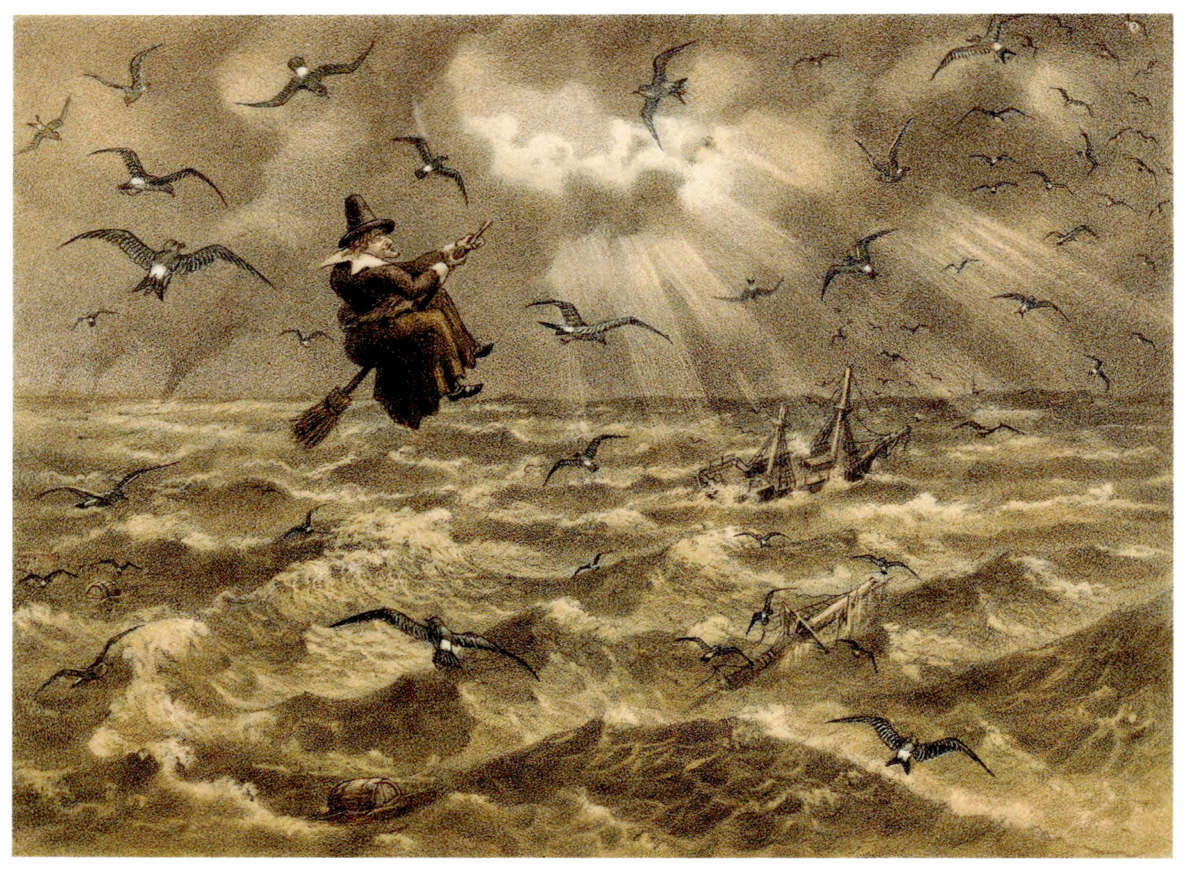

**105**  *Mother Carey and her Chickens*  1877
J.G. Keulemans (1842–1912)
Lithograph

**106**  *The 'Obby 'Oss of Padstow*  2017
Ben Edge (b.1985)
Oil on canvas

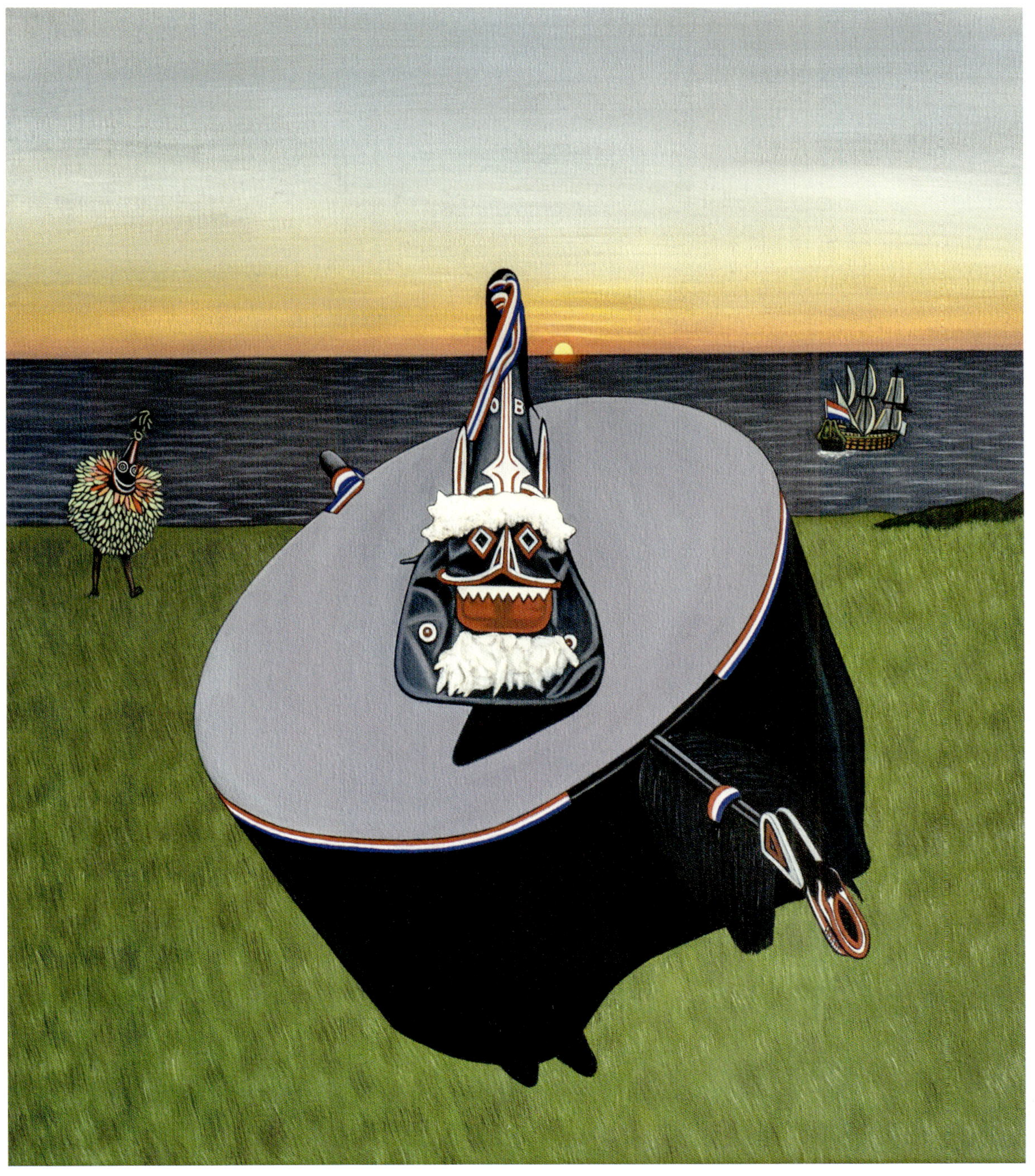

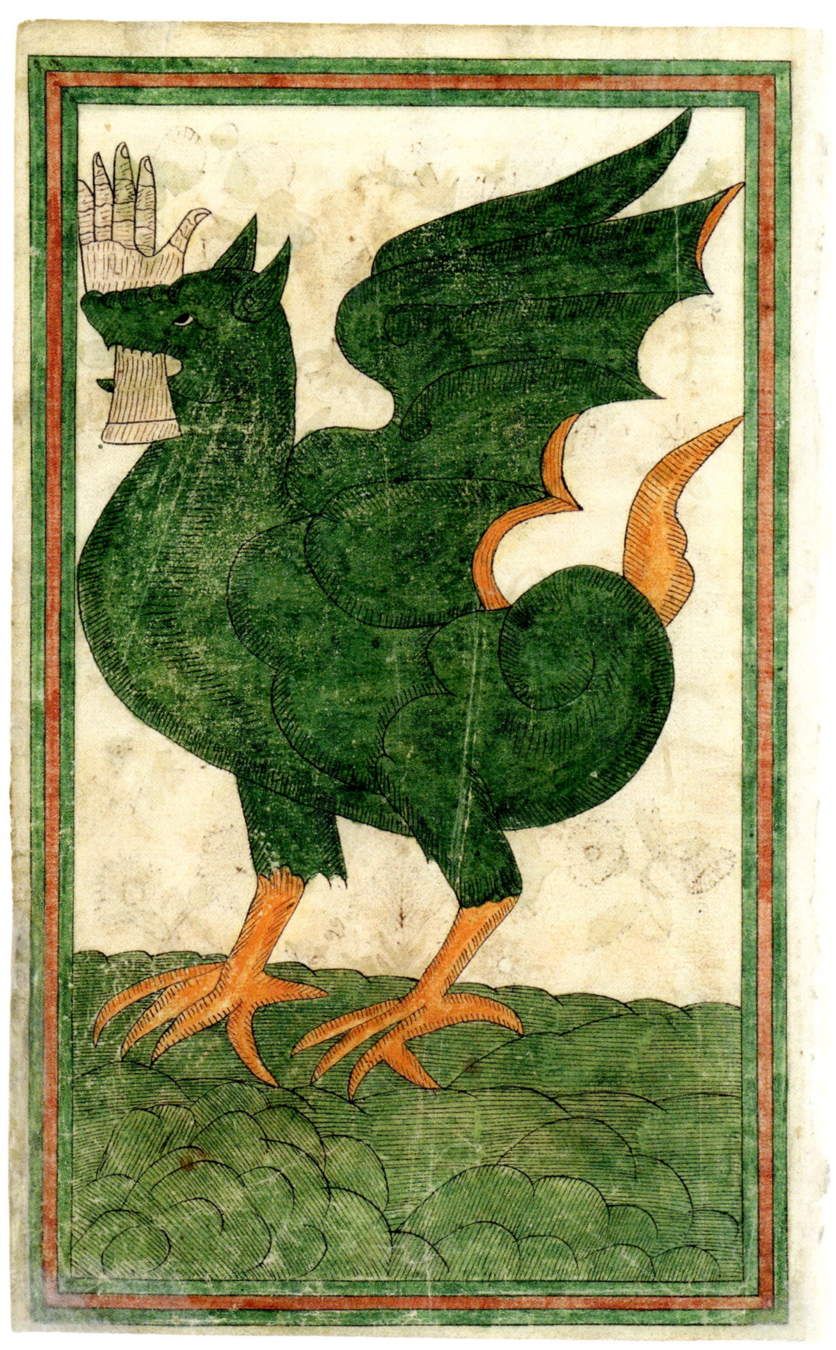

**107** *Green Dragon from* The Trevelyon Miscellany  1608
Thomas Trevelyon (b. *c.*1548)  Engraving

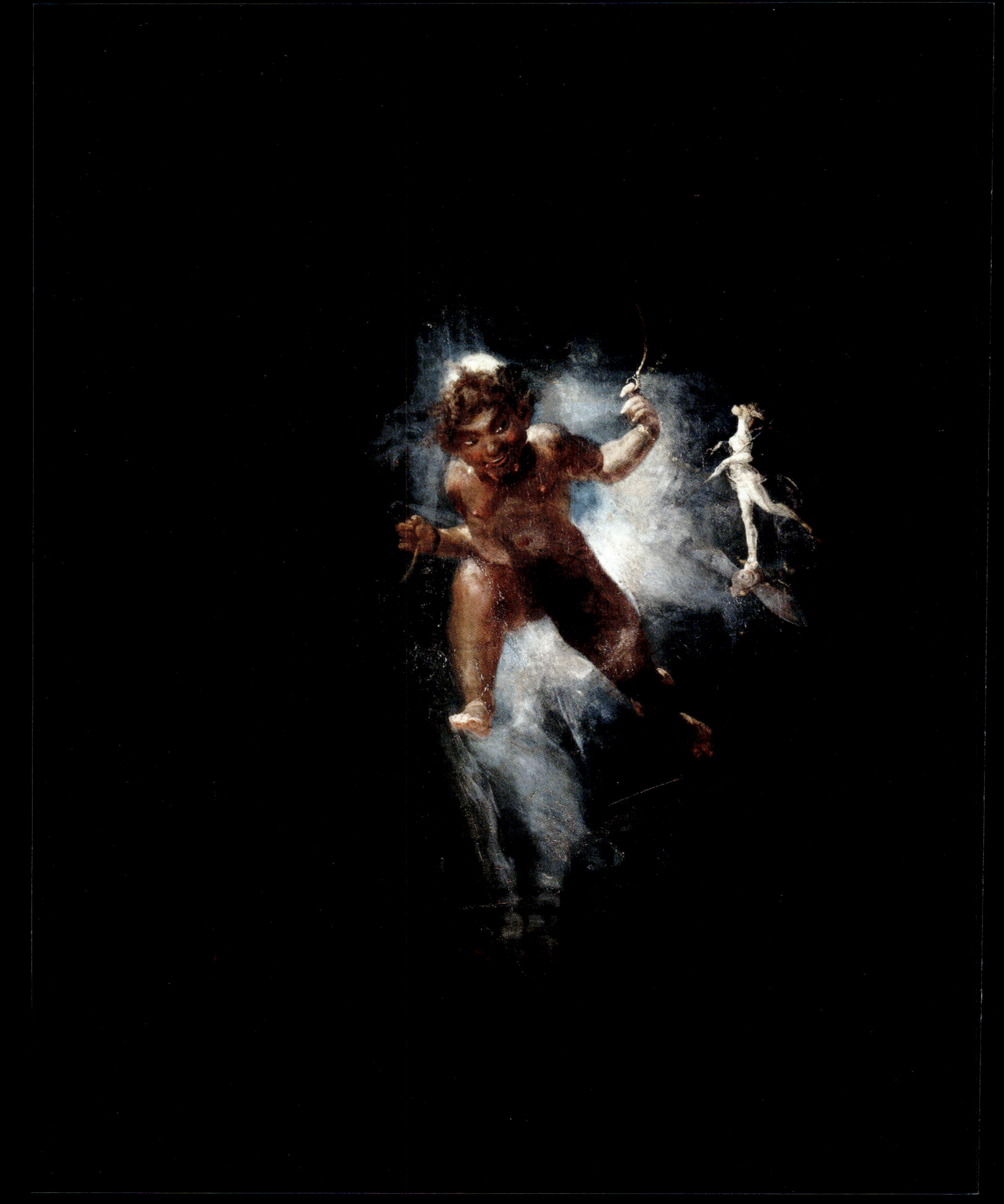

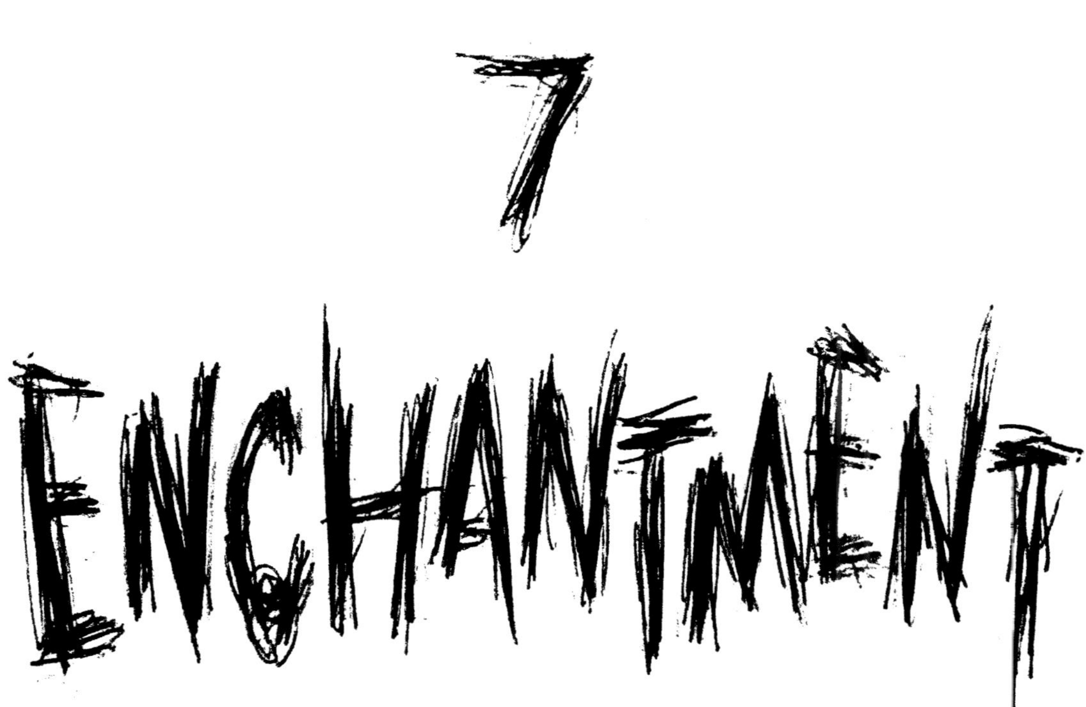

7
ENCHANTMENT

ENGLAND IS A CUCKOO, GROWN
HUGE AMONG ITS SICKLY SIBLINGS.

That's what the Tyburn boy tells us. He
rolls his eyes back in his head and says,
"I was left here by the magic folk. I have
one foot in this England and one foot in the
other." He takes our hand and says, "Close
your eyes and I'll show you the land only us
dreamers know. There are two Englands –
this one of yours in which I am marooned,
with its car parks, and miles of pylon, and
factory farms, and barbed wire and barbed
comments. With its fly-tipped white goods
like sacrificialofferings and its rows of
Chicken Cottages. And then there's another,
enchanted England."

He pulls a dandelion clock from between
the flagstones and blows. Through the
cloud of seeds we glimpse, for a moment,
a changeling land. Herds of hobby horses
gallop under tangerine trees, while flower-
petal carriages roam marmalade skies.

And then it's gone. Everything we saw
fades. A loss like innocence and immediately
a yearning to be back among the strangeness.
We crowd the boy. "Again, again," but he
shrugs and walks on.

"What's it like, the upside-down England?"
we ask, and he scratches himself.

"It's no Eden, that's for sure. As cruel as
this world and as capricious, too. But home
to wild, whirling overthrow and dancing
madness. We ride hedgehogs and vampire
bats, fly alongside dragons and butterflies.
We sleep in rings of toadstools and bathe in
rivers of wine."

He pulls us close. "But guess what? There
in the magic land, when they're drunk or
dreaming or high, it's this grey world they
see. They dream of burnt-out cars, shopping
trolleys in canals and crows eating KFC.
A cairn of nitrous canisters in the skate park.
Empty offices with window-eyes blazing,
cleaners dozing in lanyards, tramps dying
in doorways."

He wipes a hand across his eyes. "There
are rare places where the two worlds meet,"
he says. "In madness and intoxication. In the
shadow of rings of trees. In the interplay of
bassline and drum beat. In the heart of fire.
In those suburban seances that combine
England's two true loves – bureaucracy
and the occult. Only the English could see
another world in anything as mundane as
tea leaves. But our time in that other world is
short, too short, and it's only in dreams that
we ever see our true home."

England is a cuckoo that kills
the ones it loves.

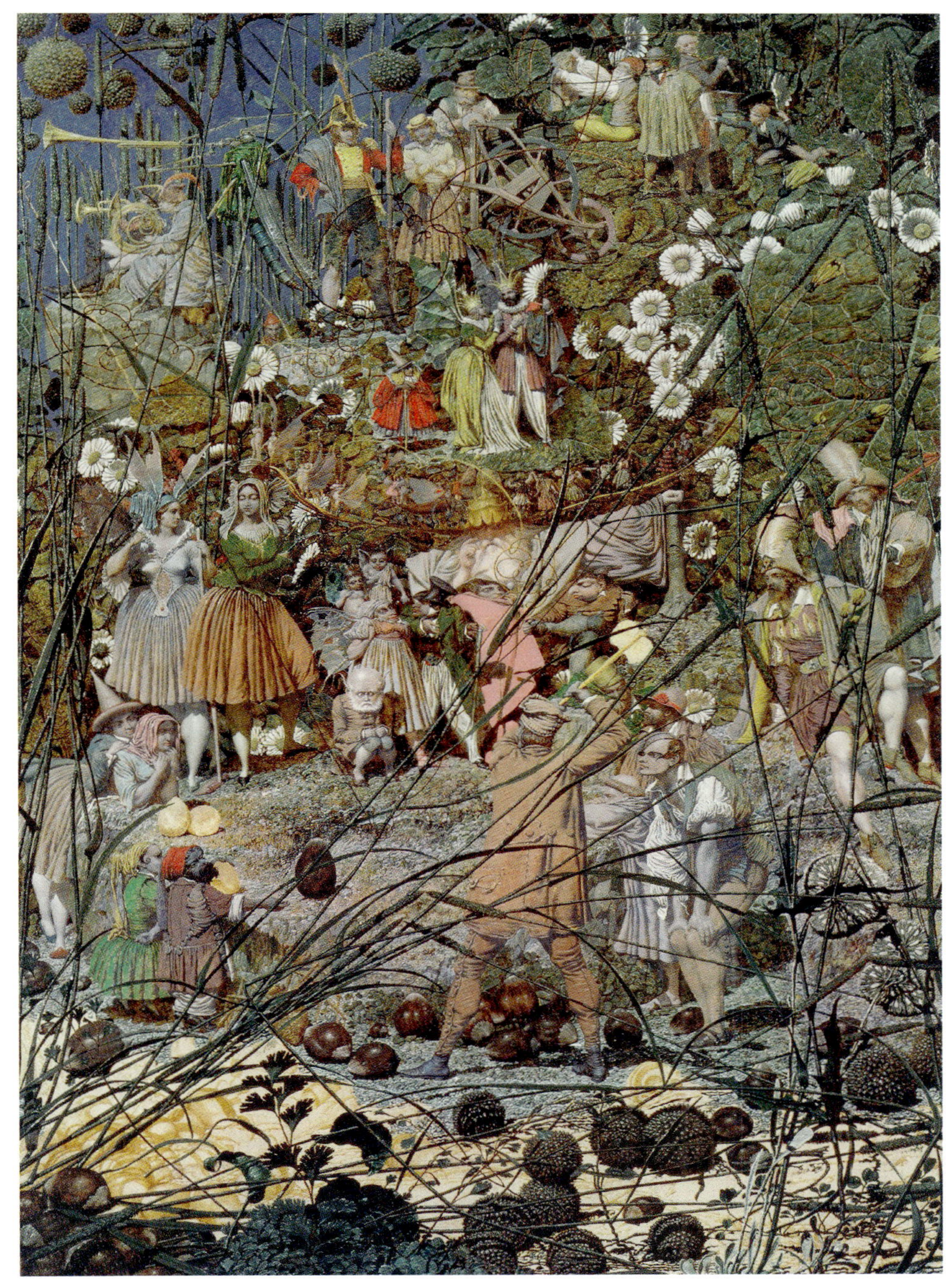

**109** *The Fairy Feller's Master Stroke* 1855–64
Richard Dadd (1817–86)  Oil on canvas

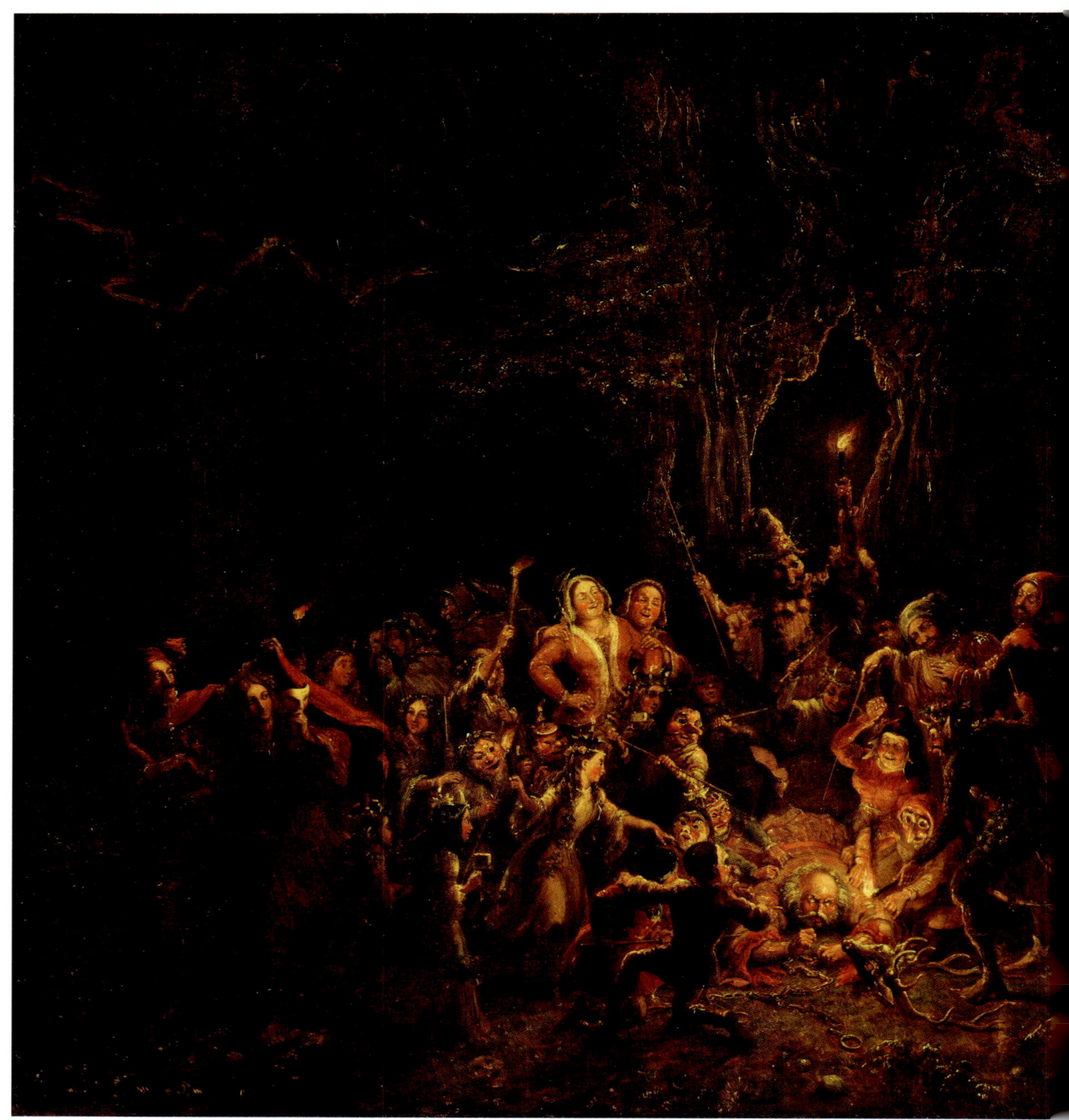

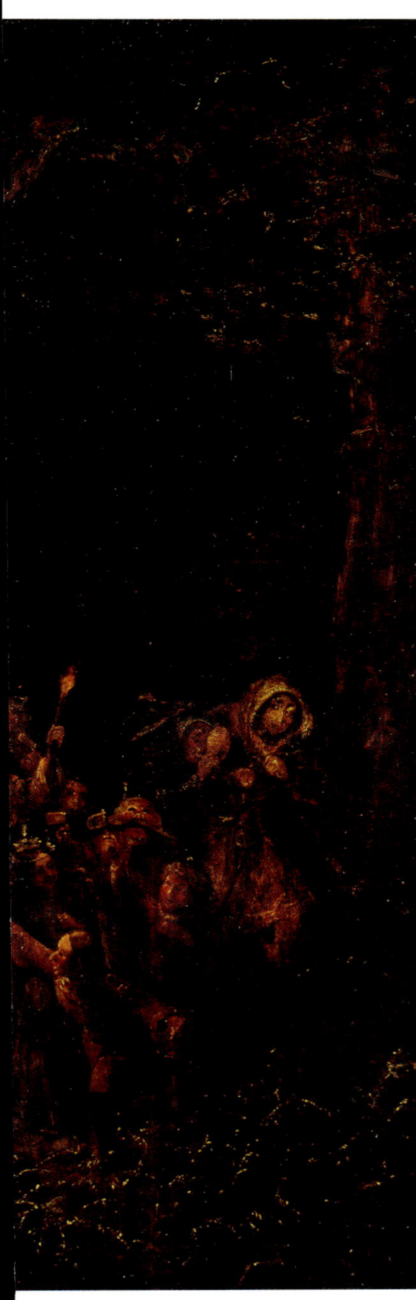

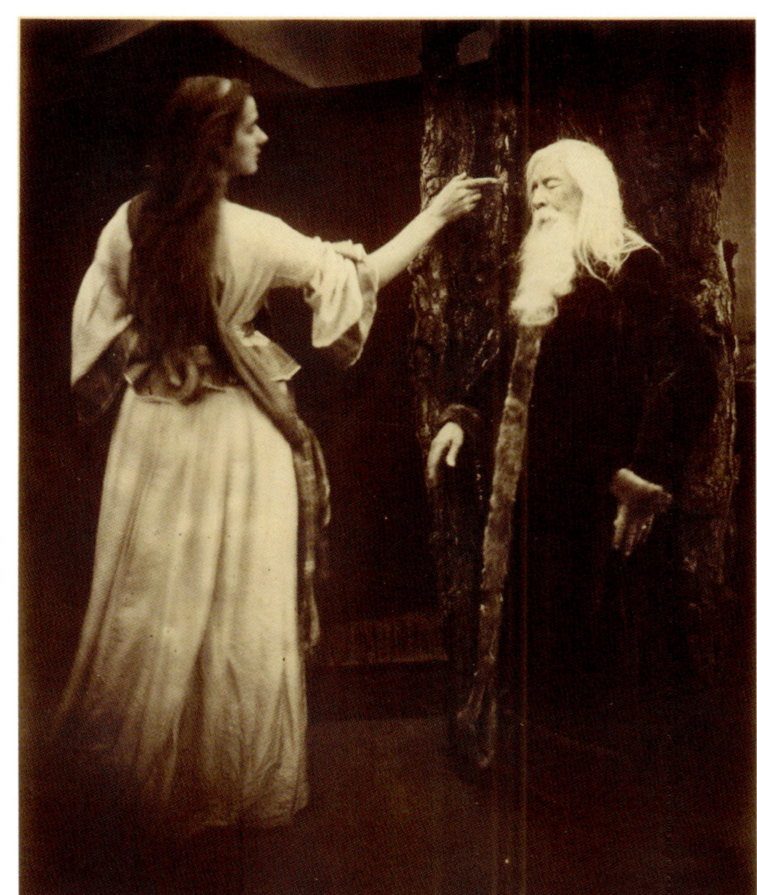

**110**  *Vivien and Merlin*  1874
Julia Margaret Cameron (1815–79)
Albumen silver print from glass negative

**111**  *Herne's Oak from "The Merry Wives of Windsor"*  c.1857
George Cruikshank (1792–1878)
Oil on canvas

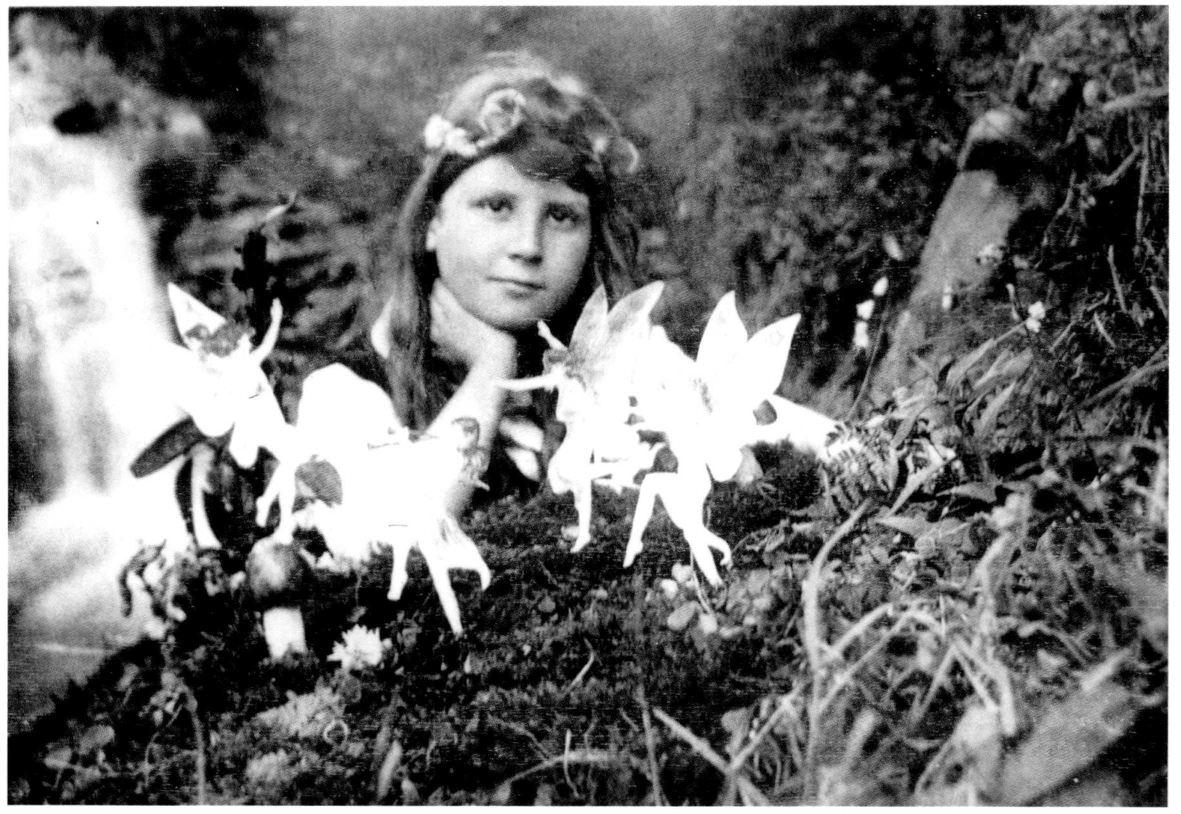



The Cottingley fairies photographs were produced in West Yorkshire in 1917 by sixteen-year-old Elsie Wright and nine-year-old Frances Griffiths. Debates over the authenticity of the photographs continued for two or three years after their initial publication, accompanied by a mass suspension of disbelief that was perhaps a symptom of the traumatic aftermath of World War I and the associated rise in spiritualism. The girls continued to maintain that their encounter with fairies had been genuine until the 1980s, when an elderly Elsie finally admitted that the faking of fairy photographs had been a fun pastime of theirs that had got out of hand.

113  *Notting Hill Carnival*  1981–2
Andrew Moore (b.1962)
Silver gelatin print

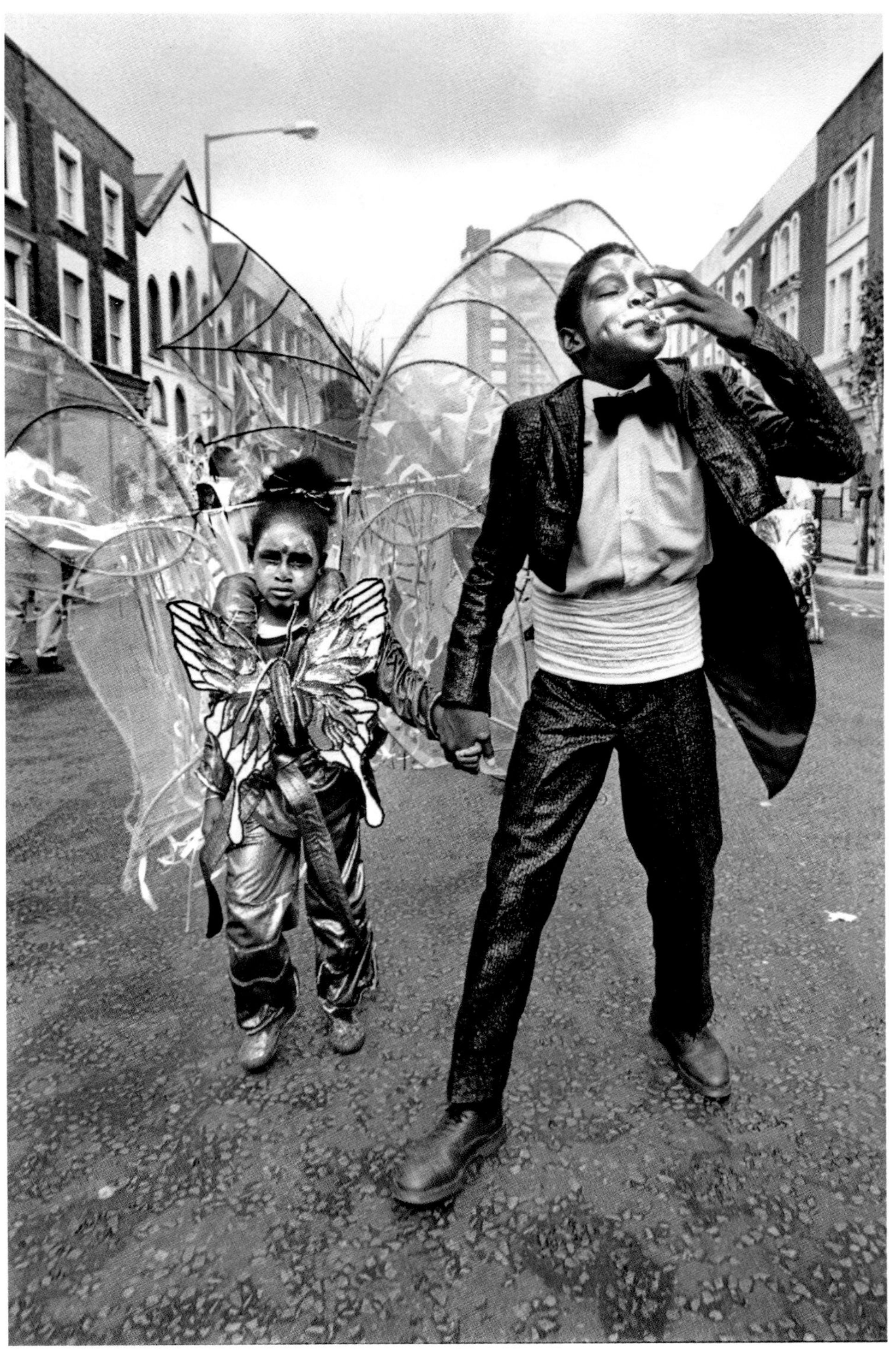

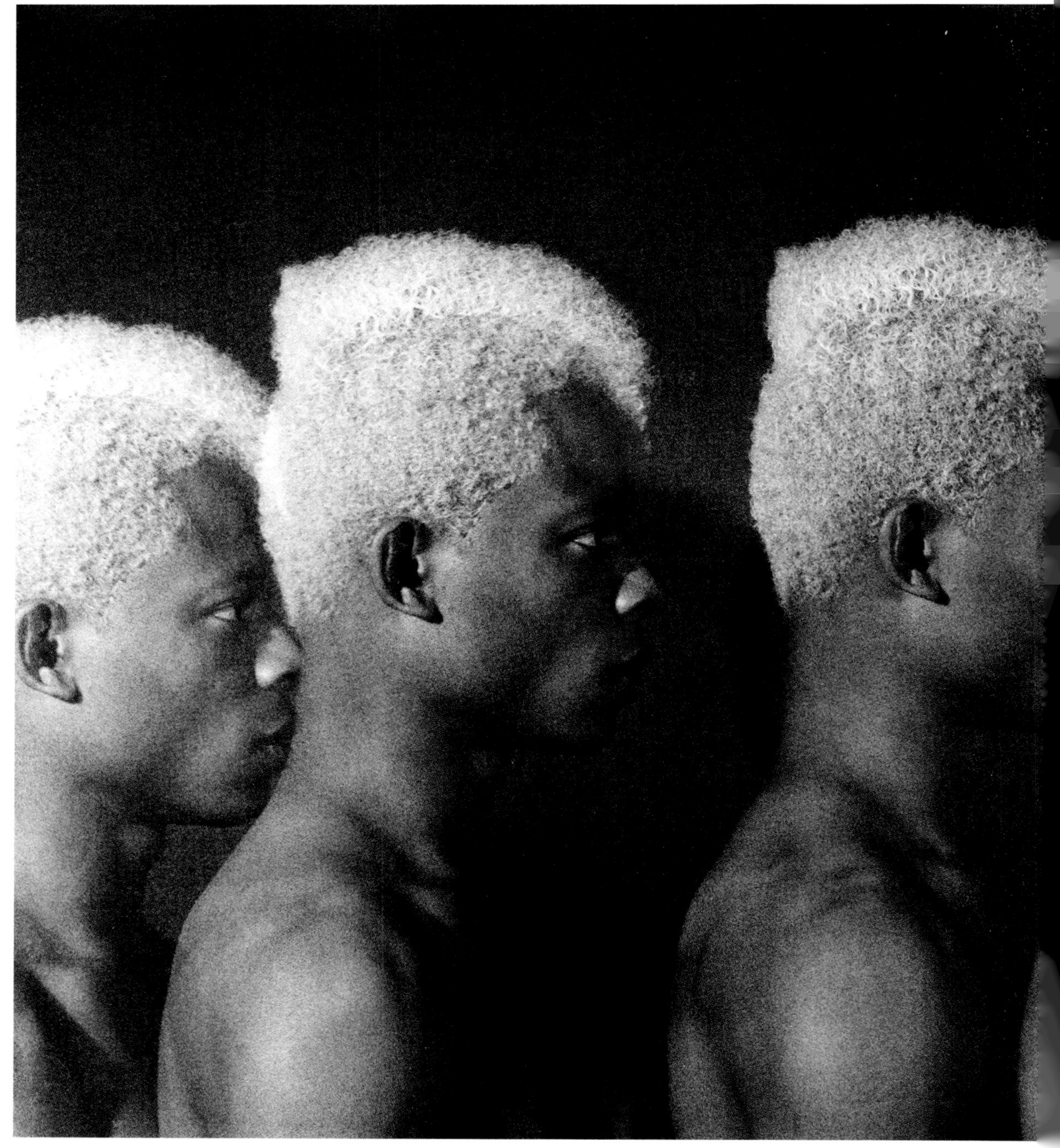

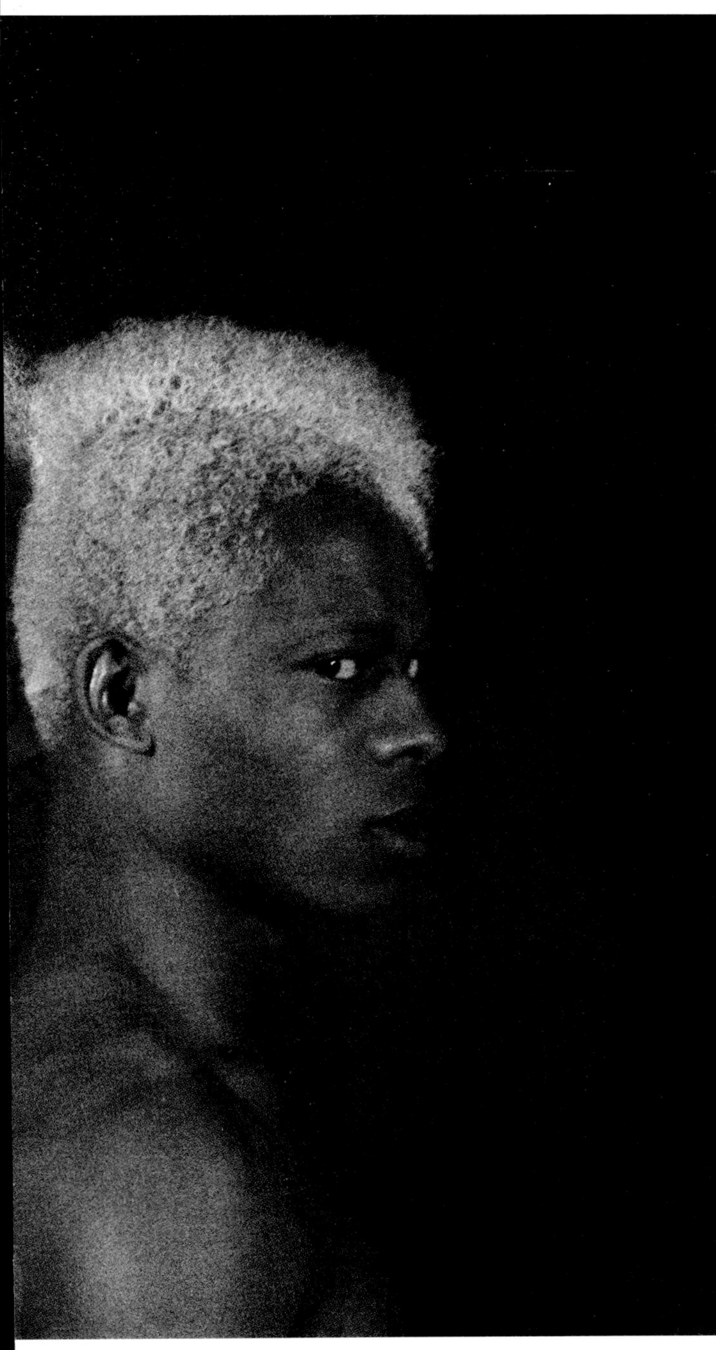



Escaping civil war, Fani-Kayode
moved to Brighton from Nigeria at
the age of eleven. In his work, largely
produced in the 1980s before his death
aged just thirty-four, he explores
the intersection of race, sexuality
and culture, particularly the tension
between his gay identity and the
Yoruba religion he was brought up
in, as well as the position of the black
body in Western imagery.

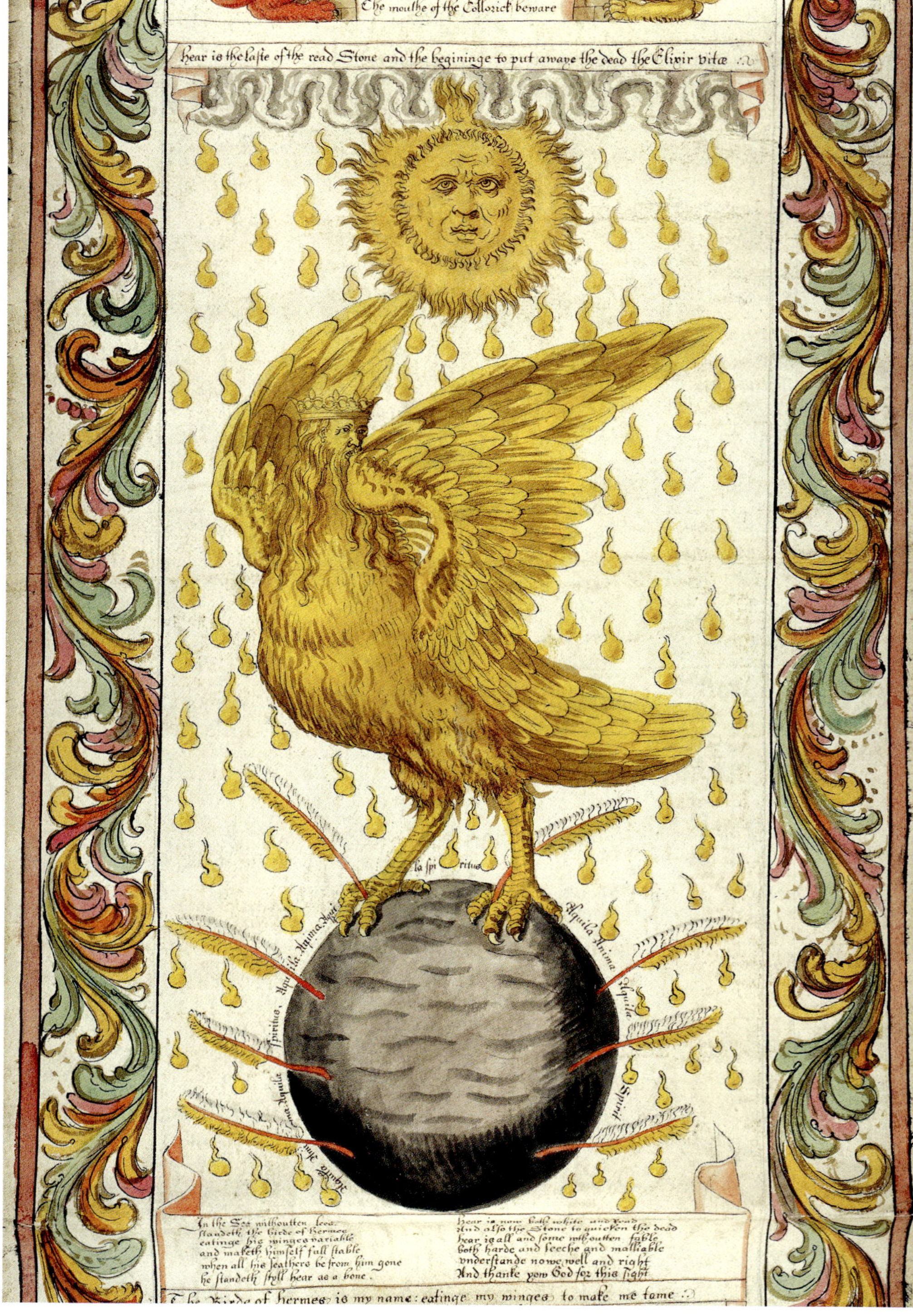

The mouthe of the Collorick beware
hear is the laste of the read Stone and the begininge to put away the dead the Elixir vitæ
la spiritus
Aquila
Aquila Anima Aquila
spiritus
Spirit
In the See withoutten leea.
standeth the birde of Hermes
eatinge his winges variable
and maketh himself full stable
when all his feathers be from him gone
he standeth styll hear as a bone.
hear is now both white and read
And also the Stone to quicken the dead
hear is all and some withoutten fable
both harde and seeche and malliable
vnderstande nowe well and right
And thanke yow God for this sight
The birde of hermes is my name: eatinge my winges to make me tame :.

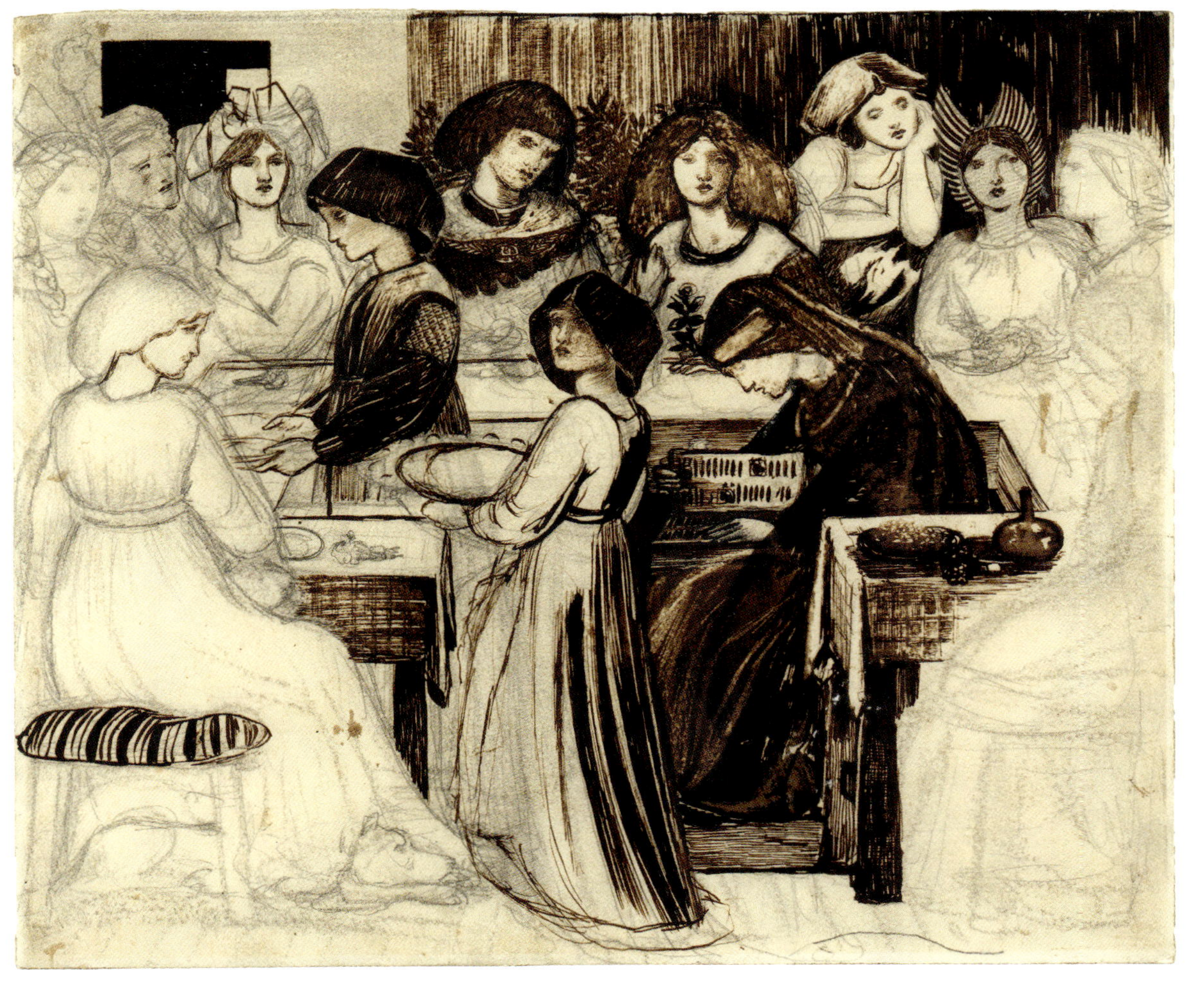

**115**  *Study for the wedding feast of Sir Degrevaunt*  Undated
Edward Burne-Jones (1833–98)
Pen, brown ink and graphite on paper

**116**  *Western Manuscript 693*
*Ripley Scroll*  *c*.16th century
Artist unknown
Manuscript

The Ripley Scroll, named after alchemist George Ripley of Bridlington Priory, Yorkshire, describes how to produce the Philosopher's Stone. This is the ultimate prize in alchemy, being the key to immortality and enlightenment, as well as having the ability to transmute base metal into gold. The scroll pairs emblematic illustrations with "Verses upon the Elixir", stating in this case that, "Heare is the last of the red stone and the beginning to put away the dead the elixir vitae".

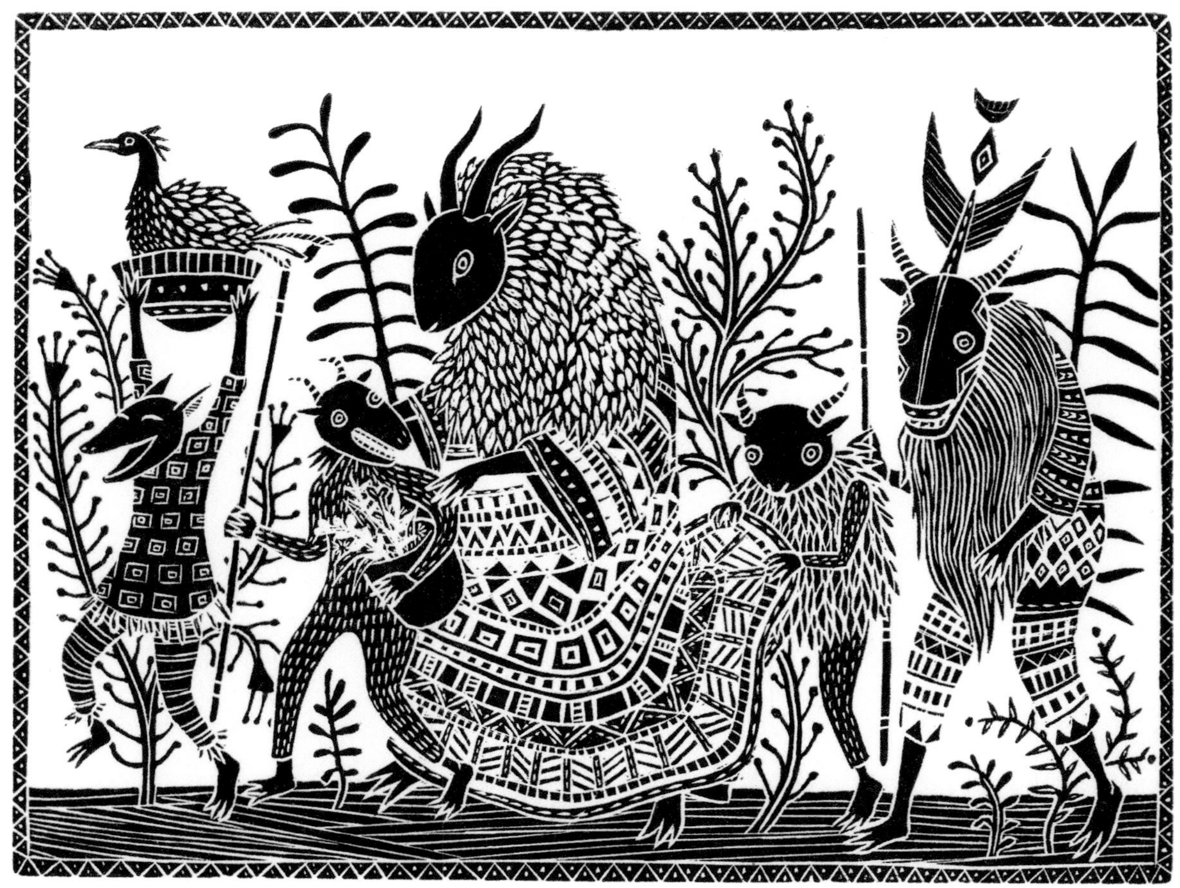

**117**  *Bwa Procession*  2017
India Rose Bird (b.1989)
Wood engraving print

**118**  *The Portrait of the Lord Jesus Christ*  1862
Georgiana Houghton (1814–84)
Watercolour

This painting is one of the numerous spirit drawings produced by Georgiana Houghton in the 1860s and 1870s. Text on the back of these paintings explains how she was guided in her painting by spirits. Often anonymous angelic beings, these also included well-known Renaissance artists such as Titian and Correggio.

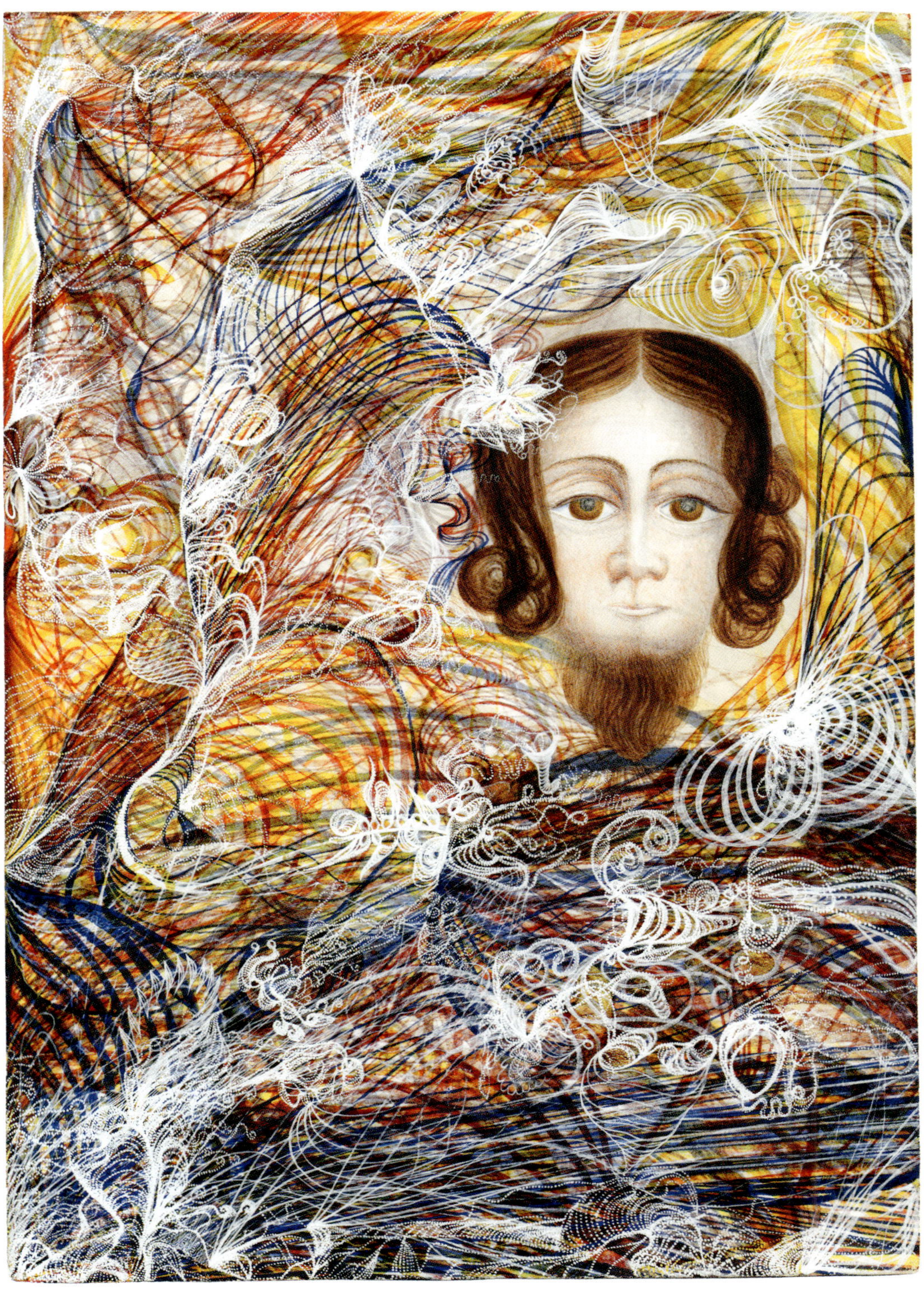

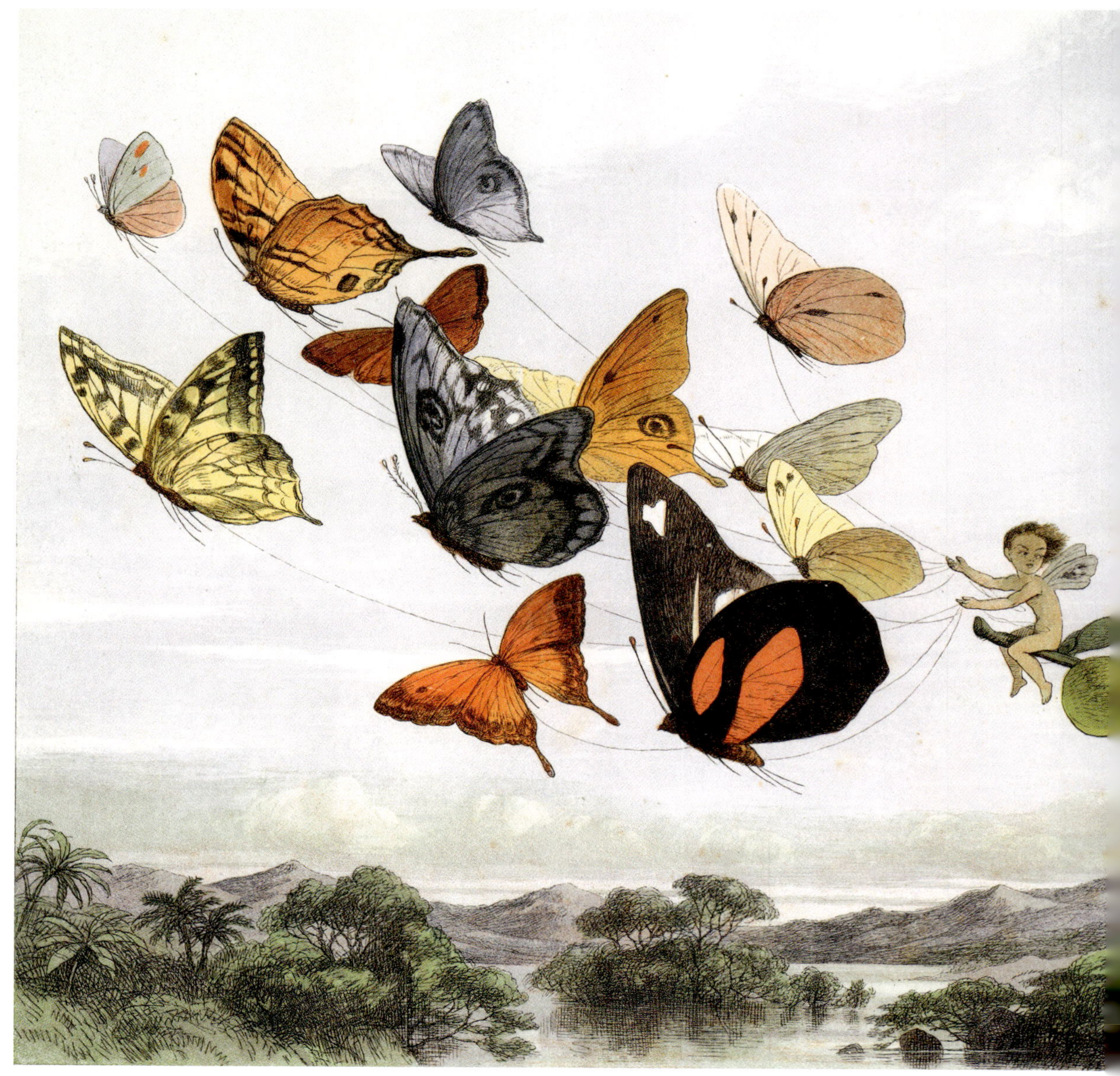

**119** *The Fairy Queen Takes an Airy Drive in a Light Carriage,*
*a Twelve-in-hand, drawn by Thoroughbred Butterflies* 1870
Richard Doyle (1824–83)
Colour wood engraving and colour lithography

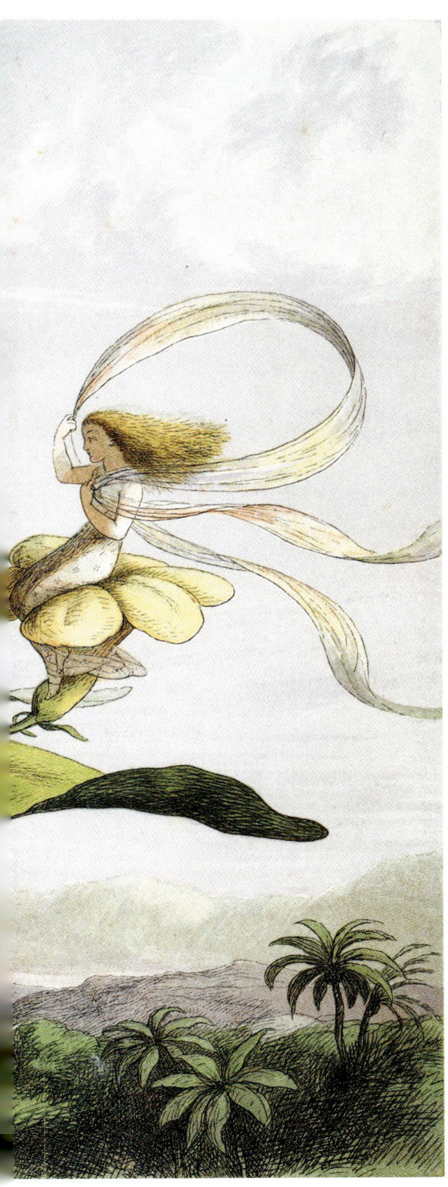

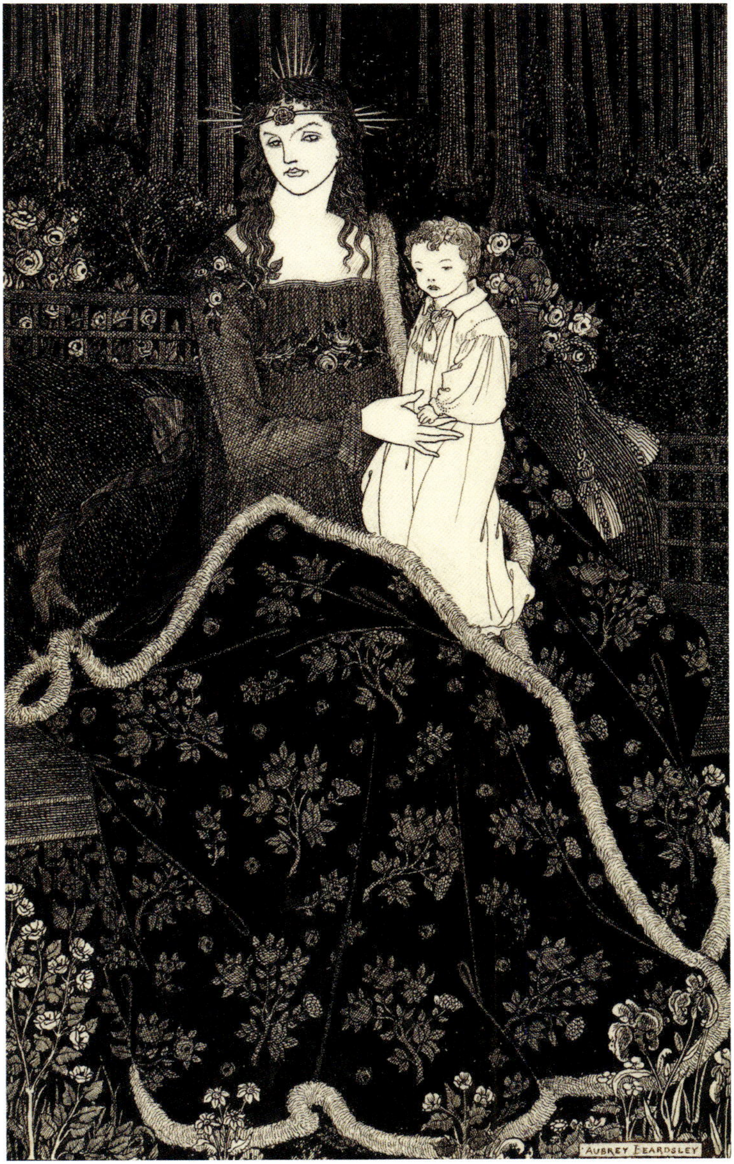

**120** *A Large Christmas Card* 1895
Aubrey Vincent Beardsley (1872–98)
Pen and black ink over graphite on paper

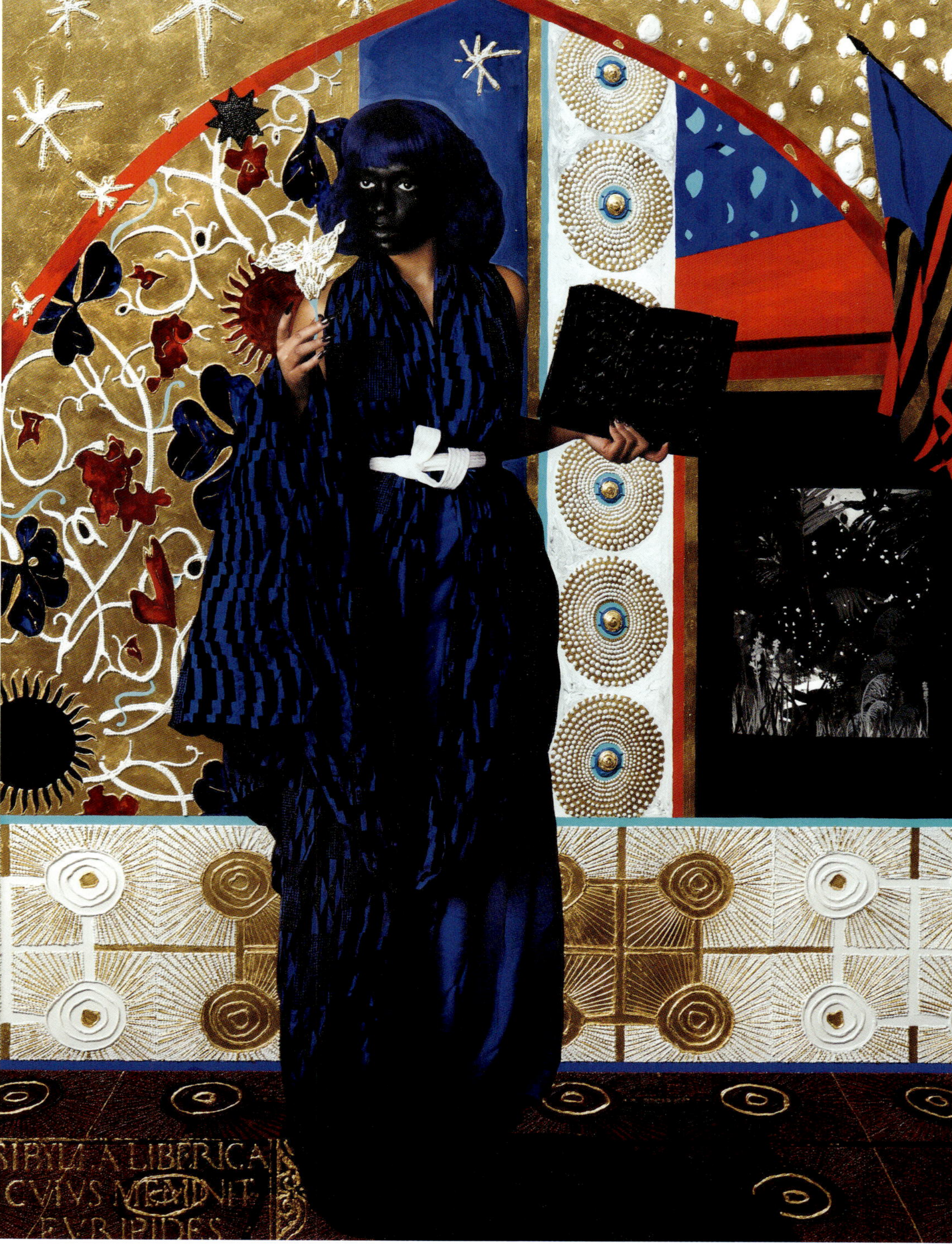

SIBYLA ·A· LIBERICA
CVIVS MEMINIT
EVRIPIDES

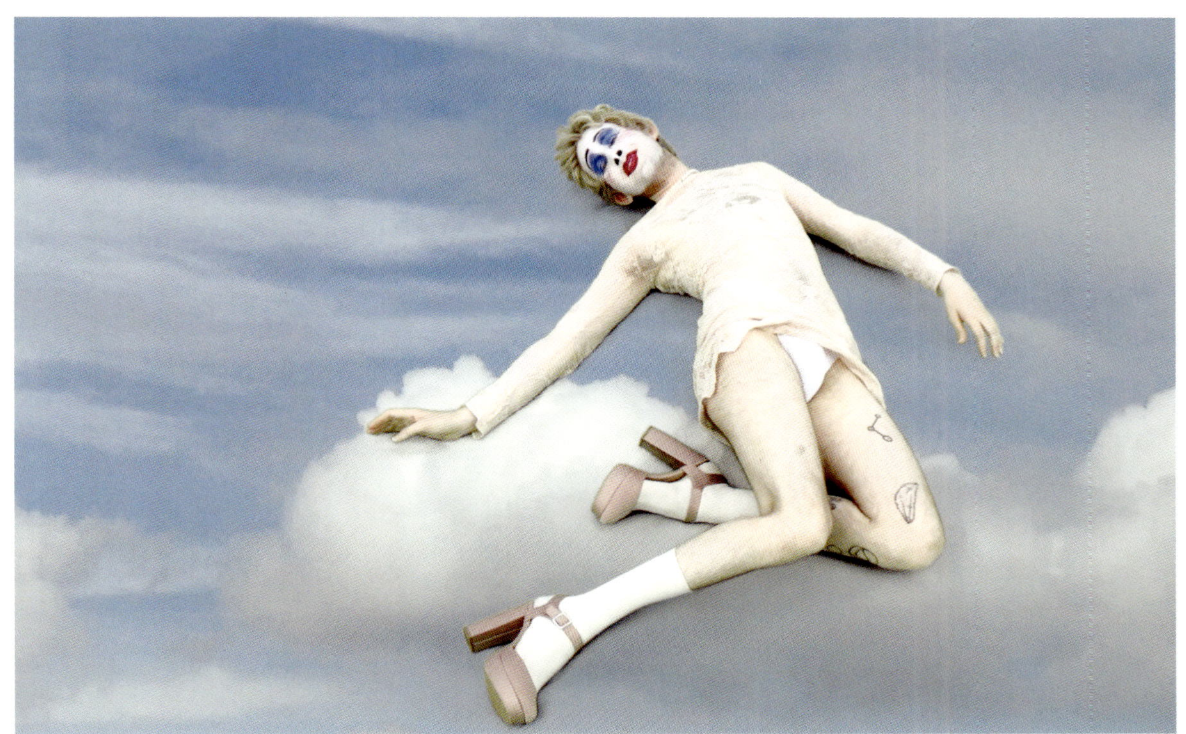

**121**  *Up Up and Away* from *Lotusland the Musical*  2017
Paul Kindersley (b.1985) and
Philip Cornett (b.1985)
Film still

**122**  *Fourth*  2017–18
Lina Iris Viktor (b.1987)
Pure 24-carat gold, acrylic, ink, gouache,
copolymer resin, print on cotton rag paper

Lina Iris Viktor, a Liberian-British conceptual and
performance artist, explores her relationship with being and
time through a multidisciplinary pairing of contemporary
and ancient art forms. She uses gold in many of her works, as
well as the ultramarine blue made famous by Yves Klein, in
a way that resembles the depictions of early modern English
monarchs by artists such as Hans Holbein the Younger.

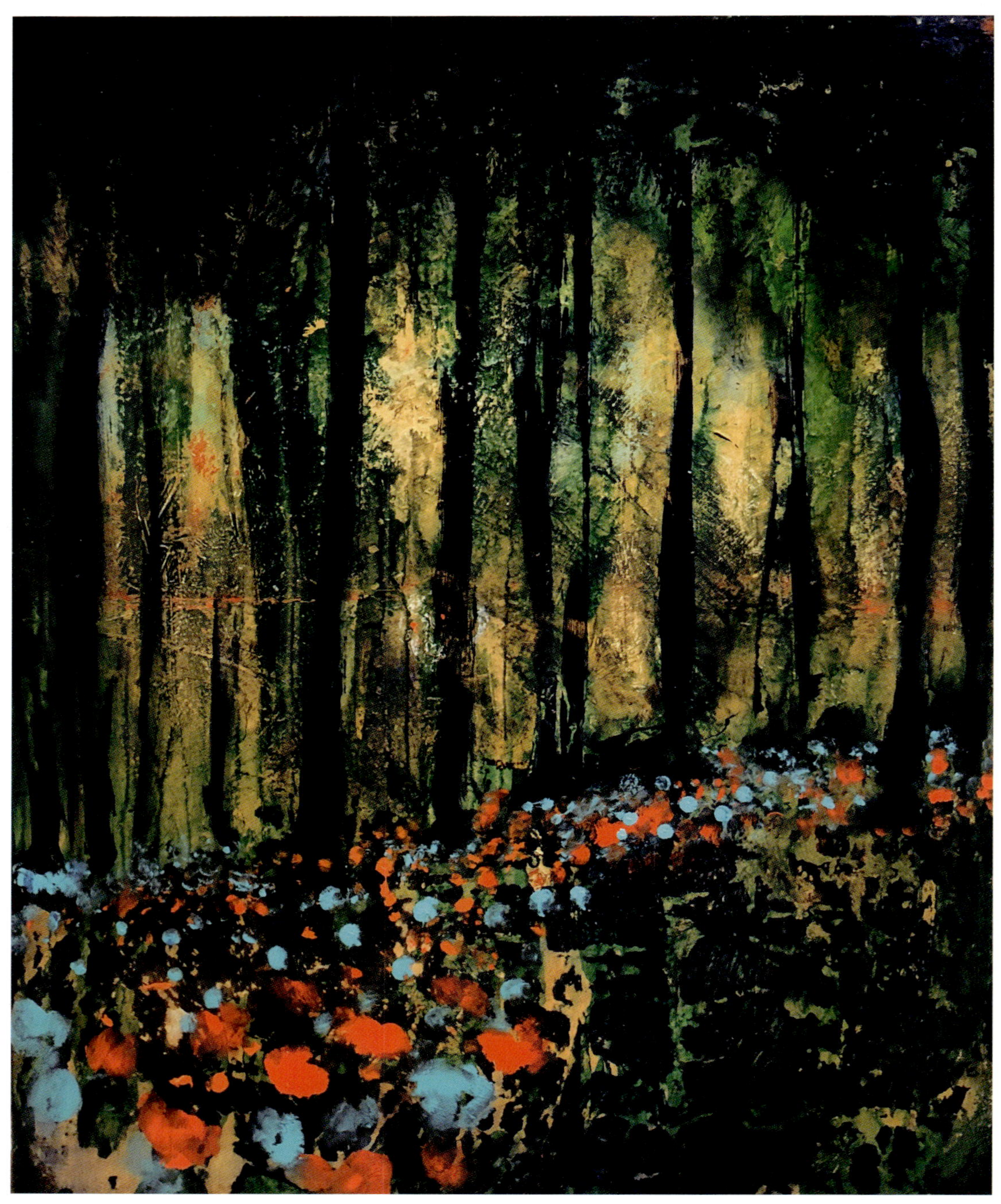

**123**  *Parade*  2019
James F. Johnston (b.1966)   Acrylic and gold paste

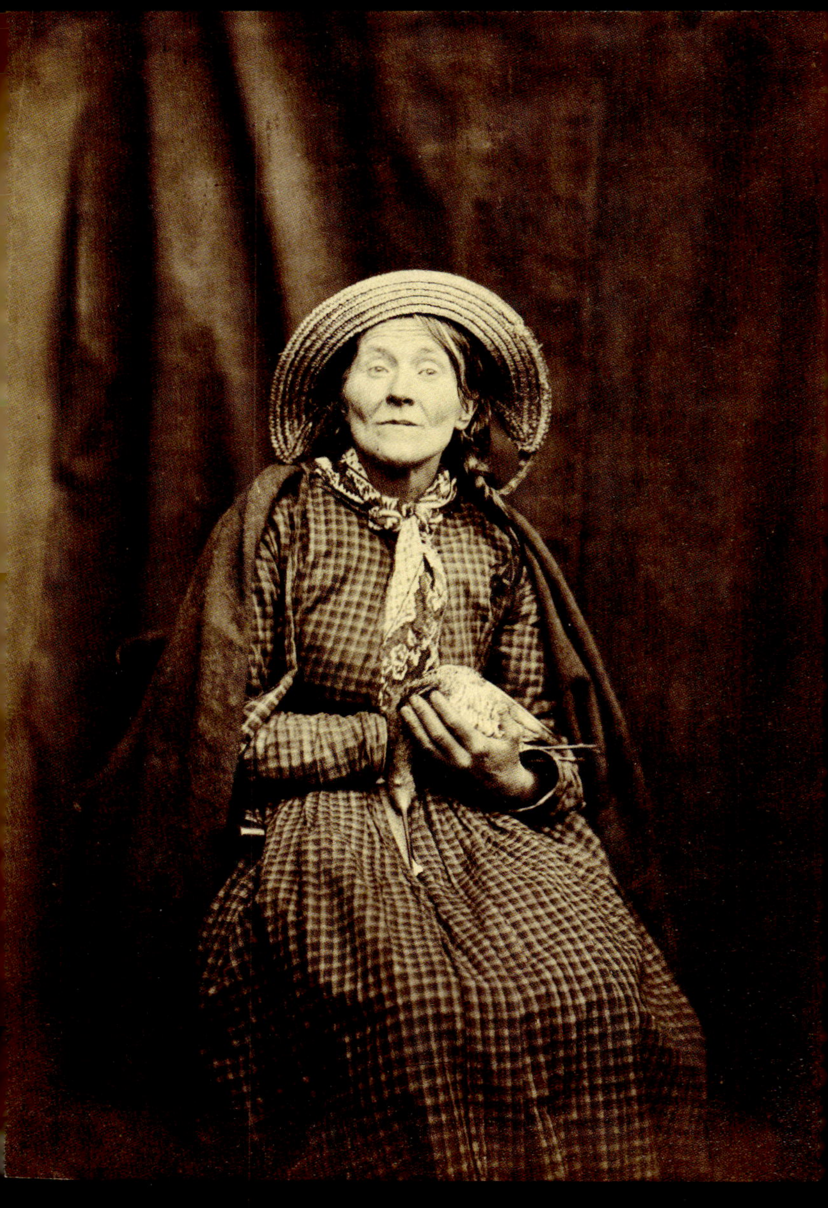

# 8

# ENCLOSURE

PREVIOUS PAGE
**124** *Seated Woman with Bird* c.1855
Hugh Welch Diamond (1809–86)  Albumen silver print

ENGLAND IS A FORTRESS AROUND A CASTLE AROUND A KEEP ABOUT A TOWER WITH A LOCKED ROOM AT ITS HEART.

The Tyburn boy urges us onward, but the castle comes no closer. Instead, fences rise up around us. Fresh gorse fences *snip snip snip* the land into neat fields. Spectral dry stone wallers *stack stack stack* the stones up around the moorlands, and what were once common lands echo to the sound of grouse shoots. Bears are led by the nose to the pits, cockerels sprout spurs. Badgers are chained and their claws sharpened to talons. Only the pylons run free, giants astride the chessboard fields.

The boy urges us on, faster and faster, as others join the throng. Everywhere we walk KEEP OUT signs bloom in front of us. "No trespassing!" they order. "No right of way". "Private land".

The fences sprout higher and our path through England narrows. Now we are part of a pulsing human mass, all making for the castle but squeezed tighter and tighter into streets lined with advertisements. The lanes have jingles for birdsong and billboards for a view, showing us what we might see if they were ever torn down.

If we could fly, we would see a land subdivided, reparcelled, bought, sold and exchanged. Shell companies own those tinkling brooks, and off-shore banks have gobbled up the mountains and valleys. *Snip snip snip* go their scissors. *Stack stack stack* goes the cash.

The Tyburn boy spray-paints slogans across the billboards: "25,000 people own half of the land in England" and "A third for the gentry, a third for the corporations and a third for the rest of us". Now the way on is so narrow that we clamber onto the shoulders of the people in front. England's arteries are squeezed sclerotic and we clog the public bloodstream.

And still ahead of us, never nearing, lies the castle.

England is a fortress and all its soldiers are fled.

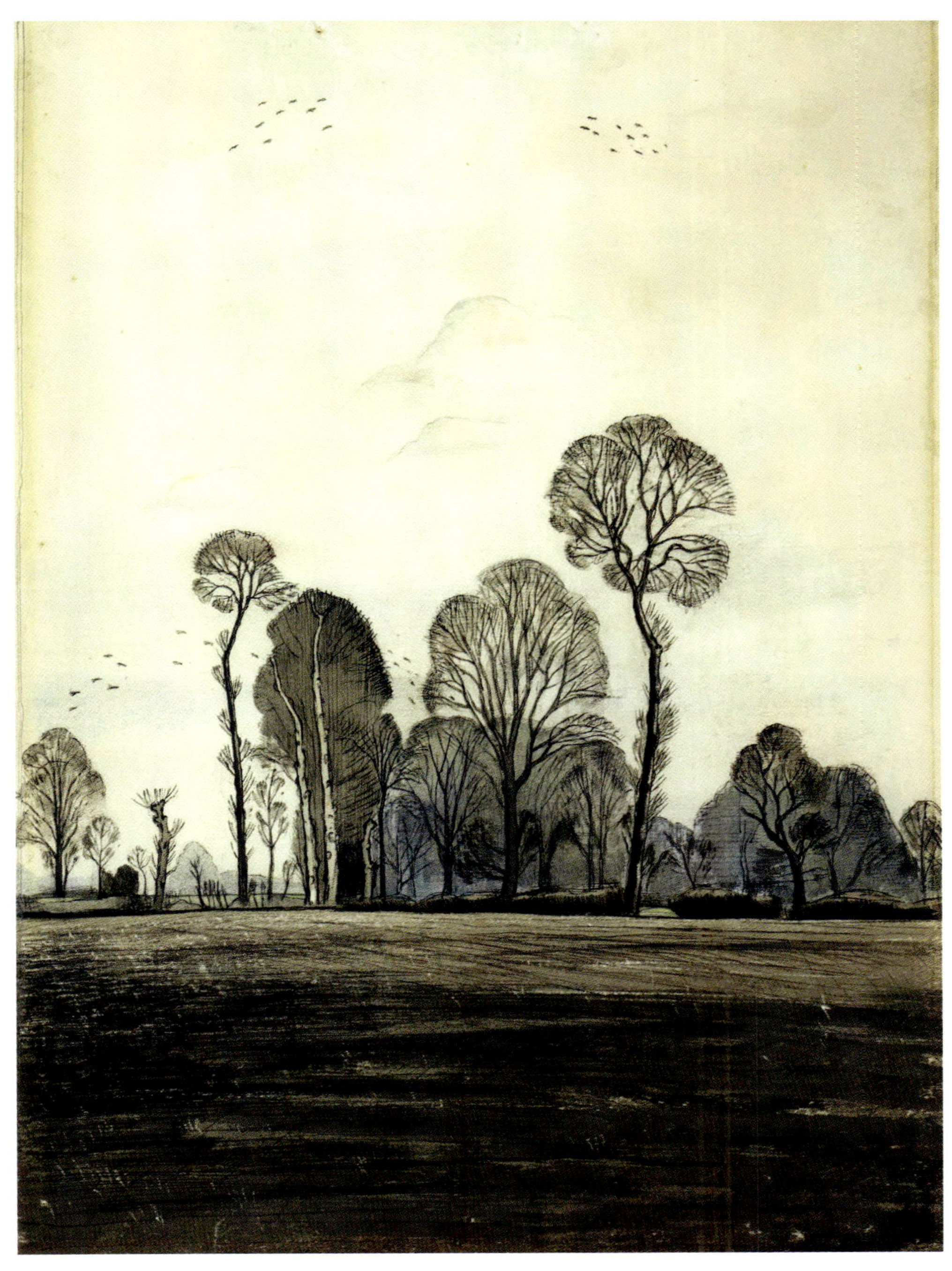

**125**  *Ploughed Fields at Iden*  c.1929
Paul Nash (1889–1946)  Pencil, wash, pen and ink and crayon

ENCLOSURE

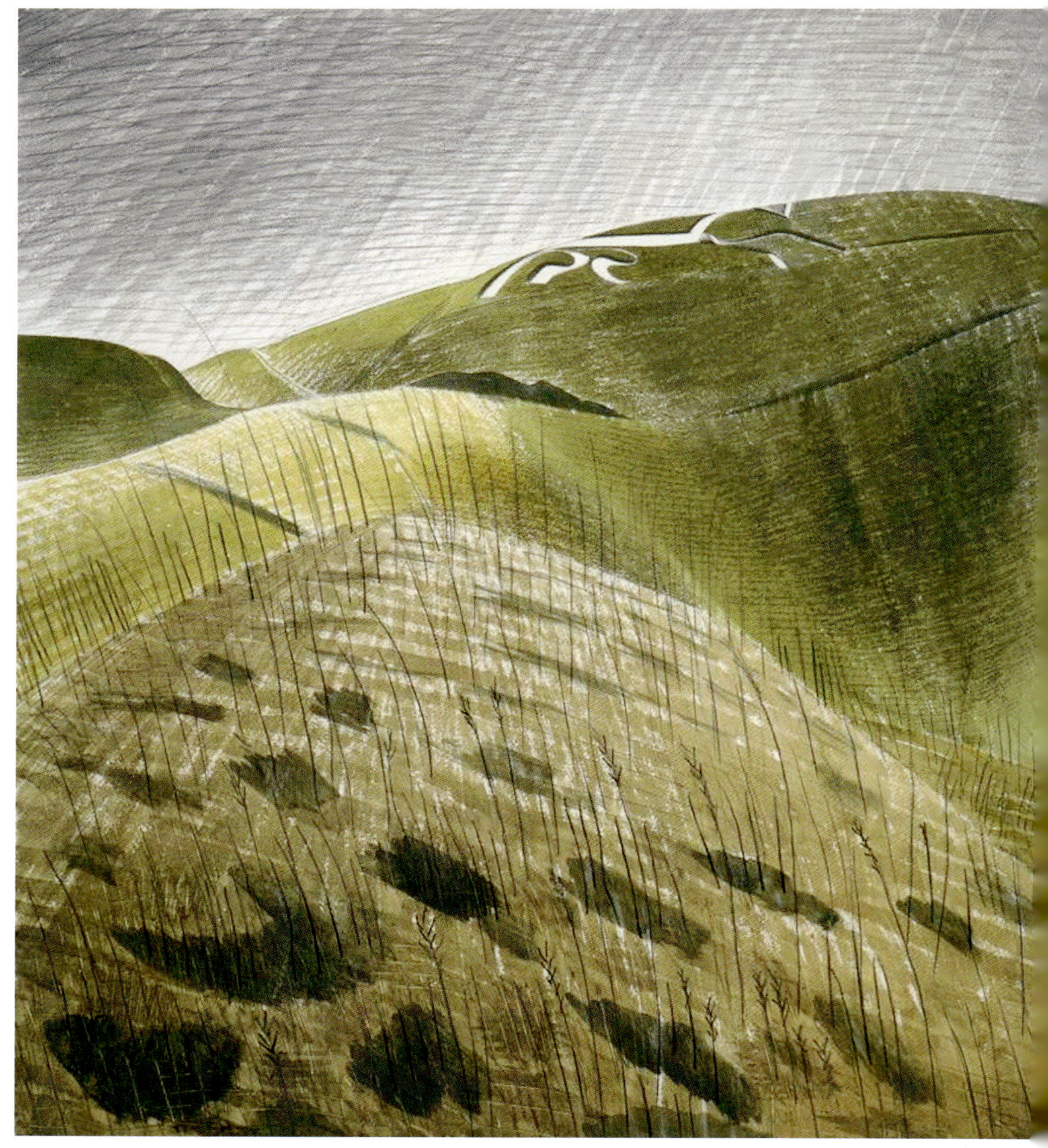

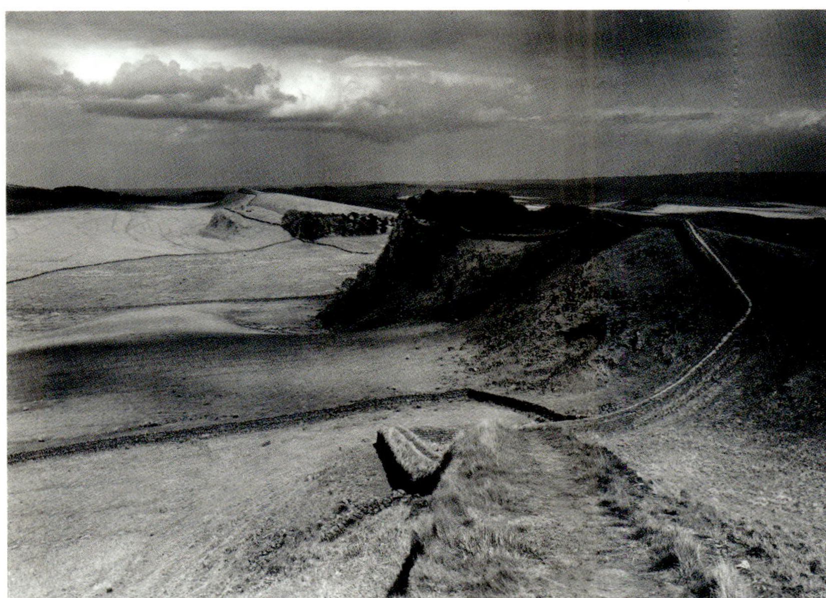

126  *Hadrian's Wall, Northumberland, Looking*
*East from Hotbank Crags*  1959
Edwin Smith (1912–71)
Black and white photograph

Edwin Smith is best known for his photographic records of mid-century Britain, and particularly his ability to capture the specifics of place and of people's everyday lives. Here, he turns his lens to Hadrian's Wall, which was built around 122 CE and was intended to secure the northern limit of the Roman Empire.

127  *The Vale of the White Horse*  c.1939
Eric Ravilious (1903–42)
Graphite and watercolour on paper

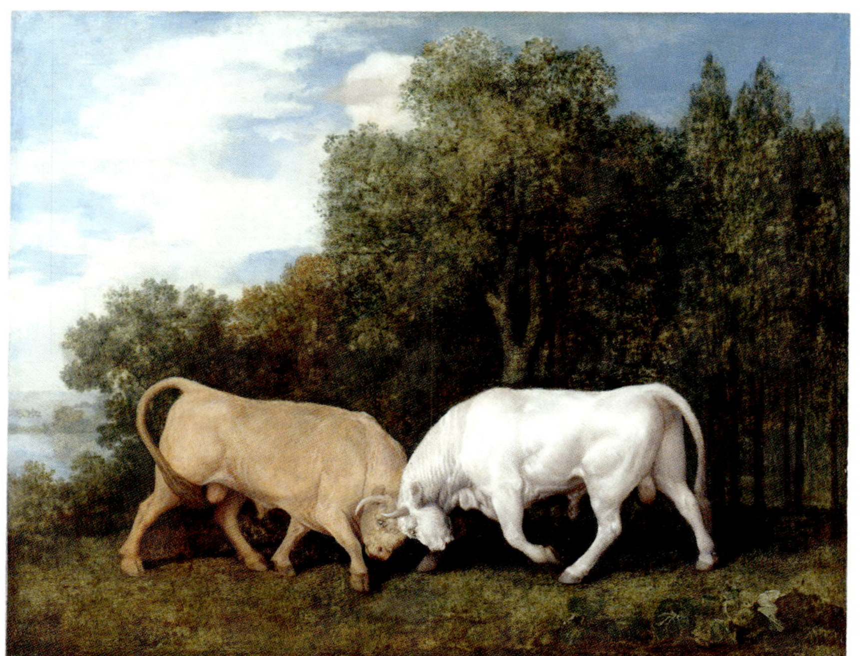

128  *Bulls Fighting*  1786
George Stubbs
(1724–1806)
Beeswax and oil
on panel

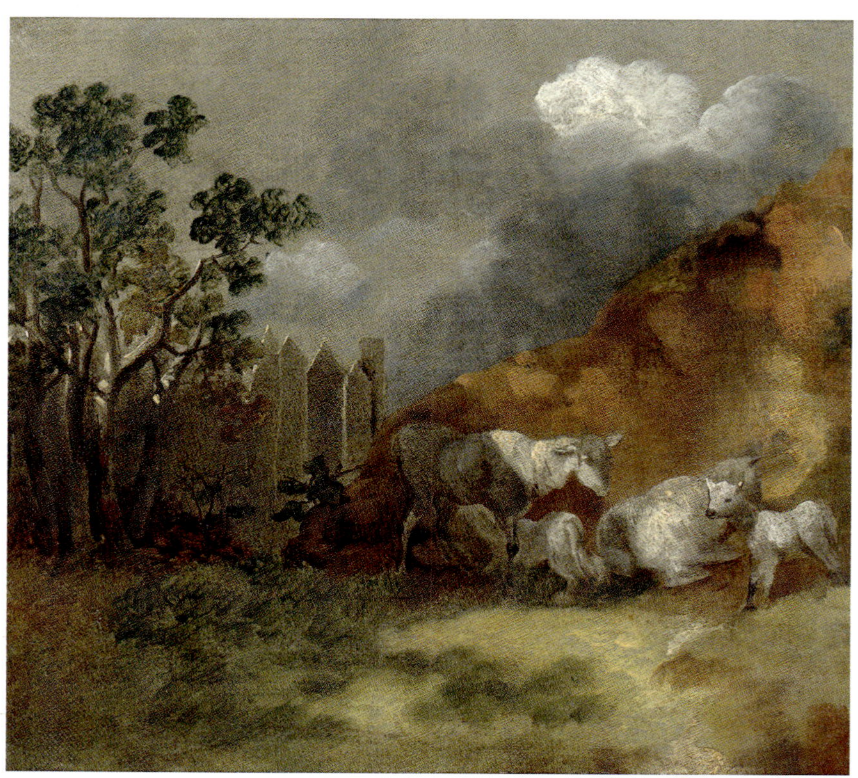

129  *Sheep and
Lambs by a
Fence*  c.1745
Thomas Gainsborough
RA (1727–88)
Oil on canvas

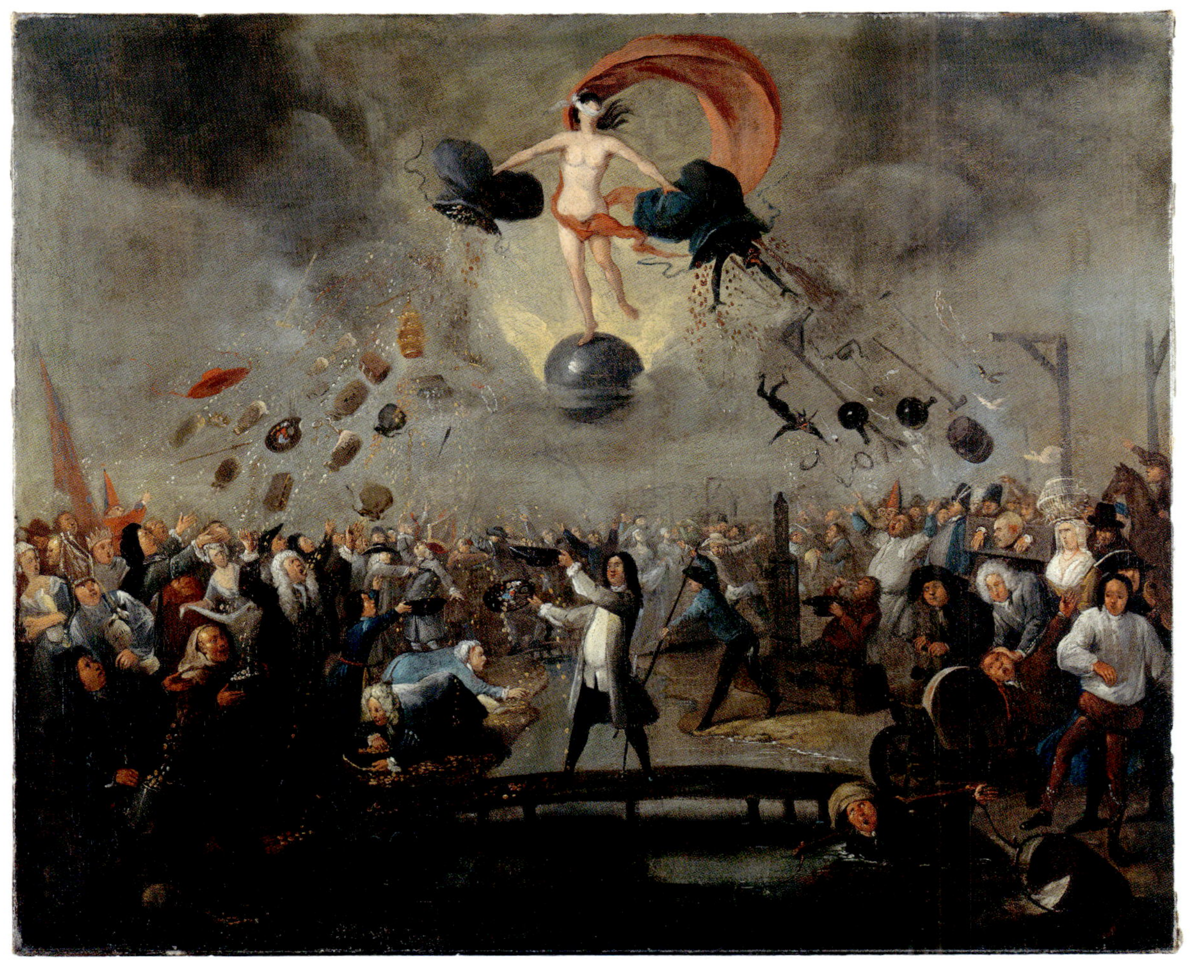

**130** *Allegory of Fortune* 1730
Balthazar Nebo (active 1730–62)
Oil on canvas

**131** *An Unknown Man, perhaps Charles Goring of Wiston*
*(1744–1829), out Shooting with his Servant*  18th century
Artist unknown
Oil on canvas

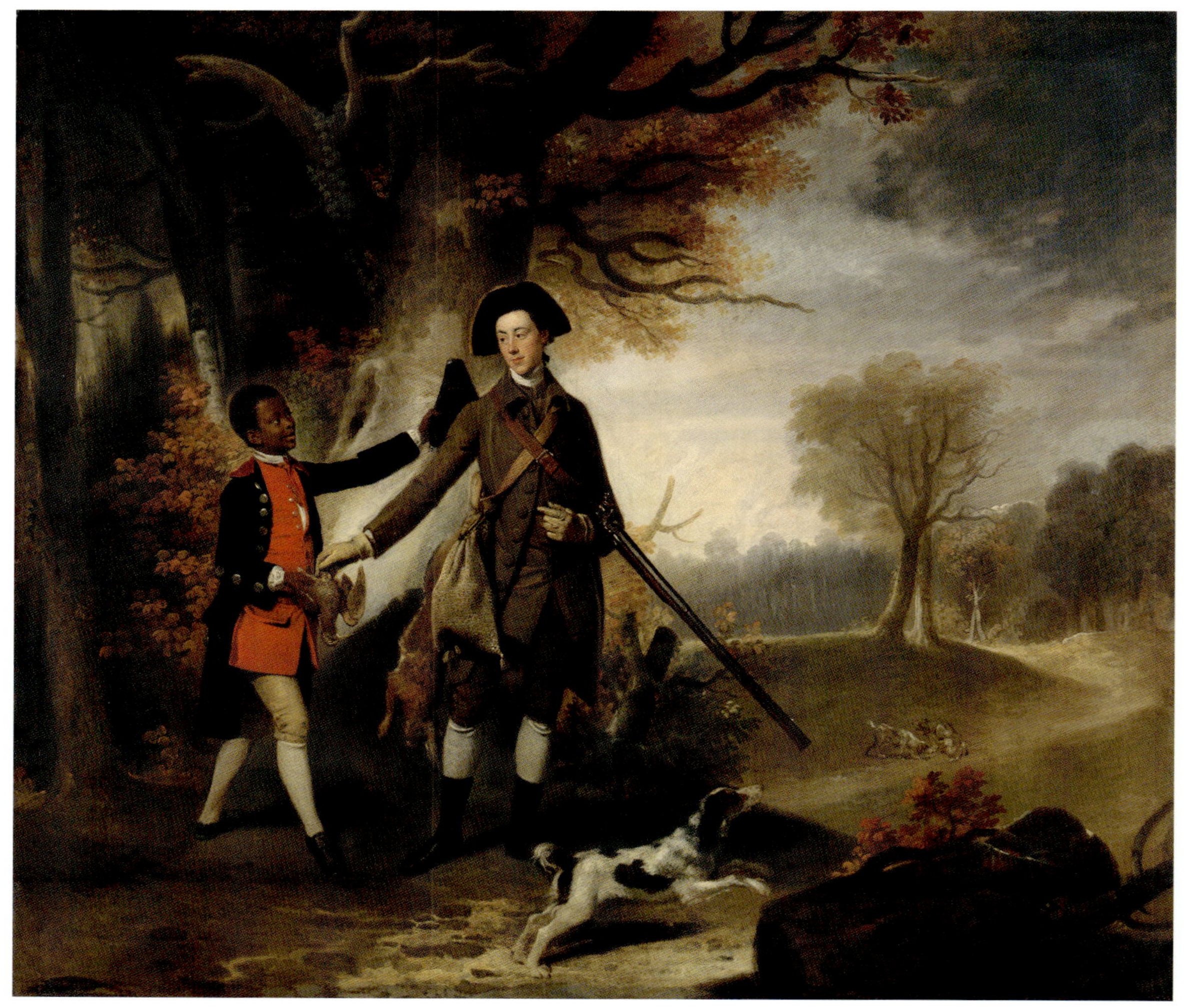

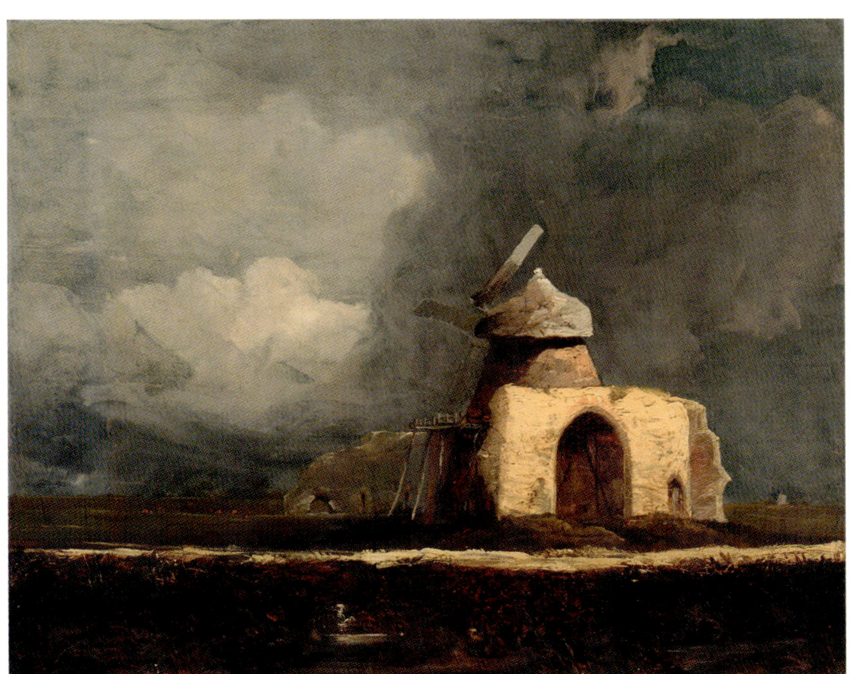

**132** *St Benet's Abbey* 1810
Attributed to John Sell
Cotman (1782–1842)
Oil on canvas

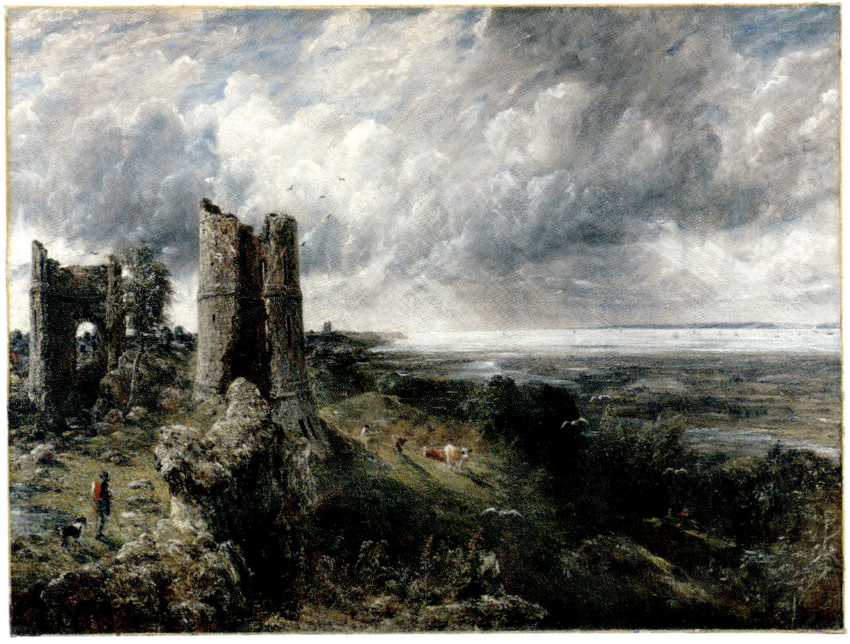

**133** *Hadleigh Castle,*
*The Mouth of the*
*Thames – Morning*
*after a Stormy*
*Night* 1829
John Constable
(1776–1837)
Oil on canvas

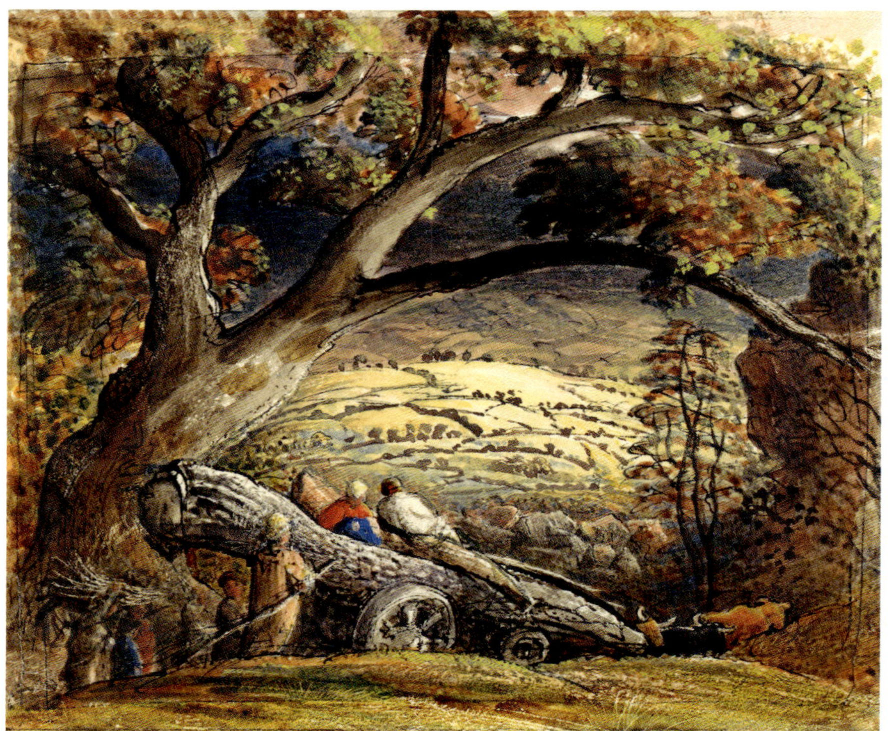

134  *The Timber Wain*  1833–4
Samuel Palmer
(1805–81)
Watercolour
and gouache
with pen and
black ink on paper

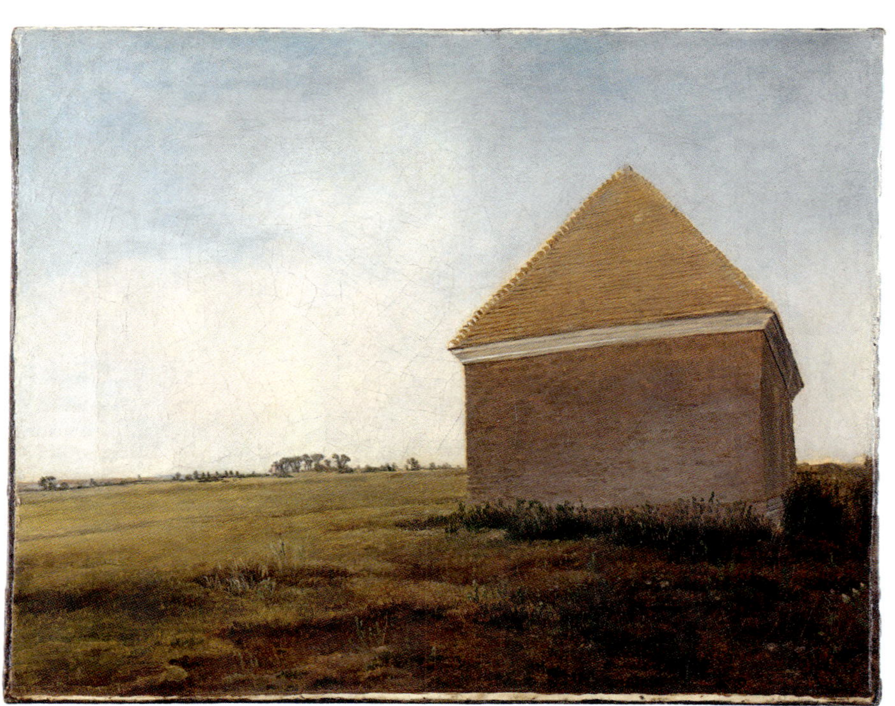

135  *Newmarket Heath, with a rubbing down house*  c.1765
George Stubbs
(1724–1806)
Oil on canvas

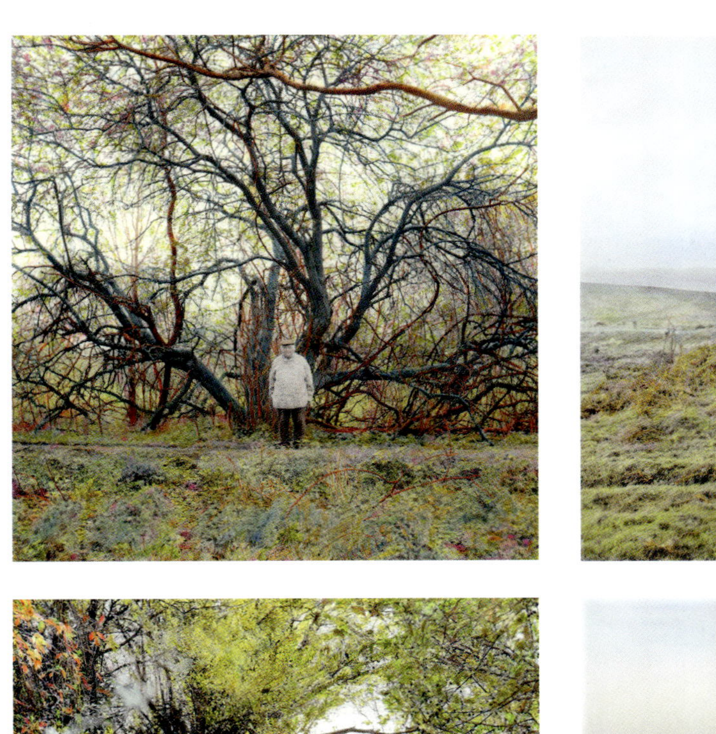

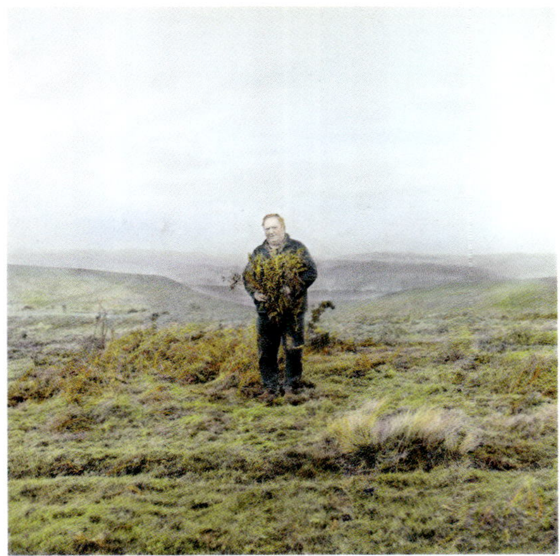

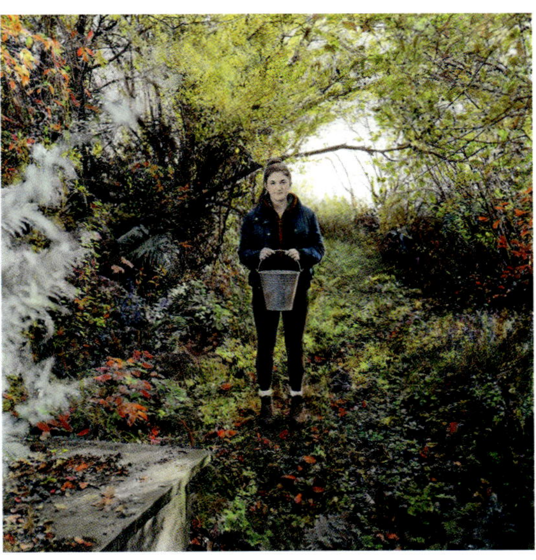

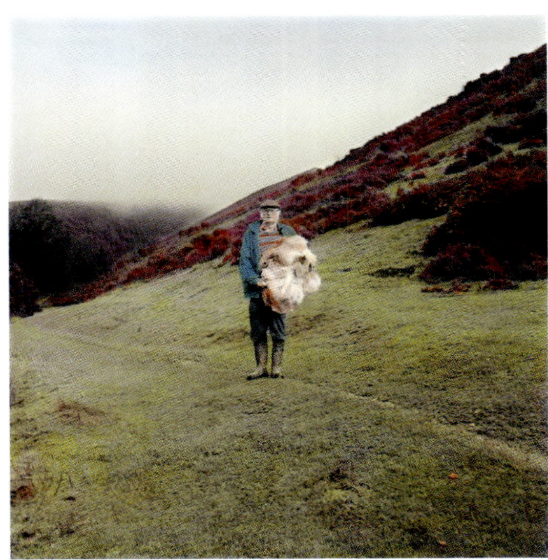

**136** *Monument to the Vanquished*  2021
Leah Gordon (b.1959)
Silver gelatin prints from black and white negatives subsequently hand-tinted with photographic dyes

Gordon's work focuses on the politics of enclosure, and the ways in which the Enclosure Acts, which saw the end of the open field system of agriculture, could be viewed in the context of the Industrial Revolution and the American and Caribbean plantation system. The acts saw the redrawing and redesignation of land across England, recalling the historian E.P. Thompson's words, "land remained the index of influence, the plinth on which power was erected". Gordon used black and white film which was then hand-tinted by Marg Duston in an attempt to breathe life into the landscapes and, in her own words, to invoke "the uncanny nature of the land".

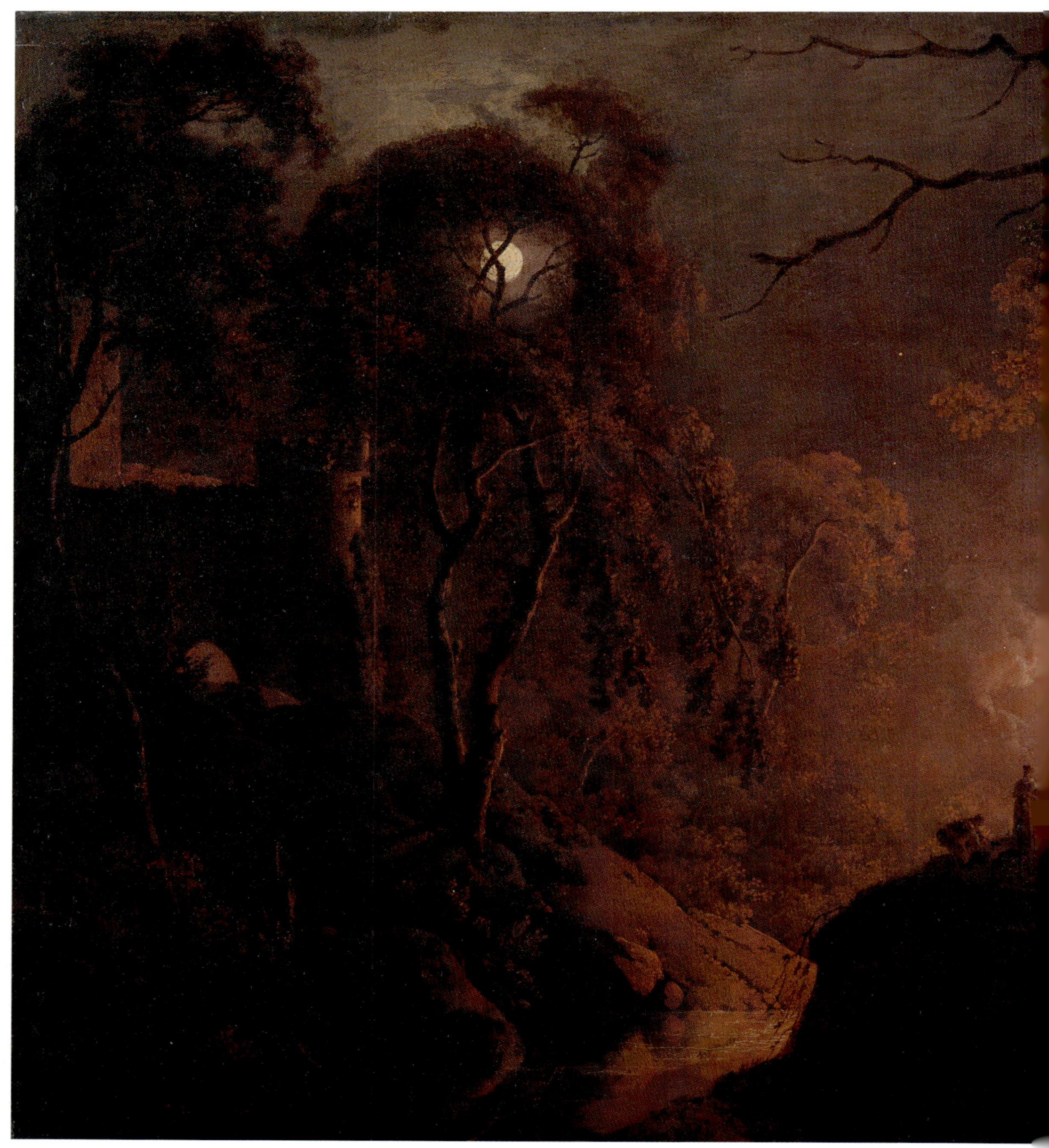

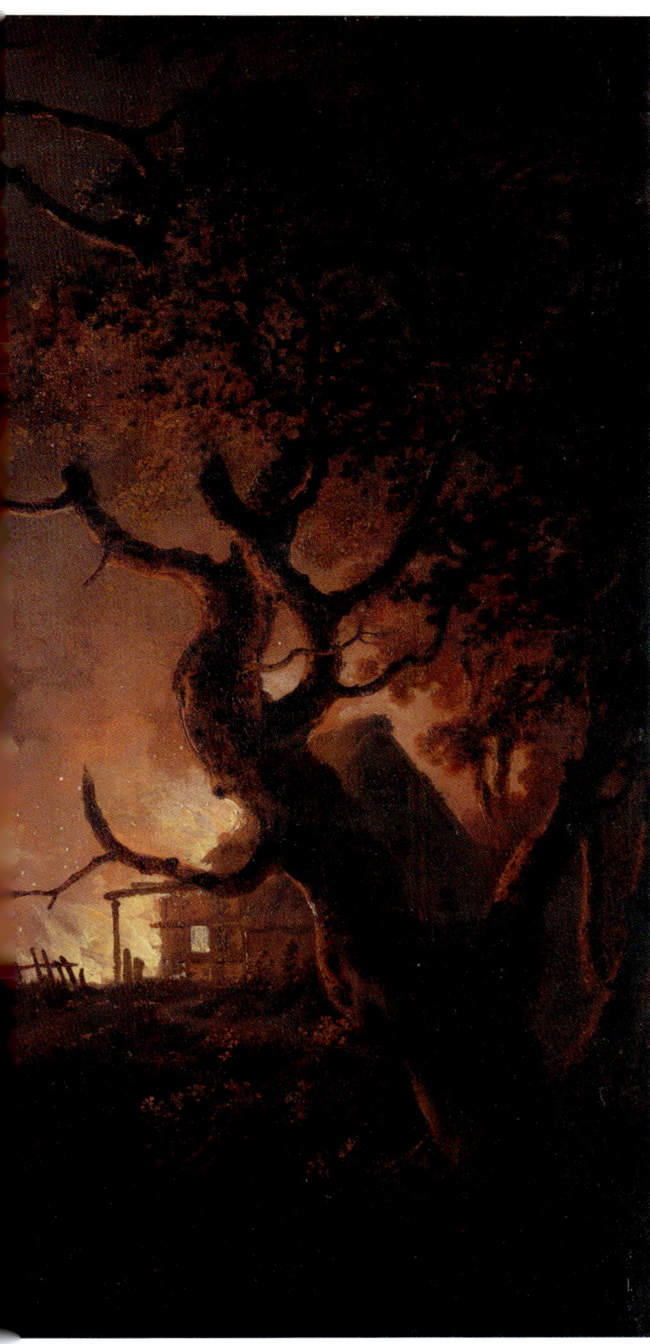

137  *Cottage on Fire at Night*  1785–93
Joseph Wright of Derby (1734–97)
Oil on canvas

Here, Wright depicts the English landscape
ablaze, a mother and child watching as
their cottage burns. Wright, known for his
impressive portrayal of light in darkness, uses
a restricted colour palette in this painting.
The light of the moon is paired with the
ferocious blaze, evocatively producing a sense
of simultaneous stillness and movement.

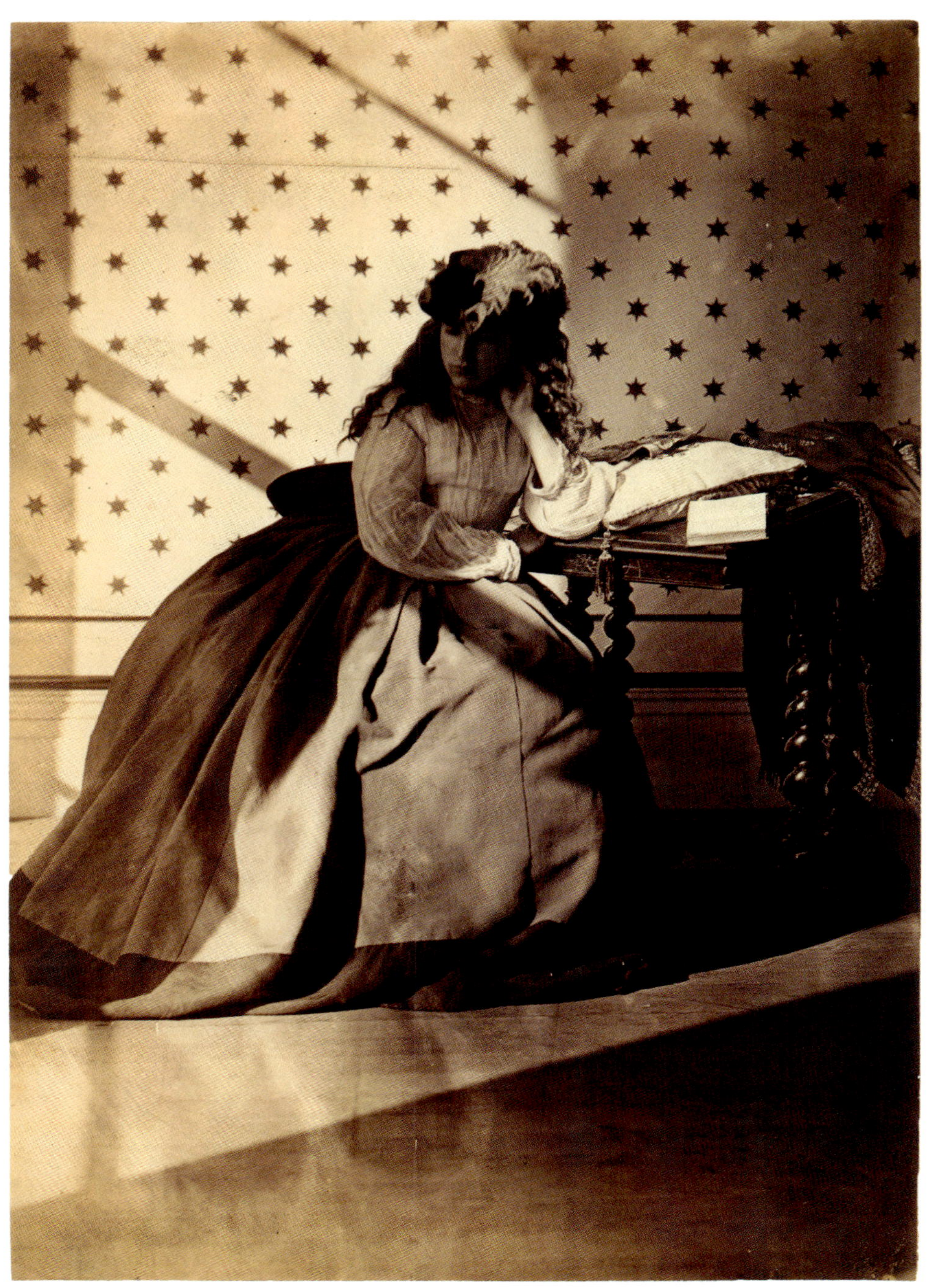

**138** *Photographic Study* *c.* early 1860s
Lady Clementina Hawarden (1822–65)
Albumen silver print from glass negative

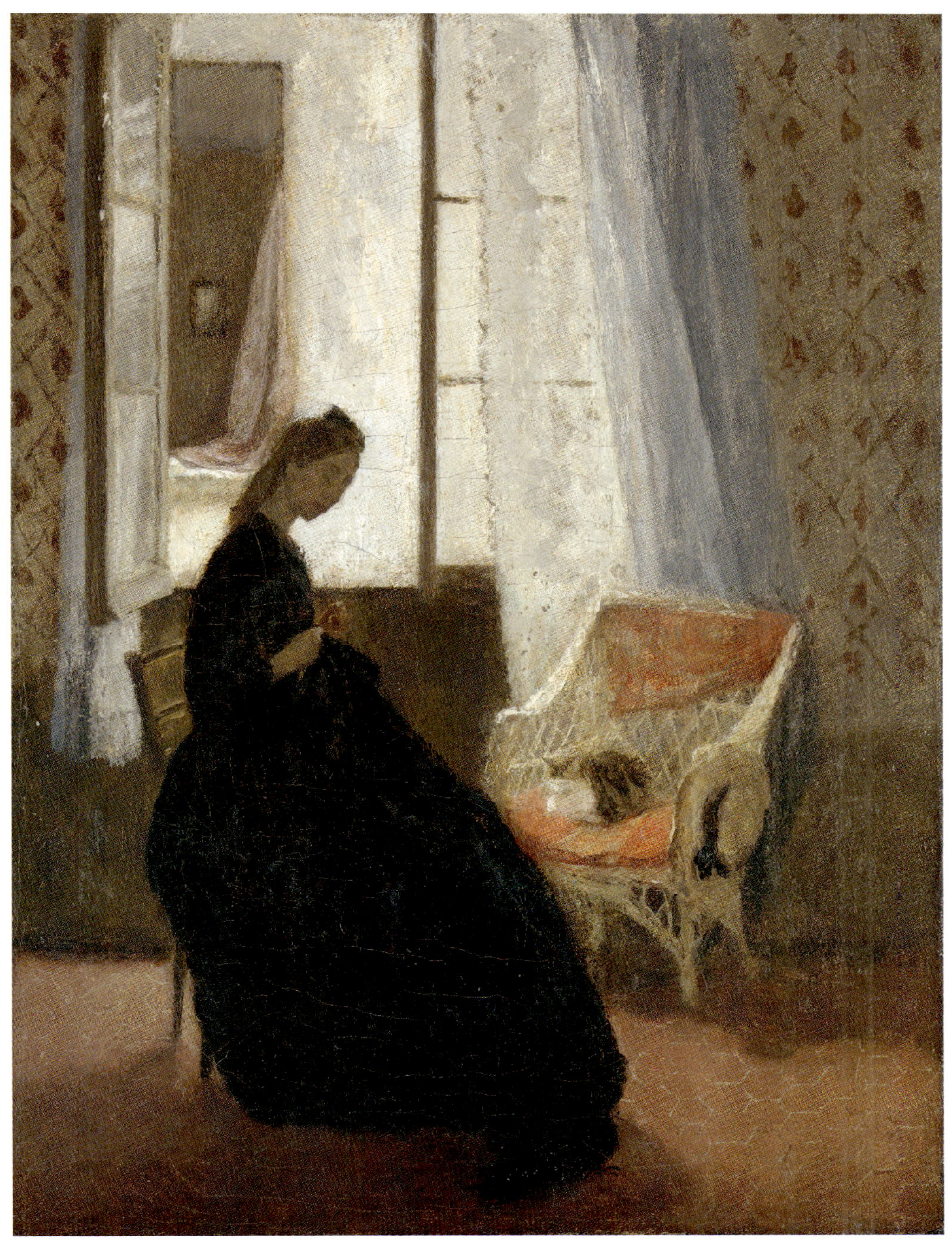

**139** *La Chambre sur la Cour*  1907–08
Gwen John (1876–1939)
Oil on canvas

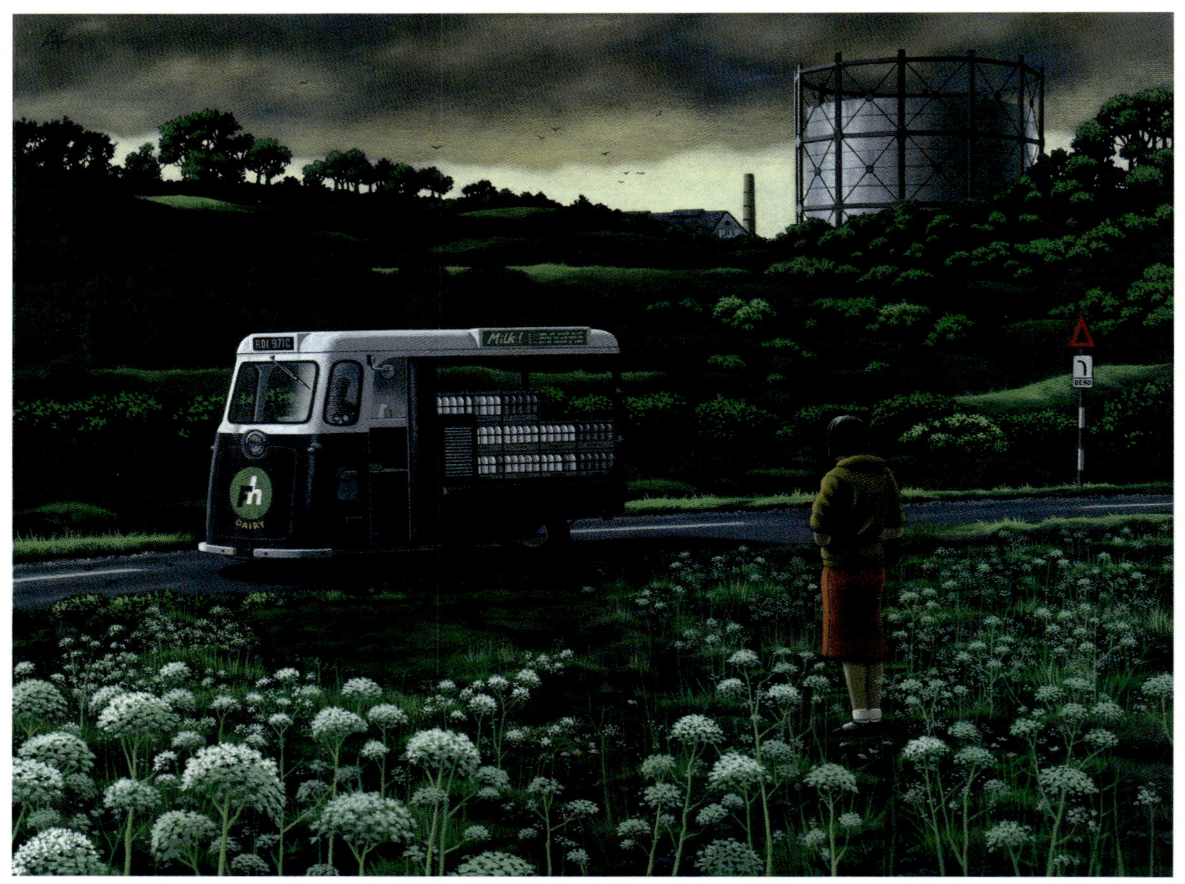

**140** *Father Figure* 2012
Christopher Noulton (b.1961)
Acrylic on canvas

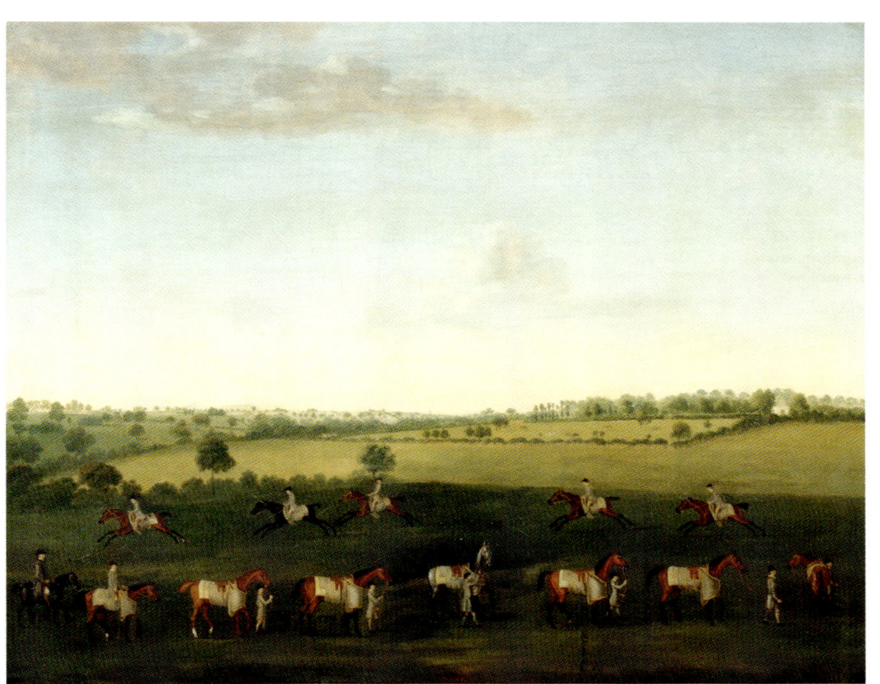

141 *Sir Charles Warre Malet's String of Racehorses at Exercise* c.1800
Francis Sartorius
(1734–1804)
Oil on canvas

142 *Coach Trip – Original London to Brighton Road* 2014
Jeff Pitcher (b.1967)
Colour photograph

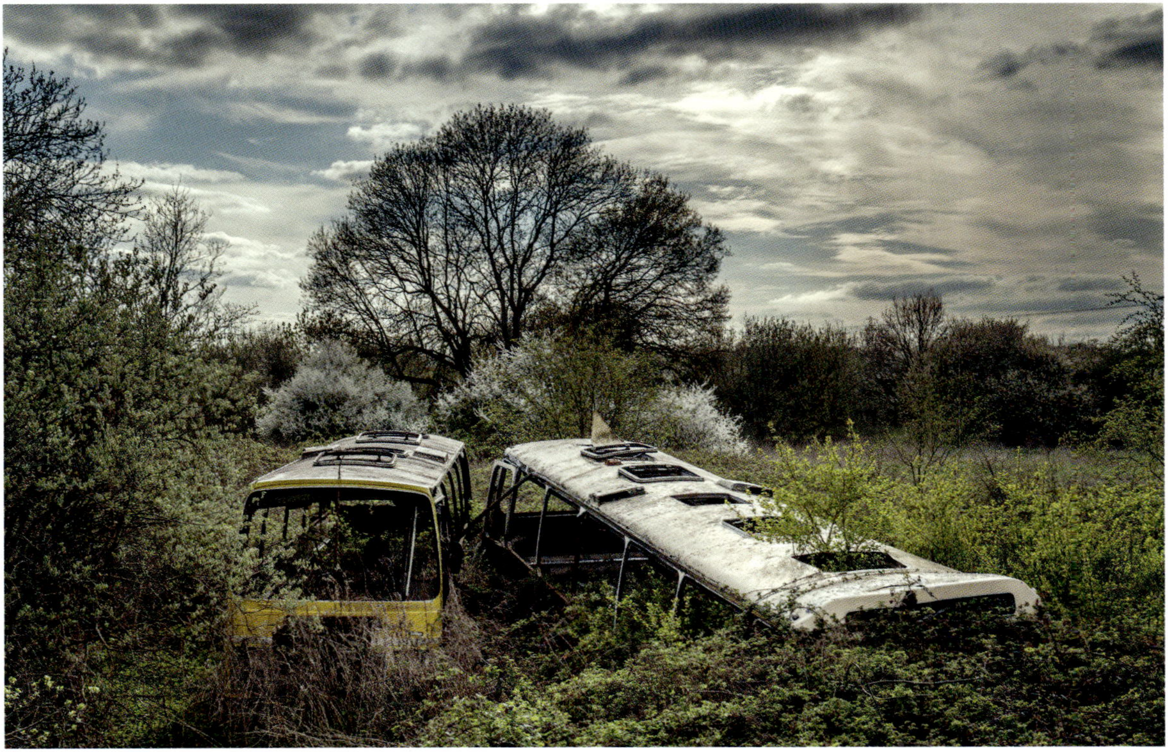

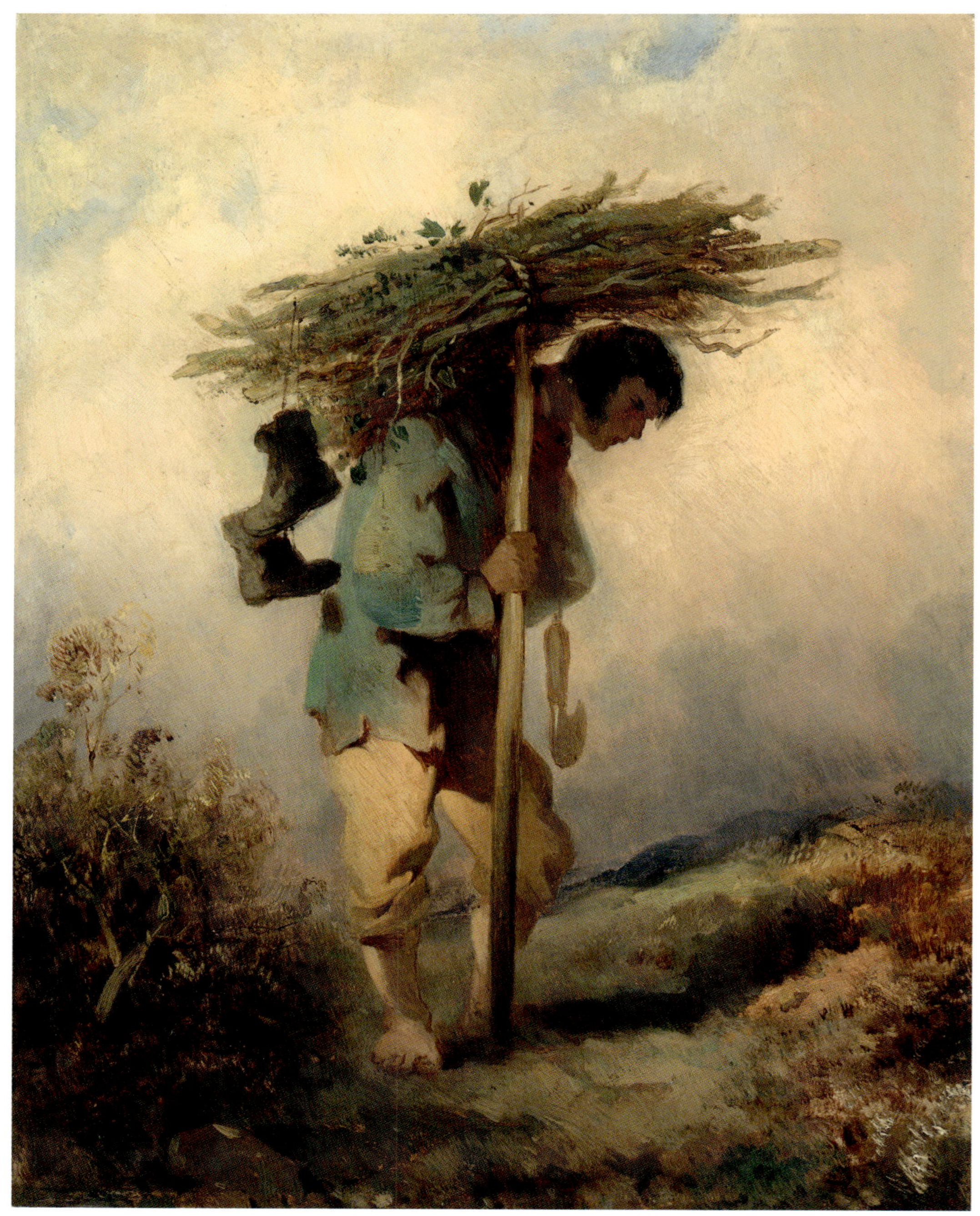

**143** *A Man Carrying Faggots*  c.1799
George Chinnery (1774–1852)
Oil on paper on board

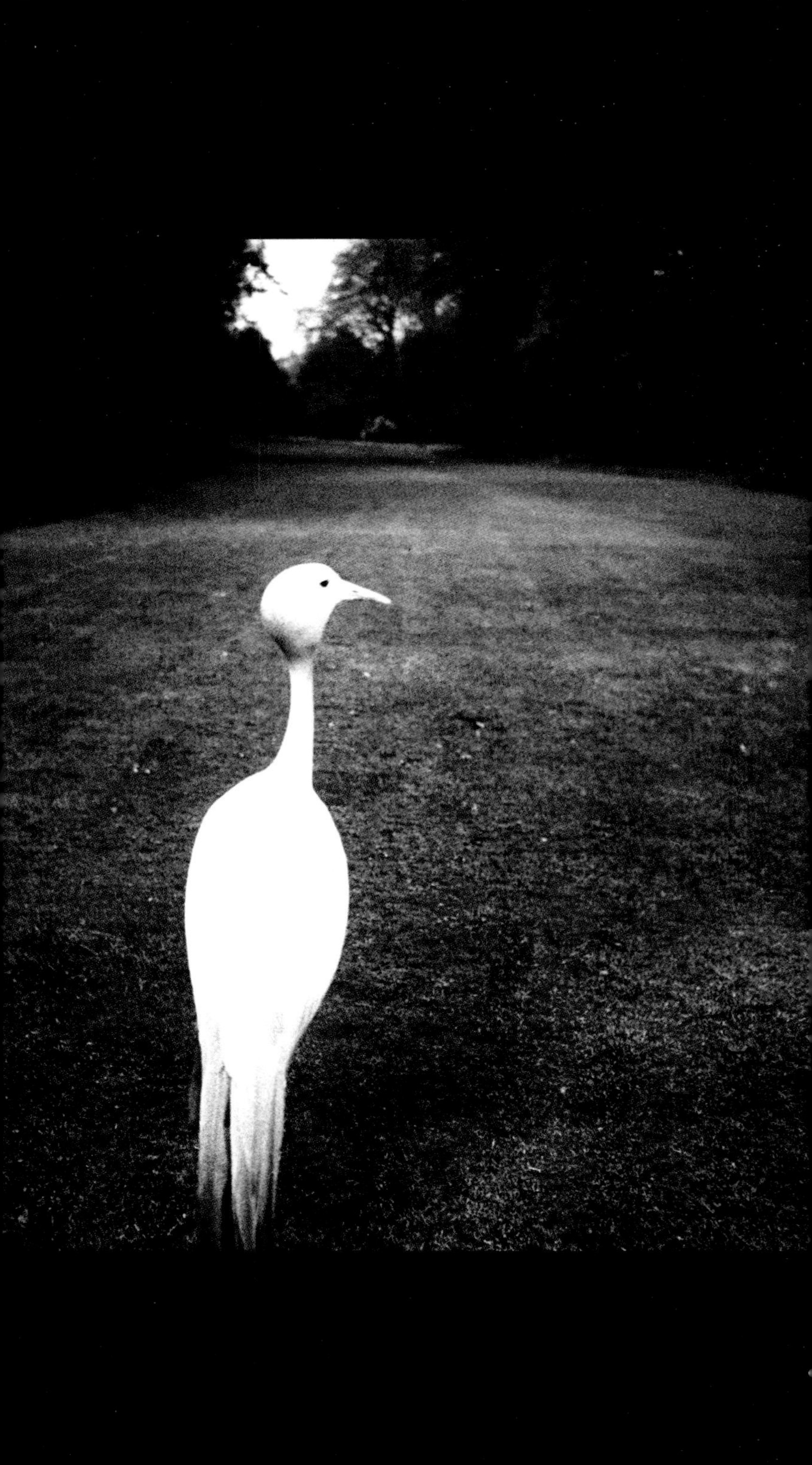

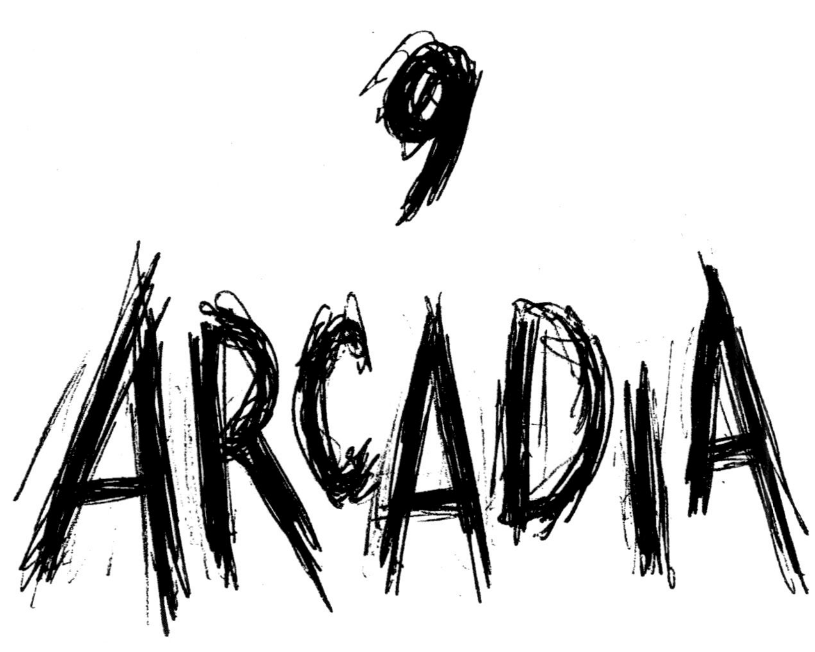
9
ARCADIA

PREVIOUS PAGE

**144** *An Evening at Kew Gardens* 1932
Bill Brandt (1904–83) Silver gelatin print

ENGLAND IS A HOTHOUSE FLOWER
THAT WOULD DIE IN THE WILD.

The Tyburn boy pushes aside waist-high thistles and says, "Do you know the difference between a weed and a flower?"

He plucks the seeds from the thistlehead and says, "Weeds are strong. They're mongrel strains that thrive everywhere. They push their fronds up through pavements and laugh at storms and rain and heat and disease. No matter what we throw at them they survive, until they've sucked down poison and turned it to wine. Weeds are scum like you and I, with no inbred pedigree lineage. But flowers ..."

He pushes the gate open. The garden is as neat as clockwork. Pineapples loll in steaming greenhouses and the grass is cut stubble-short. Knots of gravelled paths display the roses like pictures at an exhibition. Red and white: colours that once thousands died for. The Tyburn boy pulls a petal from one and whispers *loves me not*.

"These roses are the royalty of the flower world. They are bred with only their own kind, kept separate until they are as beautiful as gemstones and as weak as kittens." He pulls off another petal and says *loves me not* again. "They would die if the gardeners weren't here to keep the real world out." He kicks at a stone. *Loves me not, loves me not.*

"England loves its purebred weaklings. Behind this garden are stables of thorough-bred horses that go lame at the drop of a hat." There's a wheezing from the path and he reaches down to stroke a passing bulldog. That living symbol of England gasps for air through nostrils that have been bred modishly (and fatally) tight. The boy sighs and says, "They say England is a garden as if that's a good thing but all gardens will go to seed eventually. Out there is England's real heart; wild rebellious nature, unbroken and raw, and one day all this will belong to disorder again."

England is a hothouse flower and all the glass is cracked.

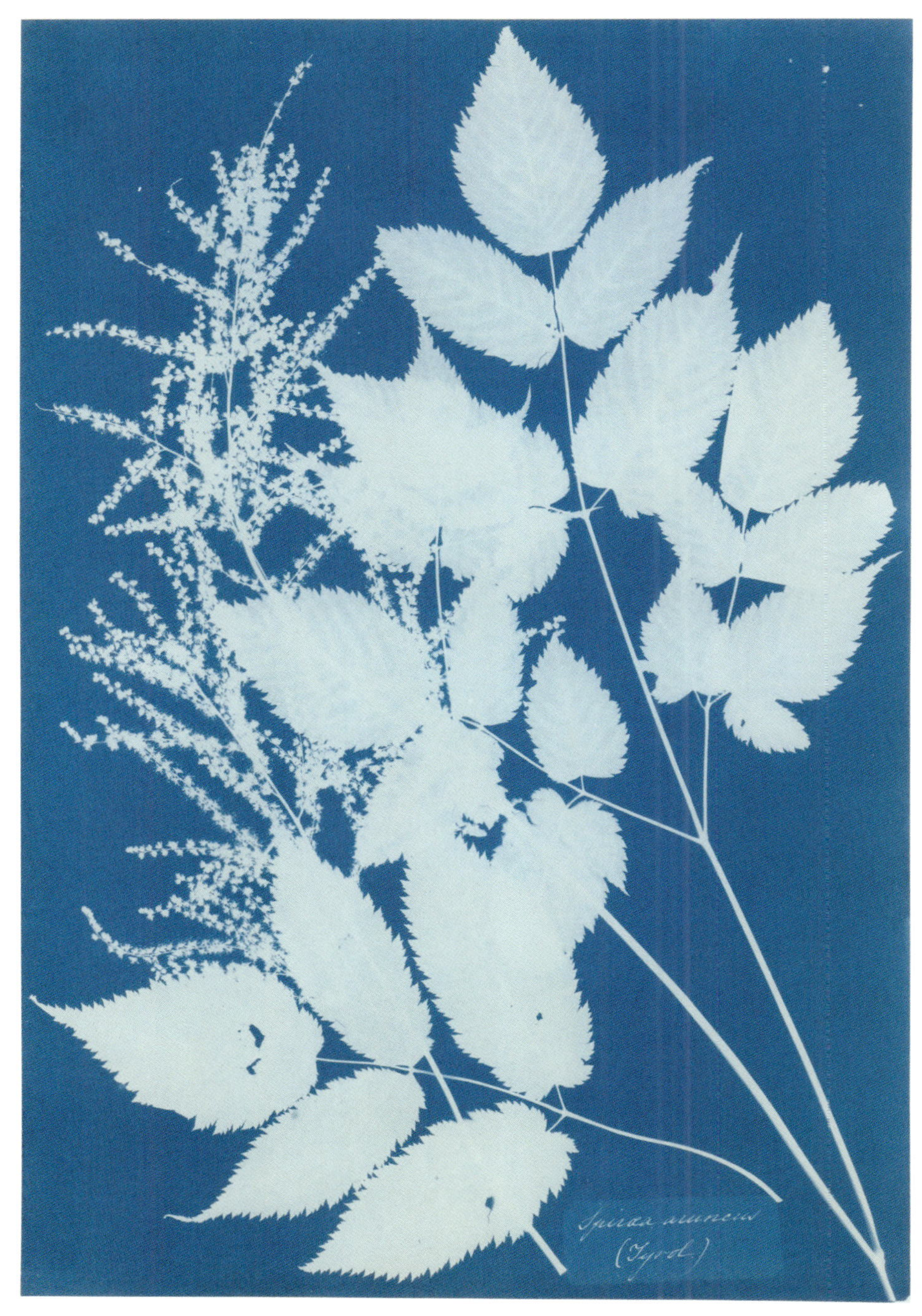


**145** *Spiraea aruncus (Tyrol)* c.1851–4
Anna Atkins (1799–1871)  Cyanotype

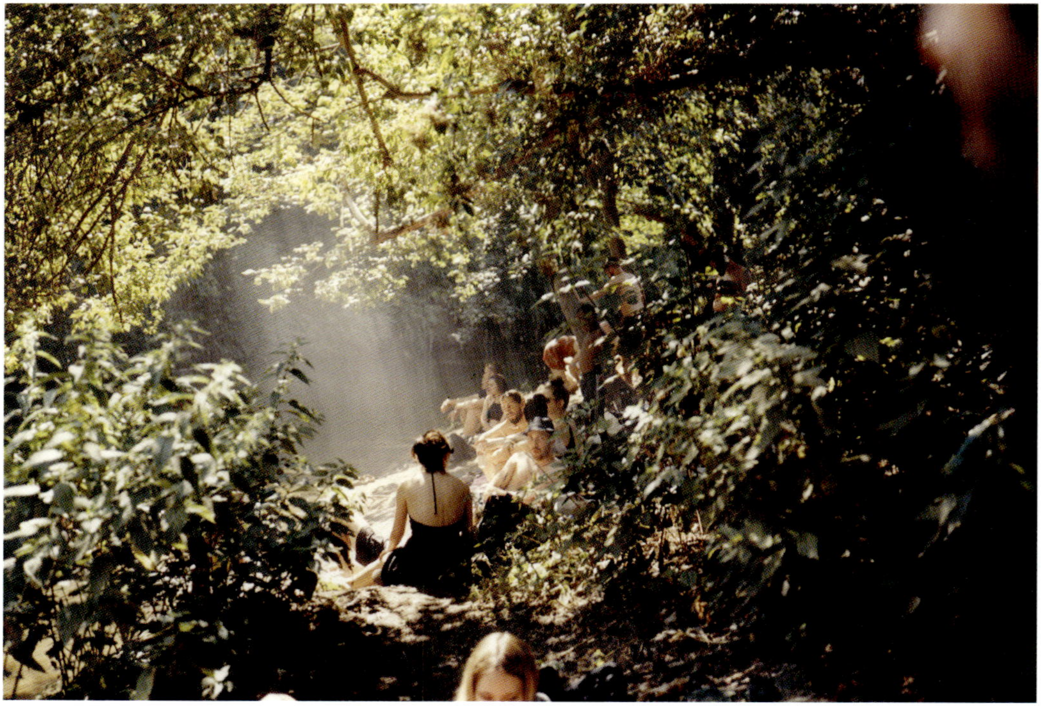

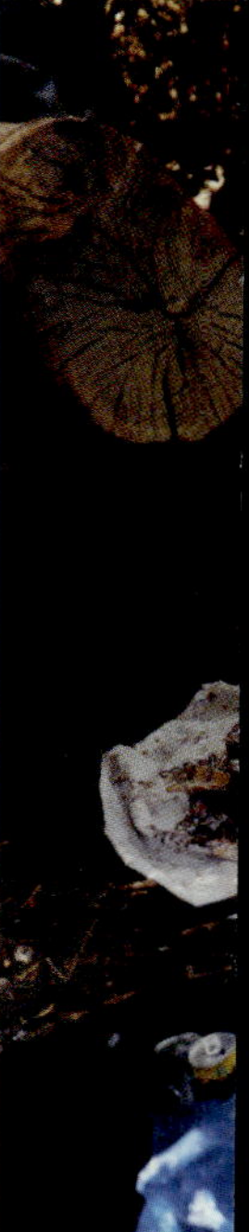

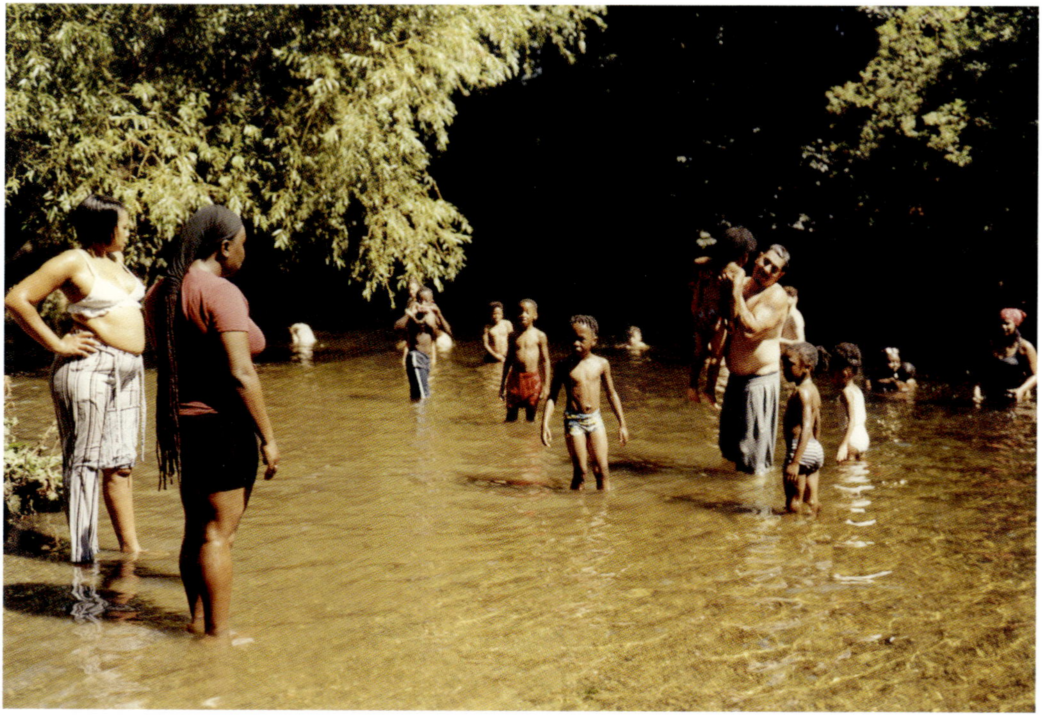

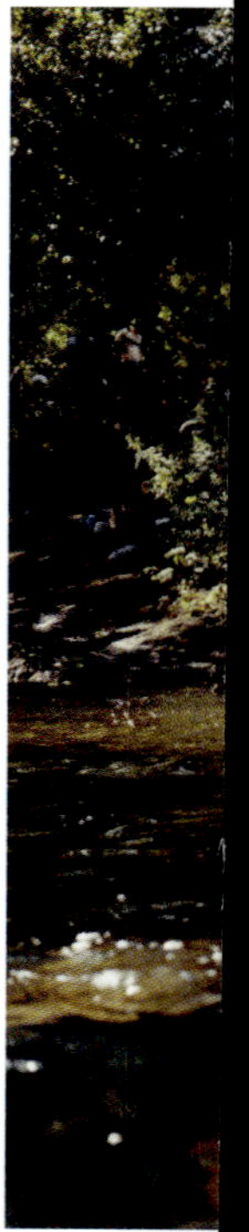

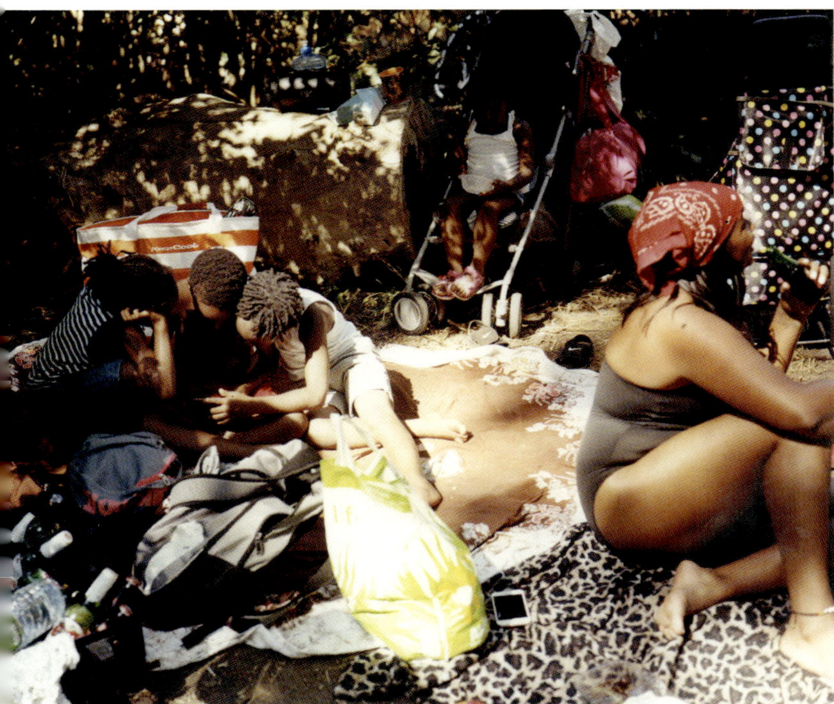

146  *Untitled from*
*Hackney Riviera*  2018
Nick Waplington (b.1965)
C-type photographs

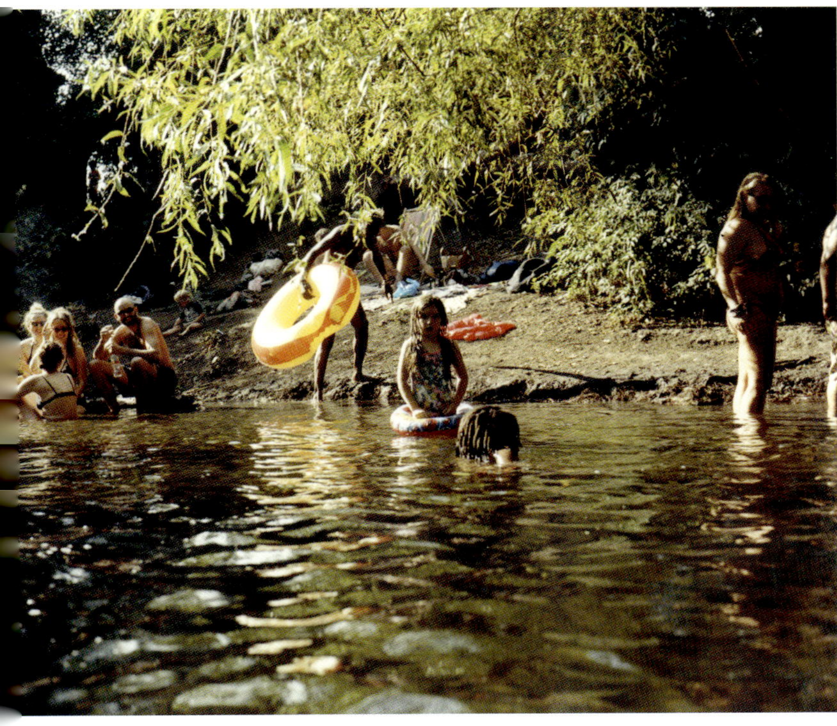

ARCADIA

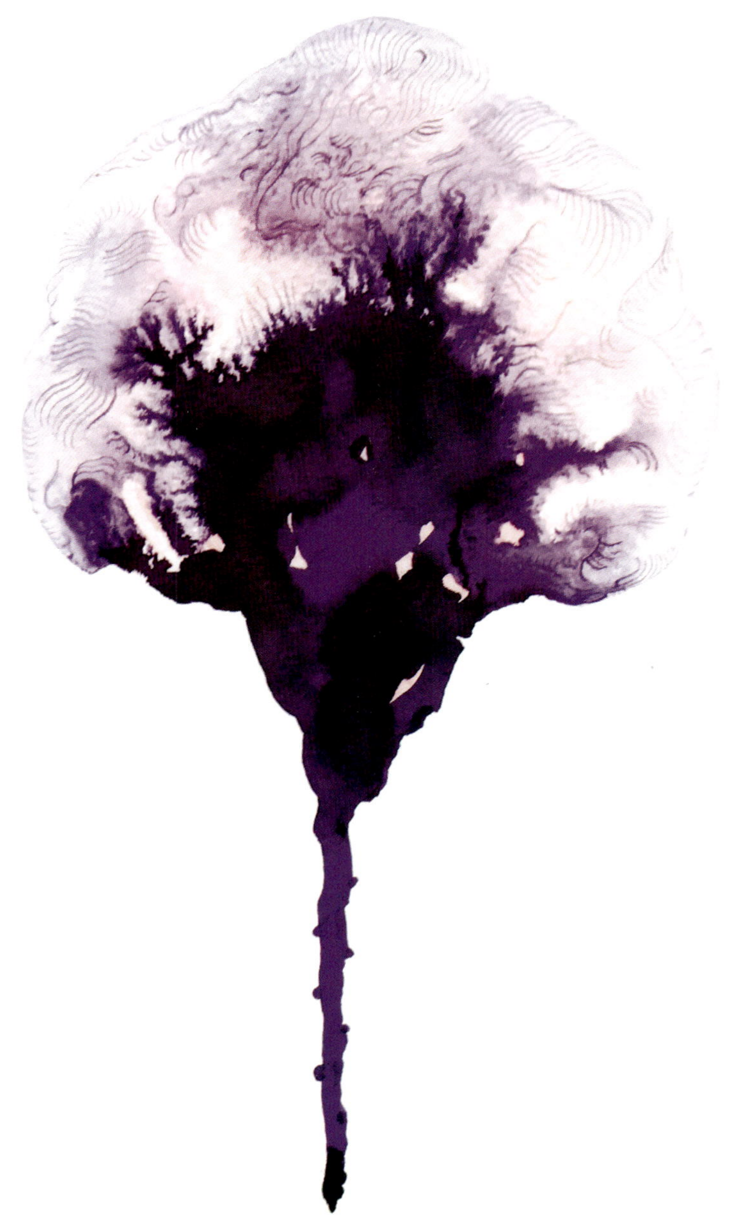

**147**  *Flower of the Future*  2018–21
Joanna Kirk (b.1963)  Ink and watercolour on acid-free, cold-pressed archival paper

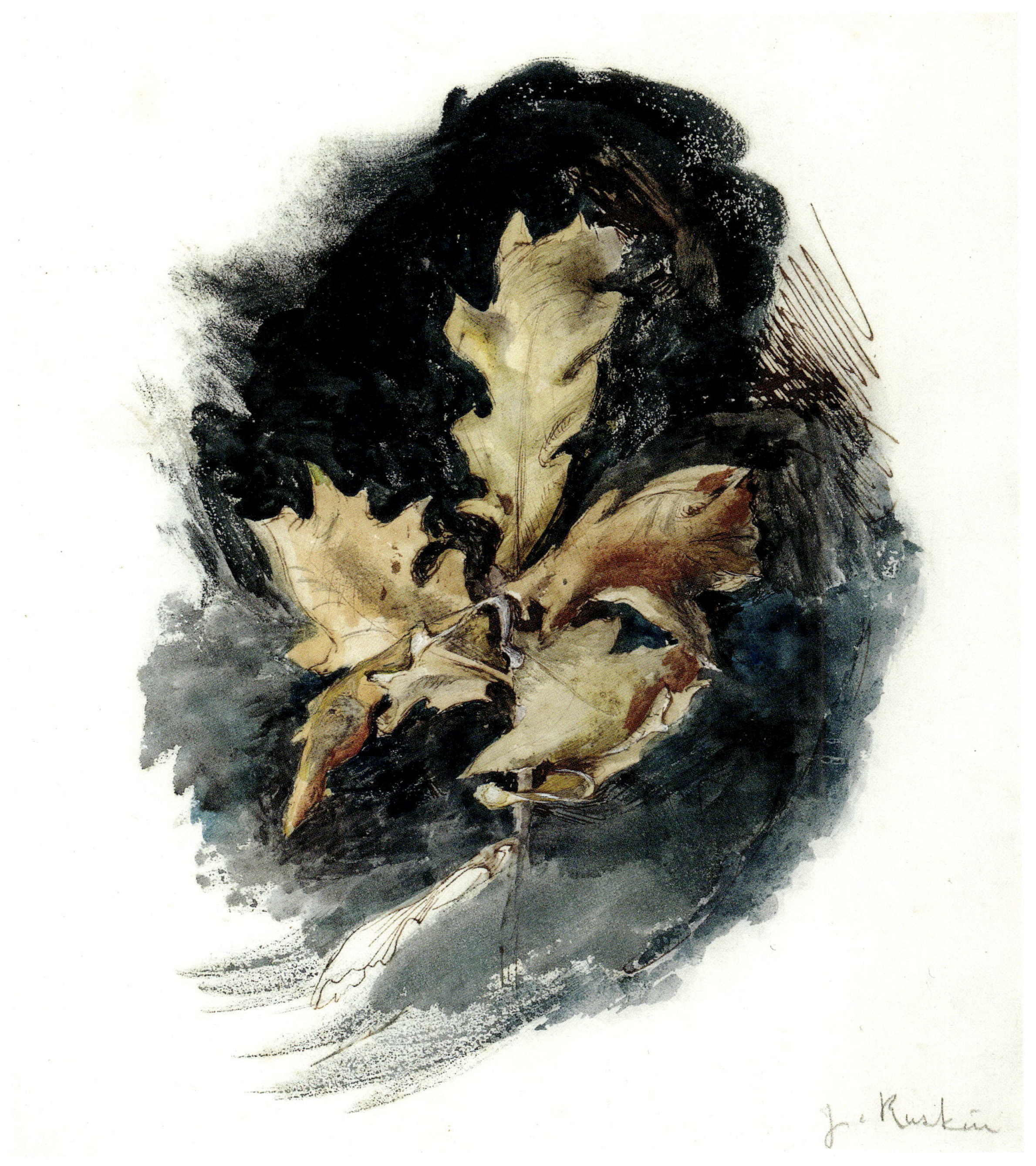

**148**  *Study of an Oak Leaf*  Undated  John Ruskin (1819–1900)
Watercolour, pen and brown ink, white gouache, gum and graphite; verso: graphite on paper

ARCADIA

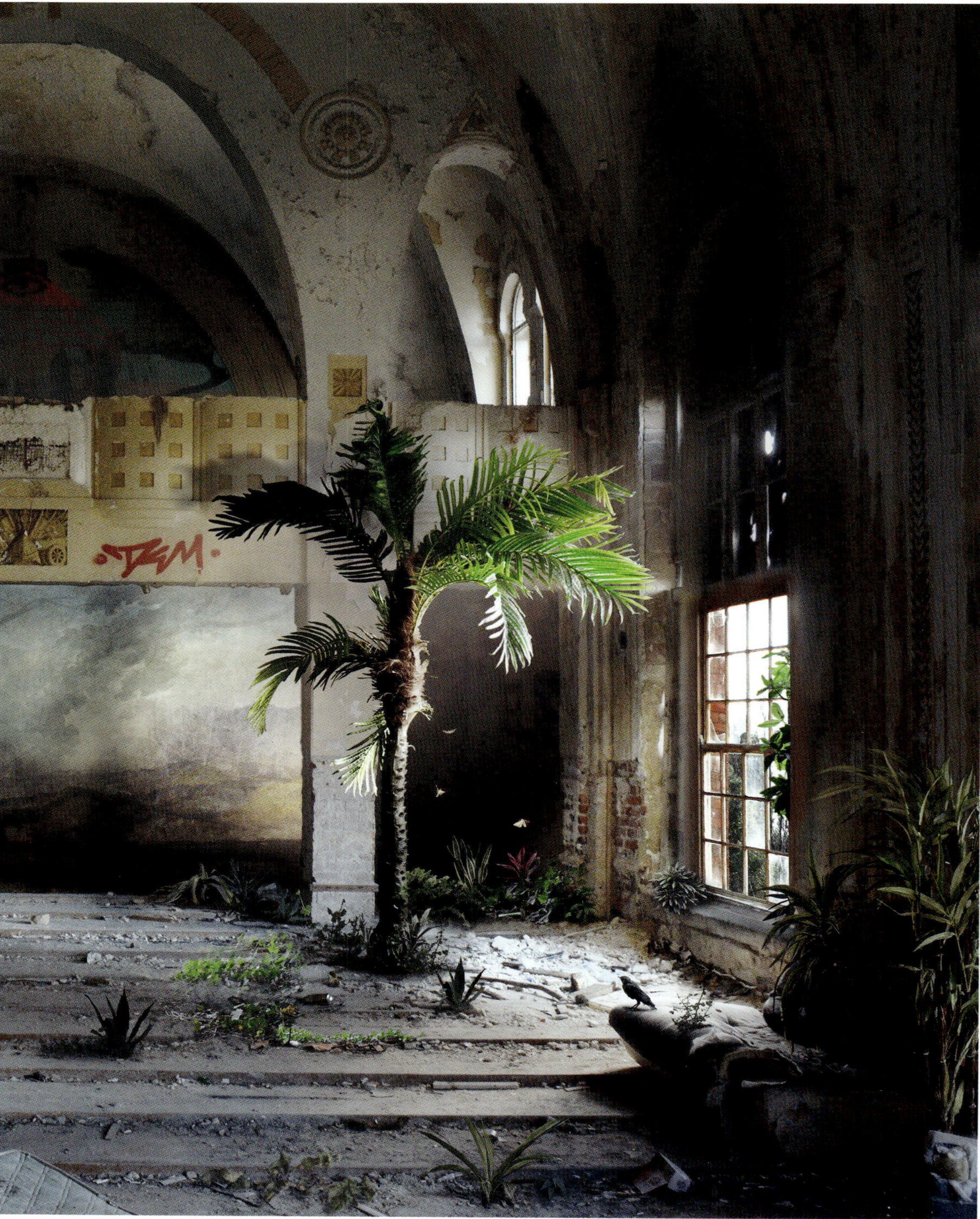

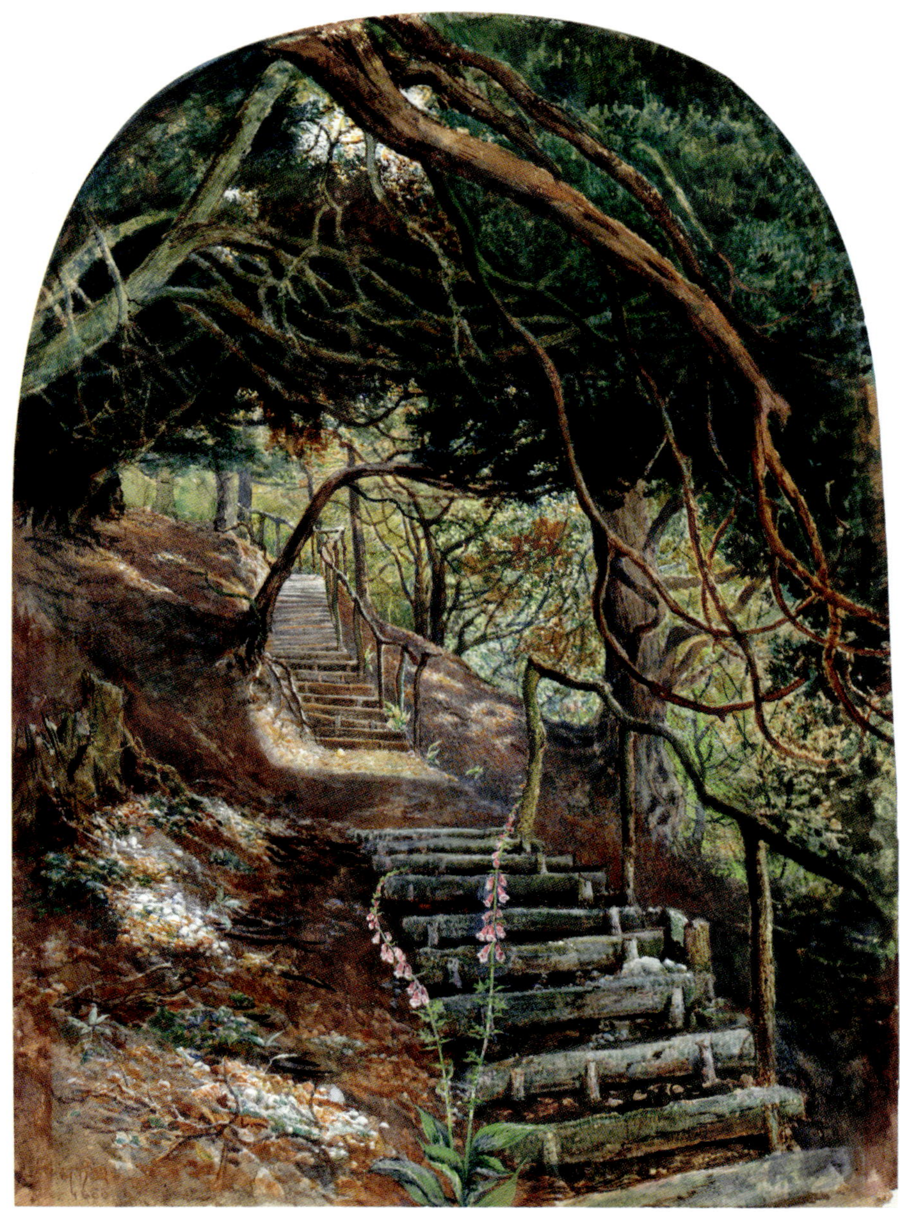

**149**  *Steps in a Garden*  1860
William Henry Millais (1828–99)
Watercolour and gouache with scratchaway technique on paper

**150**  *Palm*  2020
Suzanne Moxhay (b.1976)   Archival pigment print on Hahnemühle Photo Rag

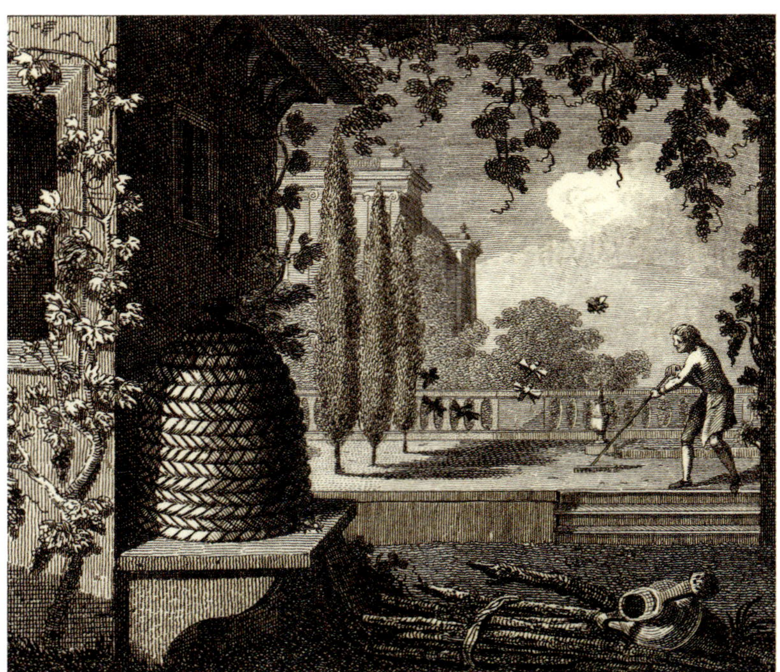


151  *The Degenerate Bees* 1793
William Skelton (1763–1848)
Etching and line
engraving on paper

Bees, a symbol of both
industry and monarchy, are
used as an allegorical tool
in John Gay's poem "The
Degenerate Bees", addressed
to Jonathan Swift. The poem,
on which this Skelton print is
based, is a political allegory for
the corruption of power, with
one cunning bee described
as scorning those who follow
honour and engaging in
industry only when there
is potential for profit.


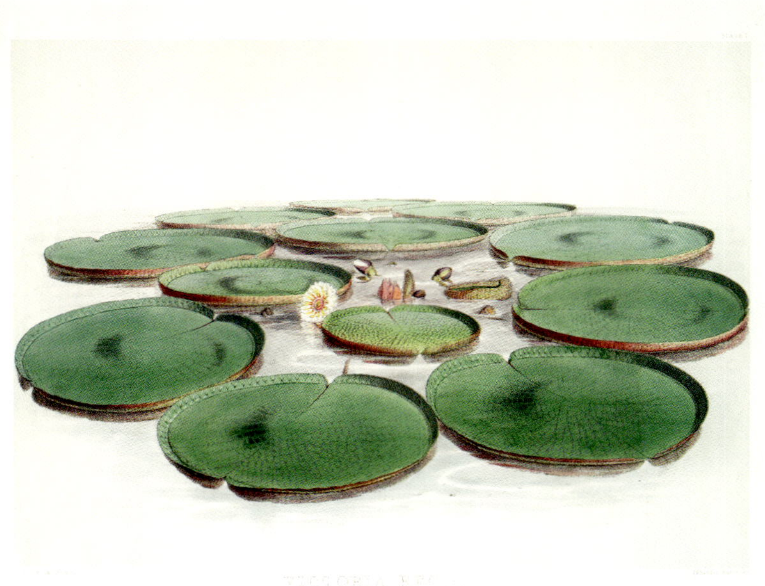


152  *Illustrations of the
Royal Water Lily from
Victoria Regia* 1851
Walter Hood Fitch
(1817–92)
Lithograph

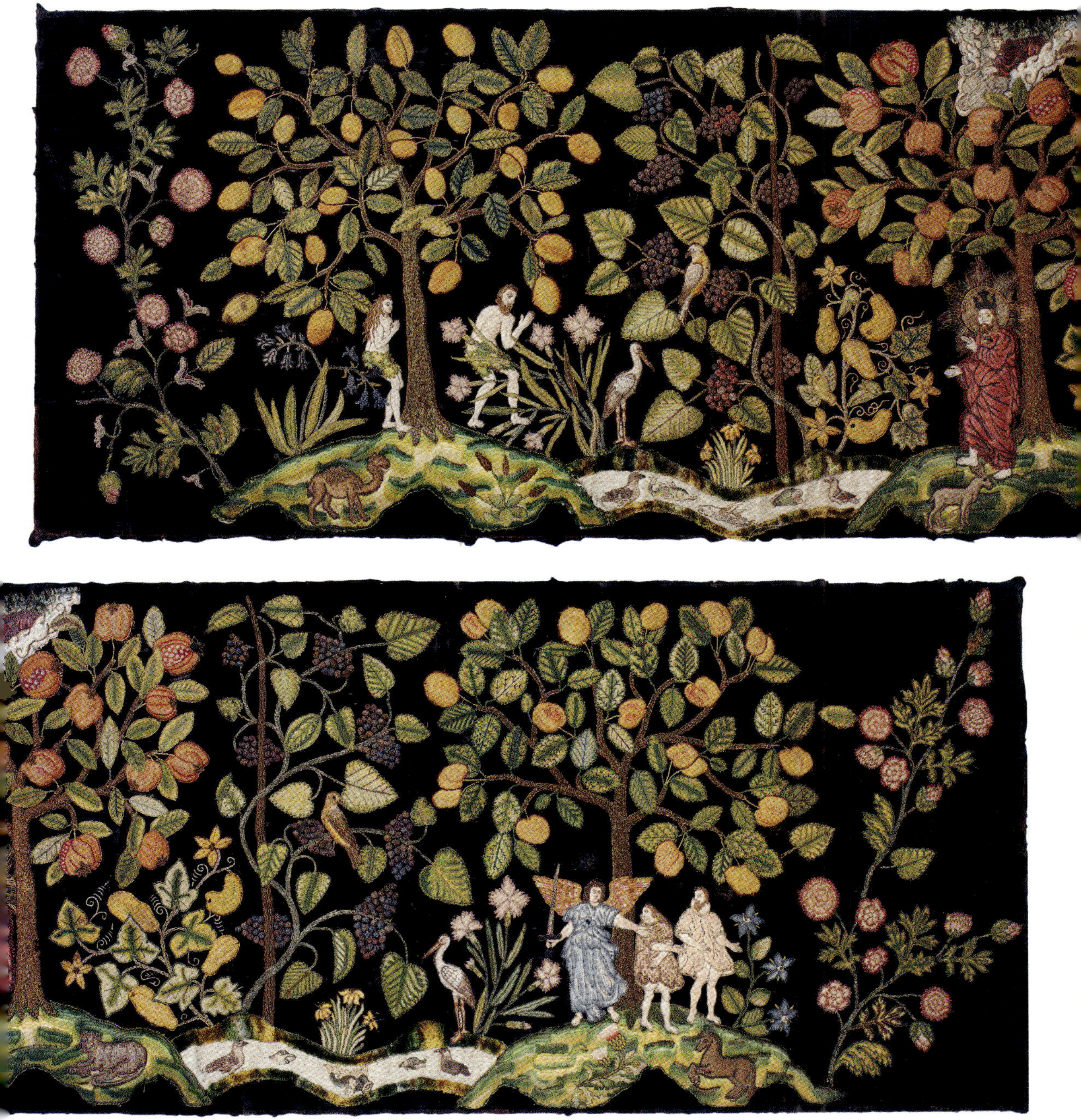

**153**  *The Garden of Eden*  Last quarter 16th century
Artist unknown  Tapestry panels

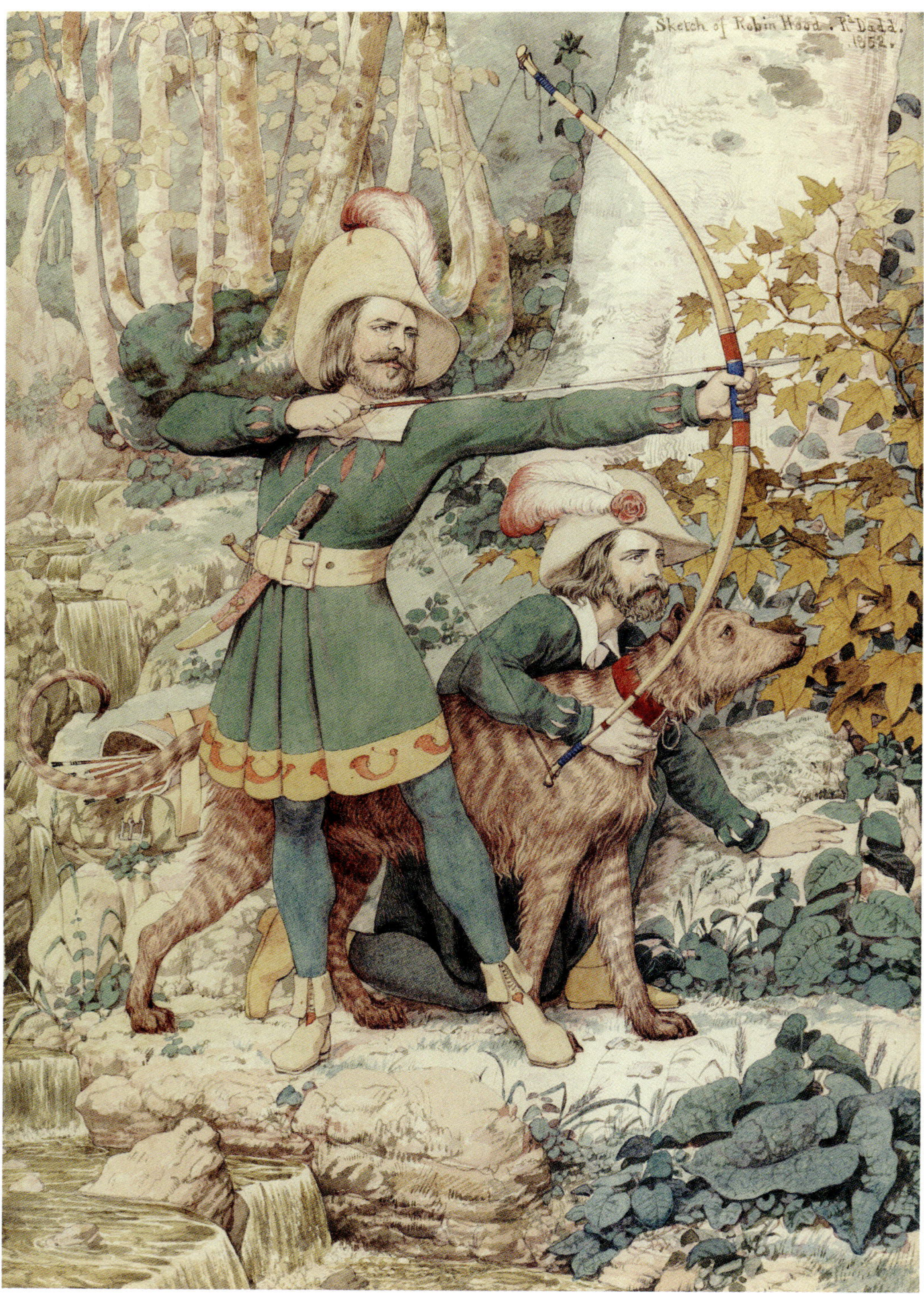

Sketch of Robin Hood . R. Dadd.
1852.

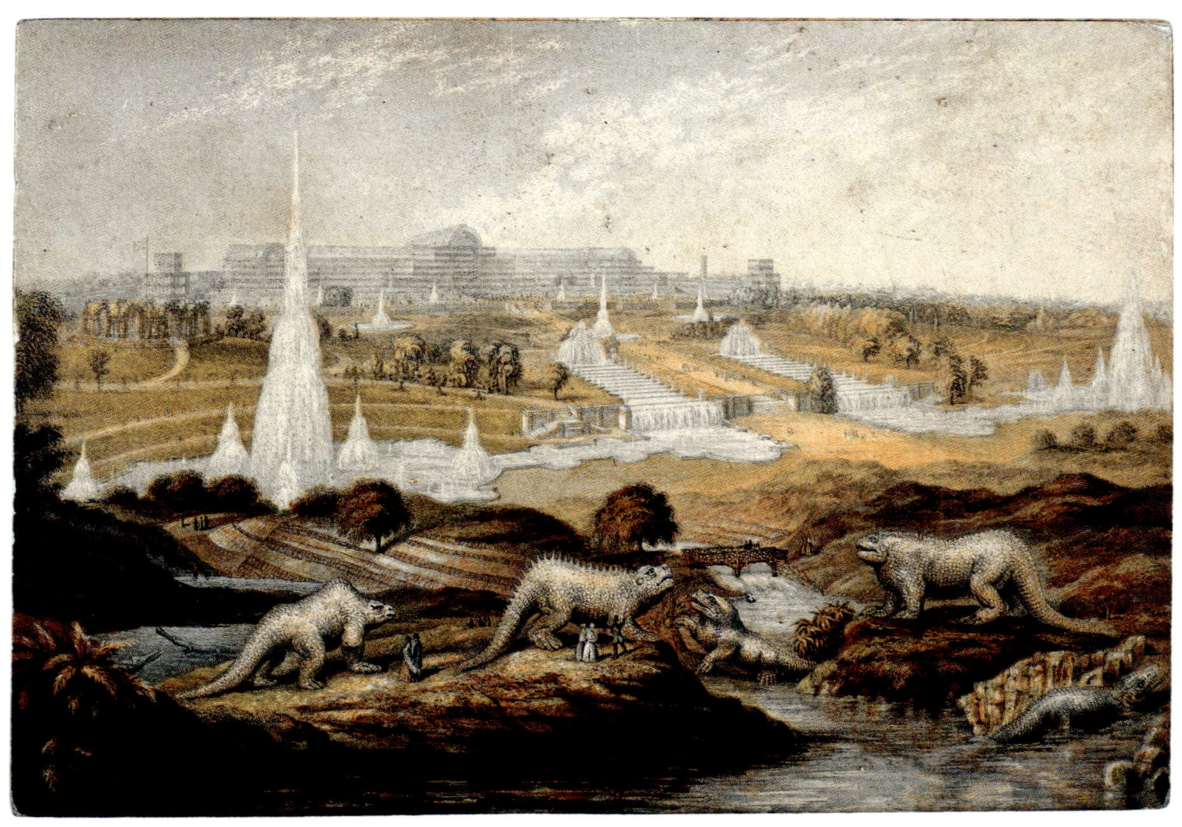

**154** *The Crystal Palace from the Great Exhibition, installed at Sydenham: sculptures of prehistoric creatures in the foreground*  c.1864
George Baxter (1814–67)
Colour Baxter-process print

In the 1850s, Benjamin Waterhouse Hawkins created over thirty sculptures of prehistoric animals to be placed in a landscape designed by Joseph Paxton at the Crystal Palace. These included creatures discovered by Mary Anning in Lyme Regis and animals such as the South American *Megatherium* (giant ground sloth), remains of which were brought to England by Charles Darwin on HMS *Beagle*. The statues are the first known attempt to construct three-dimensional, full-scale models of such creatures.

**155** *Sketch of Robin Hood*  1852
Richard Dadd (1817–86)
Watercolour and graphite on paper

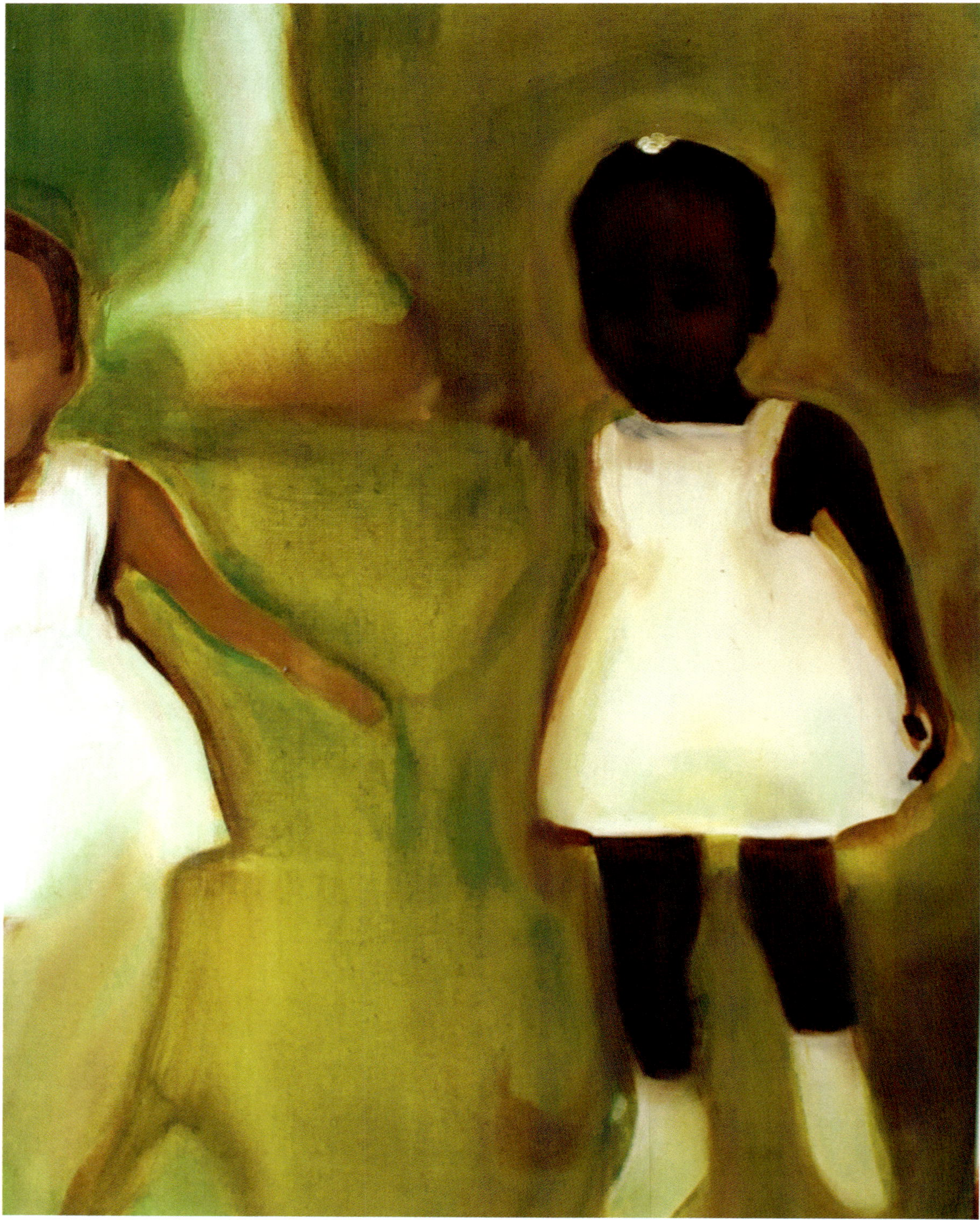

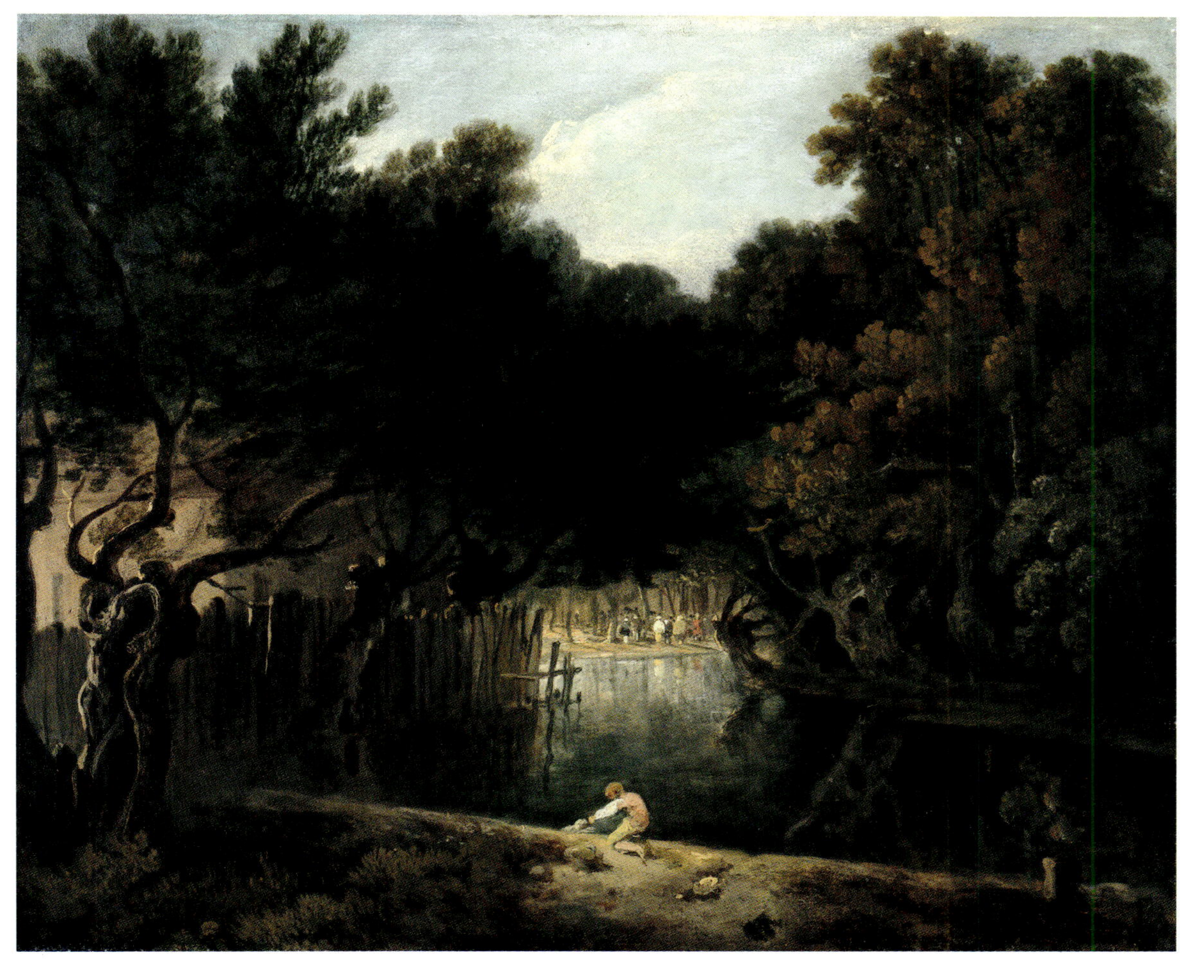

**156**  *View of the Wilderness in St James's Park*  1770–75
Richard Wilson RA (1714–82)
Oil on canvas

**157**  *In the Woods*  2021
Sikhela Owen (b.1984)
Oil on canvas

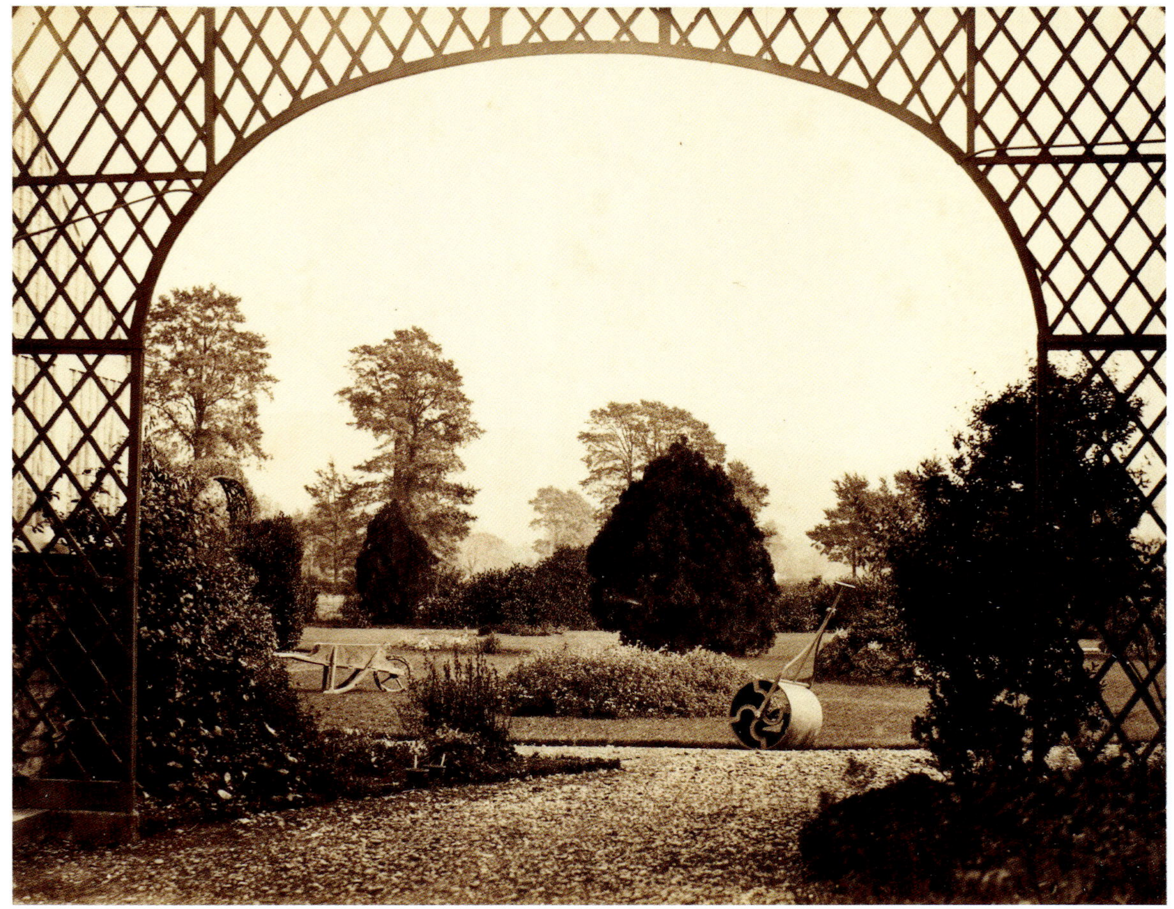

**158**  *The Hyde, Cheltenham*  1853–6
James Knight (active 1850s and 1860s)
Albumen silver print

**159**  *Spread Eagle from* The Trevelyon *Miscellany*  1608
Thomas Trevelyon (b. *c.*1548)
Engraving

Thomas Trevelyon's 1608 miscellany draws on over thirty sources, including the Bible, emblem books, almanacs and broadsides, and features various proverbs, embroidery patterns, calendars and a seventy-page chart of the early rulers of Britain, beginning with Brutus and ending with Harold. Here, he portrays the spread eagle, a traditional heraldic emblem of authority.

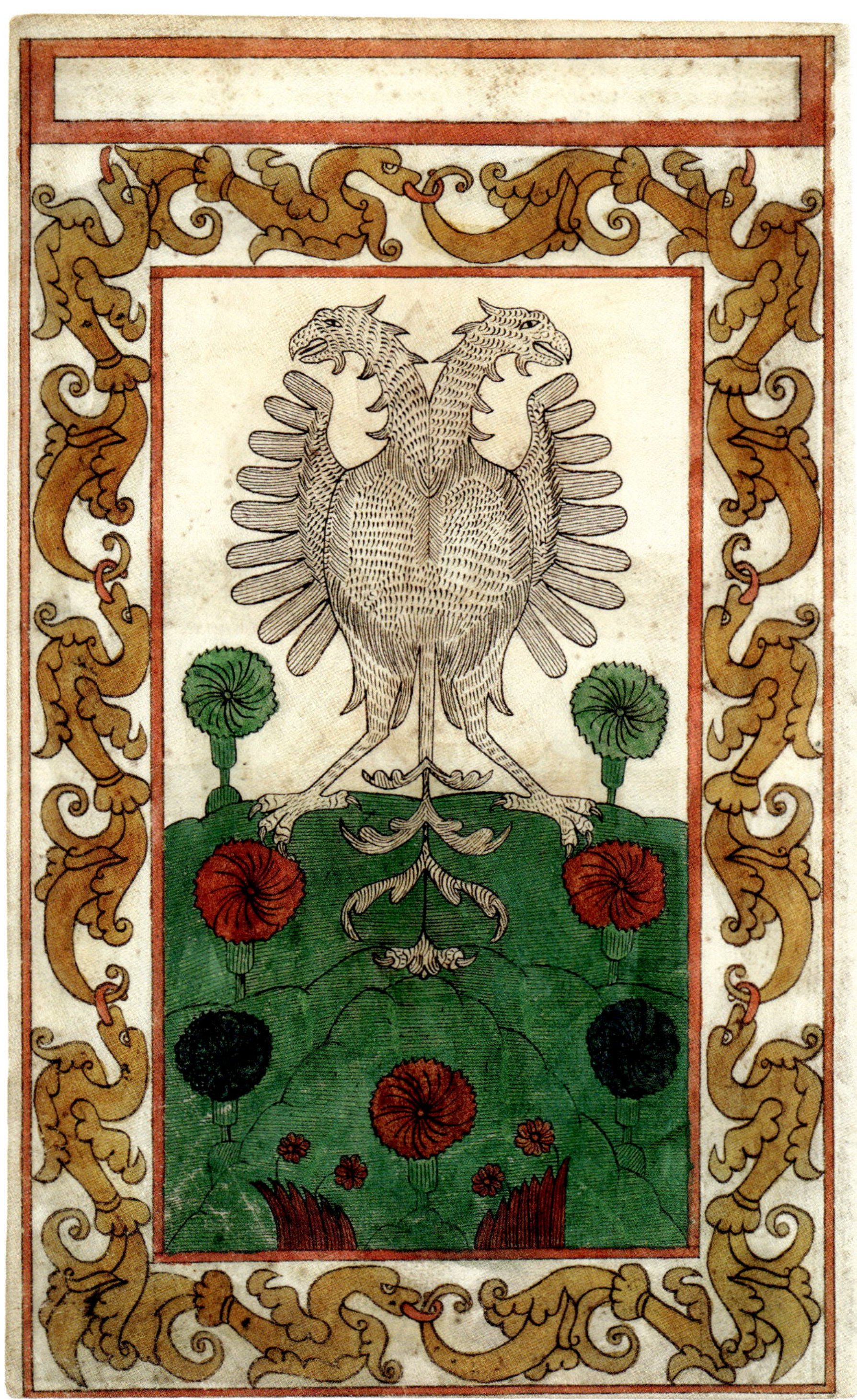

ARCADIA

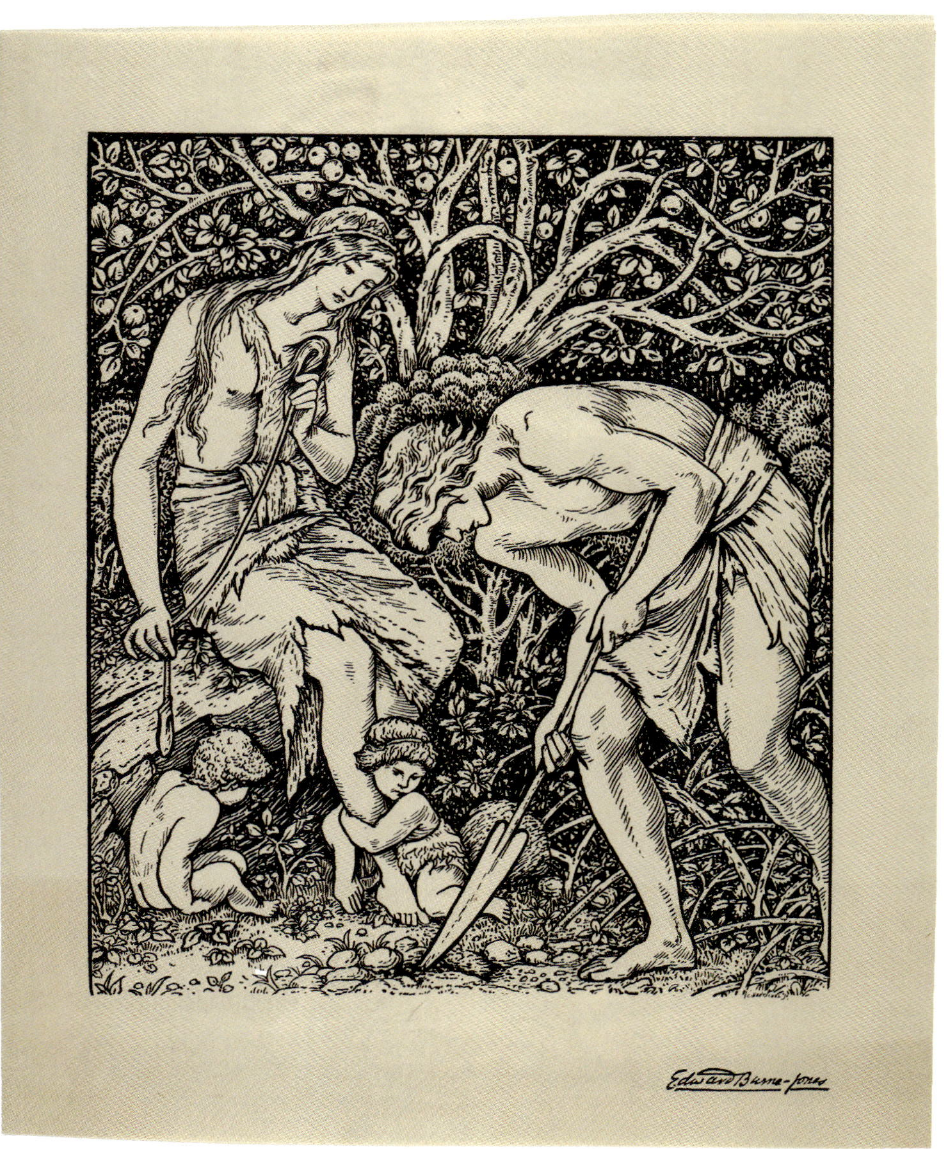

**160** *Adam and Eve (Labour: When Adam Delved and Eve Span, Who Was Then the Gentleman?)* 1895 or later
After Edward Burne-Jones (1833–98)
Process print

The subject of this woodcut comes from the famous sermon of radical priest John Ball, given to rebels on Blackheath during the Peasants' Revolt of 1381. The sermon begins with the rhyming couplet, "When Adam delved and Eve span, who was then the gentleman?" and goes on to outline the unjust bondage of men under the feudal system. Burne Jones designed this image as the frontispiece of William Morris's 1888 novel, *A Dream of John Ball*, which chronicles the fourteenth-century revolt. The image does not, however, share the same explicitly socialist message as the novel.

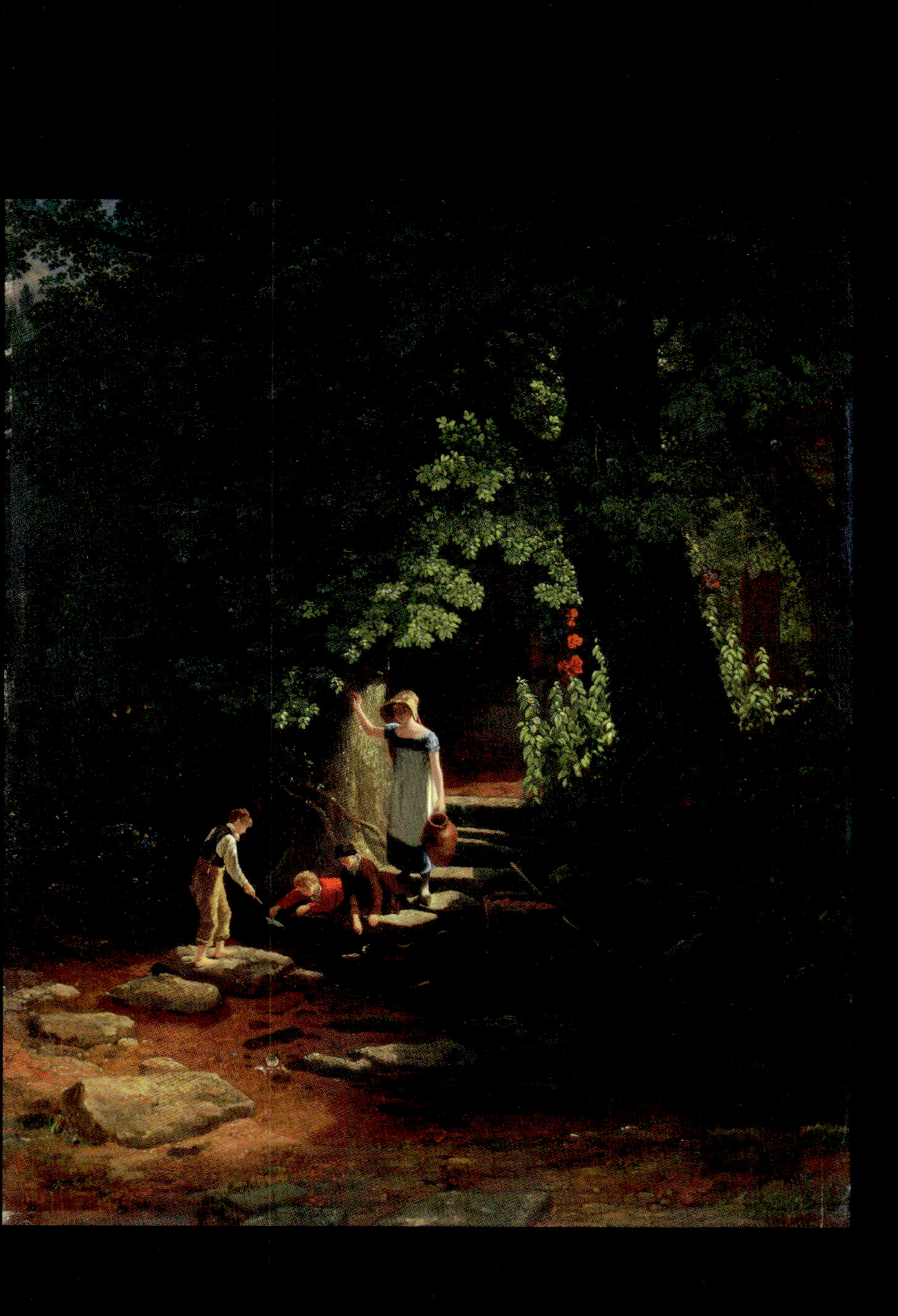

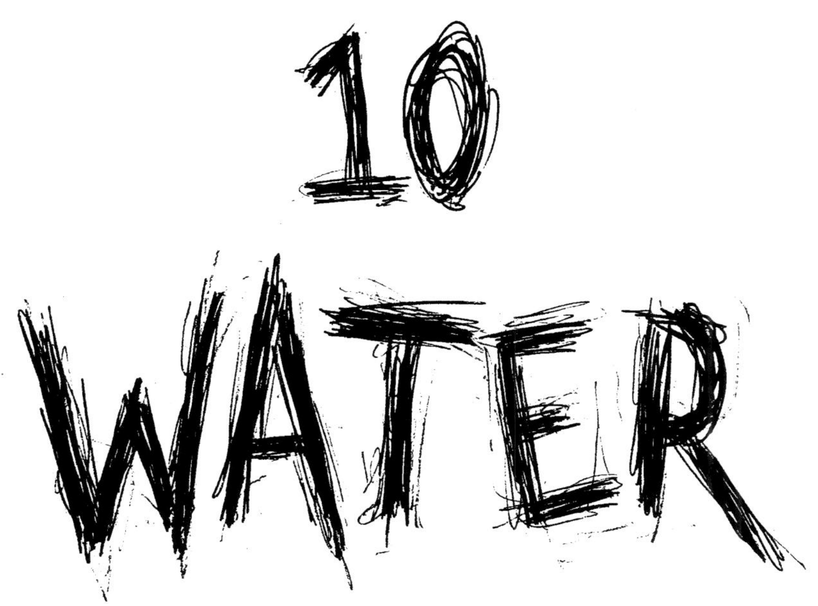
10
WATER

## ENGLAND IS A PIRATE SHIP.

We sit under the evening sun at Beachy Head, prettiest of suicide spots, and watch the country pump its boats out into the sea. Seeds on the wind. Union flags – not the skull and crossbones – flutter from the masts, but the message they send to the rest of the world is the same: lock up your valuables, the English are coming. Each ship in the armada is a floating model of the nation proper, with a captain for a king and Jack tars for the peasants. Bad food and good weapons. Rum for payment and the whip for education.

We kick our feet in the waves as the Tyburn boy builds St Pauls from the sand and laughs as the relentless waves wash it away again and again.

He says, "We're water babies, us English. Our dry land is the negative space around the real bones of Empire: the rivers and streams and brooks and burns. The lakes and ponds and puddles and gutters. All yearn for the ultimate escape – the sea. One by one, out we go, washed like flotsam into the world, carrying, hidden somewhere in our cells, the English diseases. Scurvy and envy. Single-use plastics and financial deregulation. Smallpox and big business."

He moulds the cathedral dome again, and water rushes in. "England sneezes and in Australia a million rabbits die. The London Stock Exchange coughs and a garbage dump is set on fire a thousand miles away. We export poison and what do we bring home?"

Sails reappear on the horizon. The ships lurch low in the water, weighed down with booze-cruise beer and unbranded cigarettes. England breathes in and draws them back, back through the ports and harbours, back up rivers, like salmon returning to spawn. Upstream, uphill, through streams that turn to rivulets that turn to springs. Everything dissolving until all the world is contained in one drop of water, ready to fall as rain some other day.

England is a pirate ship and it's taking on water.

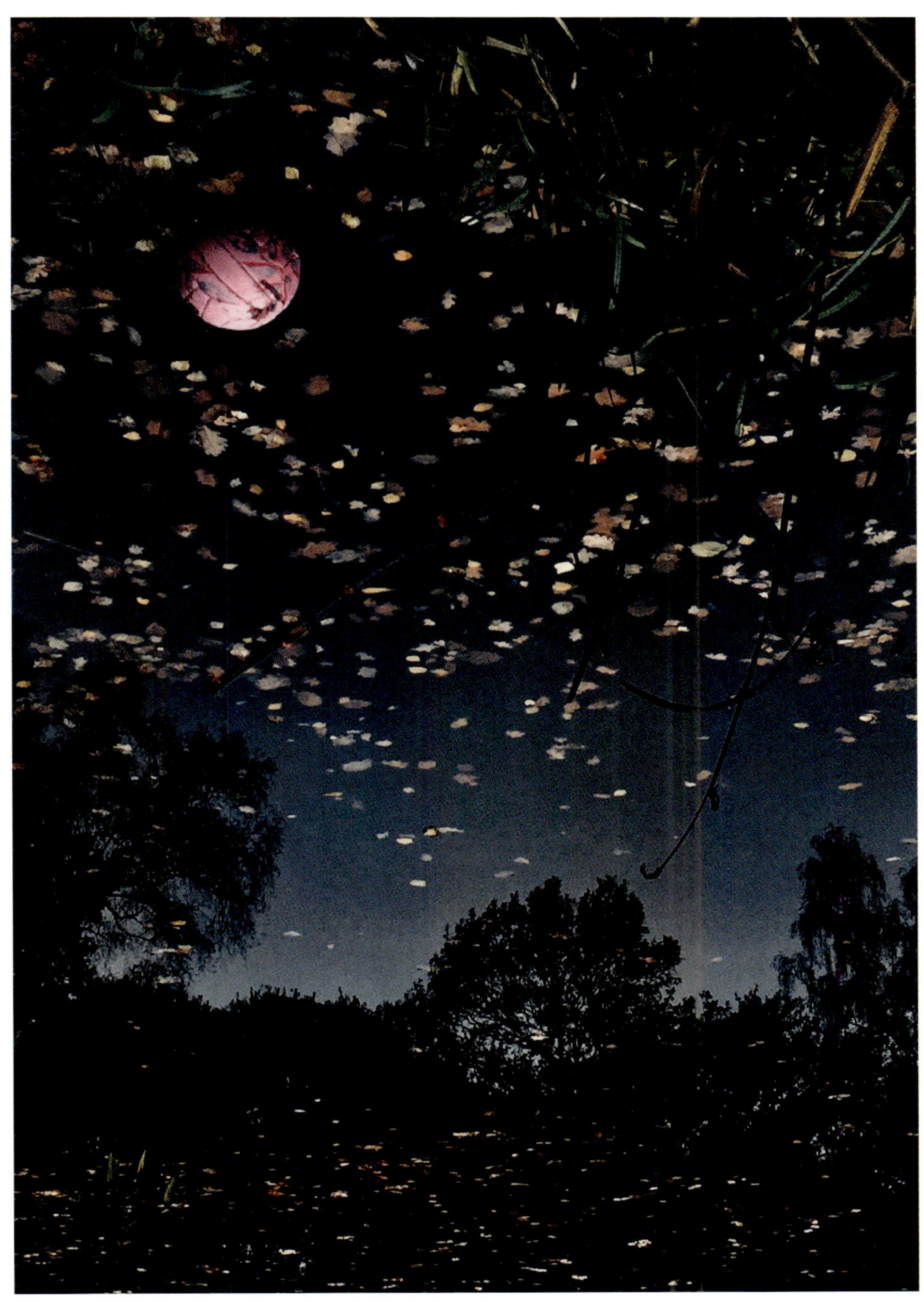

**162**  *Pink Full Moon (Hampstead Heath)*  2019
Sayako Sugawara (b.1972)  Colour photograph

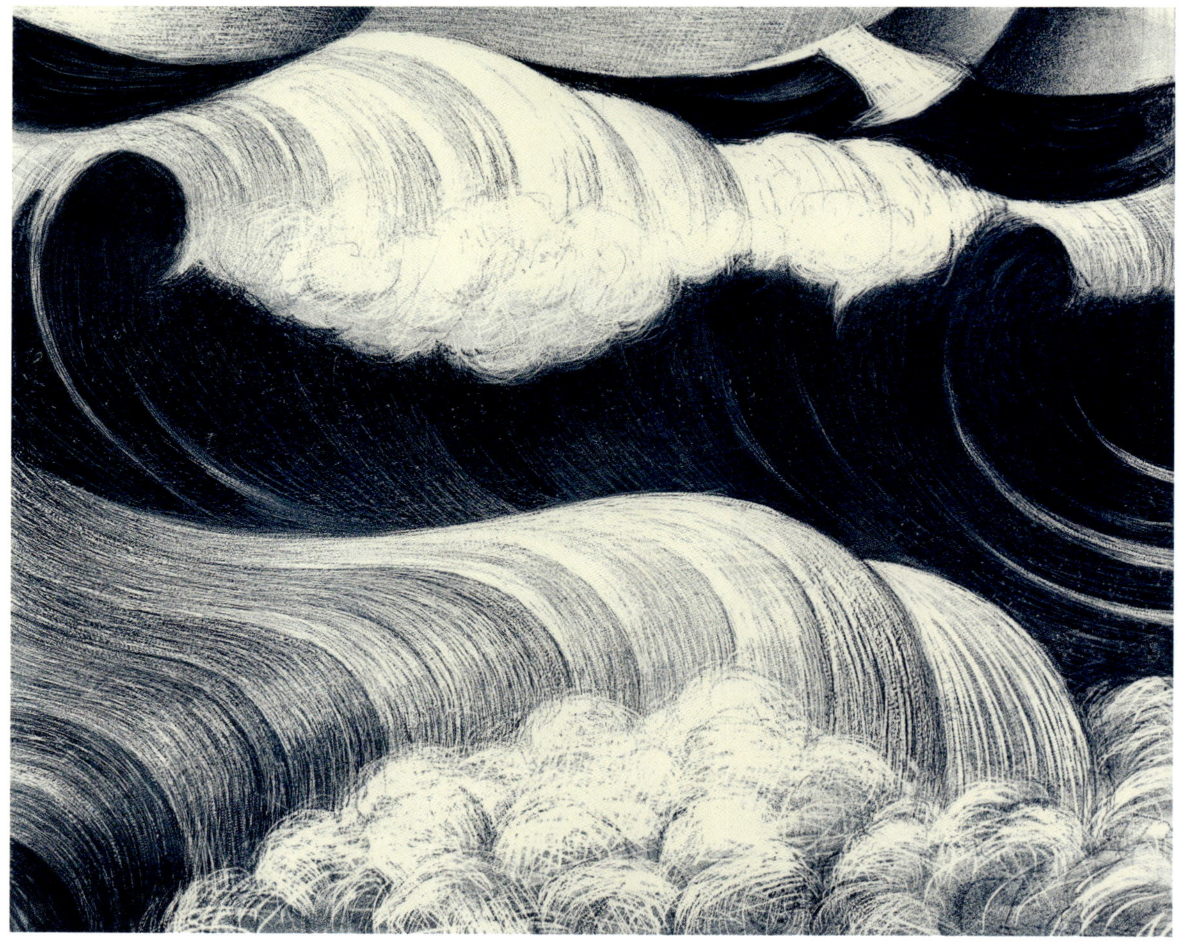

**163** *The Wave* 1917
C.R.W. Nevinson (1889–1946)
Lithograph on paper

**164** *Nelson's Ship in a Bottle* 2010
Yinka Shonibare (b.1962)
Installation

In this work, a replica of HMS *Victoria* created for Trafalgar Square's Fourth Plinth, Shonibare explores the implications of empire, tradition and cultural appropriation. The sea is viewed both as a site of journey and of violence, with colonial associations embedded in Shonibare's decoration of the ship's sails with a pattern that resembles Indonesian batik. This wax-resist dyed cloth, once mass-produced by Dutch traders and sold in West Africa, has become synonymous with African dress and identity.

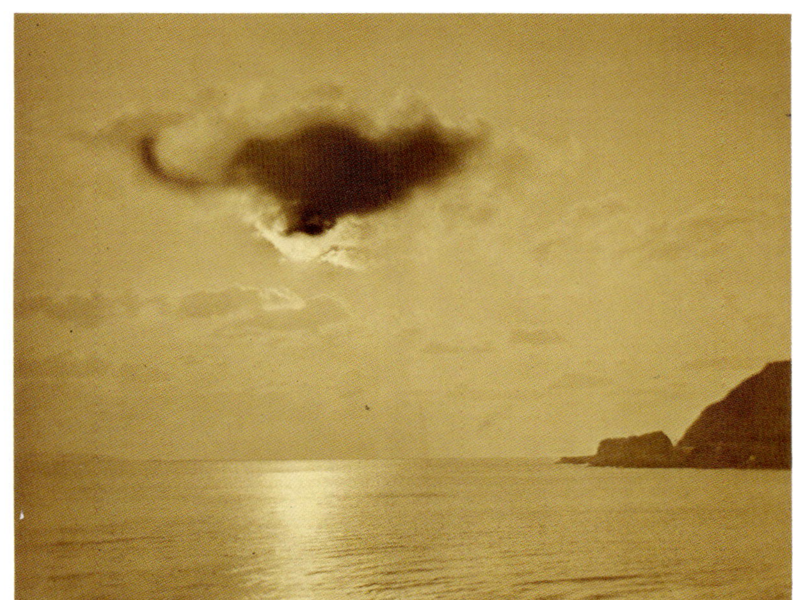

165  *The Midnight Moon
is Weaving her Bright
Chain o'er the Deep*  c.1863
Colonel Henry Stuart
Wortley (1832–90)
Albumen silver print

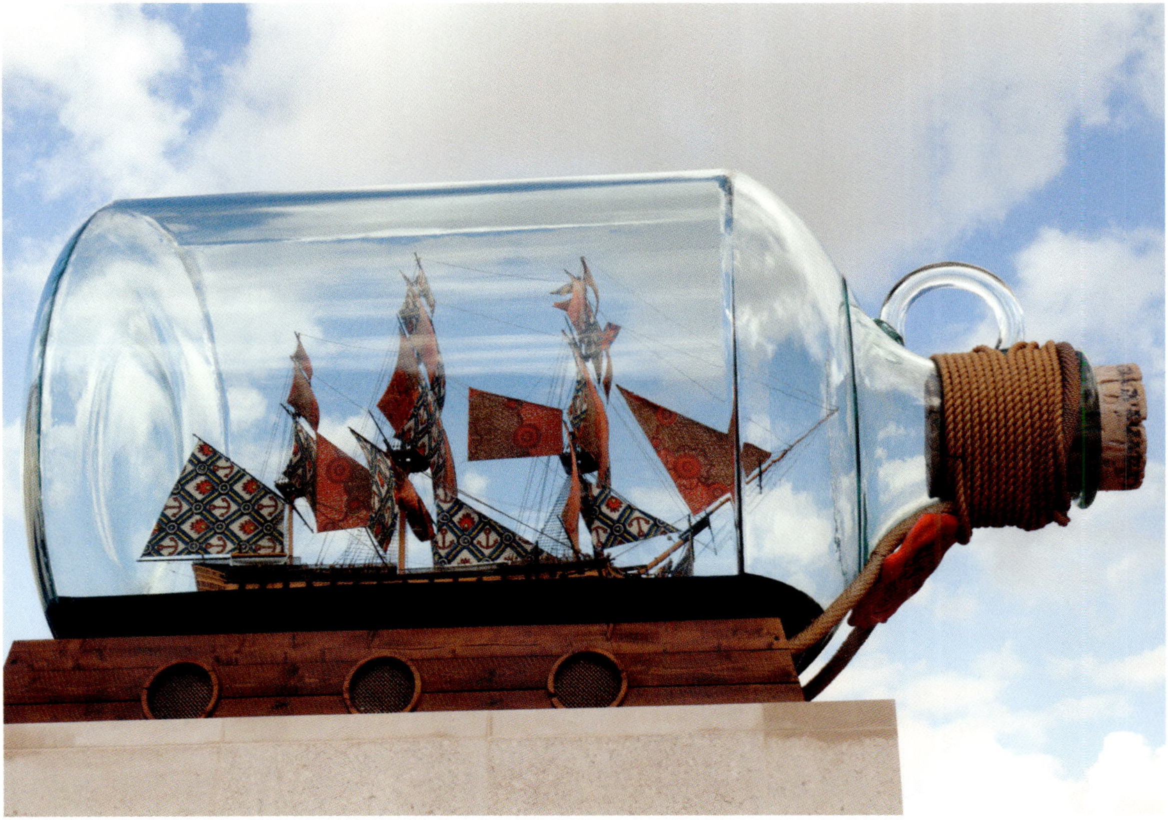

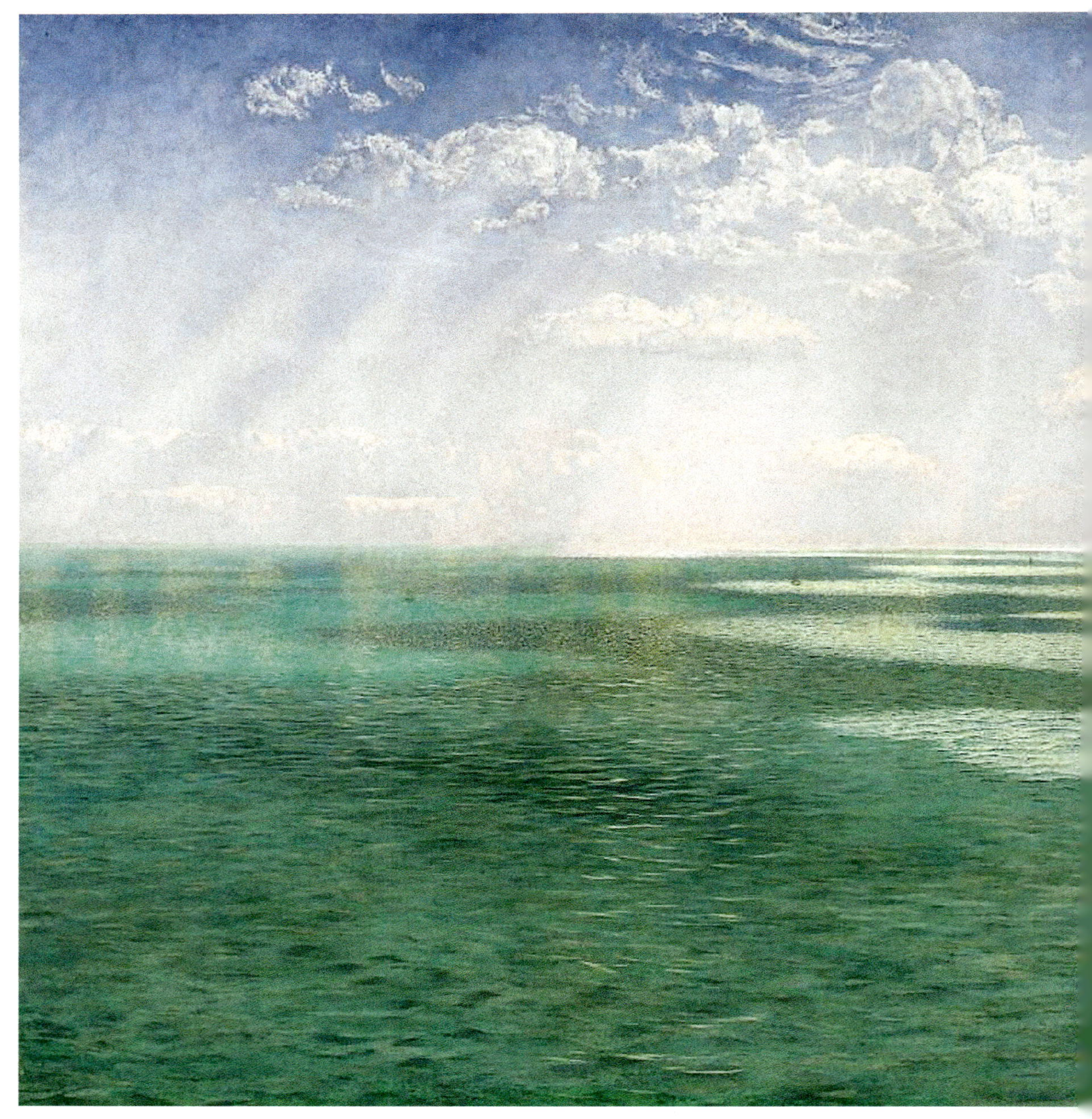

166  *The English Channel seen from the Dorsetshire Cliffs*  1871
John Brett (1831–1902)
Oil on canvas

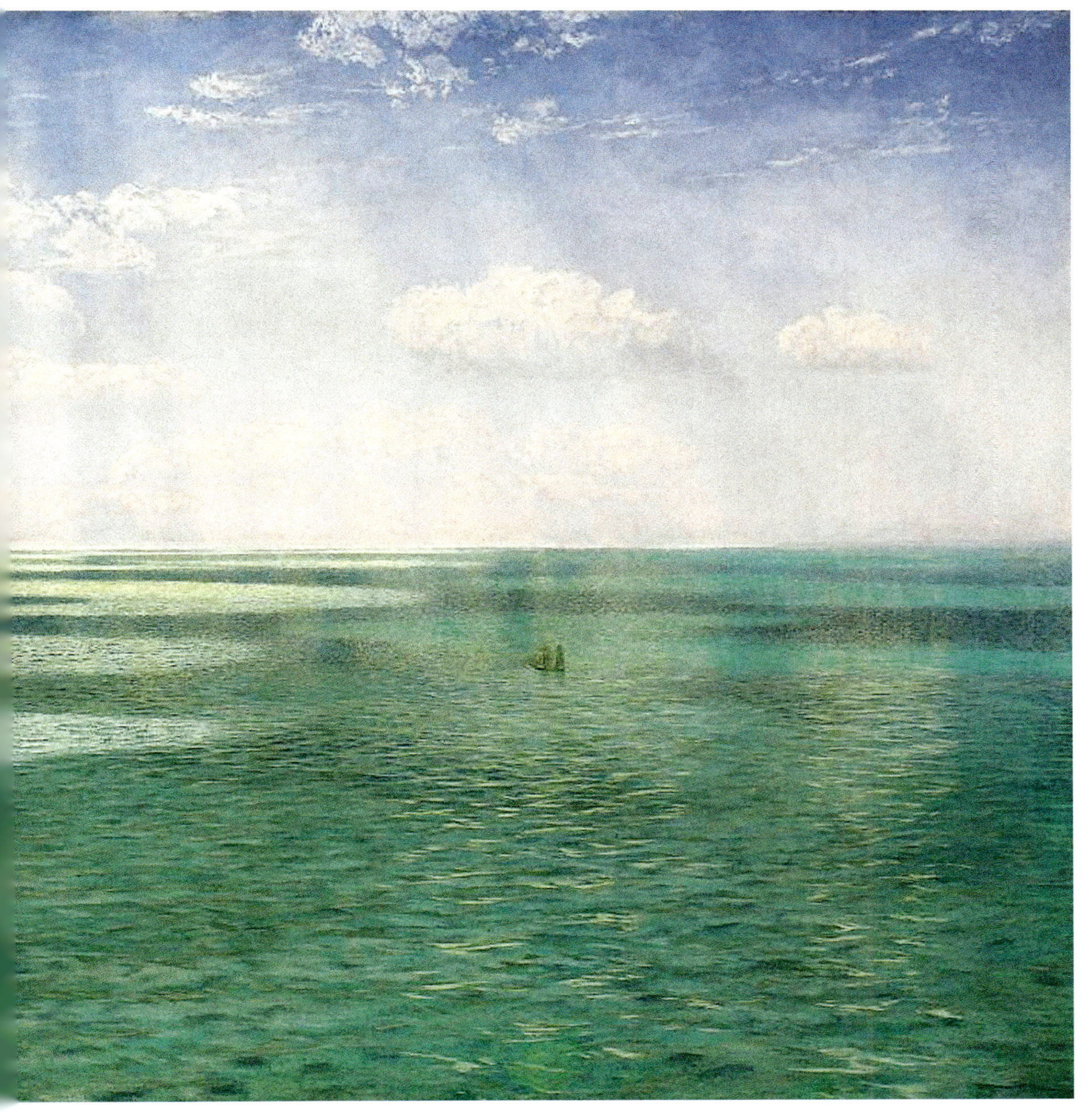

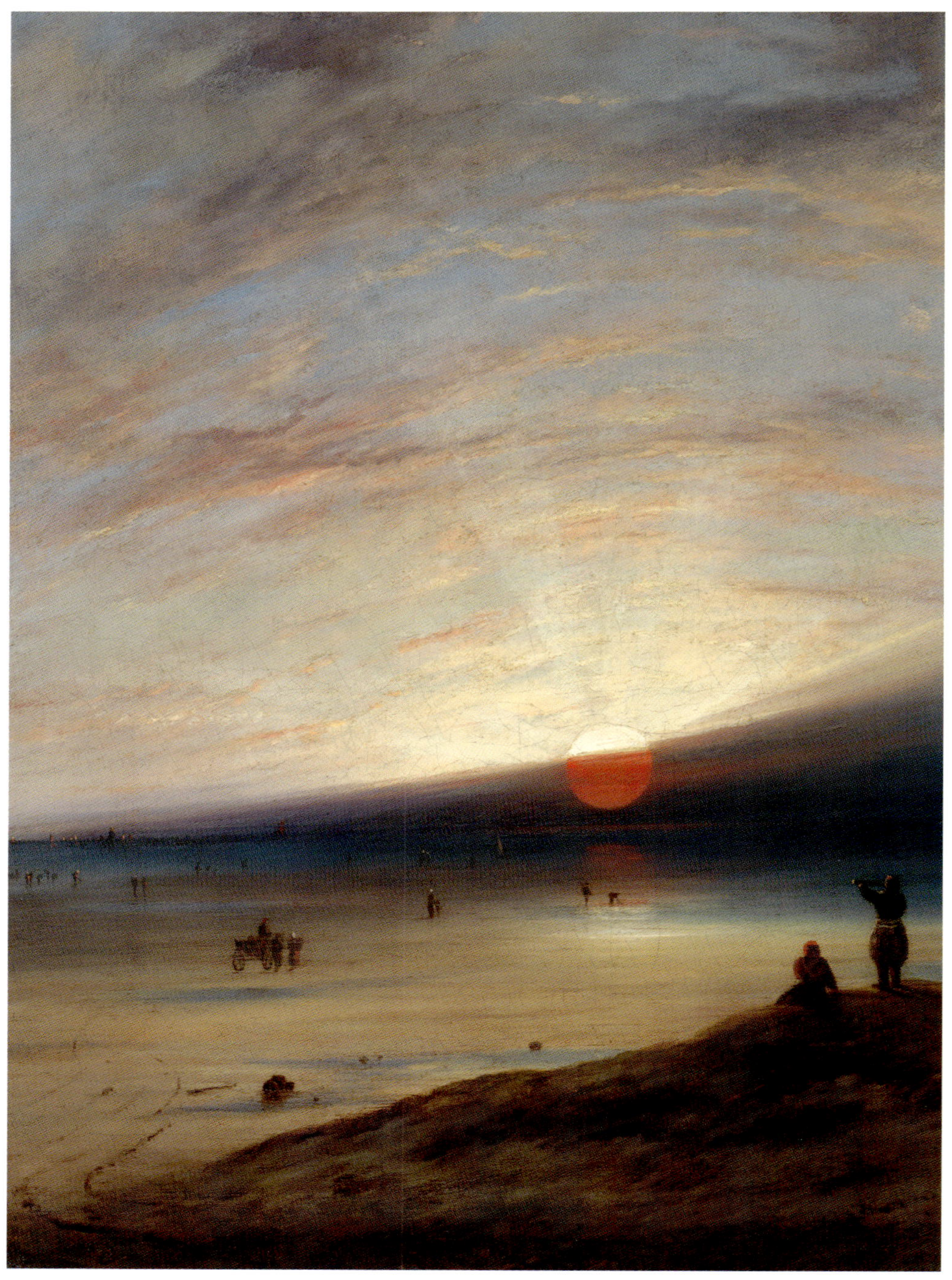

**167**  *Sunset on the Beach at Sark*  c.1850
Artist unknown  Oil on canvas

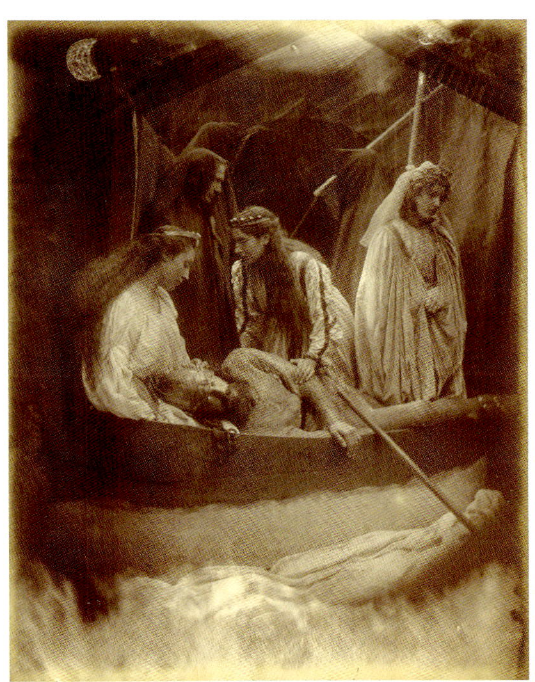

**168**  *So like a shatter'd column lay the King*  1875
Julia Margaret Cameron (1815–79)
Albumen silver print

The title and subject of this photograph come from Alfred Tennyson's *Idylls of the King*, a series of narrative poems based on Arthurian legends which Cameron was asked to illustrate, through photography, by the author himself. This scene depicts the passing of the king, as he is carried by boat from Camelot. A moon, drawn onto the negative by Cameron, shines upon the scene, creating a sense of wistfulness that corresponds to her trademark soft-focus technique.

**169**  *Whitby Harbour*  1879
John Atkinson Grimshaw (1836–93)
Oil on board

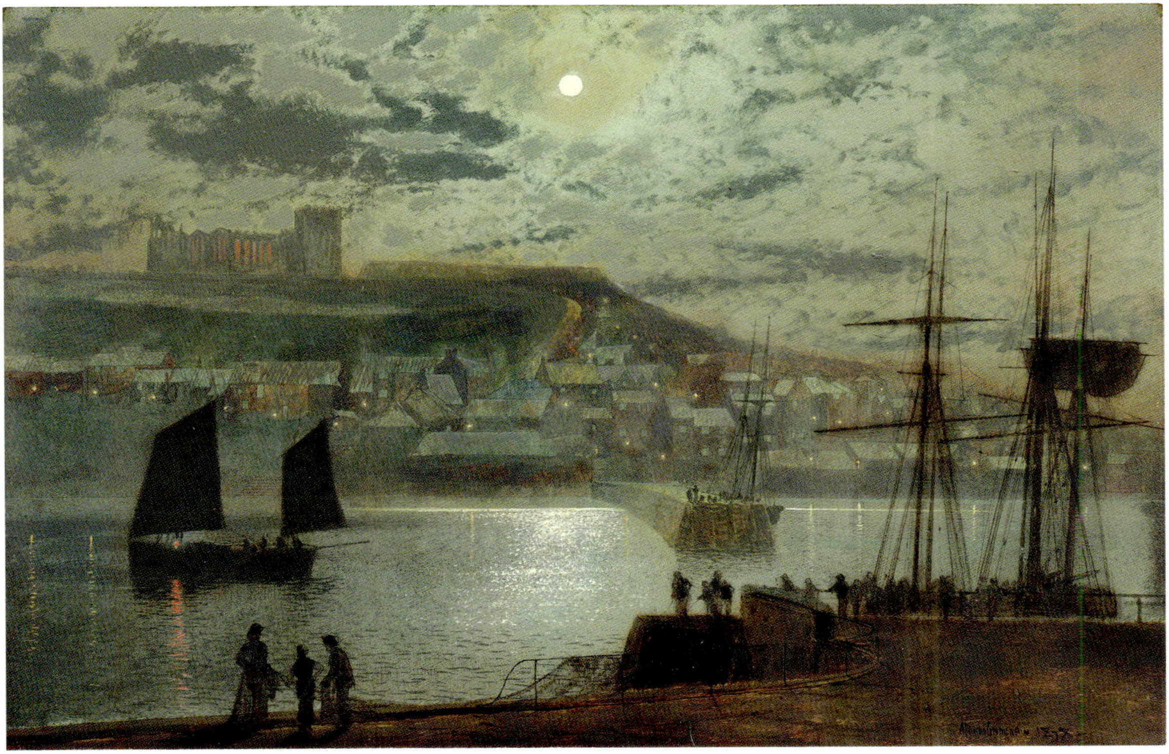

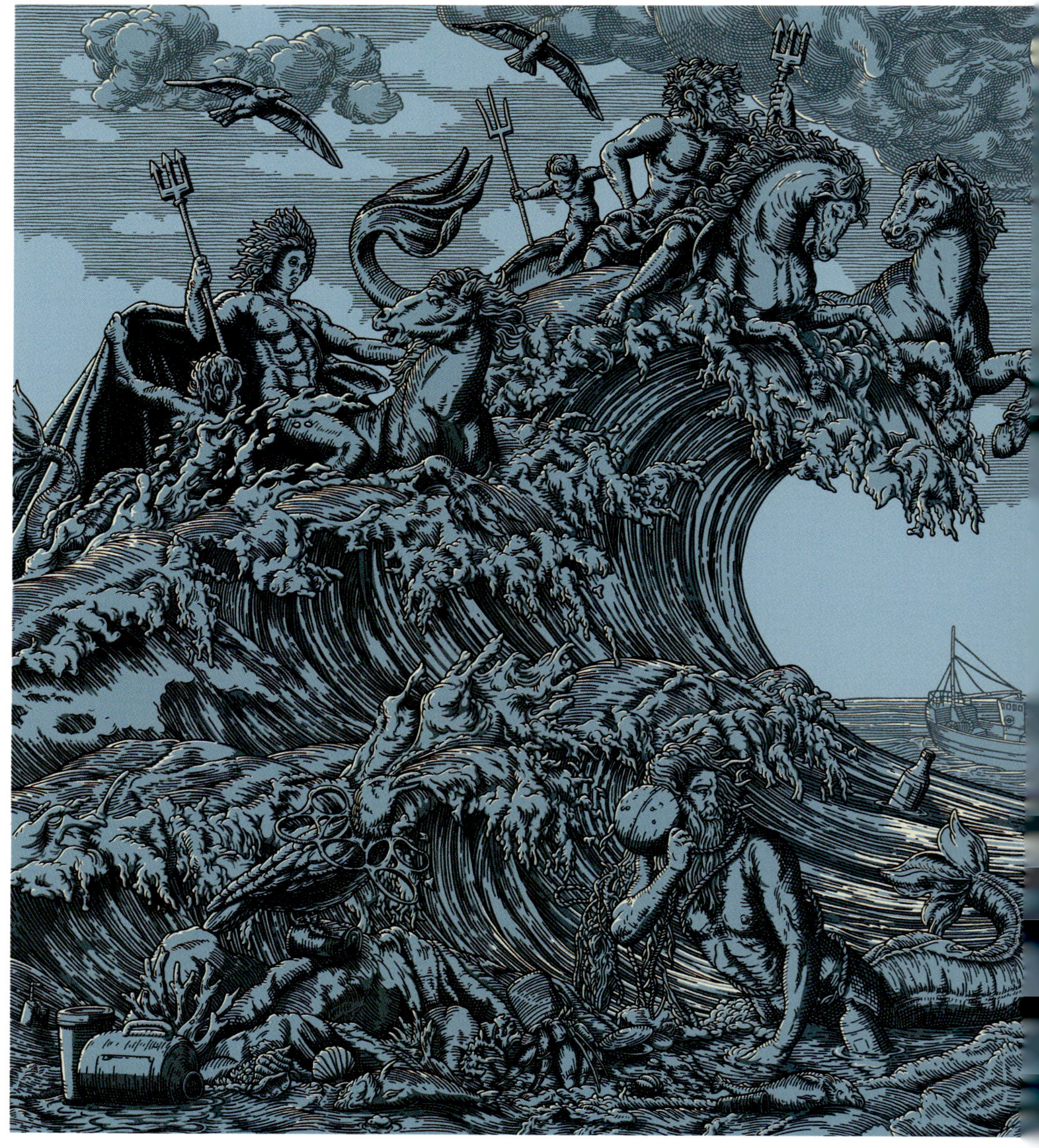

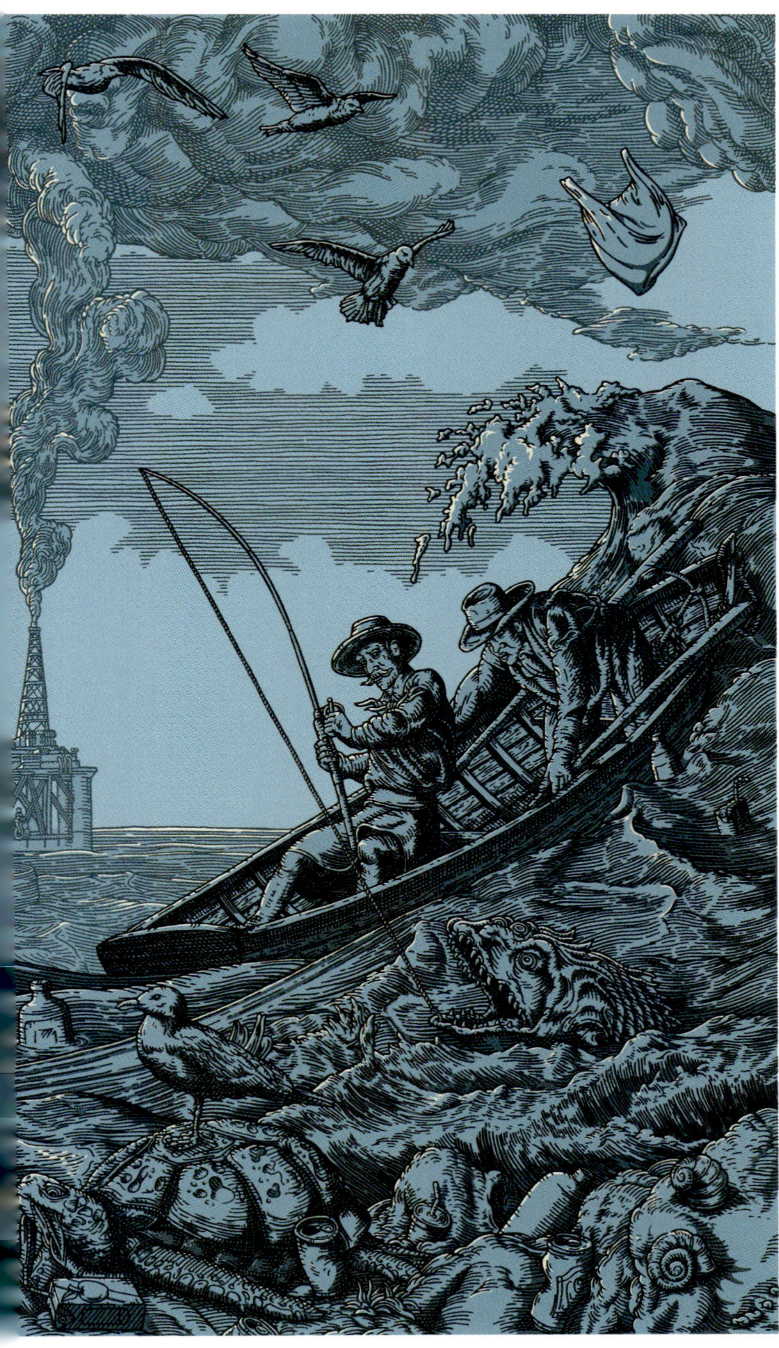

170  *Eye of the Storm*  2020
Daniel Hosego (b.1983)
Screenprint on perspex

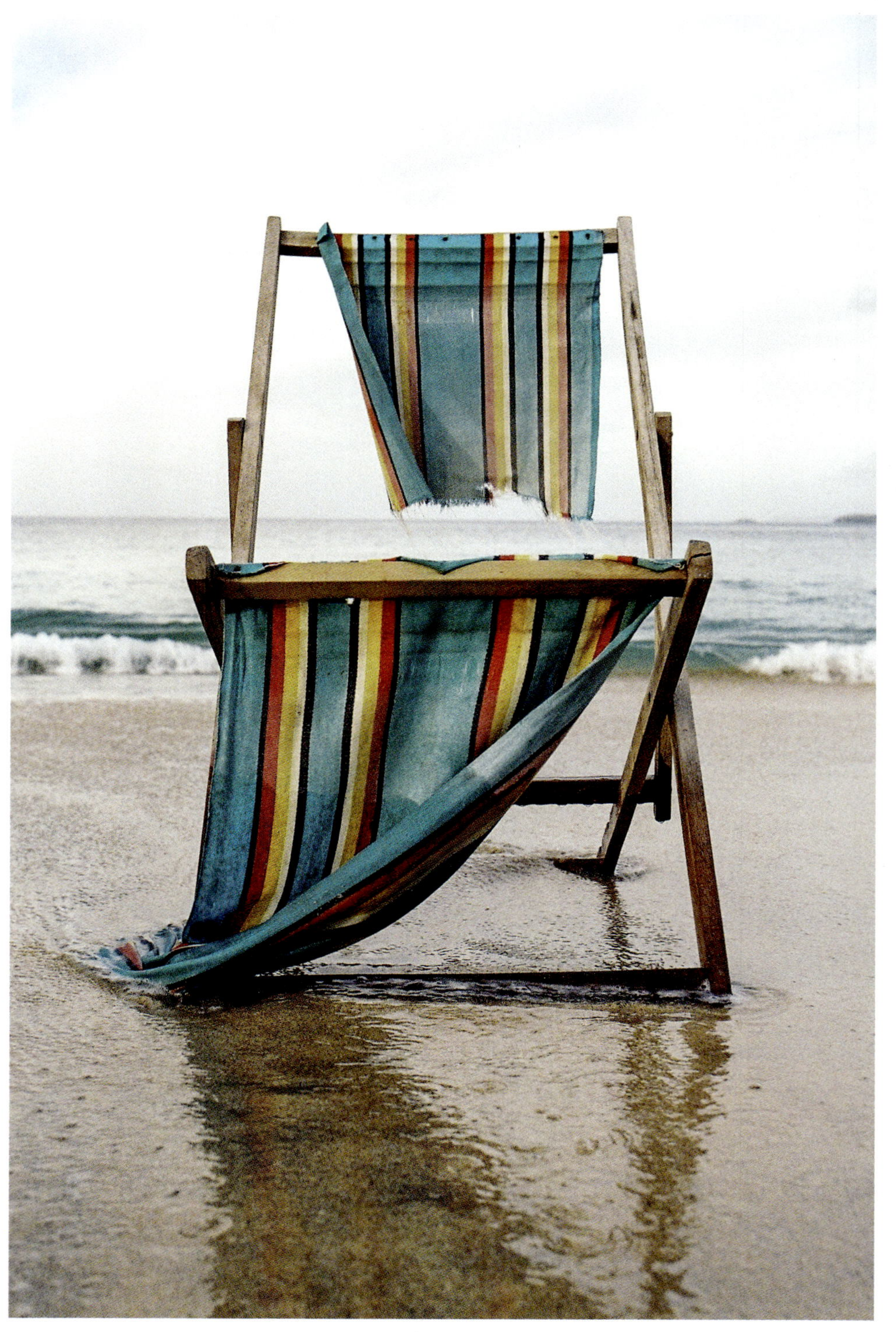

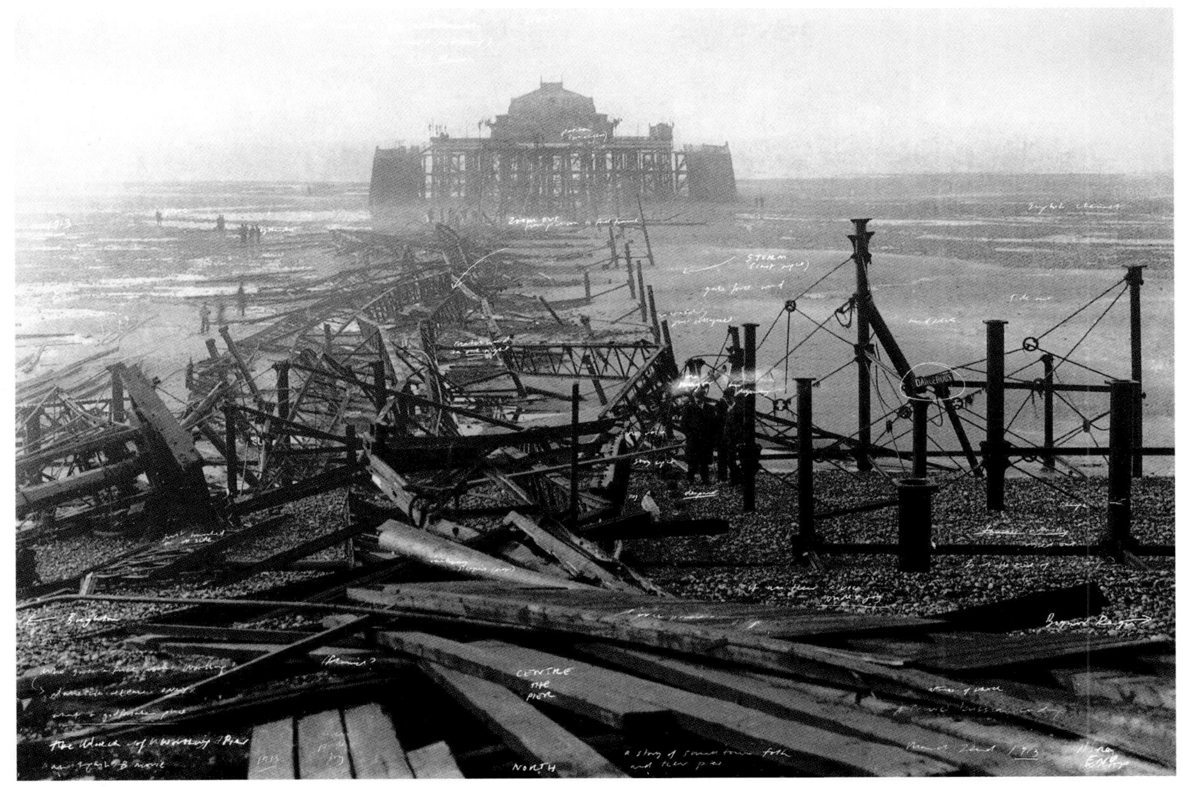

**171**  *The Wreck of Worthing Pier*
2001
From *The Russian Ending* series
Tacita Dean (b.1965)
Photo etchings on paper

This work comes from a series of twelve prints entitled *The Russian Ending*, in which Dean etches handwritten notes onto collected postcards in the style of film directions. The concept and title of the series is taken from an early Danish film technique, which involved the making of two versions of a film, one for an American audience with a happy ending, and another, far more tragic, for Russian audiences. Most of her chosen postcards depict moments of ruin; here, she uses an image which was taken following the 1913 storm that destroyed Worthing Pier. Her notes implicate the viewer in the incident, turning them into witnesses and asking them, "Is this the end of Worthing?".

**172**  *St Ives Deckchair*  2009
Jeff Pitcher (b.1967)
Kodak colour print

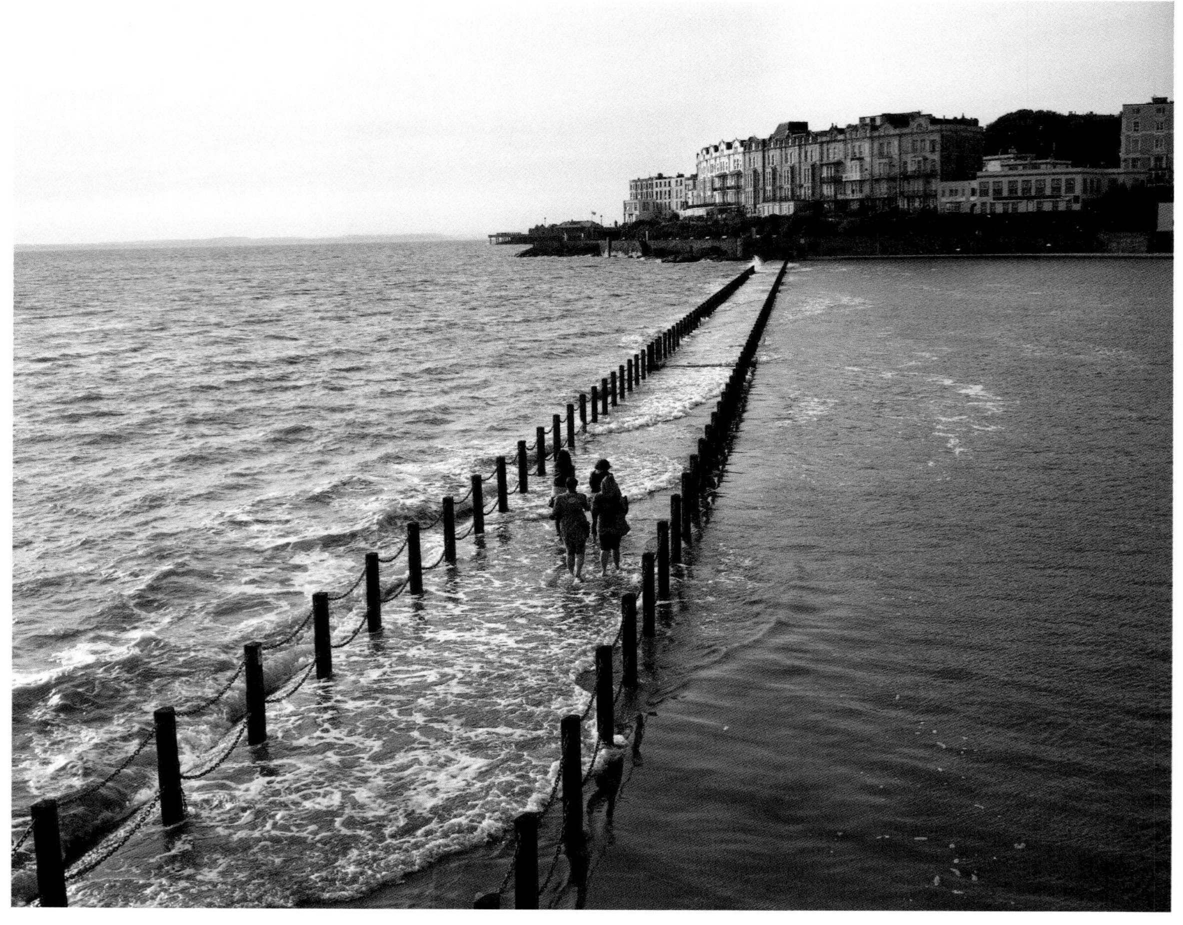

**173** *Walking on Water, Weston-Super-Mare, England* Undated
From *Tough & Tender – English Seascapes*
Sheila Rock
Photograph shot on HP5 Ilford Film on an analogue Mamiya 7 camera

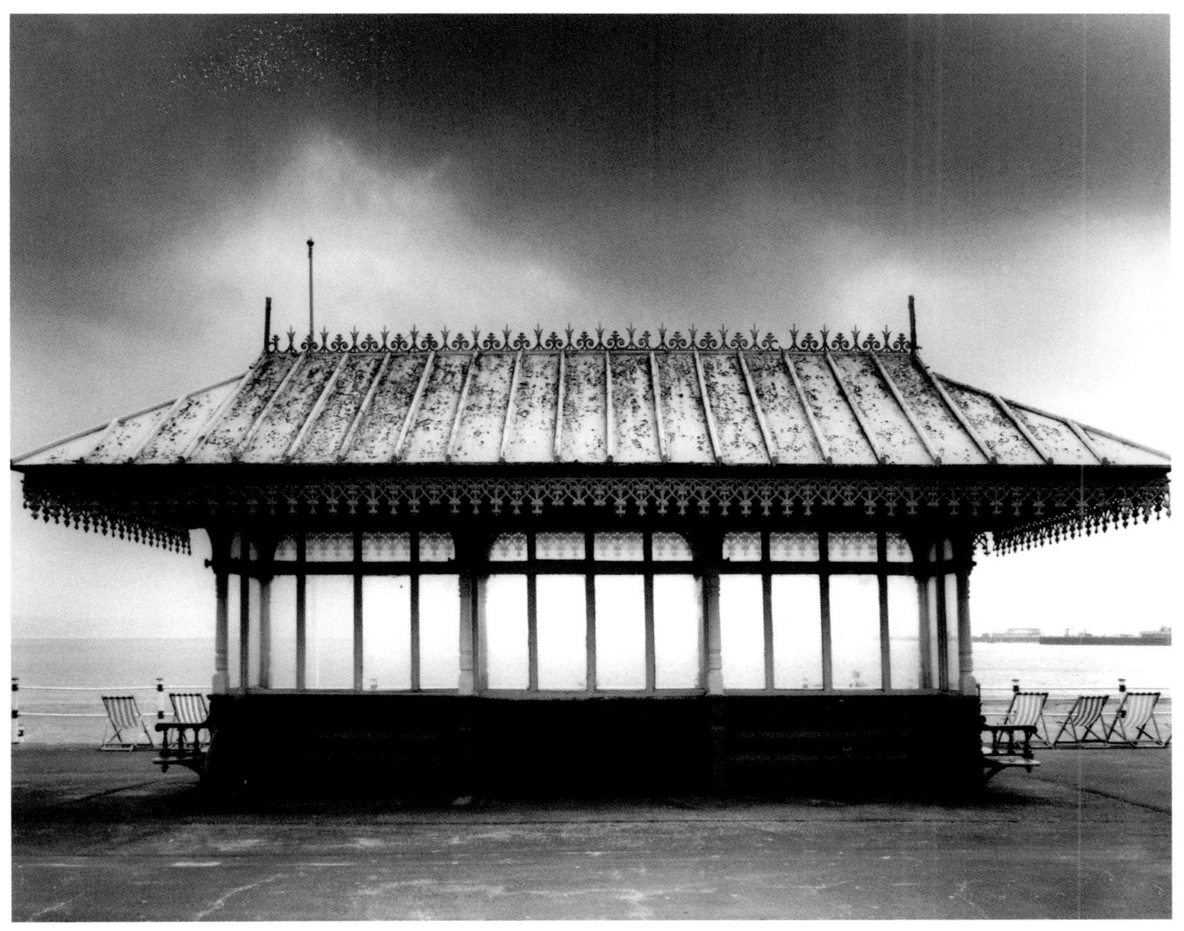

174  *Beach Shelter*  Undated
From *Tough & Tender – English Seascapes*
Sheila Rock
Photograph shot on HP5 Ilford Film on an analogue Mamiya 7 camera

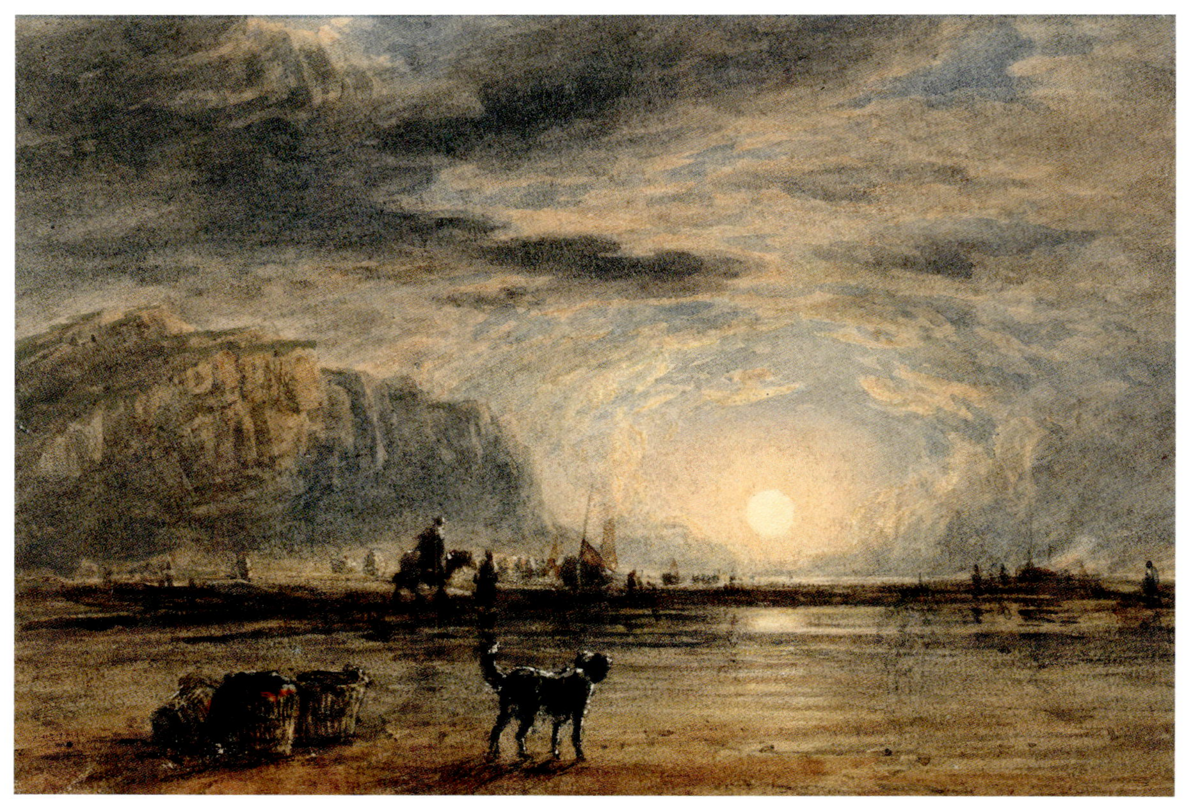

**175**  *British Beach Scene, Sunrise*  c.1820
David Cox (1783–1859)
Watercolour and graphite

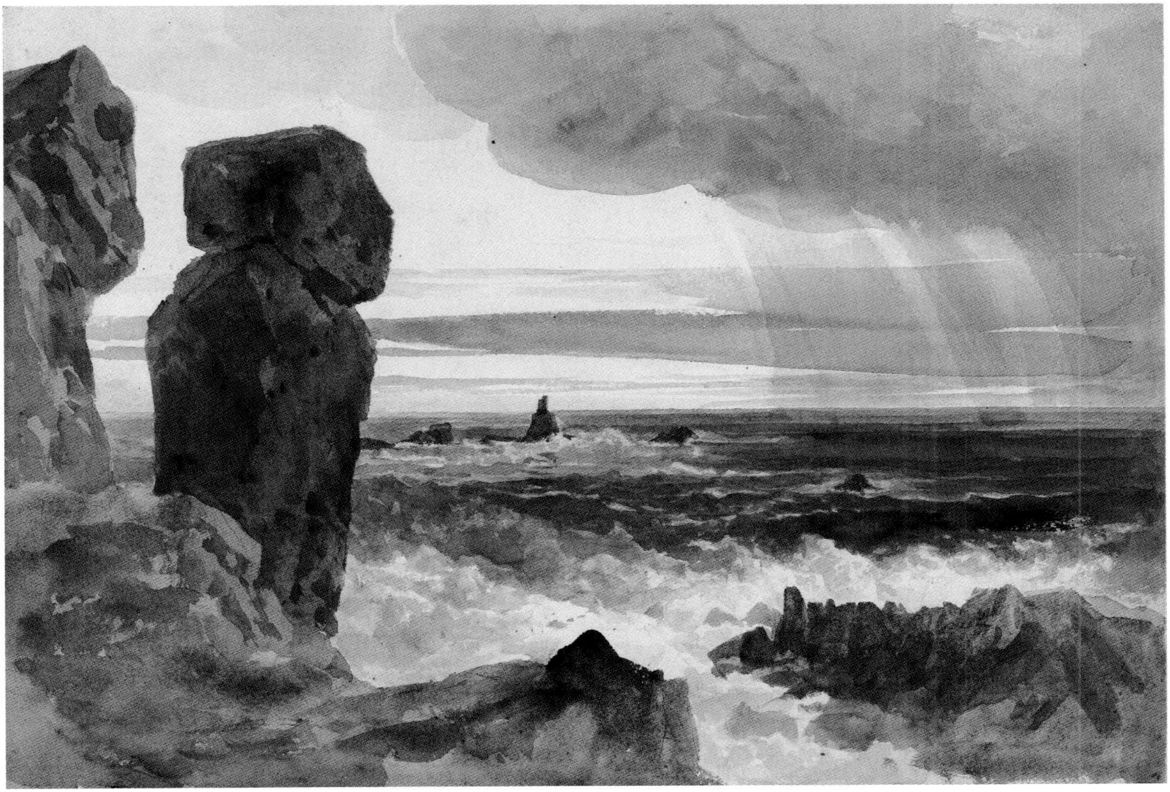

176  *British, Seascape with Rocks, Lizard, Cornwall*  Undated
Peter de Wint (1784–1849)
Watercolour over
graphite on paper

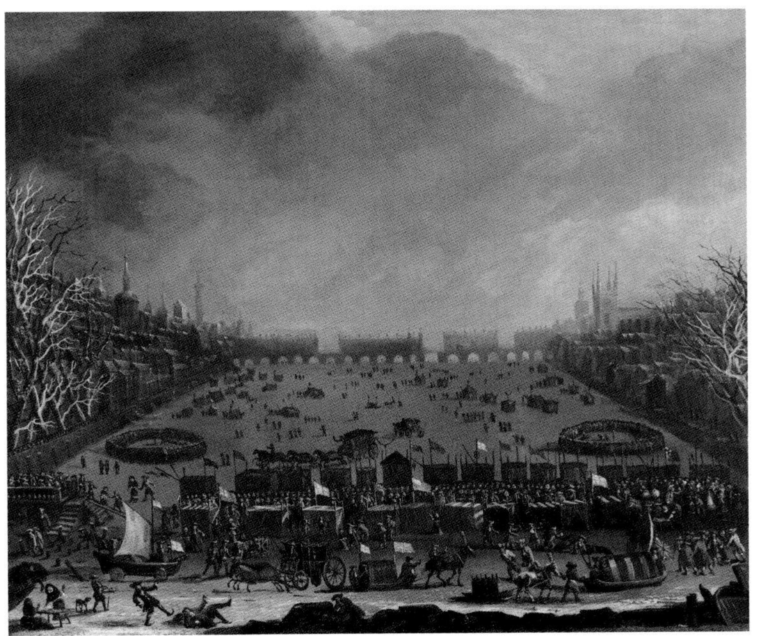

177  *Frost Fair on the Thames, with Old London Bridge in the distance*  1684
Artist unknown
Oil on canvas

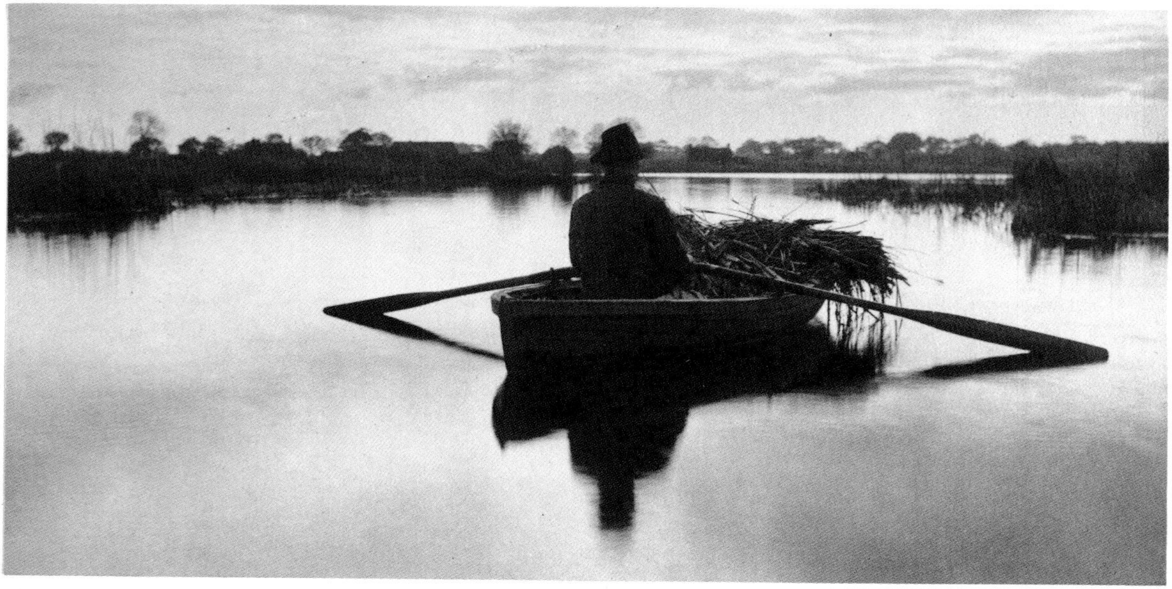

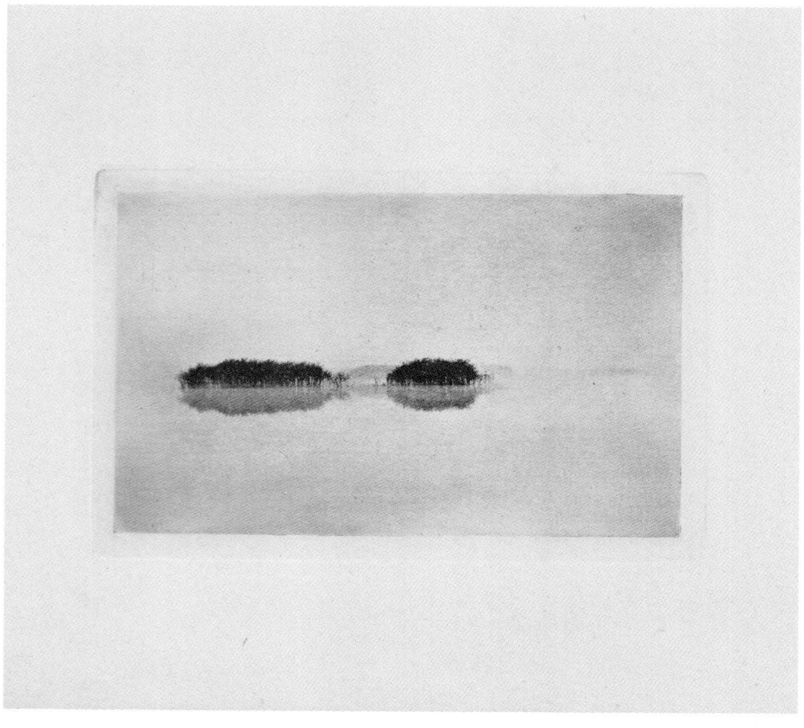

**178** *Rowing Home the Schoof-Stuff* 1886
Peter Henry Emerson
(1856–1936)
Platinum print
photograph

**179** *The Lone Lagoon* 1895
Peter Henry Emerson
(1856–1936)
Photogravure

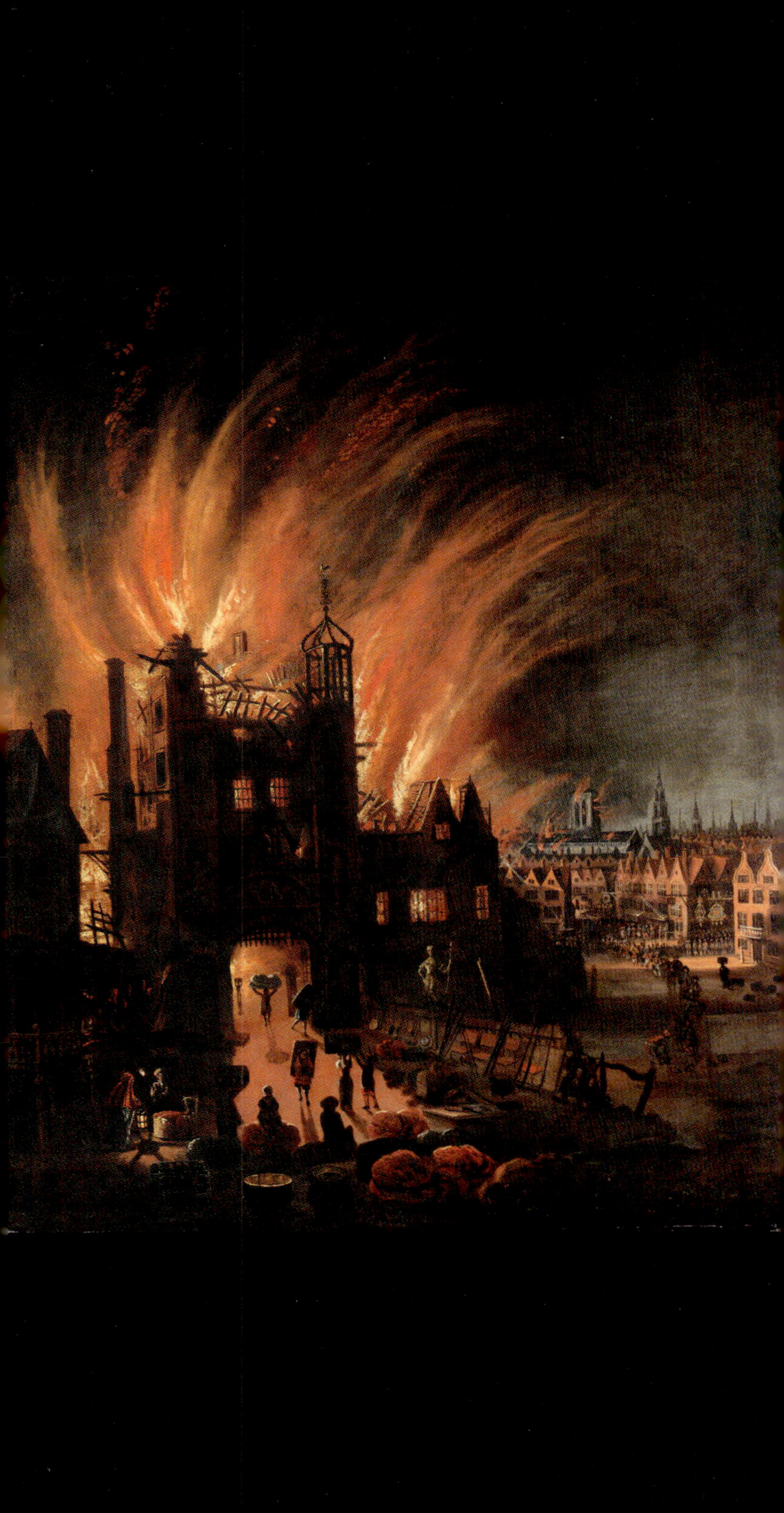

# 11

# SETTLEMENTS

ENGLAND IS A STAGE SET WITH
TRAP DOORS UNDER EVERY STREET.

Scene: Manchester, early morning. We walk through Piccadilly and rain begins to fall (surprise, surprise). Hour upon hour of rain, and the storm washes the country clean until we walk through a city that has been stripped of living beings. There's no sound bar wind through sightless windows and our lonely footsteps. This is what England will become once the human virus is wiped out. Without people, the buildings become unreadable and incomprehensible. The city resembles an uninspiring sculpture park. Office windows gleam like mirror balls, churches point out clouds. Tower blocks mass like frozen robots on the skyline, silently watching, silently judging. One skyscraper struggles on, its back-up generator straining as the still-working AC and heating battle it out for supremacy. We walk north, into the outskirts, but there is nowhere the buildings haven't reached. Dark Satanic mills are lit with shafts of weak-tea sunlight where the ivy has broken through the tiling. Big-box retail parks rear up from nowhere, the megaliths of the future, with no clue to their use bar the fading logos in letters taller than England's highest tree.

Cities are humanity's unconscious artworks, where pattern and chaos live intertwined, but when we're not there to watch, the land that spawned them claims them back. Grassy hills rise like gums around the shark's tooth of the Shard. A parliament of crows roosts in the House of Lords, on nests made with stuffing from the Woolsack. Without inhabitants, the truth is clear: buildings are machines for living. What does that make us then – those of us whose every second was spent inside these factories of the home? We thought we were the machine operators, instructing our smart houses how to weave our lives, but now, as the Arndale Centre crumbles into ruin, that seems to claim too much. Perhaps we were just code, overwritten now and dead, bringing forth blooms of chaos. Or ghosts. Ghosts in these machines, haunting our own homes as they have killed us time and time again.

England is a stage set with the curtain halfway down.

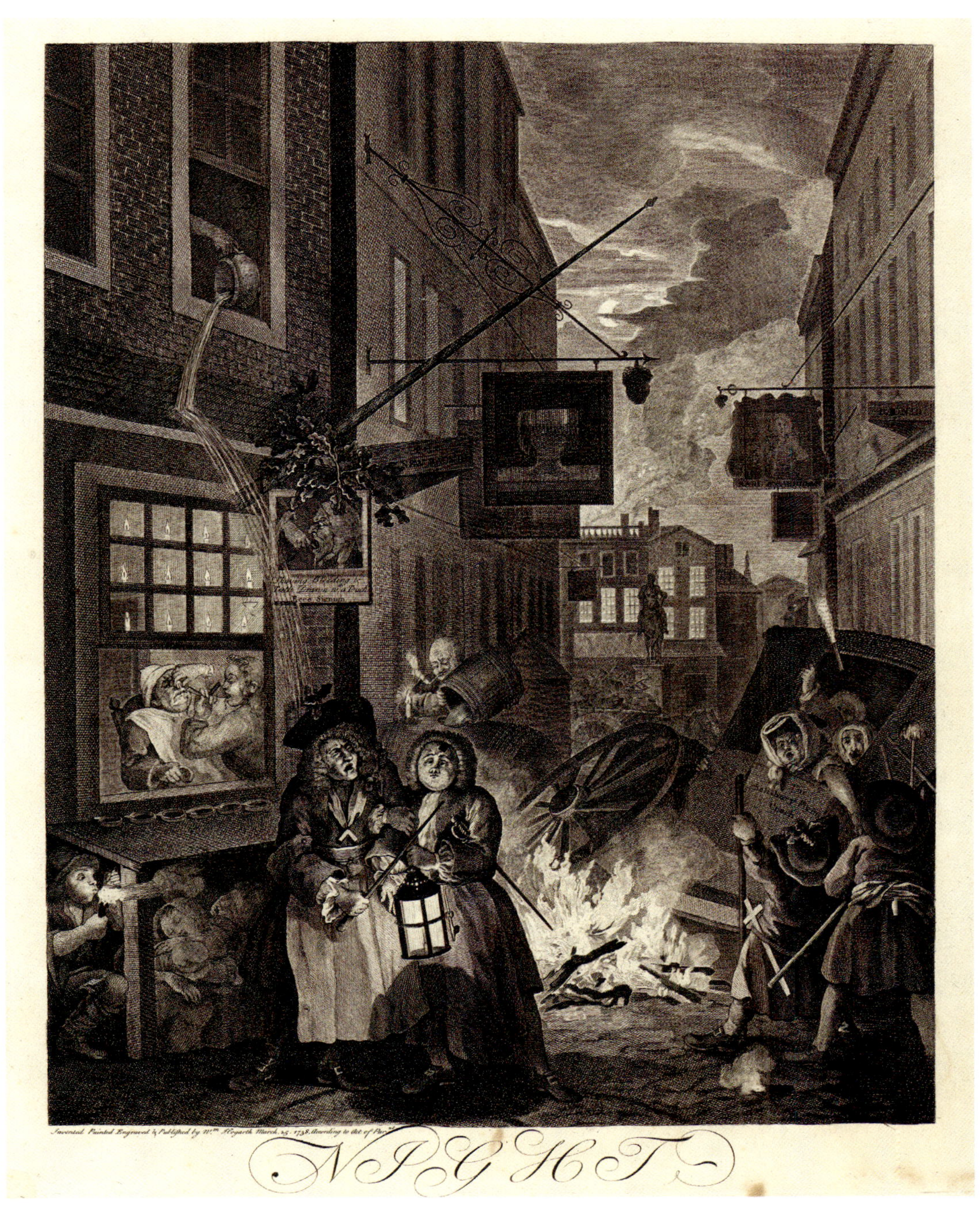


**181**  *The Four Times of Day, Plate IV: Night  1738*
William Hogarth (1697–1764)  Engraving

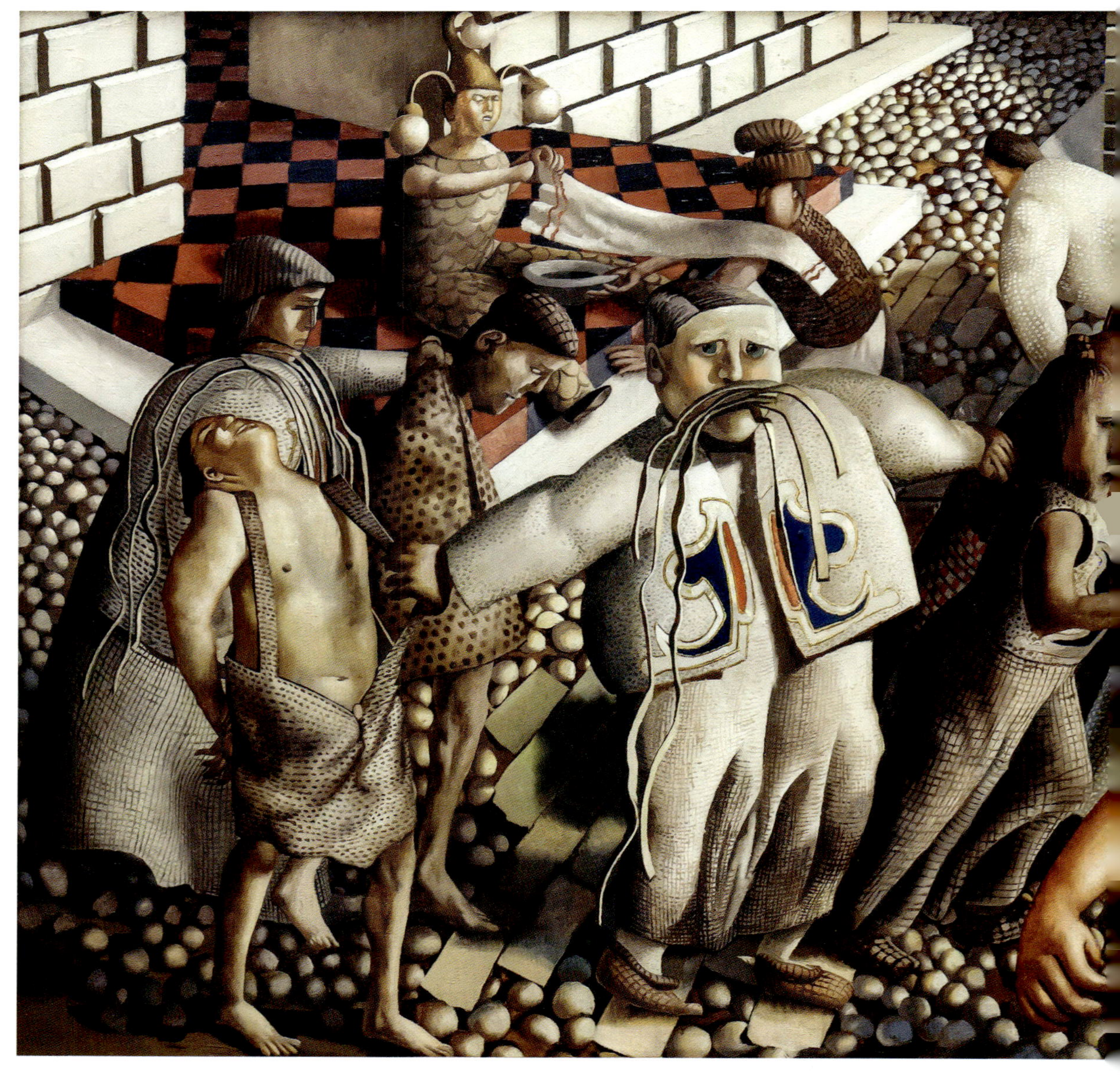

**182** *Christ Delivered to the People* 1950
Sir Stanley Spencer (1891–1959)
Oil on canvas

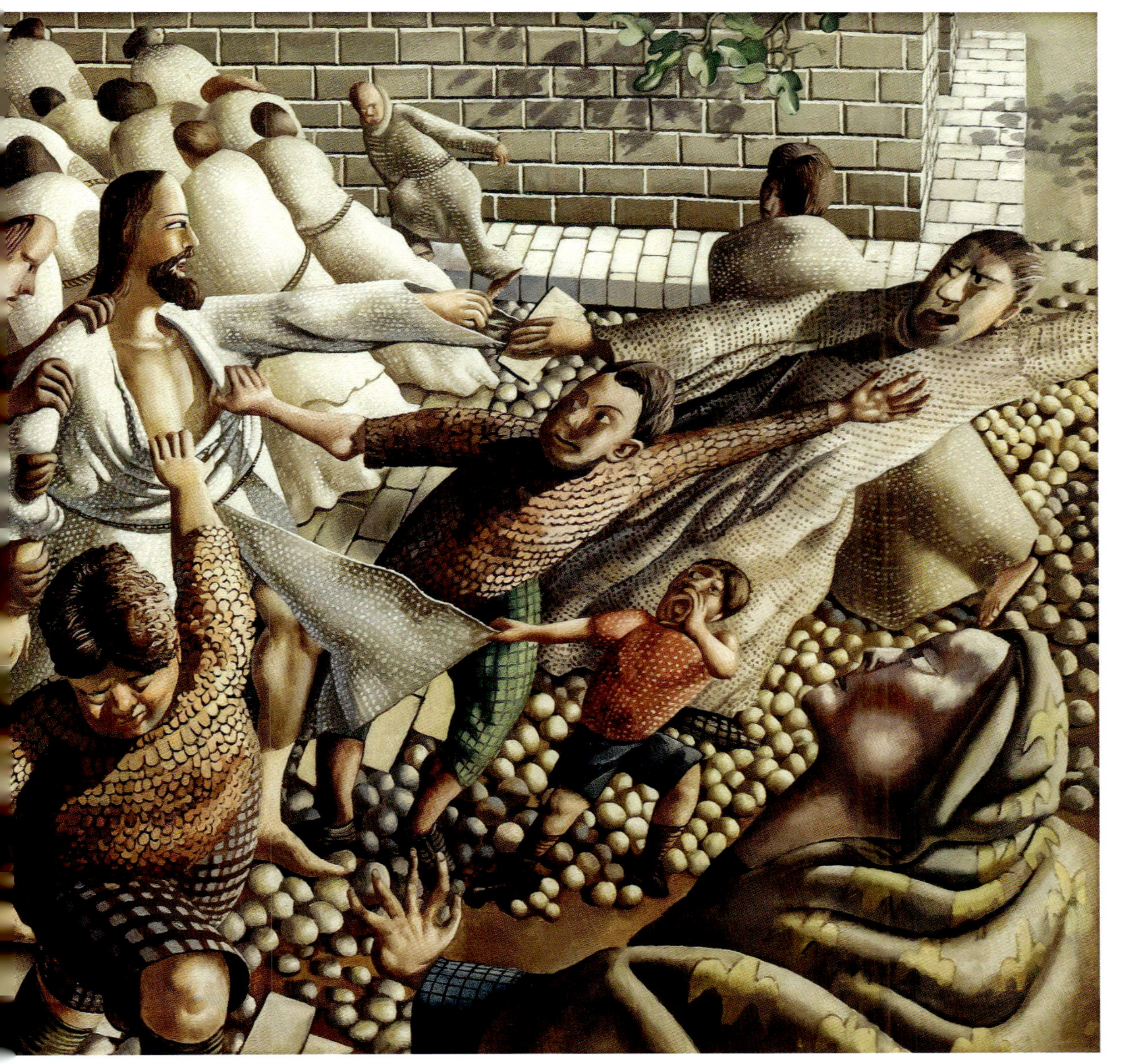

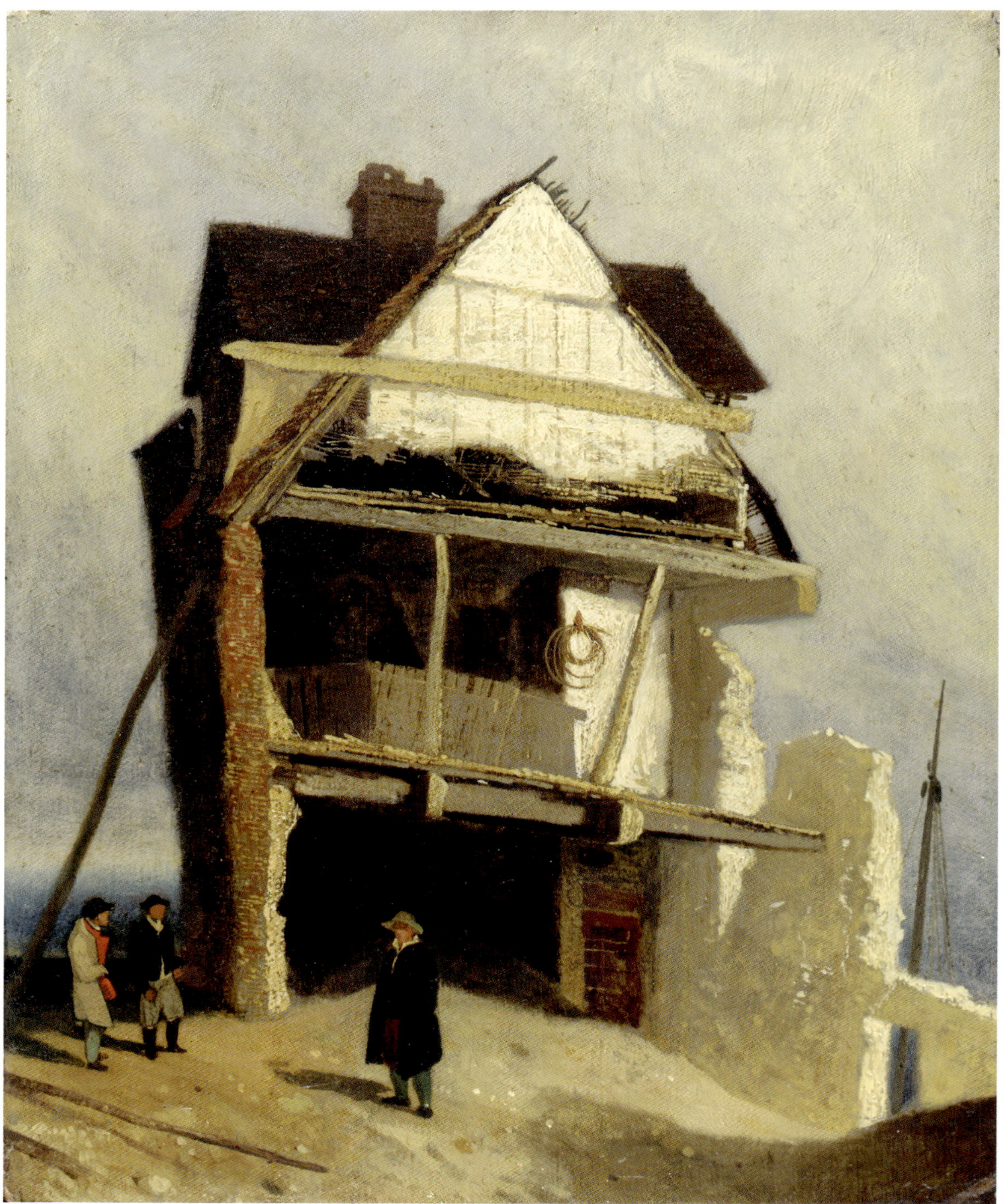

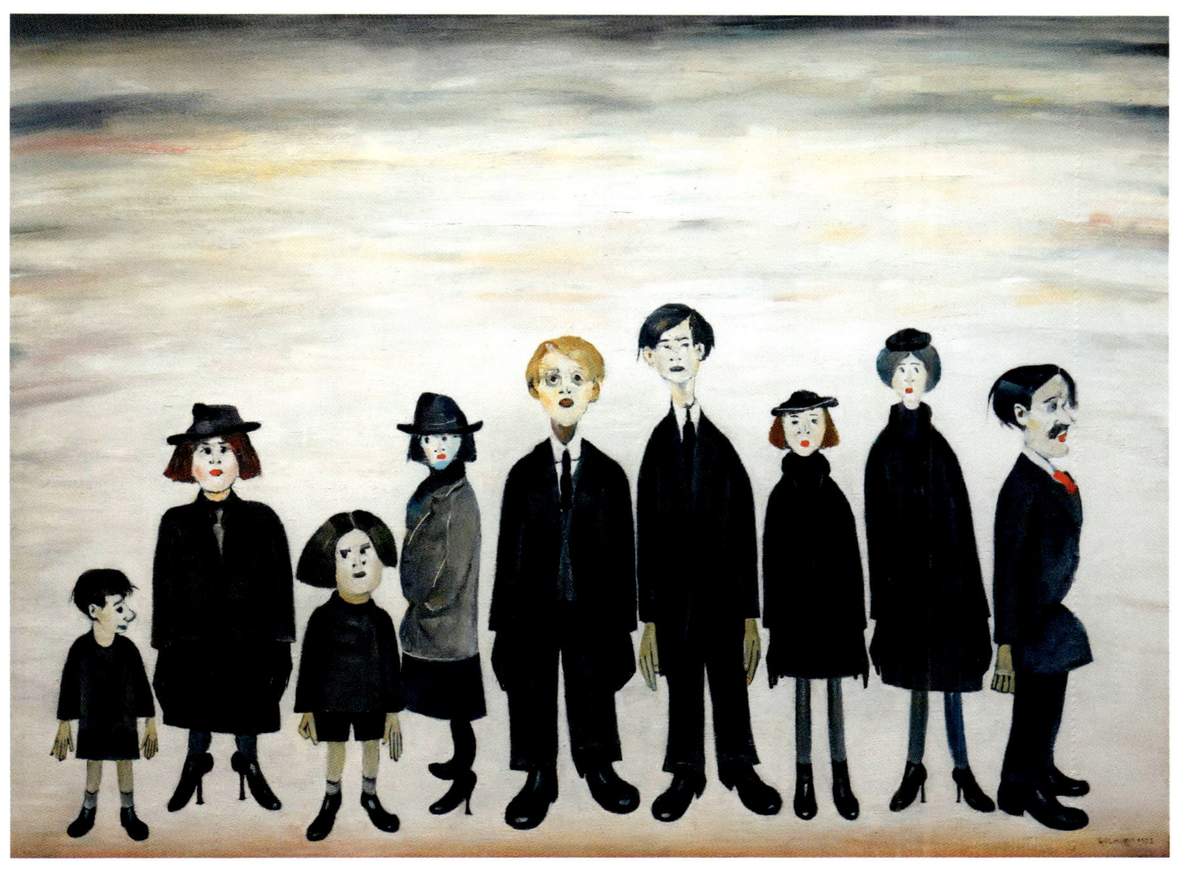

**183**  *The Funeral Party*  1953
L.S. Lowry (1887–1976)
Oil on canvas

Lowry is best known for his depictions of industrial life in northwest England. Here, he succeeds in bringing humour to a funeral scene despite the bleak colour palette and vacant stares of his shadowless "matchstick people" (as they have often been described).

**184**  *Ruined House*  1807–10
John Sell Cotman (1782–1842)
Oil on millboard, mounted on panel

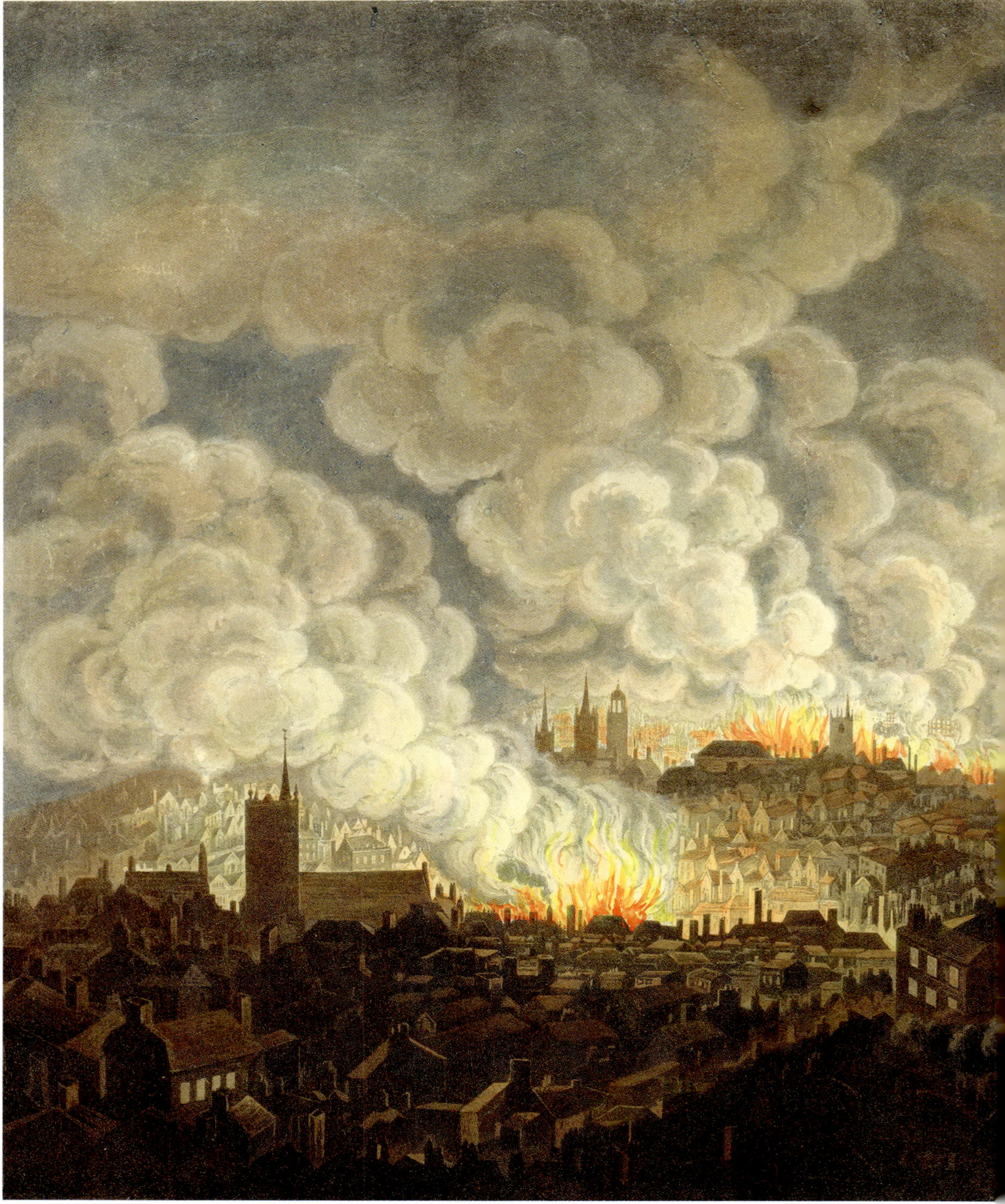

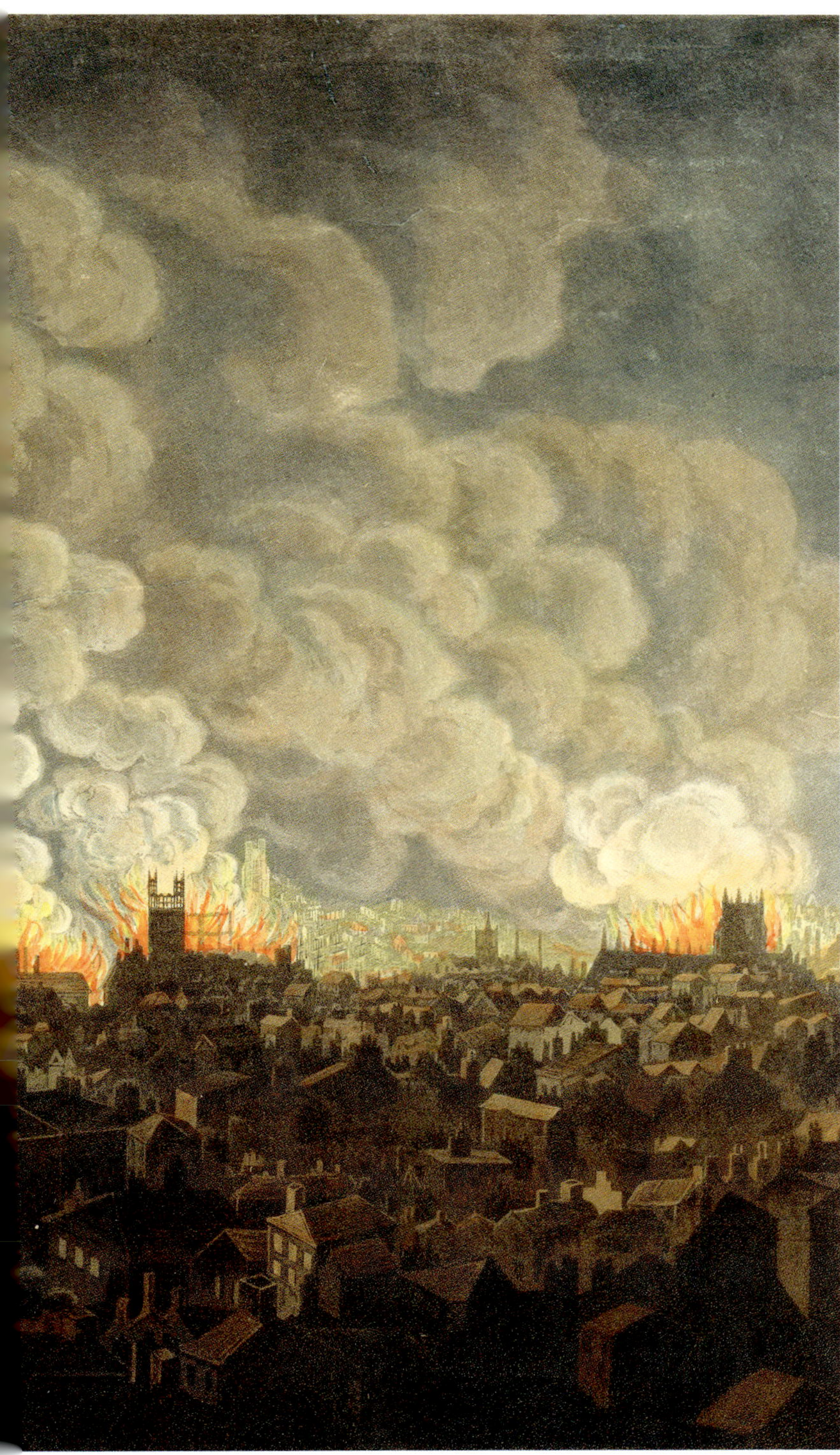

**185** *Conflagration of the City of Bristol, Taken from the Centre of Somerset Street* 1831
Charles Rosenberg
(active 1828–48)
Aquatint on paper

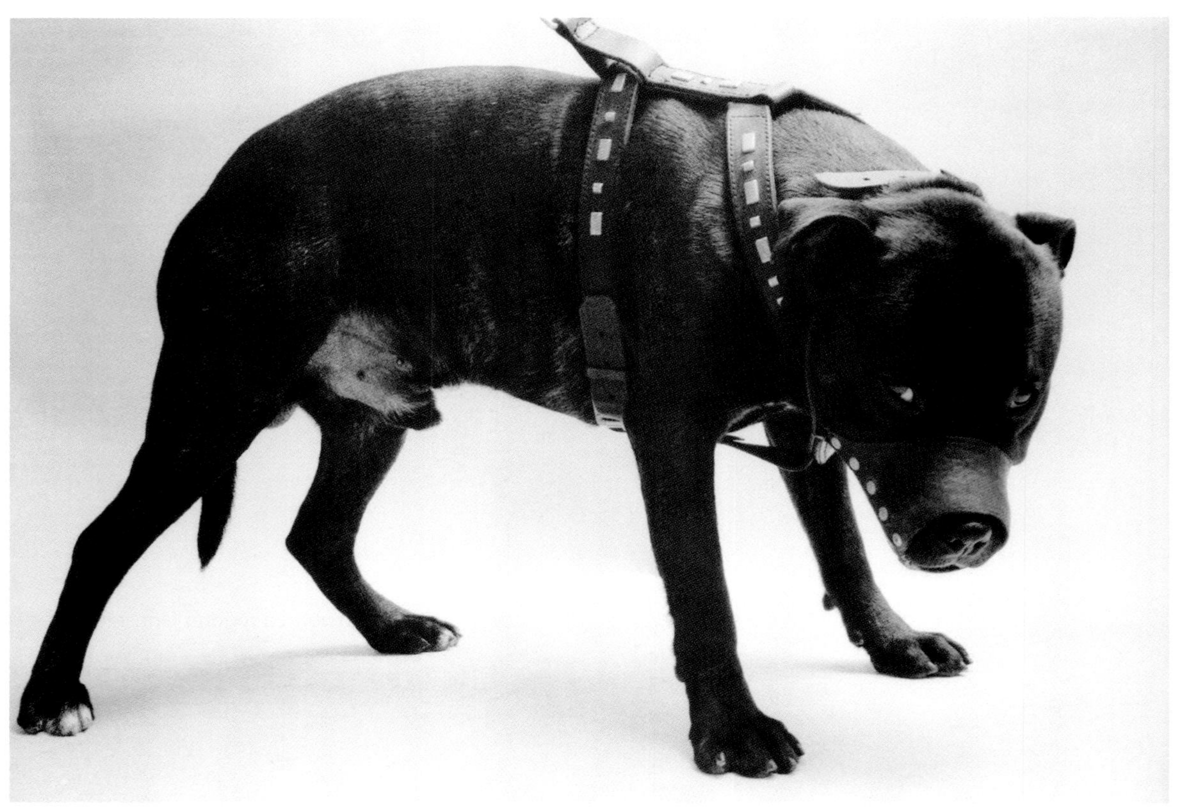

**186**  *For His Own Good*  1995
Abigail Lane (b.1967)
Black and white photograph

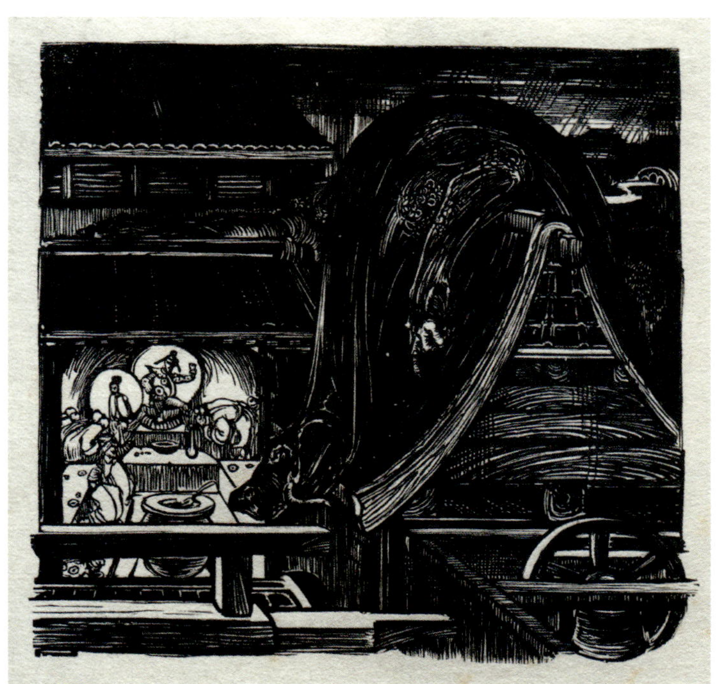

**187**  *The Dragon*  Undated
Charles de Sousy Ricketts
(1866–1931)
Woodcut

**188**  *Fire in London,
seen from Hampstead*  *c*.1826
Attributed to John Constable
(1776–1837)
Oil on paper laid on panel

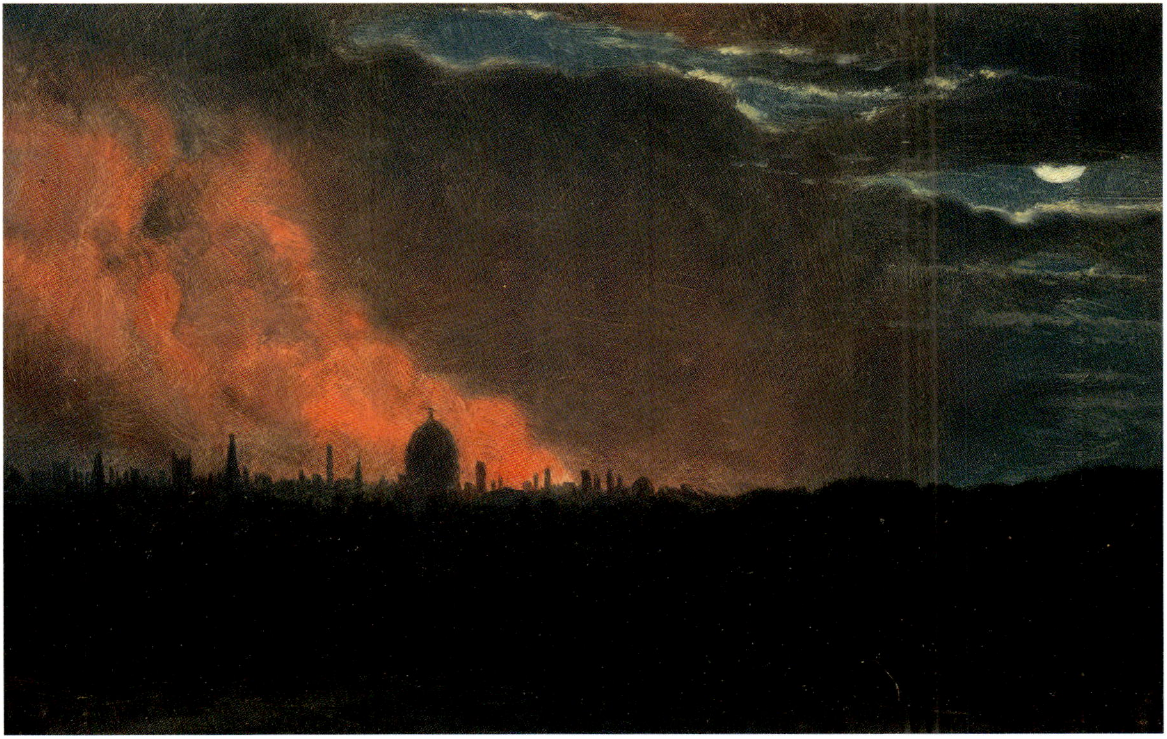

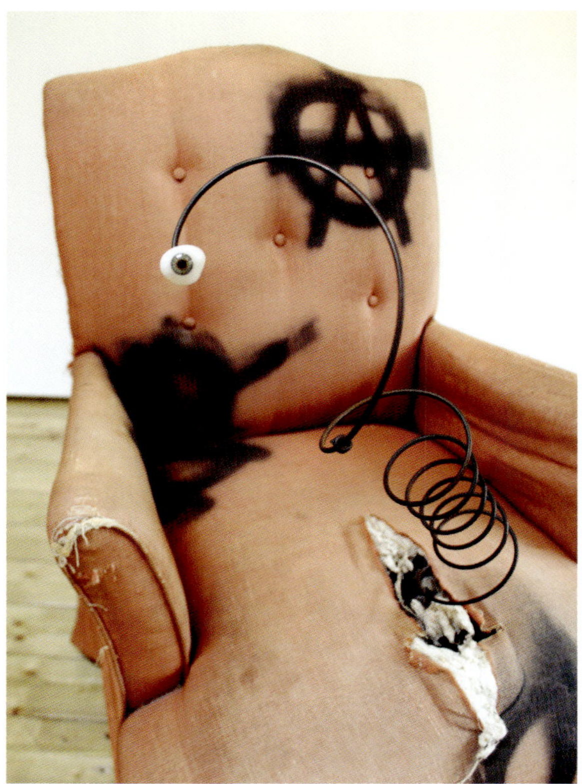

189  *Eye am the Chairman*  2004
Abigail Lane (b.1967)
Upholstered chair, graffiti,
brass wire and glass eye

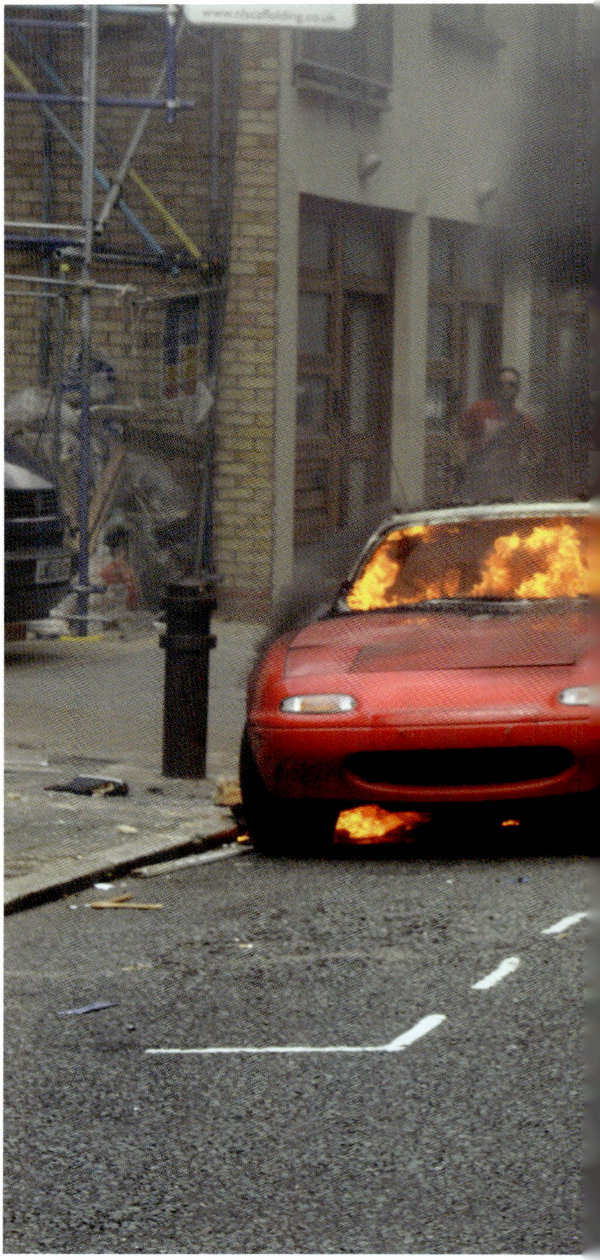

190  *Hackney*  2011
From the *King Mob* series
Max Reeves (b.1966)
Colour photograph

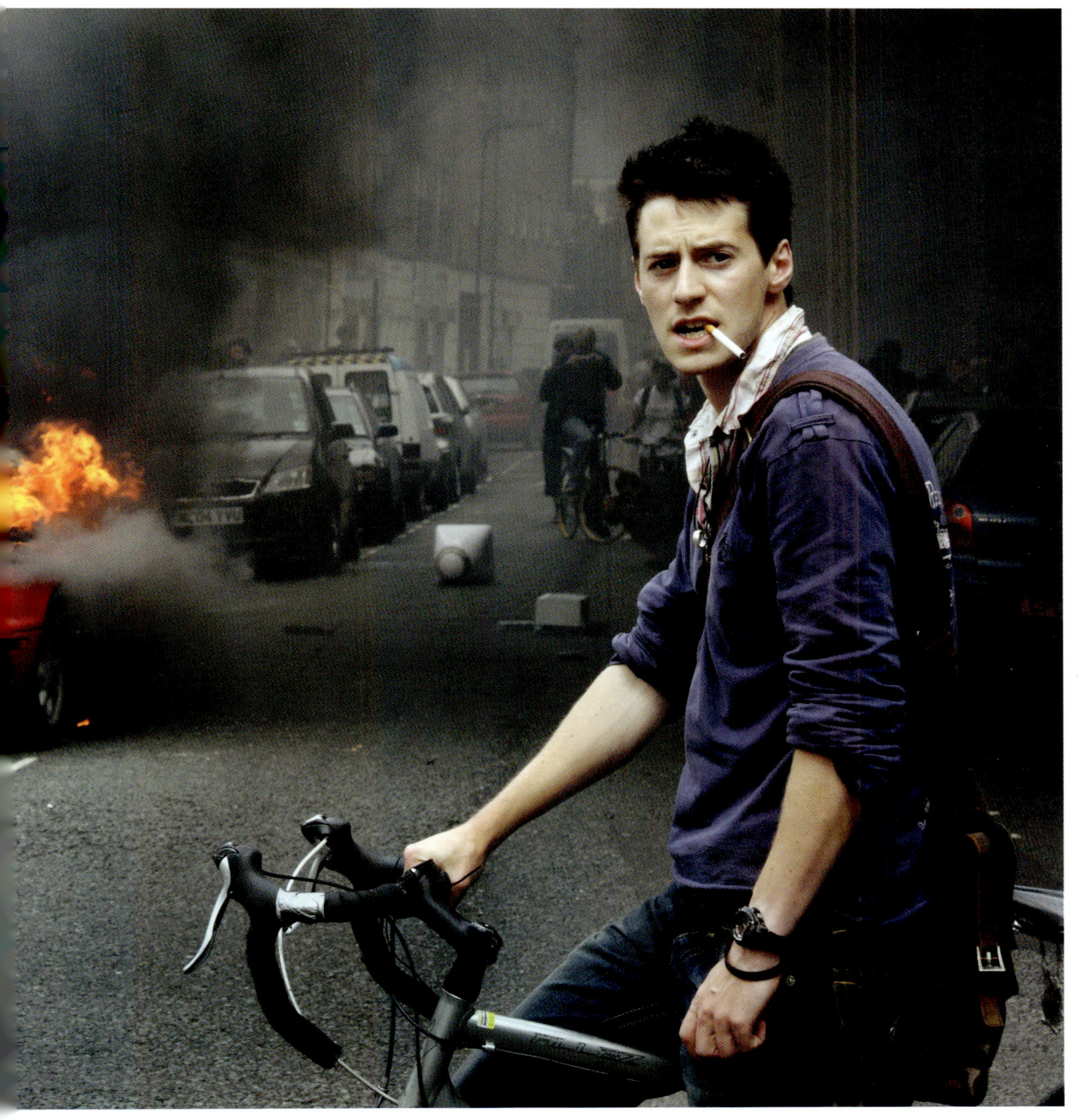

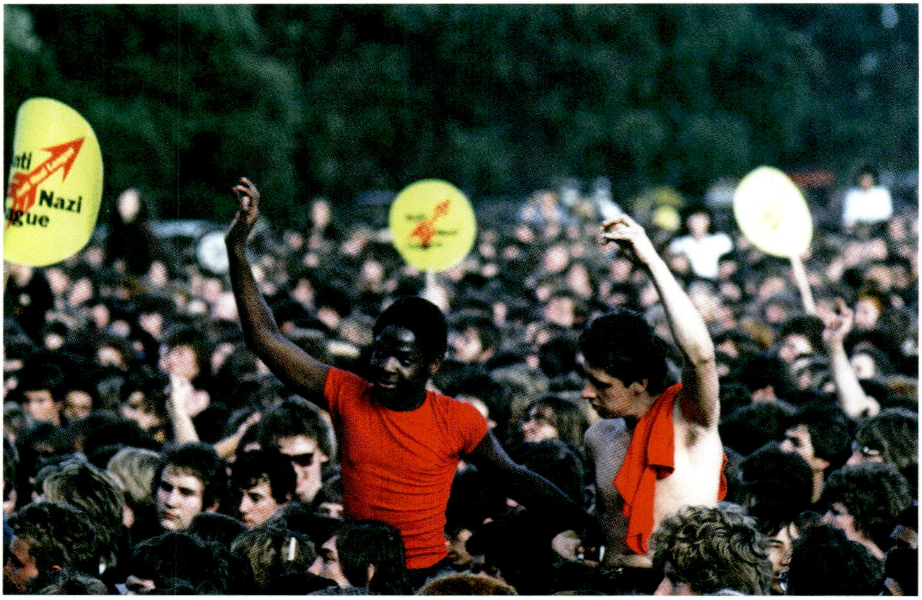
Nazi

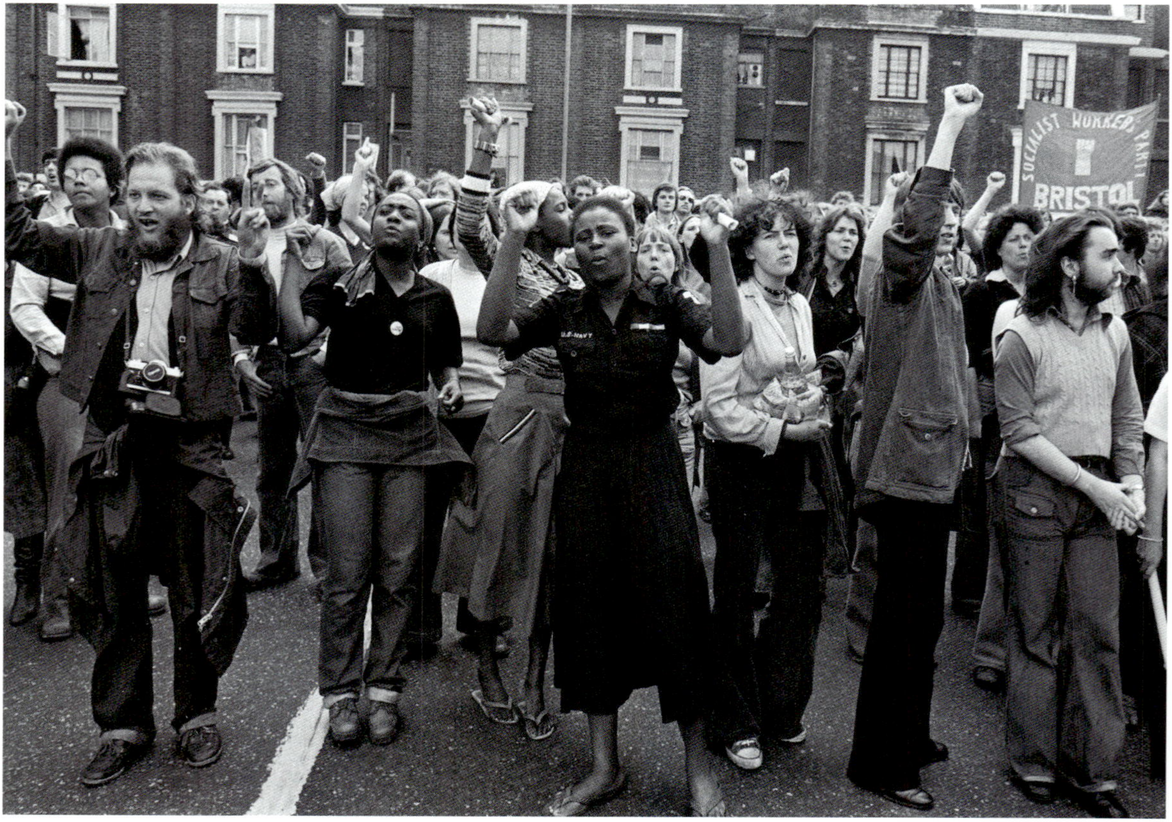
SOCIALIST
BRISTOL

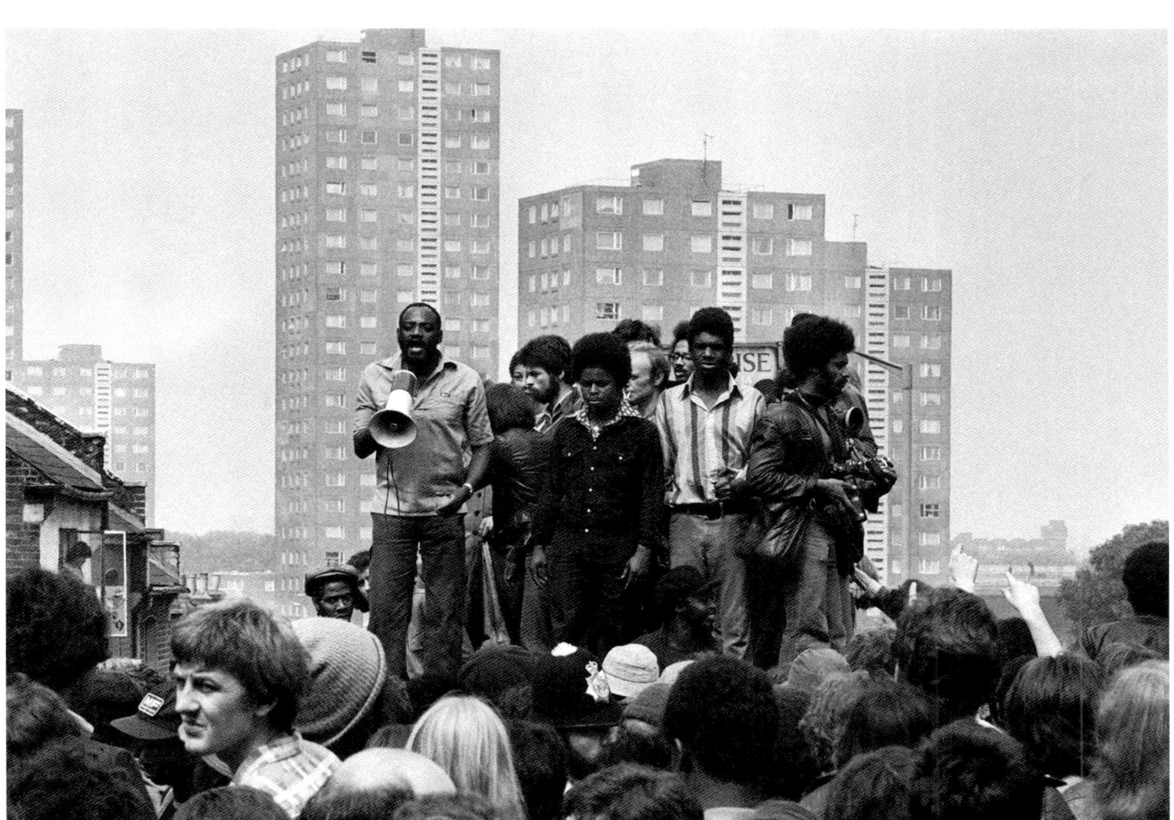

**191** (top left)
*Brixton, London*
*24 September 1978*

In the late 1970s, the hugely influential protest movement Rock Against Racism organized hundreds of anti-fascist marches, festivals, gigs and other mass protest events across Britain to urge opposition to the National Front, using music as a means to rebel against fear and hatred. Shelton was heavily involved in the movement, documenting its activities and helping to design its magazine, *Temporary Hoarding*. In September 1978, 50,000 people marched from Hyde Park to the Rock Against Racism Carnival in Brockwell Park, Brixton.

**192a** (bottom left)
*Lewisham, London*
*13 August 1977*
**b** (top right)
*Clifton Rise, Lewisham,*
*London  13 August 1977*

In 1977, Shelton photographed some of the 5,000 local people and anti-racist activists who occupied New Cross Road in south London. They had gathered to counter a National Front march that was escorted by a quarter of the Metropolitan police and their entire mounted division. Racial justice campaigner Darcus Howe addressed the anti-National Front demonstrators from the roof of a public toilet block on Clifton Rise, Lewisham.

Syd Shelton (b.1947)
Photographs

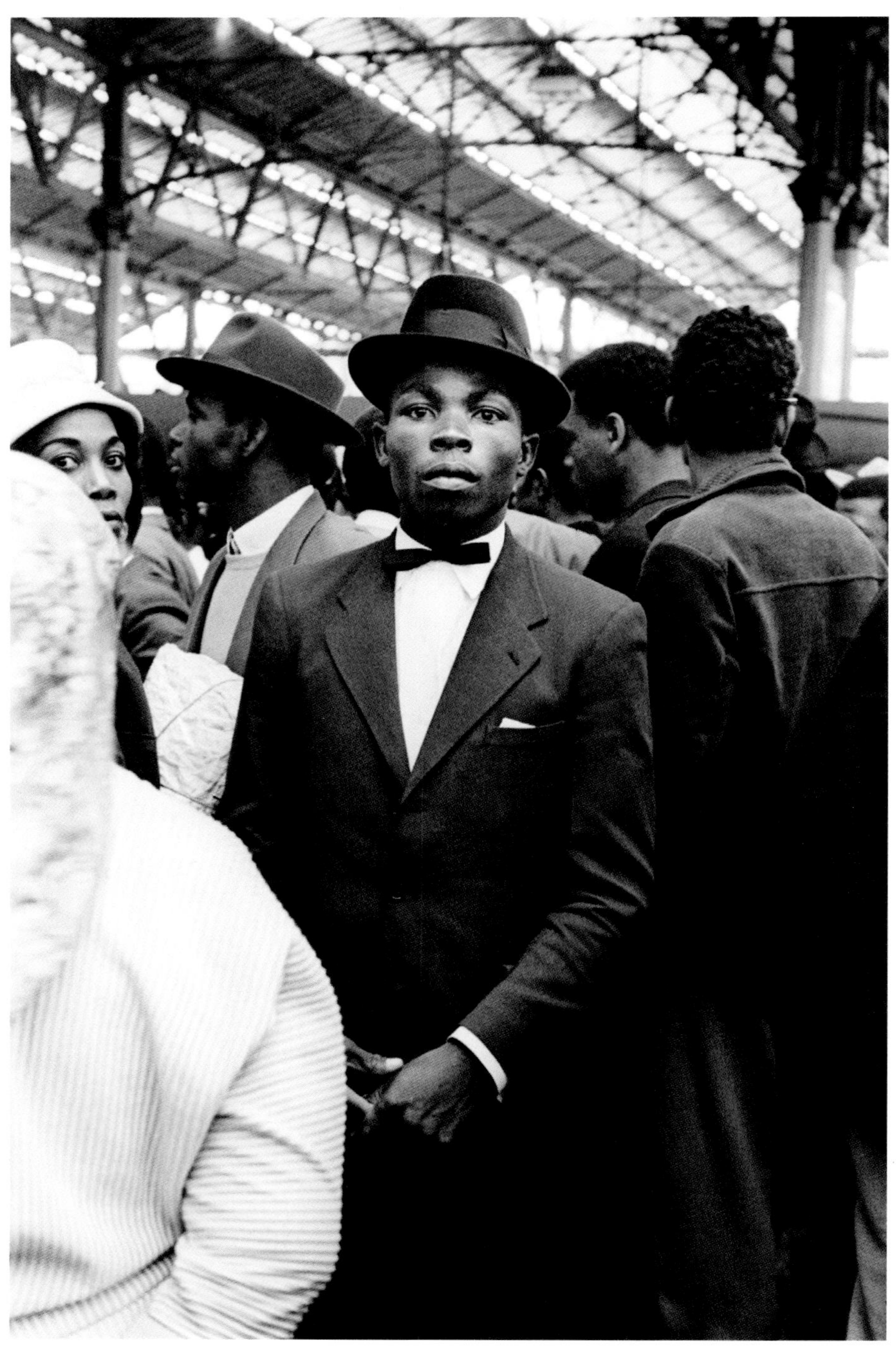

**193** *Untitled, Waterloo Station from the Arrival Portfolio* 1962
Howard Grey (b.1942)  Silver gelatin fibre-based print

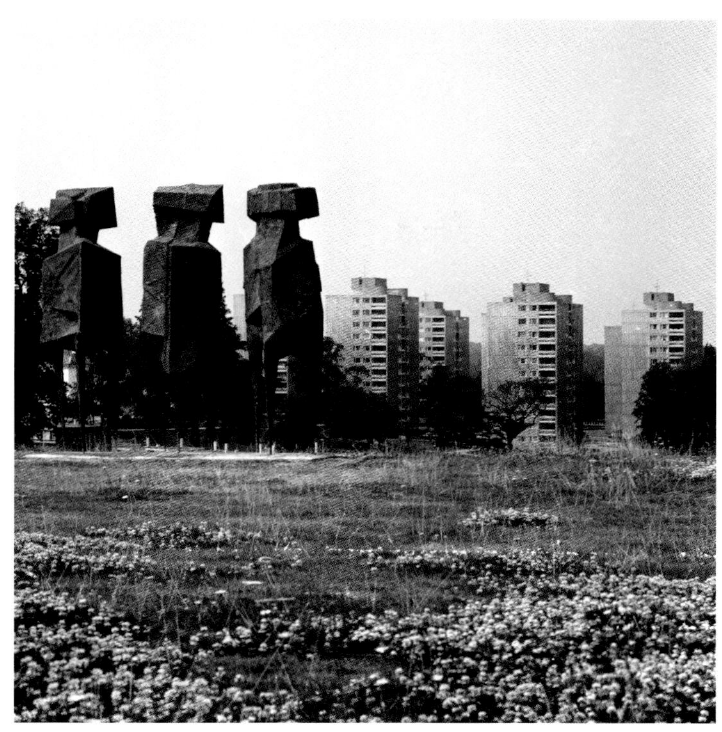



*Alton West Estate, Roehampton, London: Lynn Chadwick's sculpture* The Watchers *with the point blocks beyond*  1963
John Donat (1933–2004)
Black and white photograph

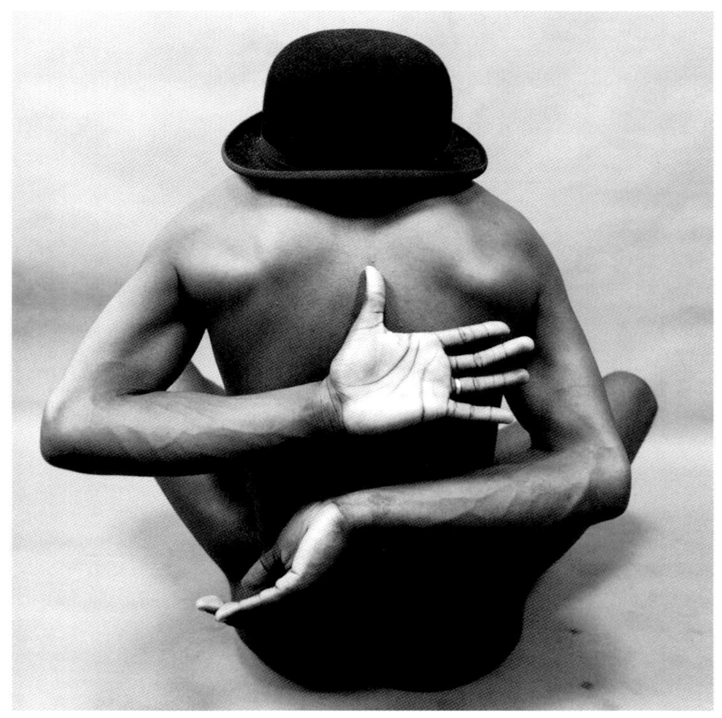

195  *City Gent*  1988
Rotimi Fani-Kayode (1955–89)
Silver gelatin fibre-based hand-print

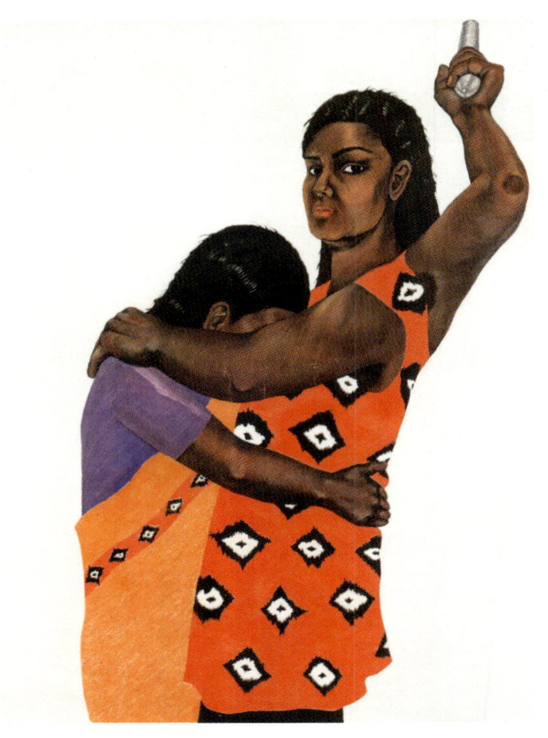



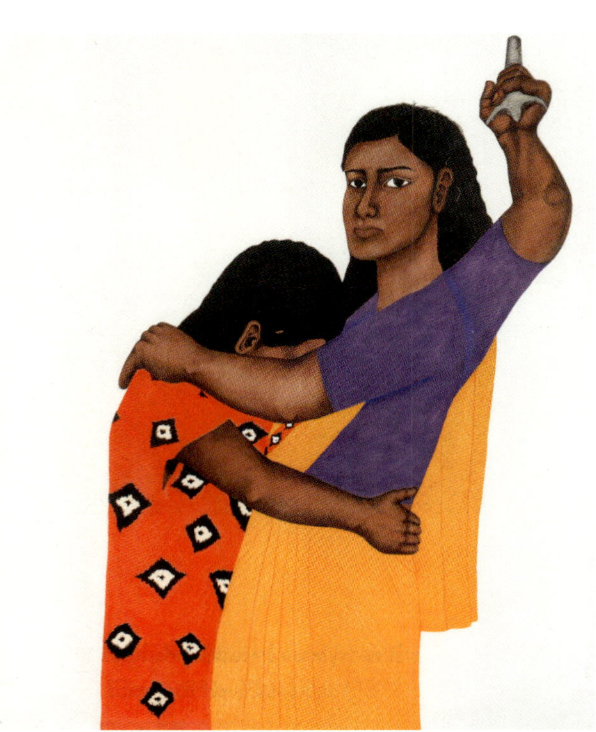

The maternal tone of this diptych highlights
Biswas's interest in foregrounding women's
stories, and, as she says, the "unheard, untold
narratives". With a background of emigration,
moving from India to Britain as a child in
the 1960s, Biswas places her own personal
memories within concepts of colonialism
and the female body.

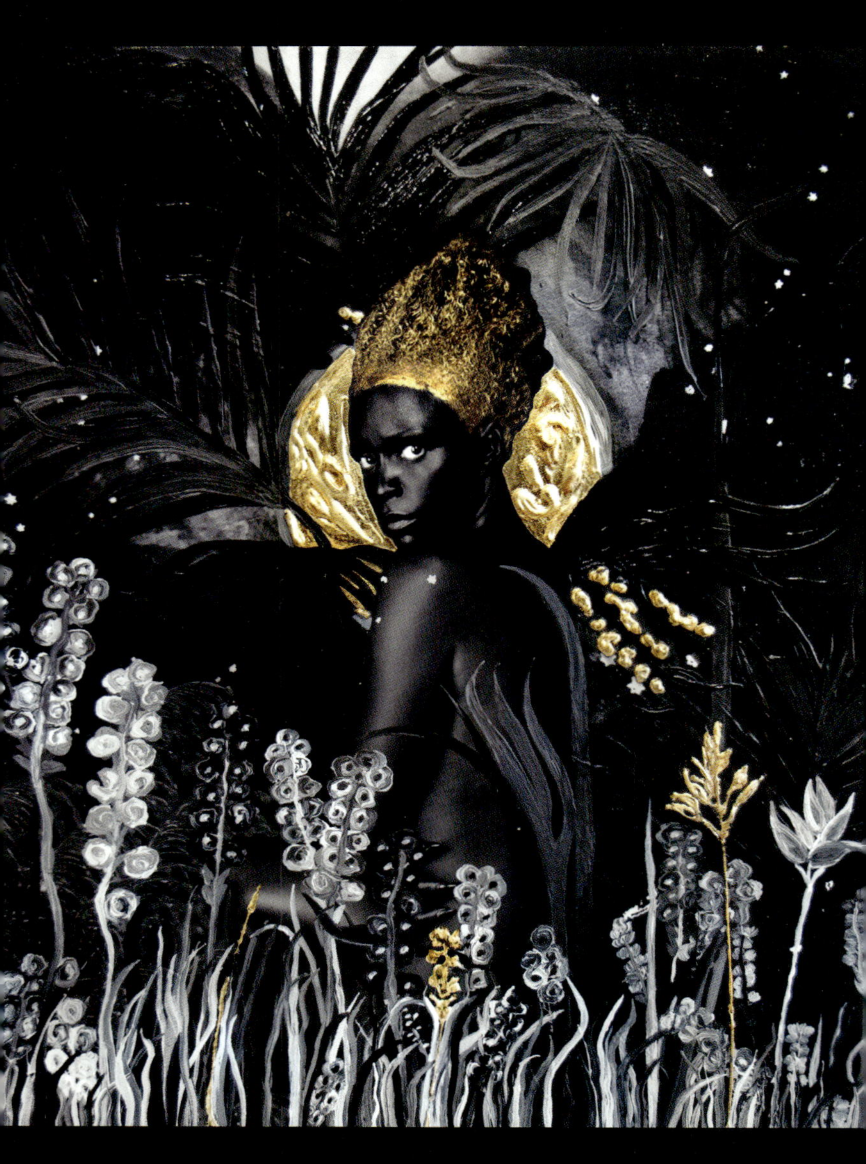

# 12 VISIONS

PREVIOUS PAGE

**197** *Refuge from the Aftermath, A Reckoning to Come* 2018–19
Lina Iris Viktor (b.1987)  Pure 24-carat gold, acrylic, ink, print on cotton rag paper

ENGLAND IS A FIREWORKS DISPLAY
THAT SETS THE NIGHT ABLAZE.

After a hundred-year sunset which slowly turns England's landscape from its cloak of green into digital greyscale, the light begins to slip away. Ghosts slink off into the black. Good night Empire, good night might. Flags are lowered. So long to the snoring galleries of dead art. Park gates wear festoons of chains. Good night Navy, good night Church.

Night falls like a curtain around us, turning every step treacherous, and we still have miles yet before we get home. Myth lit this place by day and dressed it in money-green and sun-gold, but now, at long day's end, we can see it for what it is: a dark little puddle of ghosts with no safe way off the island. A haunted, haunting, dank and dreary place.

But then, with a sound like warfare and a spray like fountains, flowers of light bloom across the clouds. *Crack* and new colours paint the sky – African reds and Indian oranges and Carnaby Street blues and submarine yellows. *Crack* and the isle is full of noises again. Catherine wheels spit with honey kisses and rockets fling themselves at the stars with idiot glee. They burst like rainstorms and die like conscripts. On and on goes the display, building to a perpetual rainbow fireball that threatens to turn midnight to midday. And everywhere that the rockets fall, they set alight an Albion wriggling with anarchy. Mushrooms burst from the corpses of the Lion and Unicorn, and slave boats are turned to fireships, fizzling as they slip beneath the kaleidoscope seas. Every new dying firework sets another city ablaze, and the hedgerows burn and shrivel and die. Now all the freaks are loose. Warrior queens paint black Union Jacks and scrawl graffiti across Britannia.

And us? We are flame-lit and bonfire-warmed. We walk in beauty like the night, secure in the knowledge that everything grows better after a wildfire; 1666 was a year of birth, not of death. Joyfully, we kick at the ashes like autumn leaves, and shoots push up through the smouldering ground. Magical artworks climb and swell and sway and bear fruit – until all of us walk through a forest of art, alight and alive, as the very land is rebuilt around us.

England is a firework that burns forever.

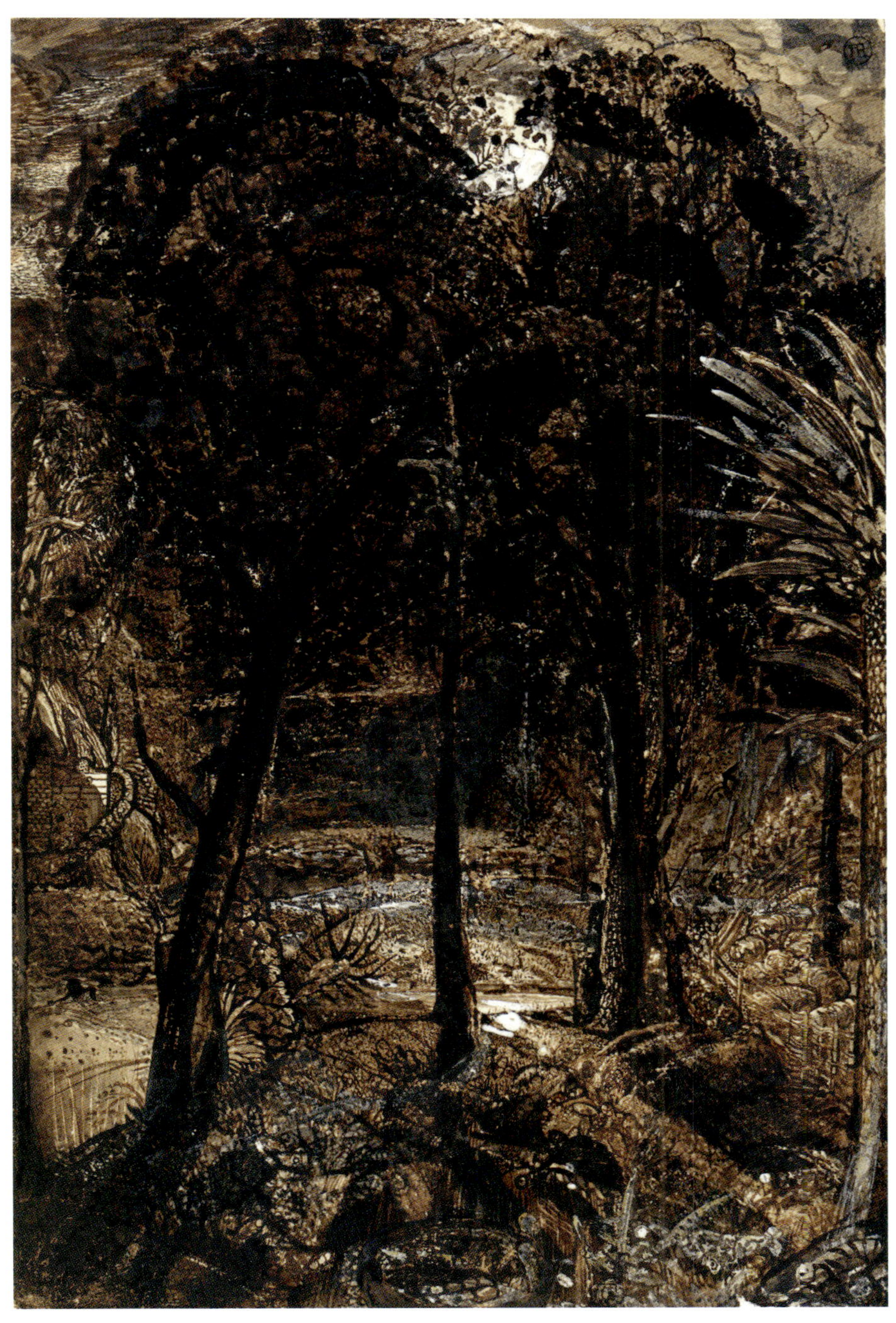

**198**  *A Moonlit Scene with a Winding River*  c.1827
Samuel Palmer (1805–81)
Black and brown wash, gouache and gum on paper

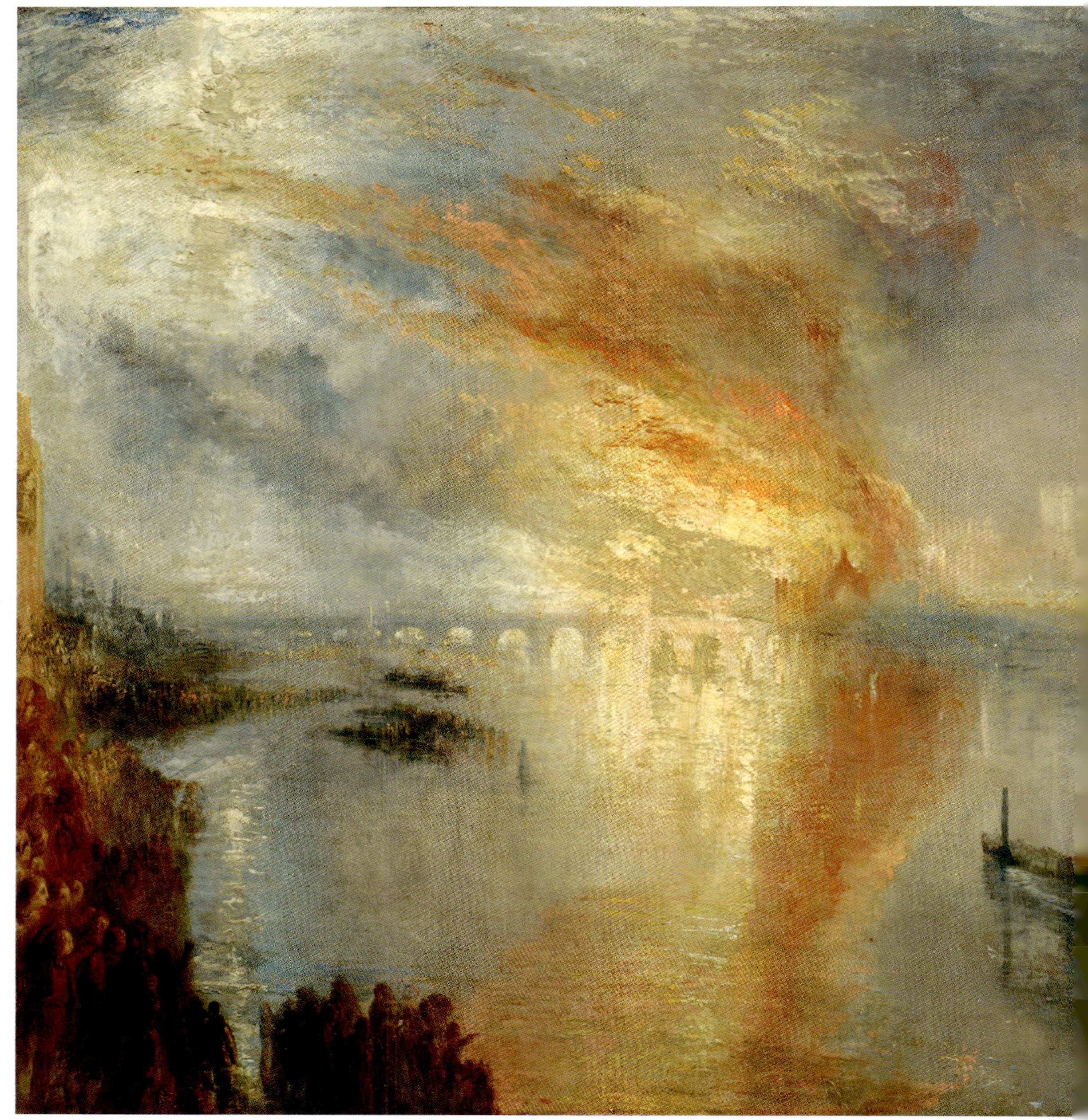

ENGLAND ON FIRE

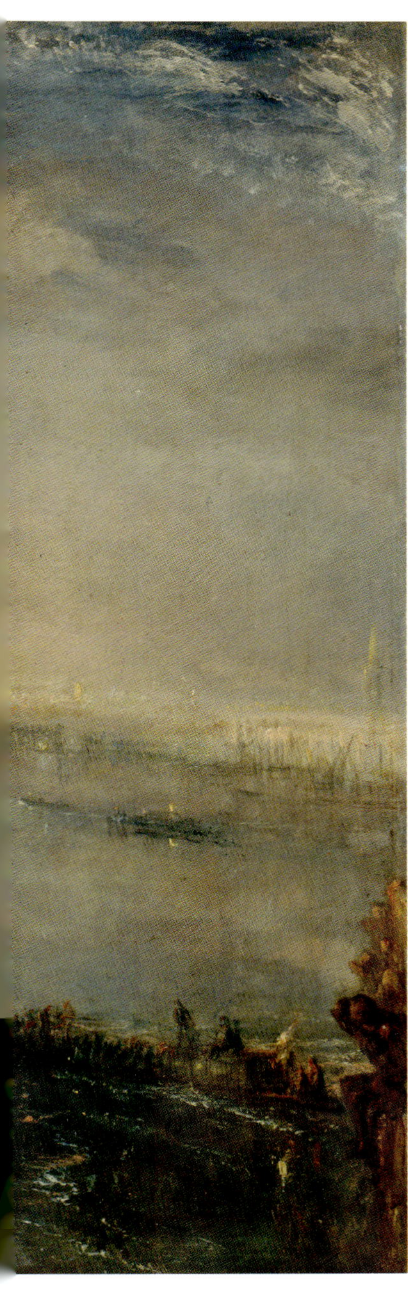

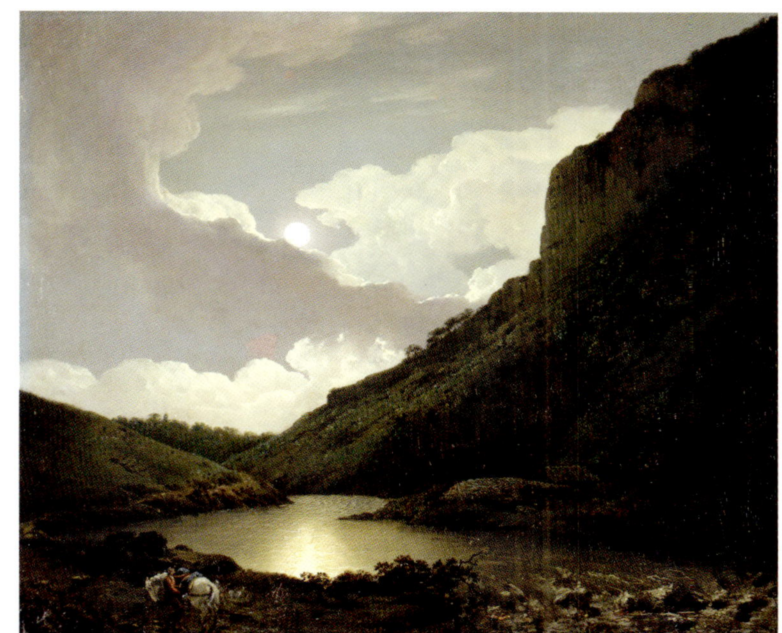

**199** *Matlock Tor by Moonlight*  1777–80
Joseph Wright of Derby (1734–97)
Oil on canvas

**200** *The Burning of the Houses of Parliament*  1834–5
Joseph Mallord William Turner (1775–1851)
Watercolour and gouache on paper

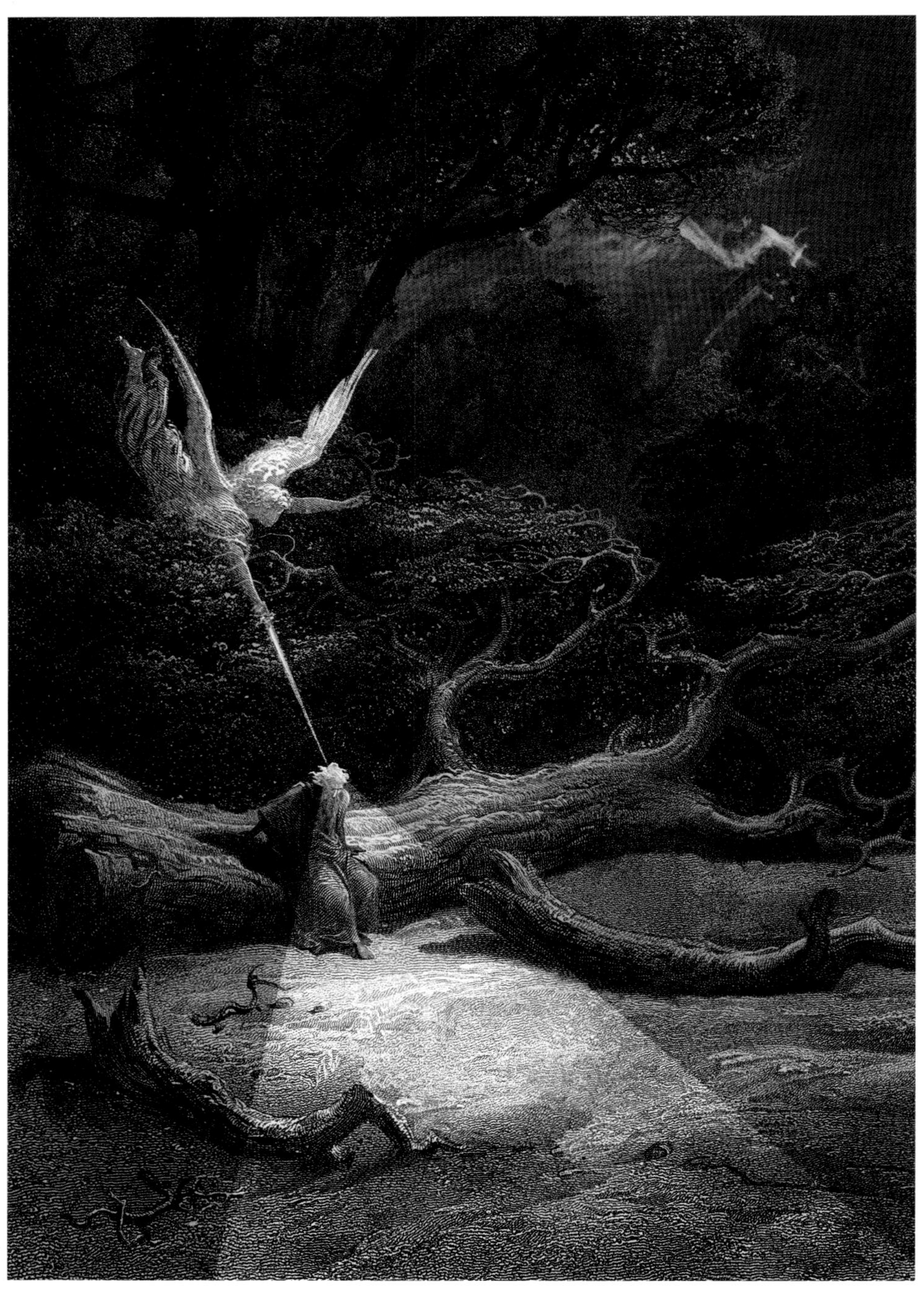

**201**  *Seer*  2021
Dan Hillier (b.1973)
Giclée print

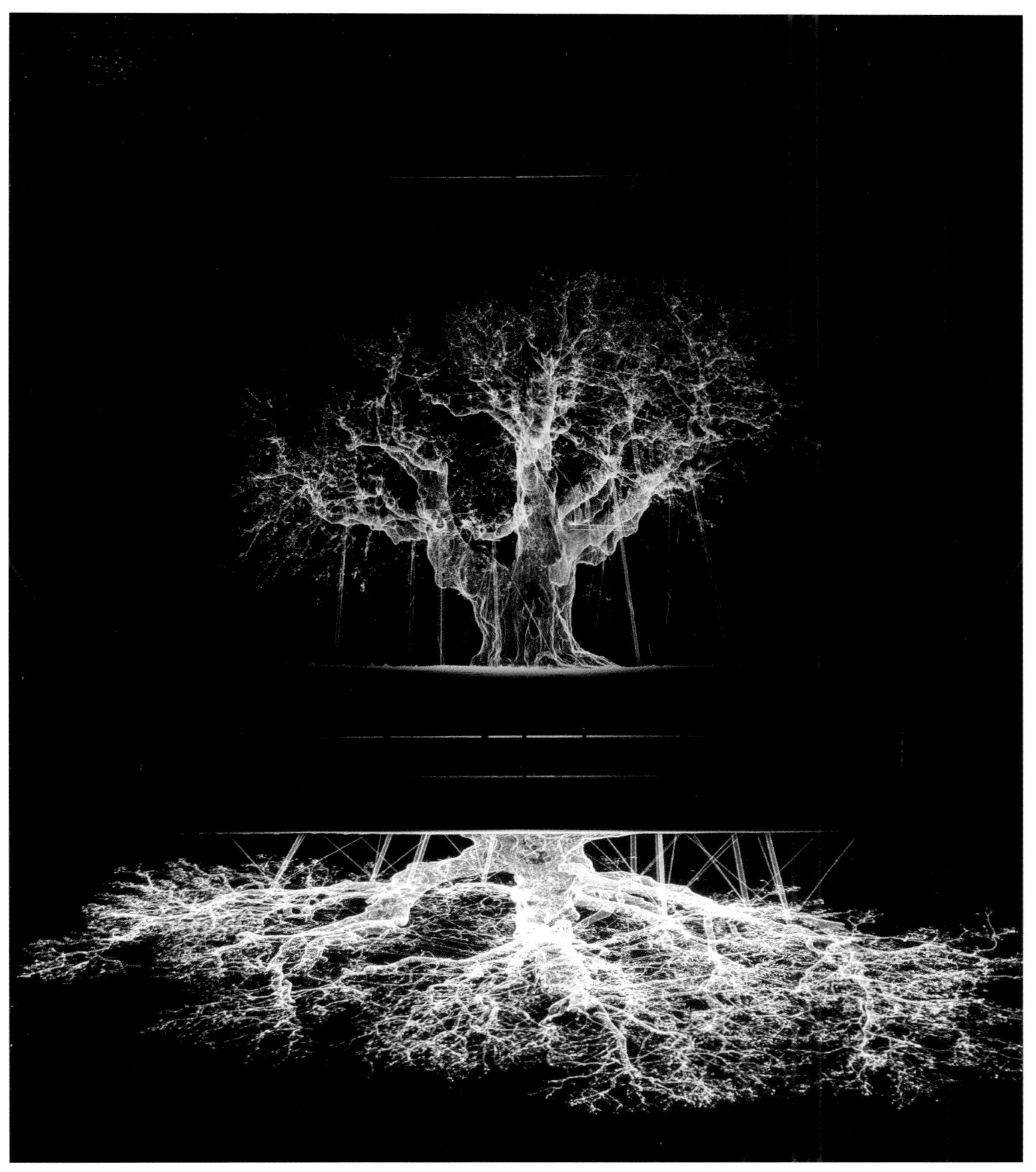

**202** *Albion* 2008
Mat Collishaw (b.1966)
Installation

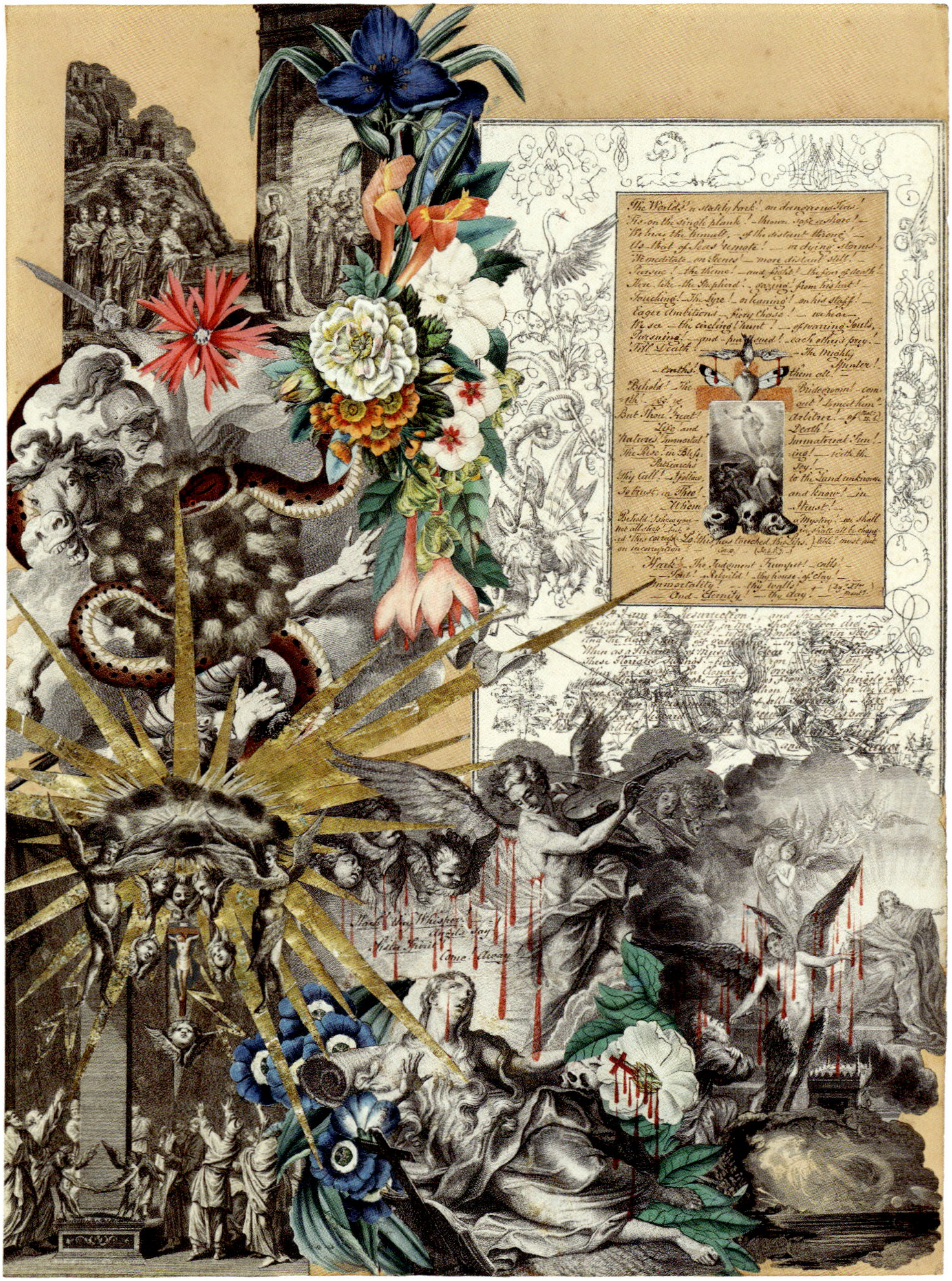

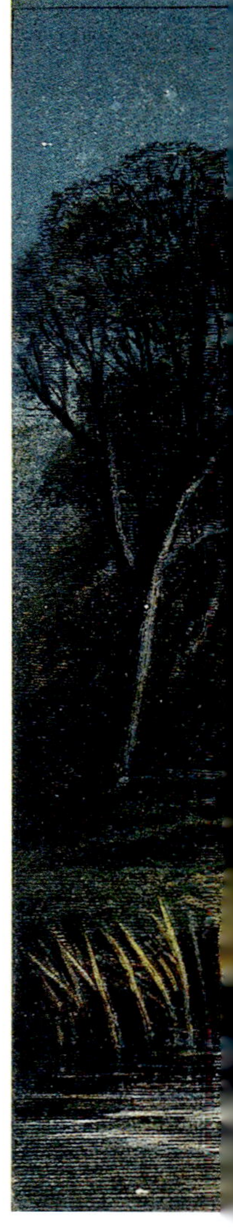

**203**  *Collage*  1850s–60s
John Bingley Garland (1791–1875)
Collage of prints and metallic foil

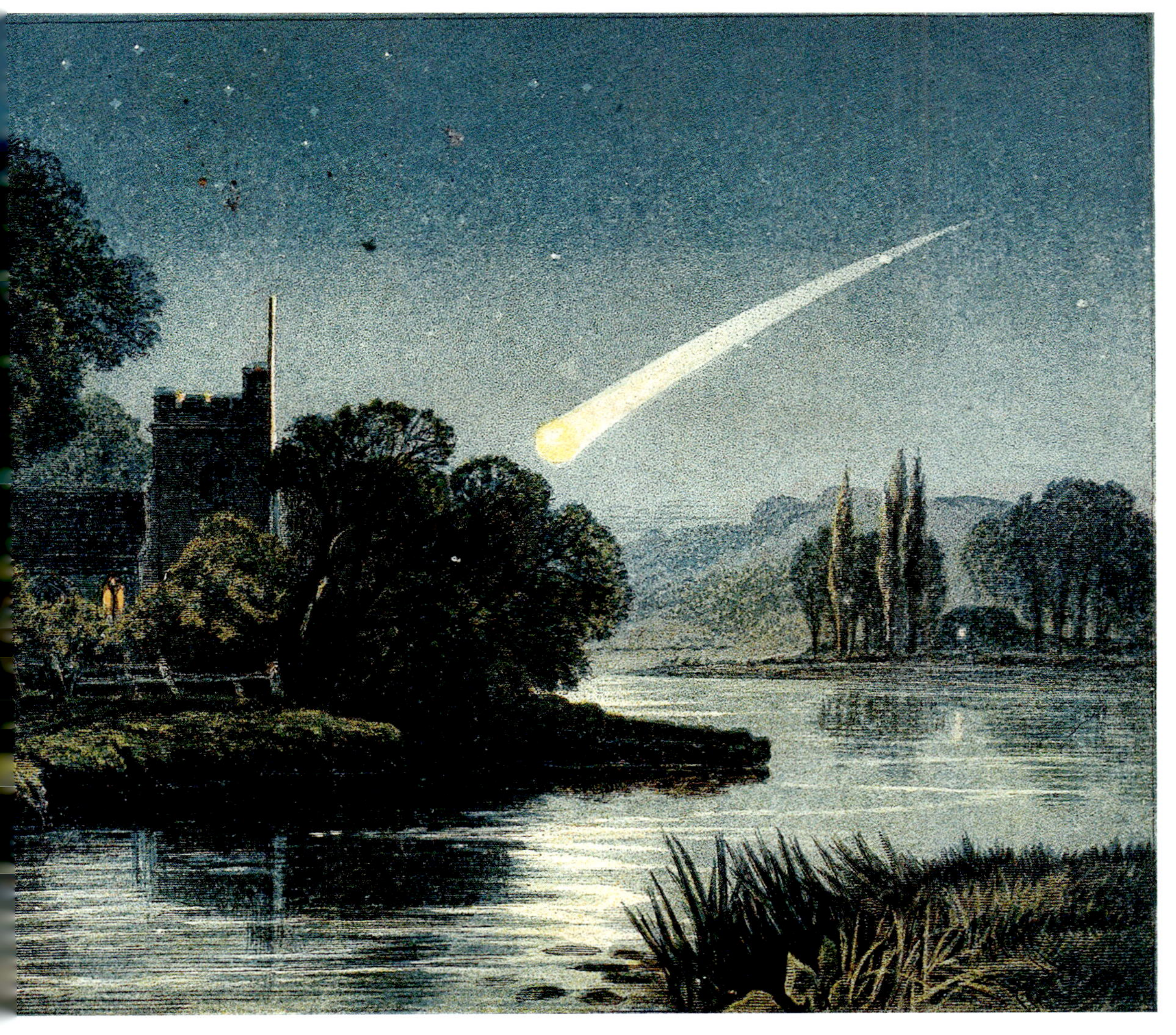

**204** *Astronomy: a Meteor in the Night Sky* 1868
Artist unknown
Coloured wood engraving

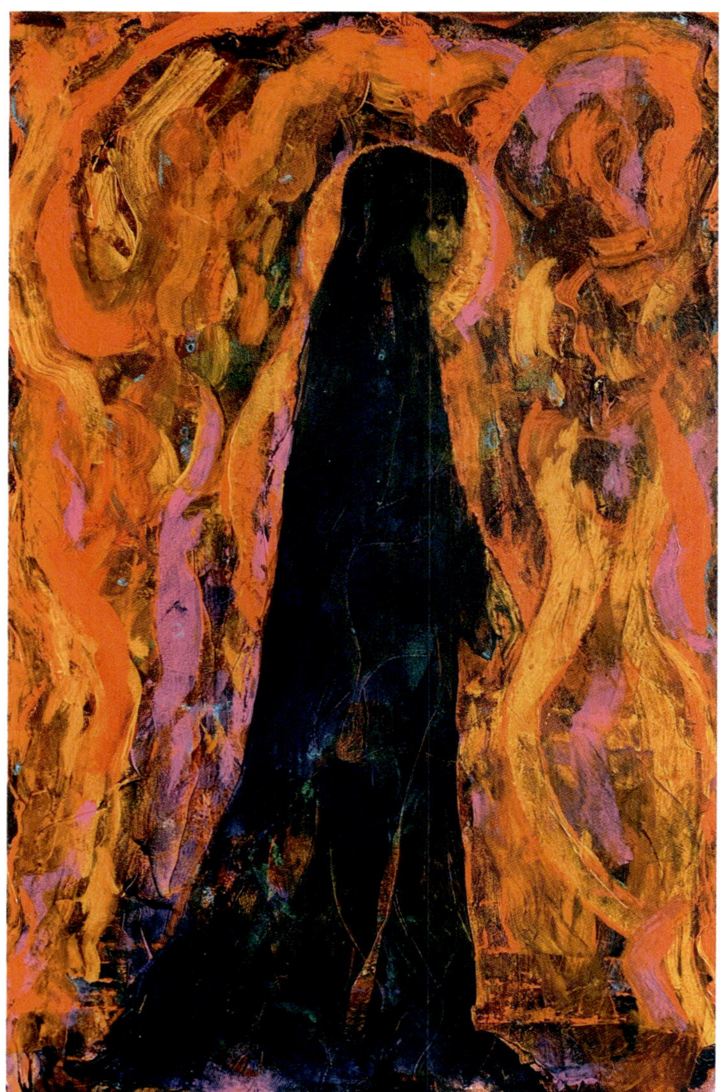

206  *Gounod (Plate G)*  1905
From *Thought Forms*
by Anne Besant &
Charles Webster Leadbeater
(1847–1933 & 1854–1934)
Drawing printed in a book

While ancestrally speaking Besant belongs to the England of big houses and conservative values, her life's work was committed to countering the damage done by the privileged few. She worked, politically and artistically, to uncover the things hidden in life. Besant and Leadbeater's *Thought Forms* sought to express the unseen world through the effects of form and colour; they show that music can muster a feeling that is, and can be expressed, beyond language.

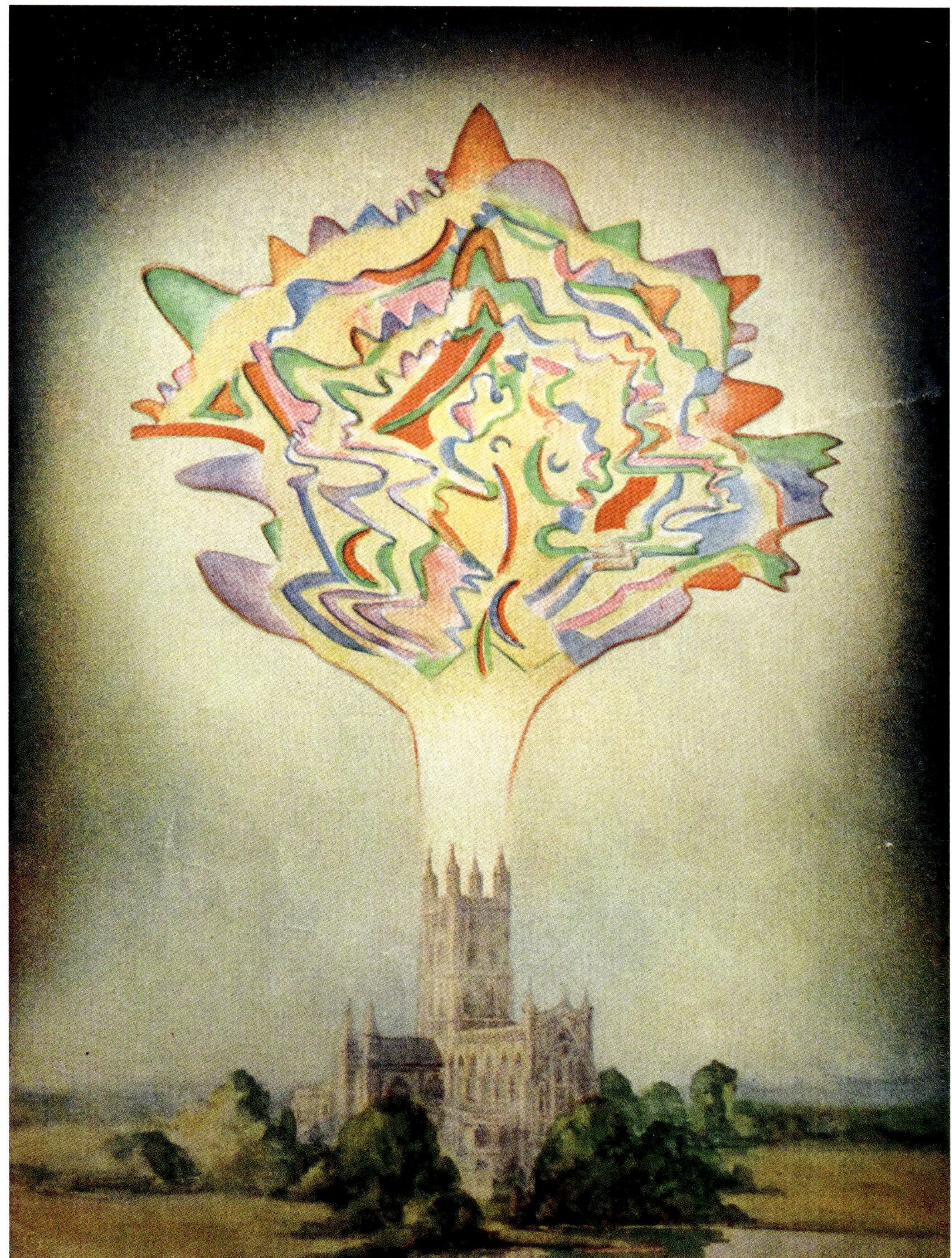

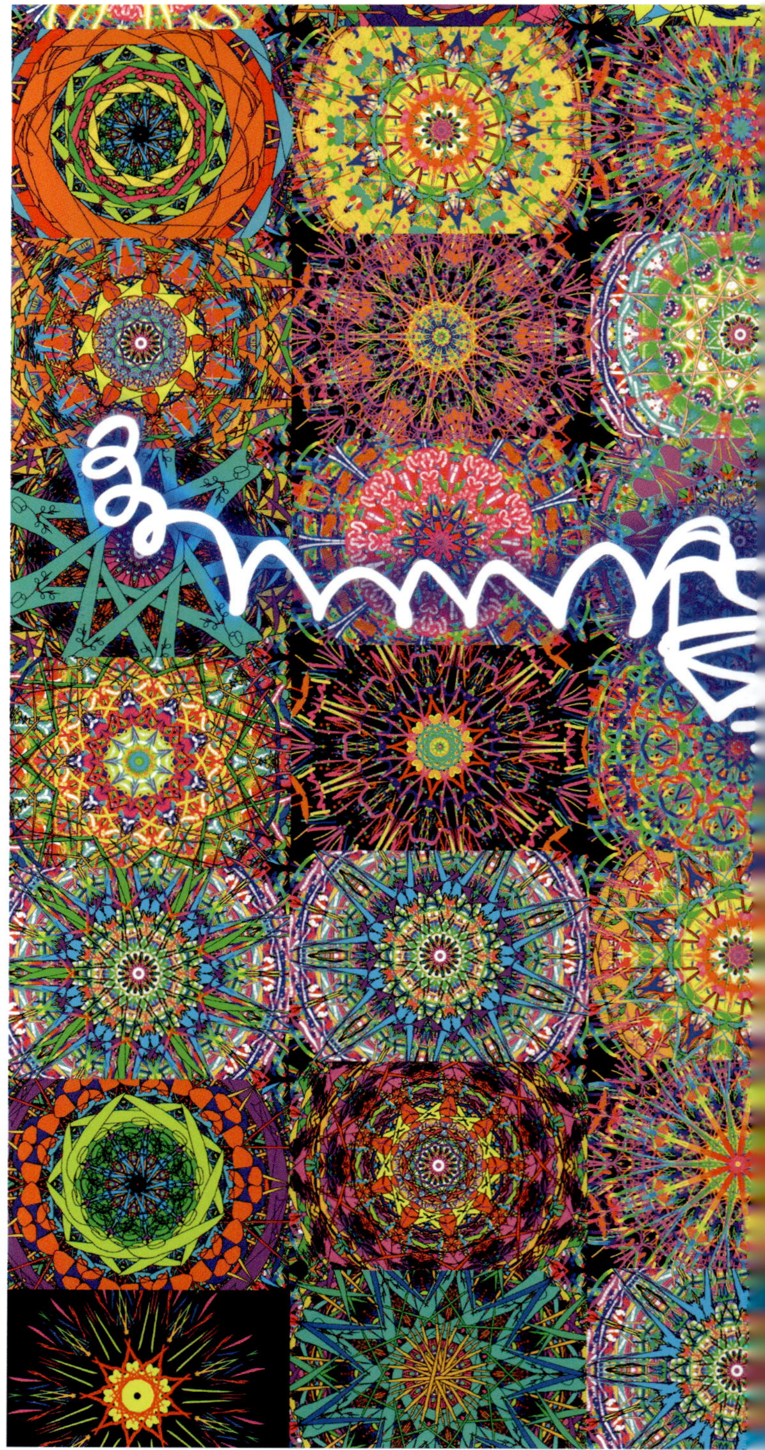

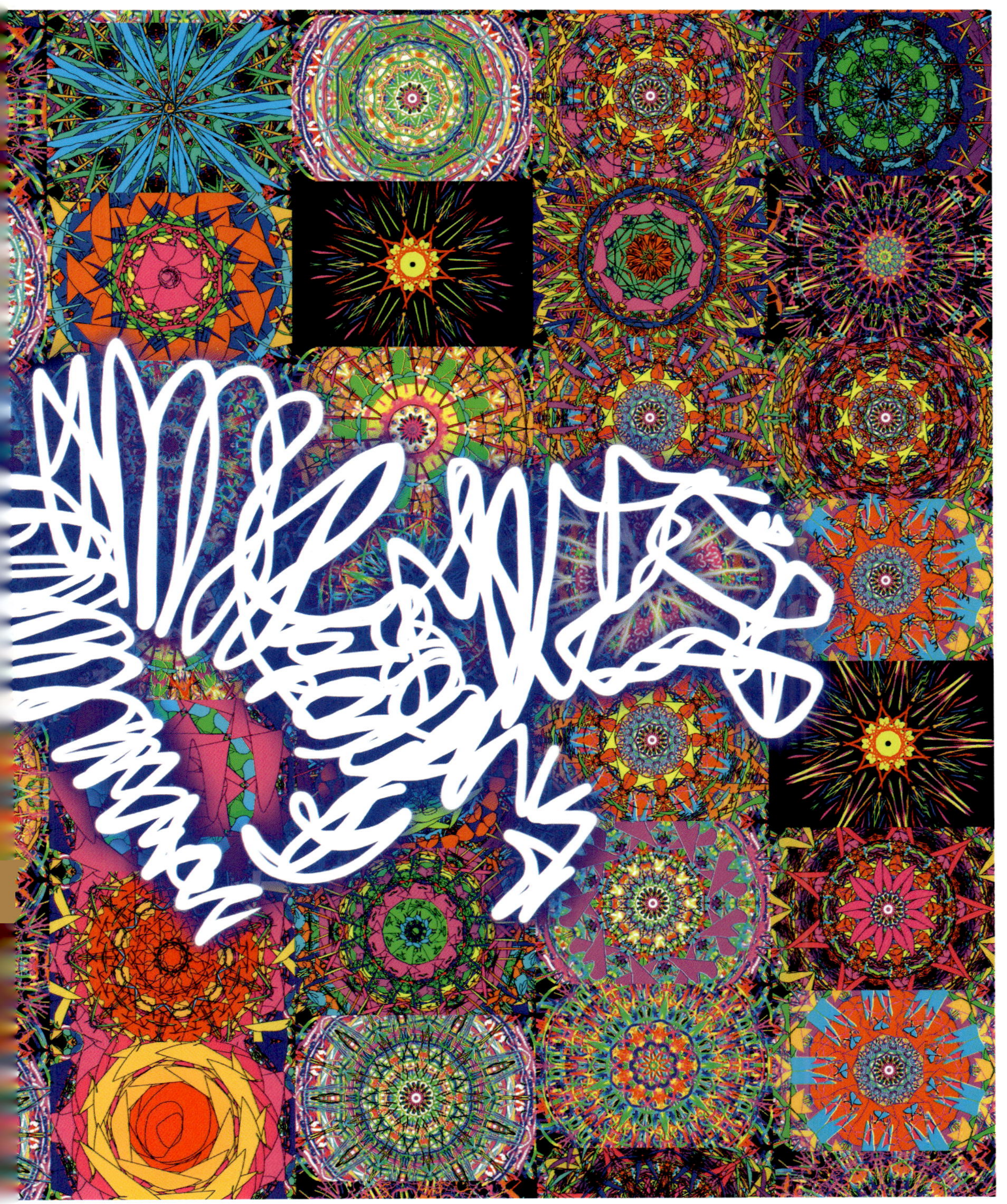

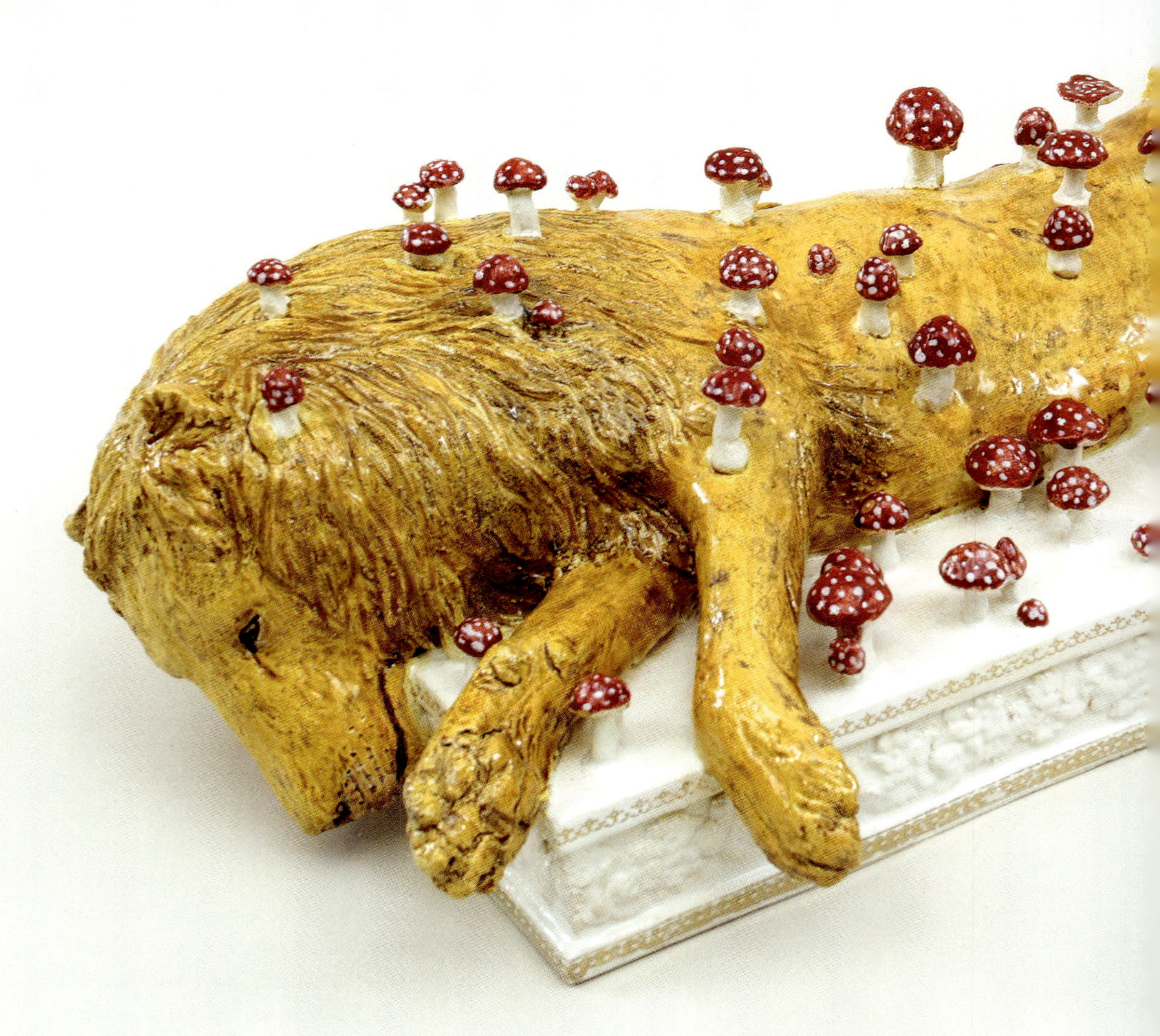

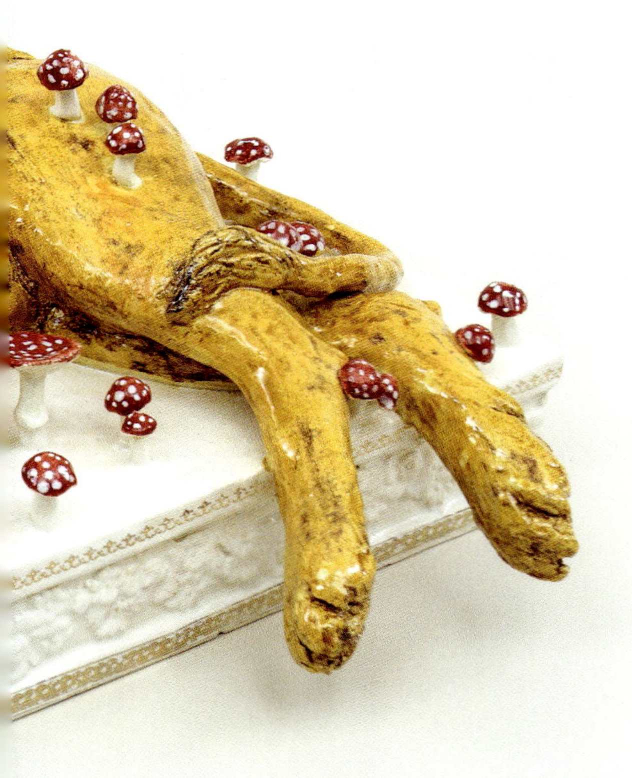



Partington's *The Red Lion*, part of an
exhibition entitled "Britainton", looks
to Britain's past with a critical eye, re-
evaluating its grandiose portrayal in art.
The lion, a potent symbol of the British
Empire, lies sleeping as nature reclaims its
place in the nation's visual history. Once
a symbol of land seizure, Partington's lion
appears now as an immobilized, dormant,
almost submissive force; set in earthenware,
the imperial institution is undermined and
relegated to the past.

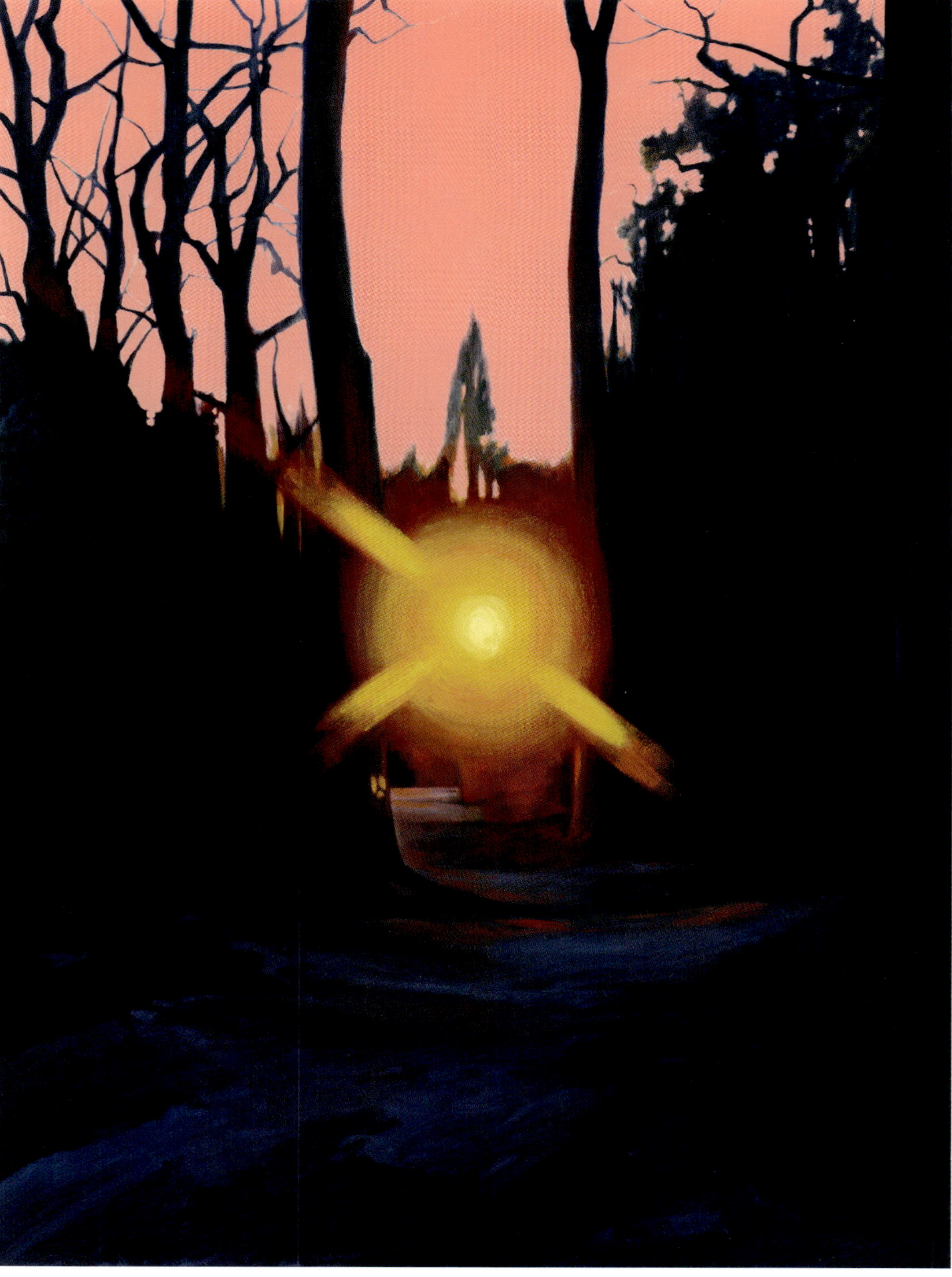

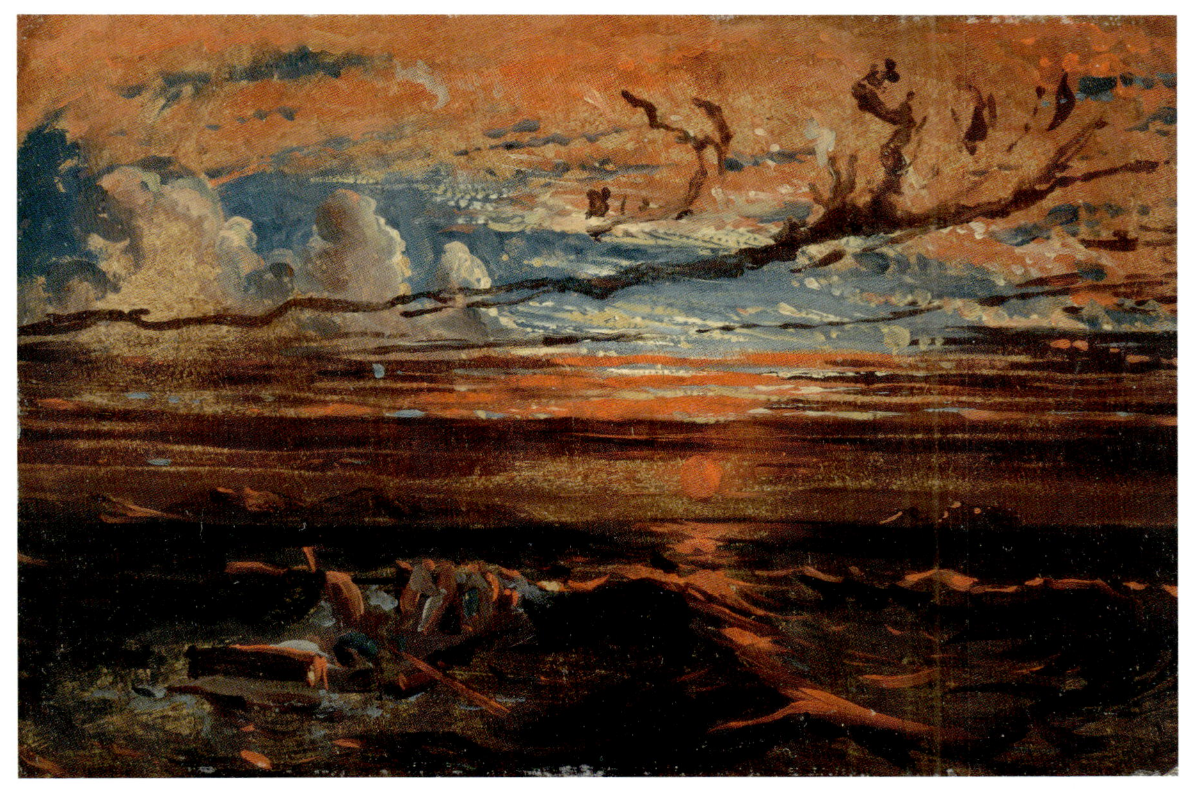

**209**  *Sunset at Sea after a Storm*  1824
Francis Danby (1793–1861)
Oil on canvas

**210**  *Day's End*  c.2015–18
George Shaw (b.1966)
Enamel on board

George Shaw marks his pots of Humbrol enamel paint with the date when he opens them, for the texture slowly coagulates with time. This conscious connection between medium and time is apparent in *Day's End*, a painting that glows with the various shades and textures of dusk. Initially recognized for his paintings of Tile Hill, the Coventry estate he grew up in, here Shaw removes himself to the open landscape, delicately portraying a sense of a hopeful ending, a natural closure.

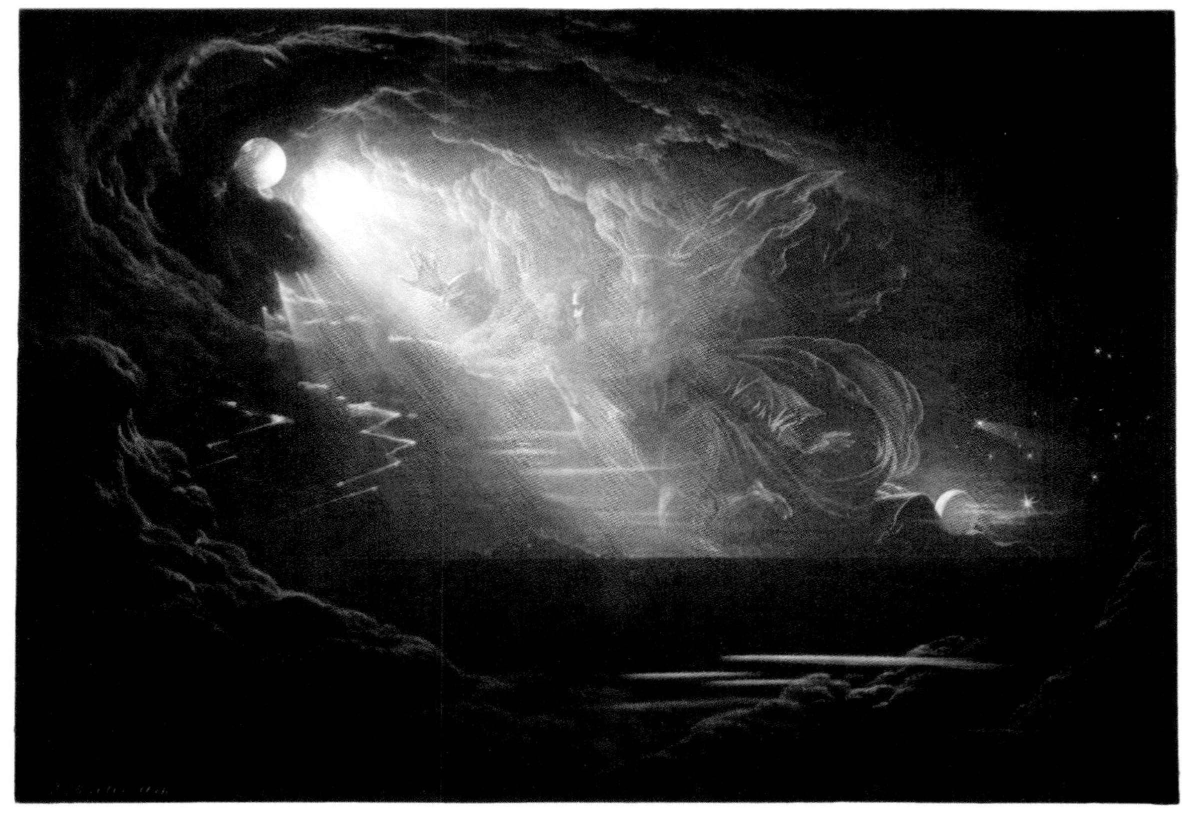

**211** *Paradise Lost – The Creation of Light*
1824, published 1825
John Martin (1789–1854)
Mezzotint

**212** *Jerusalem, The Emanation of*
*The Giant Albion* c.1804–20
William Blake (1757–1827)
Relief etching on paper

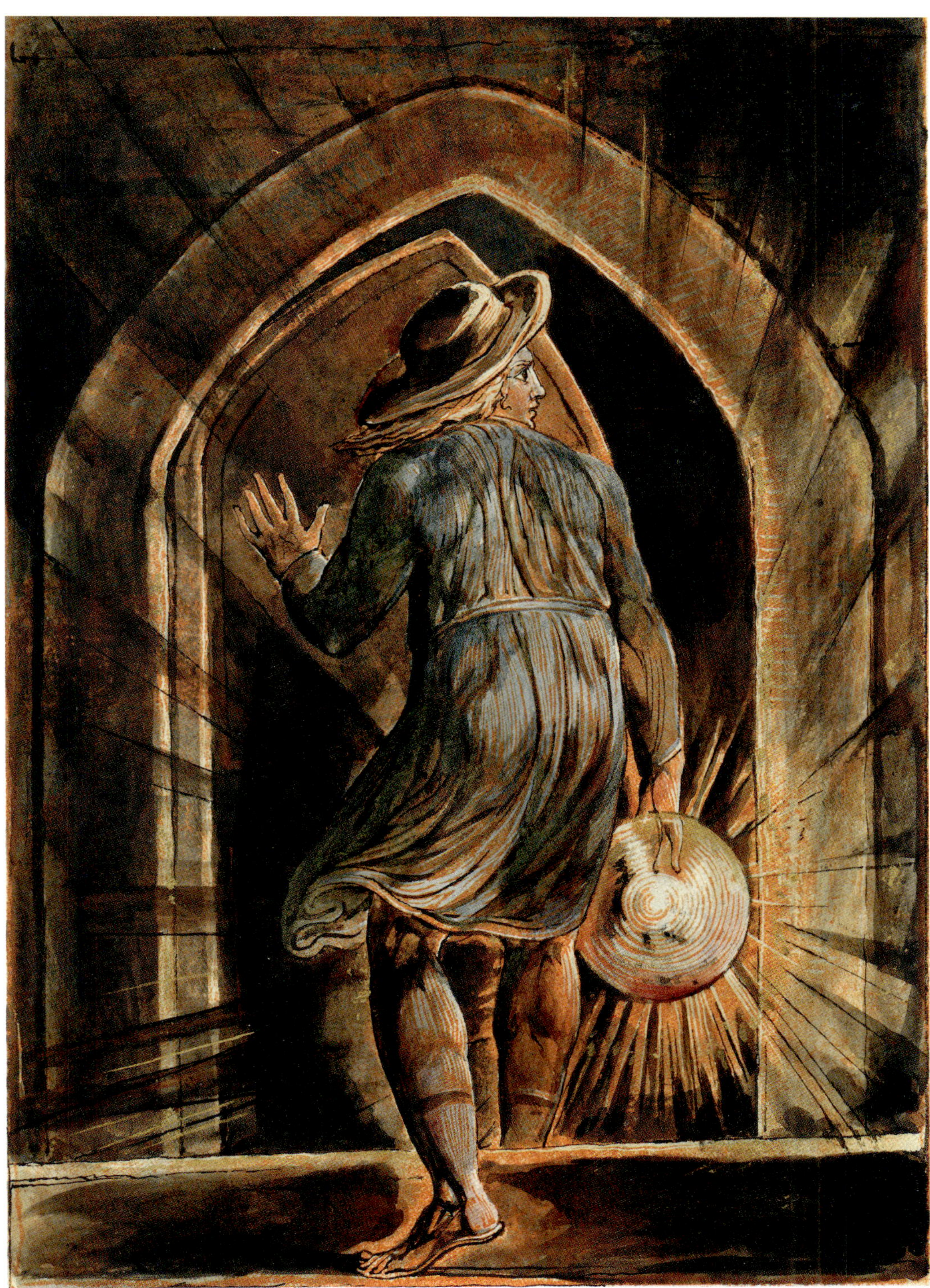

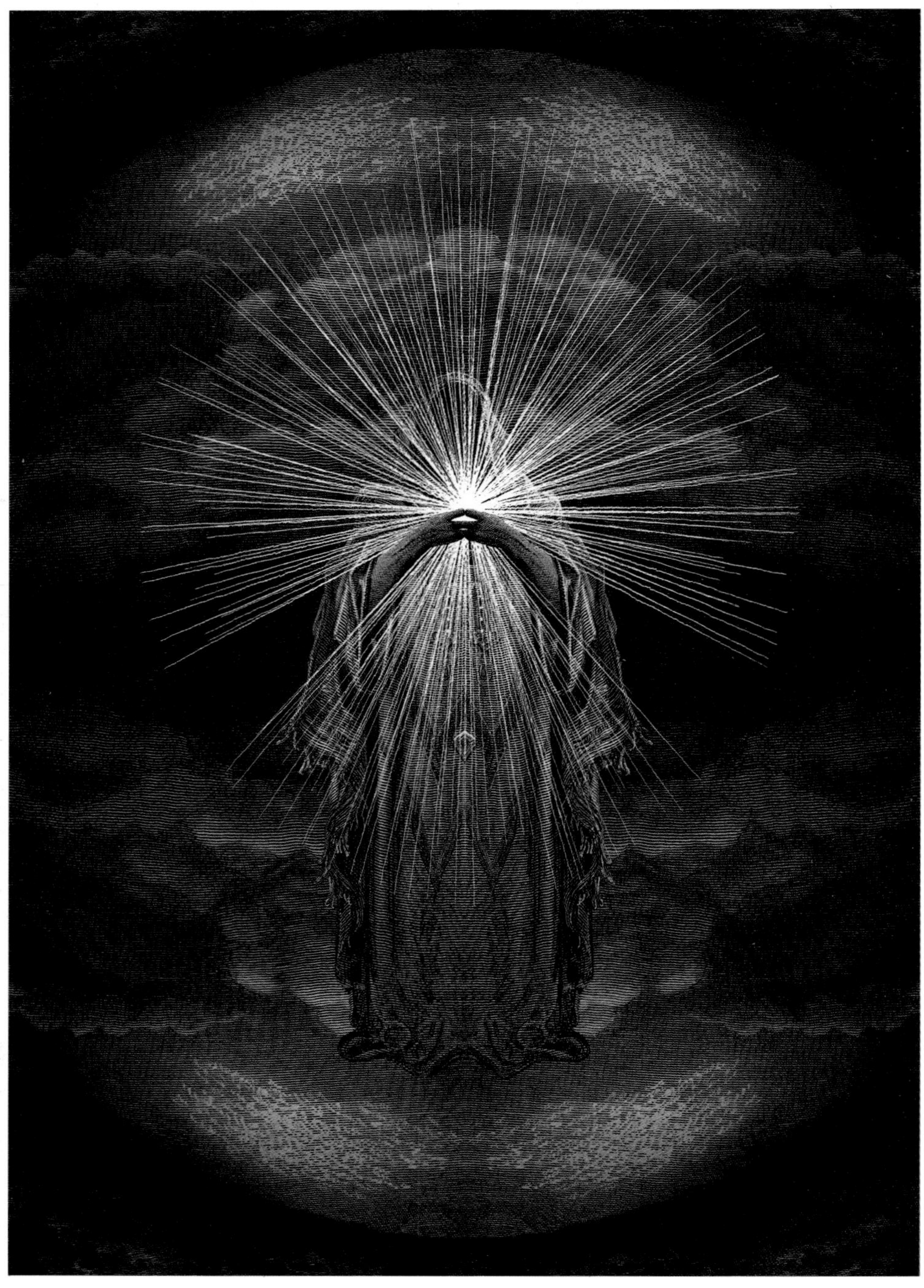

**213**  *Older Light*  2021
Dan Hillier (b.1973)
Giclée print

# INDEX OF ARTISTS

# INDEX OF WORKS

# ACKNOWLEDGEMENTS

I would like to thank Fiona Robertson for her endless patience, forbearance, support and encouragement; Mat Osman for the perfect text; Josse Pickard for inspiration, insight, inspired design and impeccable problem-solving skills; Adam Gordon for proposing the book in the first place and for overseeing its initial stages; and Maisie McGregor for the wonderful captions.

I would also like to express my deep gratitude to all the artists, creators, galleries, museums, institutions and estates who have so generously granted us permission to feature their work – this book would not exist without them.

*Stephen Ellcock, January 2022*

# PICTURE CREDITS

1 *Wolf Moon* 2020 © Cathy de Monchaux. Private collection courtesy of Ron Dennis 2 G.F.Watts, courtesy of the Watts Gallery, Compton, Surrey, UK © Watts Gallery/© Trustees of Watts Gallery/Bridgeman Images 3 John Martin, courtesy of the Yale Center for British Art, Paul Mellon Collection 4 William Blake, courtesy of the Yale Center for British Art, Paul Mellon Collection 5 Thomas Stothard, courtesy of the Yale Center for British Art, Paul Mellon Collection 6 William Blake, courtesy of the Yale Center for British Art, Paul Mellon Collection 7 *Boat and Lizard c.*1972 © Ken Kiff 8 Arthur Rackham, courtesy of The Cleveland Museum of Art. Gift of Mrs Don Hunter 9 Samuel Palmer, courtesy of The Picture Art Collection/Alamy Stock Photo 10 *Anglo Saxon Disc Brooch* courtesy of the Metropolitan Museum of Art, New York. Purchase, Joseph Pulitzer Bequest, 1987 11 *Fount* 2021 © Dan Hillier 12 William Turner of Oxford, courtesy of the Yale Center for British Art, Paul Mellon Collection 13 *Devil's Chimney,* courtesy of the Metropolitan Museum of Modern Art. Gift of Weston J. Naef, in memory of Kathleen W. Naef and Weston J. Naef Sr, 1982 14 John Flaxman, courtesy of the Yale Center for British Art, Paul Mellon Collection 15 *South Cadbury Hill* 1993 © Norman Ackroyd 16 *97. Richmond, Yorkshire, sw Quad* 1899 Courtesy of the David Rumsey Historical Map Collection www.davidrumsey.com 17 *Untitled c.*1945 by Madge Gill © Newham Heritage Service 18 Joseph Michael Gandy, courtesy of the Metropolitan Museum of Art. Harry G. Sperling Fund, 2005 19 William Heath Robinson originally published in *Twelfth Night* by William Shakespeare, Hodder & Stoughton *c.*1908, Wikimedia Commons 20 John Henry Dearle for William Morris & Co., courtesy of the Museum of Fine Arts, Boston. Charles Potter Kling Fund and Museum purchase with funds donated anonymously and from various donors 21 Hubert von Herkomer, courtesy of the Yale Center for British Art. Gift of Hans and Agnes Platenius 22 Roger Fenton, courtesy of the J. Paul Getty Museum, Los Angeles 23 Henry Peacham, courtesy of the Folger Shakespeare Library, Washington DC 24 Paul Nash © National Galleries of Scotland, Edinburgh/Bridgeman Images 25 *Journey to Avebury* 1973 © Derek Jarman, courtesy of the Luma Foundation 26 Frederick H. Evans, courtesy of the Los Angeles County Museum of Art. The Marjorie and Leonard Vernon Collection, gift of The Annenberg Foundation 27 Samuel Palmer, courtesy of the Yale Center for British Art, Paul Mellon Collection 28 *Scenes from the Passion: A Few Days Before Christmas* 2002–2003 © George Shaw, courtesy of the Cincinnati Art Museum, Cincinnati, USA/The Edwin and Virginia Irwin Memorial 29 *Crowhurst* 2006 © Tacita Dean, courtesy of the Frith Street Gallery, London and Marian Goodman Gallery, New York/Paris 30a William Henry Fox Talbot, courtesy of the J. Paul Getty Museum, Los Angeles, USA 30b *Leaf* 1839 by William Henry Fox Talbot, courtesy of the Metropolitan Museum of Modern Art. Gilman Collection 31 Peter Henry Emerson, courtesy of the J. Paul Getty Museum, Los Angeles, USA 32 *Cuckmere River* 1963 by Bill Brandt © Bill Brandt Archive 33 *Though the Way is Lost* 2015, Ink on Paper 100cm W × 60cm H © Olivia Kemp, courtesy of the James Freeman Gallery 34 John Constable, courtesy of the Royal Academy of Arts. Gift of Mr and Mrs J.H. Wade 35 Lionel Constable, courtesy of the Yale Center for British Art, Paul Mellon Collection 36 Joseph Mallord William Turner, courtesy of the Yale Center for British Art, Paul Mellon Collection 37 *Principal Eminences of the British Islands* 1852, courtesy of the David Rumsey Historical Map Collection www.davidrumsey.com 38 *Hey Diddle Diddle* 1989 from the *Nursery Rhymes* series, 51.7 × 38.1 cm © Paula Rego, courtesy of Paula Rego and the Cristea Roberts Gallery, London 39 Louis Wain, courtesy of the Wellcome Institute, Attribution 4.0 International (CC BY 4.0) 40 *Skull Vision* 1943 © Michael Ayrton, courtesy of the Estate of Michael Ayrton 41 Henry Fuseli, courtesy of the Yale Center for British Art, Paul Mellon Collection 42 Richard Dadd, courtesy of Artepics/Alamy Stock Photo 43 *Ann of Oxford Street, Ghost Baby Shelley* and *The Young Thomas de Quincey* 2018/2020/2018 © Julie Goldsmith. Photography by Ruth Ward 44 Arthur Rackham, courtesy of the Cleveland Museum of Art. Gift of Mrs Don Hunter 45 *Bird Call* 2021 © Nicola Tyson, courtesy of Sadie Coles HQ, London. Photo: Robert Glowacki 46 William O'Keefe, courtesy of the Yale Center for British Art, Paul Mellon Collection 47 *The Child's Dream of Pantomime* by Alfred Crowquill after himself for the *Illustrated Times* London Wikimedia Commons (CC BY4.0)

48 *Goblin Market* courtesy of the Metropolitan Museum of Modern Art. Gift of Walter L. Hildberg, 1937 49 W.S. Hobson, courtesy of the J. Paul Getty Museum, Los Angeles 50 *Mr and Mrs Andrews* 2021 © Claire Partington 51 *Black Shuck* sculpture series: *Saddle Shuck, Cousin of Yard Broom Shuck, Yard Broom Shuck, Tribal Shuck* © John Douglas Piper 52 *New Barnet* 2021 from *The Scarecrow* series © Max Reeves 53 *Housewives with Steak-knives* 1984–5, dimensions: 245 cm × 222 cm © Sutapa Biswas. All rights reserved DACS. From the collection of the Cartwright Hall Art Gallery, Bradford Museums and Galleries, UK. Photo credit: Andy Keate 54 Aubrey Beardsley, courtesy of the Metropolitan Museum of Art, New York. Gift of Albert Gallatin, 1919 55 *Ghost* 2016 © Dan Hillier 56 *Stonehenge under Snow* 1947 by Bill Brandt © Bill Brandt Archive 57 *Druidesque* 1955 by Austin Osman Spare. Kenneth and Steffi Grant Archive, courtesy of FULGUR PRESS 58 *The Devil's Den* 2021 © Ben Edge 59 Frederick H. Evans, courtesy of the Los Angeles County Museum of Art. The Marjorie and Leonard Vernon Collection, gift of The Annenberg Foundation and Carol Vernon and Robert Turbin 60 Roger Fenton, courtesy of the J. Paul Getty Museum, Los Angeles 61 *Coldrum Long Barrow, Kent* 2021 and *Kit's Coty House, Kent* 2021 from *The Book of Charles* series © Max Reeves 62 William Turner of Oxford, courtesy of the J. Paul Getty Museum, Los Angeles 63 *Labyrinth Stones: the path and the walls* 2021 © Jackie Morris 64 Ithell Colquhoun. Image © The Tate 65 Bryan Wynter © The Estate of the Artist, courtesy of the Yale Center for British Art, Gift of George E. Dix 66 Stills from *Journey to Avebury* 1973 by Derek Jarman, courtesy of the Luma Foundation 67 *Single Form by Barbara Hepworth, Battersea Park* 2008, photo © Michael Gray 68 Frederick H. Evans, courtesy of the Los Angeles County Museum of Art 69 *When the Earth had Many Moons* 1990; 420 × 594 mm © Jamie Reid, courtesy of the John Marchant Gallery 70 *Celtic Head* courtesy of the Cleveland Museum of Art. Gift of Dr and Mrs Jacob Hirsch 71 Frederick H. Evans, courtesy of the Los Angeles County Museum of Art. The Marjorie and Leonard Vernon Collection, gift of The Annenberg Foundation 72 *Curse English Heritage* 1990; 297 × 420 mm © Jamie Reid, courtesy of the John Marchant Gallery 73 *Queen of the Planets* 1977 © Ken Kiff 74 Samuel Palmer, courtesy of the Yale Center for British Art, Paul Mellon Collection 75 John Atkinson Grimshaw, courtesy of the Yale Center for British Art 76 William Stukeley, courtesy of the Houghton Library, Harvard University via Wikimedia Commons 77 *The Pilgrim's Way* 1950 by Bill Brandt © Bill Brandt Archive 78 Paul Nash, courtesy of the Cleveland Museum of Art, Gift of Mrs Henry A. Everett for the Dorothy Burnham Everett Memorial Collection 79 George Barret Jr, courtesy of the Yale Center for British Art, Paul Mellon Collection 80 Samuel Palmer, courtesy of the Yale Center for British Art, The G. Allen Smith Collection, transfer from the Yale University Art Gallery 81 Edward Francis Burney, courtesy of the Yale Center for British Art, Yale Art Gallery Collection, Gift of Abel Cary Thomas 82 Frederick H. Evans, courtesy of the J. Paul Getty Museum, Los Angeles 83 Frank Meadow Sutcliffe, courtesy of the J. Paul Getty Museum, Los Angeles 84 *The mowing-Devil, or, Strange news out of Hartford-Shire...* 1678, artist unknown, courtesy of the Folger Digital Image Collection, Attribution 4.0 International (CC BY 4.0) 85 Spencer Gore, courtesy of Alamy Stock Photo/The Art Gallery of New South Wales 86 *The Maze from* The Trevelyon Miscellany 1608 by Thomas Trevelyon, courtesy of the Folger Digital Image Collection, Attribution 4.0 International (CC BY 4.0) 87 Roger Fenton, courtesy of the J. Paul Getty Museum, Los Angeles 88 *Punchinello-graphy of England* 1808 by John M. Wauthier, courtesy of the David Rumsey Historical Map Collection www.davidrumsey.com 89 *The Cosmati pavement at Westminster* Abbey laid in 1268 under the supervision of Odoricus of Rome. Dimensions: 24 feet 10 inches (11.73 metres) square. Image © Westminster Abbey 90 *Corn Maiden* 2015 © Cathy Ward 91 *Romans Destroying the Druids* from *The Book of Similitudes* 1860 by John Warner Barber, courtesy of the Internet Archive 92 *Fred Mizen aged 60 from Bardfield, Braintree, Essex, with straw effigies of the Lion and the Unicorn c.*1951 by John Tarlton, courtesy of The Museum of English Rural Life, University of Reading 93 Arthur Rackham, courtesy of the LUNA: Folger Digital Image Collection, Attribution 4.0 International (CC BY 4.0) 94 *Mari Lwyd revellers conjured in stop-motion maquettes made for the first performance of "The Mare's Tale"* 2013 © Clive Hicks Jenkins 95 *Warrior (Possibly St George) Fighting a Dragon* courtesy of the Cleveland Museum of Art. Purchase from the J.H. Wade Fund 96 *The Lion and the Unicorn* 2013 © Claire Partington. Lion: H81cm × W28cm × D28cm Unicorn: H 85cm × W 29cm × D 29cm 97 *Abbot's Bromley Horn Dance c.*1900 by John Benjamin Stone. Image sourced from Wikimedia Commons 98 *Long Parish Mummers* by George Long, courtesy of The Museum of English Rural Life, University of Reading 99 Thomas Henwood, courtesy of the Yale Center for British Art, Paul Mellon Collection 100 *Disparate Remedies* 2006, C-Type photograph 60 × 40 inch © Nick Waplington 101 C. Turner, courtesy of the Wellcome Collection, Attribution 4.0 International (CC BY 4.0) 102 *The Seed Guardian* 2021 © Holland Otik 103 Lewis Carroll, courtesy of the J. Paul Getty Museum, Los Angeles 104 *Green Man Searches for Wilderness* 2020 © Pinkie Maclure 105 *Mother Carey and her Chickens* 1877 by J.G. Keulemans, courtesy of Biodiversity Heritage Library 106 *The 'Obby 'Oss of Padstow* 2017 © Ben Edge 107 Trevelyon Miscellany, courtesy of the Folger Digital Image Collection 108 Henry Fuseli, courtesy of the Folger Digital Image Collection 109 Richard Dadd, courtesy of Album/Alamy Stock Photo 110 Julia Margaret Cameron, courtesy of the Metropolitan Museum of Art. David Hunter McAlpin Fund, 1952 111 Cruikshank, courtesy of the Yale Center for British Art, Paul Mellon Fund 112 *Cottingley Fairies* series by Elsie Wright, courtesy of the Granger Historical Picture Archive/Alamy Stock Photo 113 *Notting Hill Carnival* 1981–2 © Andrew Moore 114 *Four Twins, Trickster* 1988 © Rotimi Fani-Kayode, courtesy of Autograph, London 115 Burne-Jones, courtesy of the Yale Center for British Art, Paul Mellon Fund 116 *Western Manuscript 693 Ripley Scroll c.*16th century, artist unknown, courtesy of the Wellcome Trust, Attribution 4.0 International (CC BY 4.0) 117 *Bwa Procession* wood engraving print 2017 © India Rose Bird 118 *The Portrait of the Lord Jesus Christ* 1862 by Georgiana Houghton. Courtesy of the Victorian Spiritualists Union Inc, Melbourne, Australia 119 Richard Doyle, courtesy of the Metropolitan Museum of Art. Gift of Lincoln Kirstein, 1970 120 Aubrey Vincent Beardsley, courtesy of the Yale Center for British Art, Paul Mellon Fund 121 *Up Up and Away*, film still from *Lotusland the Musical* 2017 © Paul Kindersley and Philip Cornett 122 *Fourth* 2017–18. 40 × 52 in./101.6 × 132.1 cm © Lina Iris Viktor 123 *Parade* 2019. Acrylic and gold paste on 61 cm × 46 cm canvas © James F. Johnston 124 Hugh Welch Diamond, courtesy of the J. Paul Getty Museum, Los Angeles 125 Paul Nash, courtesy of Alamy Stock Photos/Asar Studios 126 Edwin Smith, courtesy of the the RIBA Collection 127 Eric Ravilious, courtesy of Alamy Stock Photo/Steeve-x-art 128 George Stubbs, courtesy of the Yale Center for British Art, Paul Mellon Collection 129 Thomas Gainsborough, courtesy of the Yale Center for British Art, Gift of Lowell Libson & Jonny Yarker in honor of Amy R.W. Meyers, Director of the Yale Center for British Art 130 Balthazar Nebo, courtesy of the Yale Center for British Art, Paul Mellon Collection 131, Artist unknown, courtesy of the Yale Center for British Art, Paul Mellon Collection 132 John Sell Cotman, courtesy of the Yale Center for British Art, Bequest of Richard L. Purdy 133 John

Constable, courtesy of the Yale Center for British Art, Paul Mellon Collection **134** Samuel Palmer, courtesy of the Yale Center for British Art, Paul Mellon Collection **135** George Stubbs, courtesy of the Yale Center for British Art, Paul Mellon Collection **136** 4 photographs from *Monument to the Vanquished* 2021 © Leah Gordon. Text: Annabel Edwards **137** Joseph Wright of Derby, courtesy of the Yale Center for British Art, Paul Mellon Collection **138** Lady Clementina Hawarden, courtesy of the Metropolitan Museum of Art. Gilman Collection, Purchase, Harriette and Noel Levine Gift, 2005 **139** Gwen John, courtesy of the Yale Center for British Art, Paul Mellon Collection **140** *Father Figure* 2012. Acrylic on canvas 61 × 46 cm/78 cm w × 63 cm h framed © Christopher Noulton, courtesy of the John Freeman Gallery **141** Sartorius, courtesy of the Yale Center for British Art, Paul Mellon Collection **142** *Coach Trip – Original London to Brighton Road* 2014 © Jeff Pitcher (Website pitcherphotography.org |Instagram @pitcher_post |Facebook @pitcherphotos **143** *George* Chinnery, courtesy of the Yale Center for British Art, Paul Mellon Collection **144** *An Evening at Kew Gardens* 1932 by Bill Brandt © Bill Brandt Archive **145** Anna Atkins, courtesy of the Metropolitan Museum of Art. Purchase, Alfred Stieglitz Society Gifts, 2004 **146** *Untitled from Hackney Riviera* 2018, C-type photographs © Nick Waplington **147** *Flower of the Future* 2018−21 © Joanna Kirk **148** John Ruskin, courtesy of the Yale Center for British Art, Paul Mellon Collection **149** William Henry Millais, courtesy of the Cleveland Museum of Art. Gift in memory of Helen Borowitz **150** *Palm* 2020. 33 cm w × 42 cm h image size: 43 cm w × 52 cm h with white border. Archival Pigment Print on Hahnemühle Photo Rag © Suzanne Moxhay, courtesy of the James Freeman Gallery **151** William Skelton, courtesy of the Yale Center for British Art, Gift of Kenneth D. Rapoport, MD **152** Walter Hood Fitch, courtesy of the New York Public Library **153** *The Garden of Eden*, courtesy of the Metropolitan Museum of Art. Gift of Irwin Untermyer, 1964 **154** George Baxter, courtesy of the Wellcome Collection **155** Richard Dadd, courtesy of the Yale Center for British Art, Paul Mellon Collection **156** Richard Wilson, courtesy of the Yale Center for British Art, Paul Mellon Collection **157** *In the Woods* 2021. 19 7/10 × 15 7/10 in/50 × 40 cm, oil on canvas © Sikhela Owen, courtesy of the James Freeman Gallery **158** James Knight, courtesy of the Metropolitan Museum of Modern Art. Gilman Collection, Gift of The Howard Gilman Foundation, 2005 **159** The Trevelyon Miscellany, courtesy of the Folger Digital Image Collection, Attribution 4.0 International (CC BY 4.0) **160** Burne-Jones, courtesy of the Metropolitan Museum of Art. Rogers Fund, 1921 **161** Francis Danby, courtesy of the Yale Center for British Art, Paul Mellon Collection **162** *Pink Full Moon (Hampstead Heath)* 2019 © Sayako Sugawara **163** C.R.W. Nevinson, courtesy of the Yale Center for British Art, Paul Mellon Fund **164** *Nelson's Ship in a Bottle* 2010 © Yinka Shonibare, courtesy SJ Images/Alamy Stock Photo **165** Colonel Henry Stuart Wortley, courtesy of the J. Paul Getty Museum, Los Angeles **166** *The English Channel seen from the Dorsetshire Cliffs* 1871 by John Brett, courtesy Alamy Stock Photo/Ivy Close Images **167** *Sunset on the Beach at Sark*, courtesy of the Yale Center for British Art, Paul Mellon Collection **168** Julia Margaret Cameron, courtesy of the J. Paul Getty Museum, Los Angeles **169** John Atkinson Grimshaw, courtesy of the Yale Center for British Art, Gift of Michael D. Coe, Yale MAH 1968 **170** *Eye of the Storm* 2020 © Daniel Hosego, courtesy of the James Freeman Gallery **171** *The Wreck of Worthing Pier from The Russian Ending* 2001; 21 ¼ × 31 ¼ in/54 × 79.4 cm © Tacita Dean, courtesy of the artist, Frith Street Gallery, London and Marian Goodman Gallery, New York/Paris **172** *St Ives Deckchair* 2009 © Jeff Pitcher (Website: pitcherphotography.org | Instagram @pitcher_post | Facebook @pitcherphotos) **173** *Walking on Water, Weston-Super-Mare, England* undated © Sheila Rock. From *Tough & Tender – English Seascapes* **174** *Beach Shelter, Weymouth, England* undated © Sheila Rock. From *Tough & Tender – English Seascapes* **175** David Cox, courtesy the Yale Center for British Art, Paul Mellon Collection **176** Peter de Wint, courtesy of the Yale Center for British Art, Paul Mellon Collection **177** *Frost Fair*, Courtesy of the Yale Center for British Art/Paul Mellon Collection **178** Peter Henry Emerson, courtesy of the Cleveland Museum of Art. Bequest of Edgar A. Hahn **179** Peter Henry Emerson, courtesy of the J. Paul Getty Museum, Los Angeles **180** *The Great Fire of London,*, artist unknown, courtesy of the Yale Center for British Art, Paul Mellon Collection **181** William Hogarth, courtesy of the Yale Center for British Art, Paul Mellon Collection **182** *Christ Delivered to the People* 1950 by Sir Stanley Spencer, courtesy of Alamy Stock Photo/Photosublime **183** *The Funeral Party* 1953 by L.S. Lowry, courtesy of Alamy Stock Photo/Peter Barritt **184** John Sell Cotman, courtesy of the Yale Center for British Art, Paul Mellon Collection **185** Charles Rosenberg, courtesy of the Yale Center for British Art, Paul Mellon Collection **186** *For His Own Good* 1995 © Abigail Lane. All Rights Reserved, DACS/Artimage 2022 **187** Charles de Sousy Ricketts, courtesy of the Cleveland Museum of Art. Gift of The Print Club of Cleveland **188** John Constable, courtesy of the Yale Center for British Art, Paul Mellon Collection **189** *Eye am the Chairman* 2004 © Abigail Lane. All Rights Reserved, DACS/Artimage 2022. Photo: Sam Lawrence **190** *Hackley* 2011 from the *King Mob* series © Max Reeves **191** Brixton, London 24 September 1978 © Syd Shelton **192a** Lewisham, London 13 August 1977 © Syd Shelton **192b** Clifton Rise, Lewisham, London 13 August 1977 all copyright © Syd Shelton **193** *Untitled, Waterloo Station from the Arrival Portfolio* 1962 © Howard Grey **194** *Alton West Estate, Roehampton, London: Lynn Chadwick's sculpture* The Watchers *with the point blocks beyond* 1963 by John Donat, courtesy of the RIBA Collection **195** *City Gent* 1988 © Rotimi Fani-Kayode, courtesy of Autograph London **196** *As I Stood, Listened and Watched, My Feelings Were This Woman is Not for Burning...* c.1985−6. Dimensions: 183 cm × 91 cm © Sutapa Biswas. All rights reserved DACS. Image from the collection of the Cartwright Hall Art Gallery, Bradford Museums and Galleries, UK. Photo credit: Paul Thompson **197** *Refuge from the Aftermath, A Reckoning to Come* 2018−19 © Lina Iris Viktor **198** Samuel Palmer, courtesy of the Yale Center for British Art, Paul Mellon Collection **199** Joseph Wright of Derby, courtesy of the Yale Center for British Art, Paul Mellon Collection **200** Joseph Mallord William Turner, courtesy of The Cleveland Museum of Art, Bequest of John L. Severance **201** *Seer* 2021 © Dan Hillier **202** *Albion* 2008 © Mat Collishaw **203** John Bingley Garland, courtesy of The J. Paul Getty Museum, Los Angeles. Purchased with funds provided by the Disegno Group **204** *Astronomy: a Meteor in the Night Sky* 1868, artist unknown, courtesy of the Wellcome Collection, Attribution 4.0 International (CC BY 4.0) **205** *Garden* 2021 © James F. Johnston **206** Gounod (Plate G) from *Thought Forms* by Anne Besant & Charles Webster Leadbeater 1905, courtesy of The College of Psychic Studies, London. © The College of Psychic Studies. Photo: Andy Sharp **207** *Tiger, I Love You* 2021 © Chila Kumari Singh Burman **208** *The Red Lion* 2021 © Claire Partington **209** Francis Danby, courtesy of the Yale Center for British Art, Paul Mellon Collection **210** *Day's End c.* 2015−18 © George Shaw, courtesy of the Anthony Wilkinson Gallery, London. Photography by Matthew Hollow **211** John Martin, courtesy of the Cleveland Museum of Art, Mr and Mrs Charles G. Prasse Collection **212** William Blake, courtesy of the Yale Center for British Art, Paul Mellon Collection **213** *Older Light* 2021 © Dan Hillier